AMER A DREAM COME TRUE

By
Susan Haven

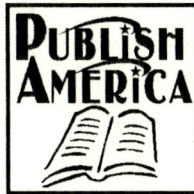

PublishAmerica
Baltimore

First printing

At the specific preference of the author, PublishAmerica allowed this work to remain exactly as the author intended, verbatim, without editorial input.

ISBN: 1-4137-9433-5
PUBLISHED BY PUBLISHAMERICA, LLLP
www.publishamerica.com
Baltimore

Printed in the United States of America

This book is dedicated to the memory of my husband Les and my daughter, Ann-Marie.

ACKNOWLEDGMENTS:

Kristin Slater who encouraged me to turn my notes into a book, my nephew Stephen Coombs, Pat Roberts from Maryland, and Sue Catmur, who all gave me invaluable help, as well as Andy Bucksey for escorting me round America.

.

FOREWORD

In September 2001, six days after the tragedy of two planes being deliberately flown into the Twin Towers in New York, and four days late, the Virgin Atlantic flight to England landed at Heathrow airport, with clapping and cheering from the passengers.

****

Ever since I can remember, horses, and cowboys and Indians, became part of my dreams. It became apparent to my mum and dad that dolls were not for me, I was far happier playing in the dirt with my brother and his cars, or talking about horses. Luckily for me I was indulged, for at Christmas the presents in my stocking included plastic cowboys and Indians on horseback, mingling with the nuts, oranges, pens and puzzles. If the people detached from the horses, then I had herds of horses neatly corralled in folds in the blankets on my bed.

I was also lucky that my paternal grandfather had lots of books, westerns amongst others. These were shelved in a glass and wood fronted cabinet in their front parlour in Tottenham, London. The parlour was special in those days, rarely used except for very special occasions. The drawn curtains and the musty smell made it very forbidding and I remember feeling overawed when I was allowed in there.

I can't remember when I first saw the books, but I know that when I was allowed to touch them, I took them out very, very carefully, almost reverently. And I grew up reading William McCloud Raine, the Hopalong Cassidy books by Clarence E Mulford, and my favourite author, Zane Grey. I learned about the Code of the West where a man's word was his bond, that 'good' women were unmolested, actually revered, and how cowboys stayed true to their friends and the ranches they worked for.

But I always had a strange pleasure in championing the Indians. As young as I was, I was profoundly upset that they lost their lands and their way of life, sad that they couldn't live the way they wanted.

When I was about twelve, my grandfather died and I was so proud to be able to take my beloved books home. I still have several, although over the years some have been lost. Through reading them, I began to learn bits of Spanish. Sometimes no explanation came with the words, so I went and bought a Spanish-English dictionary, but I only ever learnt one phrase that was rude!

I watched every western on TV that I could, Wagon Train, Bonanza, Wells Fargo, Bronco, Sugarfoot and my all time favourite, Laramie. How I wished I had a horse to ride, walking and cycling miles to find the nearest one in a field to pat. Mum and dad always laughingly said that I could find a horse if there was one within five miles. I loved the countryside, being taken to the common at Chislehurst, Kent where we first lived, watching with envy the riders going by. Then, when I was seven we moved to Wilmington a few miles outside Dartford surrounded by green fields and footpaths. I played out all the time when the weather was fine, cycling to the heath with my brother Ian and a group of boys from the new estate, choosing to play cowboys and Indians whenever I could.

As I grew up, I often found it hard to sleep at night, tossing and turning for what felt like hours. Then, when I was about twelve, I hit on the idea of making up a cowboy 'day dream.' I knew that girls couldn't be cowboys, they were boring; cooking, cleaning and wearing dresses, so although my heroine was a girl called Susan Haven, I had her brought up by her father like a boy, and laughingly called Curly because of her short, curly hair. She helped her father on a small farm where he taught her to rope and ride.

One day, her father received papers to say that they had been left a ranch by a rich uncle. He refused to go to the wilds of Texas and so the property was left untended. When Curly's father died, the Texas ranch had been willed on to her, so she went and took it over, dressing as a boy. The cowboys working there were ones from all the TV series'. For a long time 'he' was not found out to be a she, until I decided that Jess Harper would find out by accident so there would be a little romance, especially as he was my favourite actor. The brand of the ranch became the Boxed C (a C inside a box.) This brand became reality when I had my horses, all the rugs and saddle blankets having this stitched on in red ribbon.

Friends at school became interested when I told them what I was doing, and I began writing the story down by torchlight under my bedclothes for them. It actually became a pleasure to go to bed, although my short sightedness probably started because of it. Curly had all sorts of adventures with baddies, usually ones from the TV, like Jack Elam trying to take the ranch from her. She rode a beautiful palomino stallion she'd rescued called Golden Prince, and had a big German shepherd dog, Buster. By the time I left school my writing must have reached almost two feet off the ground, written on scraps of paper torn from school books and notepads, almost anything that could be written on. I wish I could find them now just to see what I had done, but they were lost many years ago when my parents moved.

Slowly, over the years I accumulated lots of cowboy books, many Zane Grey's in paperbacks and a few in hardback, although I'm still searching for the rare ones that are out of print. Then, when I began working in London, bored by the travelling, I began buying books by a new writer, J T Edson.

After I married, with my husband Les and our daughter Ann-Marie, we had a holiday at Ross-on-Wye, Hereford, visiting Hay-on-Wye the biggest book selling town in Britain. Shops and even old barns were stacked full of books. It would have taken years to get round everything, and boy, was I was willing to stay. I was lucky to find a couple of Zane Grey's that I hadn't already got, and also bought two Time Life books, one on Outlaws and one on Ranchers. (Years later I managed to buy a set of twenty.) One year, Les bought me a beautiful book on America's countryside.

Wandering round boot fairs, I was really pleased to find a book by Andy Adams, 'The Log of a Cowboy,' and also 'The Thundering Herd' that told of the birth and heyday of the cattle industry. I learnt all I could about the American Wild West, knowing more about America than I ever did about Britain. The wide, open spaces and the scenery always beckoned invitingly.

I discovered through books written by people who had actually been out there in the eighteen hundreds that the 'Code of the West' was actually true, and that thousands of dollars, and even millions of acres of land, really did change hands with just a handshake. That cowboys really did 'ride for the brand,' giving their allegiance to their ranch work mates. A horse was essential for getting from place to place, to be without one meant almost certain death, so a horse thief was considered a 'murderer' and was always hanged when caught. Water rights made most of the feuds, as without water, you could not raise cattle or horses, or even live, and to cut off a person's water was also considered about the lowest thing a person could do.

The cowboy loved to grandstand, especially in front of dudes, and how Easterners loved to watch the cowhands show off. To the cowboys, the horse, the gun and the lariat were the tools of their trade and they took great pride in showing how good they were with them. This was how the rodeo was born.

Clothes became a product of the cowboys' work: the Stetson keeping the sun and rain from faces and necks. The bandanna, or neckerchief, could be used to wipe sweat from faces, cover mouths and noses from dust, used to tie a tourniquet, and even used to tie over the hat and under the chin to keep ears from getting frostbite.

The vest (waistcoat) had pockets to carry their 'smokings,' pants or jeans had turn ups to carry nails if they were mending fence. Chaps were made from leather hide to protect legs in undergrowth and thickets. Boots had big heels to stop the feet from sliding through the stirrups, and to dig into the ground when trying to hold a roped horse or steer, but were almost useless for walking. No cowboy walked when he could ride. Even the one-piece wool underwear soaked up sweat in summer, kept them warm in winter, and easy to wash out when they came across a creek or river. Spurs were ornate and some had 'jingle-bobs,' small metallic drops that tinkled when they walked, and the larger the rowels, the bigger the impression. Cowboys were notoriously vain.

Les took me one day to a shop in Sussex for my birthday, buying me an imitation Colt Navy .45 and a brown gunbelt. Then, when the Sun newspaper had a Wild West week, I bought a beige felt cowboy hat through them. Over the years we went to a couple of fancy dress parties, and it was of no surprise to anyone that I was dressed as a cowboy. Later on, I was given an engraved, black gunbelt by my brother-in-law, which almost went round me twice.

For a year I worked in Canterbury at a saddle shop, where Les bought me a western saddle, bridle, breast collar and flank cinch, my pride and joy. I spent hours oiling it, and when Les was out, I put it on a stool and watched TV sitting on it.

Aged only 41, Les died from cancer. He'd had a lung removed at Guy's hospital, and despite the dreadful radiotherapy afterward, had fought the illness with his typical bravery. I was devastated, and Ann-Marie took it very badly, too.

A few months later, I was lucky to be left some money in a will from an elderly aunt. Ann-Marie's first boyfriend, Keith, who she'd met at school, told her his sister had been bought a pony. She mentioned that I'd always loved horses, so I was invited up to Woodcroft at Herne Bay, to see it. That was it. I wanted one. I started scouring newspapers for a horse of my own. I had no luck with the usual advertisements and got in touch with an agency that helped you find one.

Eventually, they showed me little white Charlie, a 13.3hh pony, and a demon. He was difficult to catch unless several of you came at him in a pincer movement, although I did manage to get round this with bribery and leaving the head collar on, but if he caught you off guard, he whipped his head round and ran off to the grass. He took to the western saddle easily, and with a lariat I'd bought, one day I even roped fallen branches when they'd landed in the riding area after bad gales. It was fantastic to dress and ride like a real cowboy and I had trouble changing into normal clothes to go to work.

Not long after we had Charlie, Keith was killed in a bad car accident by the dangerous driving of a lad he was travelling with, but some time after, Ann-Marie met Andy, who lived at the farm where I kept Charlie.

I decided after nine months that I was ready for a bigger horse and sold him on. I found a pretty little 14hh palomino, a child's first pony and bombproof, on the Isle of Sheppey, getting her checked out by a vet from Maidstone. The first time I rode her out, she fell onto her knees on the road. Thinking she'd slipped, I bought her knee boots, but she did it a couple more times. I got the vet out again and he said that he didn't know what was wrong with her, and to try corrective shoeing. But she still did it. Despite this, I rode around the roads and fields, getting to be quite well known because of the western attire.

I put out an advertisement several times to teach western riding and Pat, an American living in England, got in contact. She really taught me more than I did her, and we became good friends.

When Goldie finally fell, whilst trotting out in our field at the stables luckily, I got out another vet. He saw immediately that her flexor tendons had gone. Sadly, I retired her as a pet. Although I sued the original vet through the small claims court, I lost because I should have had another vet out in the beginning,

Then, one day, I was stuck by another tragedy. I came home from work and hearing the TV on in Ann-Marie's room, I called out, but she didn't answer. I was suddenly worried, as since her early teens, she had suffered dreadfully with period pains. Doctors had been called out quite often but they all insisted that it was just normal. Finally, after collapsing several times, she had been rushed to hospital, where they discovered she had something called endometriosis. She had to stop riding because of the pain, she couldn't cycle, and I even had to drive really carefully round corners while we were out in the car because the pressure hurt. The drugs she had to take were dreadful, with awful side effects. She had been to the doctor's that morning but had insisted that she could go by herself, not wanting me to have time off work perhaps.

When I got no answer to my banging on the door and threatening to knock the door down, I grabbed a hammer and chisel, and began tearing off the architrave, expecting her to shout and tell me to go away. Nothing. When I broke in, she was asleep on her bed. But her eyes were open. She had taken tablets and half a bottle of wine. The note she left said that due to her bad mood swings while on the drugs, she couldn't keep treating Andy and I so badly anymore, and she wanted to be with her dad. After she died, I lost interest in everything and Goldie was sold as a companion.

One day, six months later, Pat phoned me to say that western lessons were being given only about seven miles away from me. I told her what had happened and that I was out of riding. But the bug had started, and two weeks later I went to watch. Two weeks after that, I booked a lesson. Three weeks later in answer to an advertisement in the paper, I went to look at a three year old grey/white white cob gelding. I fell in love and named him Grey Cloud, although he was eventually referred to as Blue Boy. He was very difficult at first as I'd never had an untrained horse before, but he learned to respect me and then we became almost inseparable. He knew almost nothing, and I had to start training him from scratch.

Cloud had been very badly frightened when brought down by trailer from Swanley to Herne Bay, and it took me months to get him to travel in a horse trailer. We slowly began hacking out alone, and then I was introduced to pleasure rides, anything from ten to sixteen miles, usually sponsored. He was slow being a cob, but we ambled round by ourselves, putting in reasonable times, but mainly enjoying being somewhere different. It was a wonderful way to see the countryside and areas you couldn't see from the road. He carried not only me and the saddle, but a lariat, canteen and saddlebags. We became very well known in the area—or at least he did.

We took part in the Save the Kent and Canterbury Hospital marches several times, and with me carrying a banner, he took me safely through the traffic on Saturdays. We even had a lope on the grass alongside the old stone

Canterbury city wall. We took part in a day's ride in Epping Forest with a few others when one was organised. The following year I wanted to go on a ride in Hyde Park, London but unfortunately, had to miss it due to my car breaking down. Apparently, the western horses had caused quite a sensation.

I had been going to watch rodeos held in Essex for a couple of years, but it wasn't until I took some friends with me and they asked why I wasn't going in for it, that I finally plucked up the courage to book to enter the next one. These took place twice yearly, run by Leslie and Stuart Powell of the-S-Ranch based at Fawkham, near Longfield in Kent.

When I arrived at the first one, it was like joining a big family, everyone was so friendly and helpful, even the brilliant riders. I tried everything, from flag racing, barrel racing, bending, trail (an obstacle class,) showing-in-hand (horsemanship,) and even cattle work.

When Cloud got worried about being with the cattle the first time, I was advised not to force it, he would get used to it as he gained more experience. He never really got on with other animals including horses, and the cattle were no exception. If he thought they weren't moving out his way quickly enough, he wasn't particular about using his teeth, which would have meant being disqualified. One particular steer known as Bully, had a reputation of being rather stubborn, and the crowd were in hysterics when Cloud decided that as teeth weren't allowed, a hoof would—narrowly missing Bully's nose. A more surprised steer you never saw, and he actually gave ground! As Cloud slowly improved in confidence, I took him in the trailer up to Leslie and Stuart's for lessons.

At the rodeos three of us girls, June, Juliet Smith and I, began to team up for the cattle penning and cattle driving, even getting rosettes at a couple of shows. One time we amassed enough points to win a lovely sash as the Cowgirl of the Rodeo. It was great fun, I felt just like a cowboy.

I used to take my dogs with me, Brough a border collie and Callie, a small brown dog. Unfortunately, Brough, who was 14 ½, became very disabled with arthritis and had to be put to sleep, leaving Callie desperately unhappy. In desperation because I thought I'd lose her, I searched a local newspaper and saw an advertisement for Border Collie puppies, not far away in Deal. Going to see them, I came back with one that I named Cody.

It took Callie three days of being chased and bitten by Cody before she began to perk up and play with him, and they began to end up in rough and tumbles as she used to shake him by the throat. He loved it all.

I worked in the afternoons, and having no idea where to leave him as there was no fencing round my big caravan at the time, especially as he was so young and had had a couple of 'accidents' indoors, I tried tying him to a stake on the grass outside. It seemed to work while I was there and watching him, so I felt fairly safe and drove off.

Kristin, who owned the site had heard him barking later, came down to investigate, and found Cody had tied himself up in knots. Taking him back across the field to her house she met up with some people from a caravan at the top of the field. They adored dogs and took him off her for the rest of the afternoon.

Coming in the gate after work, I was mortified to find out that he'd got himself in such a mess but to my delight, Daphne, Tony and their son, Daniel were some of the nicest people I'd ever known, and we became firm friends. As they adored dogs, they were only too happy to help look after Cody and Callie from time to time when they were staying in their caravan, and Daniel would often come down to play with them.

Then, listening to a friend at work who came to show me his photographs of America and tell me of his travels, I began to dream of going—to actually visit places I'd only read about in books-but how? I decided to sell my bungalow and go, for I was spending so much time at the stables it was being badly neglected. It took six months before anyone was really interested in it.

I was nervous about going, especially as I was terrified of flying and asked a riding friend, Sarah Chapman, if she'd like to come with me. She jumped at the chance. I also mentioned it to Andy, who had always kept in touch with me after Ann-Marie died. As a builder and decorator, he had been brilliant at helping me out with electrical and plumbing faults around the bungalow, and he said he'd love to go as well. I was pleased as I felt it would be much safer travelling with a man.

I decided where I wanted to go, which included a week on a ranch, and he went to a travel agents to see if they could organise the trip. After a lot of manipulating, as they were more used to set tours not a DIY one, it was all arranged. As the time drew closer, I got more and more excited, reading more books about where I was going, wondering what it was really like over there and if I would I see real cowboys! If only there had been no flying involved.

And then the day arrived. A real life adventure.

HOLIDAY 1999

Chapter 1

A Dream Come True.

Monday 13th September

By late afternoon, I was packed and very, very nervous. I was absolutely petrified of flying, never even having dared to go abroad to Spain or Portugal with my parents and my brother and sister and their families, and here I was heading for America. On top of that, newspapers had always pointed out how dangerous it was in America. People had been shot and robbed at gunpoint, car doors always had to be locked, you should never stop at the side of the road, and what about road rage etc (none of which we ever saw.) But my desire to go there far outweighed the risks. Nothing was going to stop me.

I had already taken Callie and three month old Cody to local kennels just outside Whitstable, Kent, off the Thanet Way. My father often left his dog there, so I was sure they'd be looked after properly. Unfortunately, Callie had had a re-occurrence of an ear problem over the weekend and I had taken the drops with me that I got from the veterinary that morning. The elderly people assured me that they could deal with her. I also gave them written confirmation of the vet's number and address with and permission to call them out if necessary.

I sat and re-checked that I had my tickets and travellers' cheques, and my passport, the first ever. Oh, the photo. Despite having sat in the booth a couple of times, the photos still looked awful, as I'd been warned by friends. How the passport controllers would recognise me I had no idea.

Over the months, I had carefully made a list of things to take as well as do before I left home. And as I had decided to make notes while on holiday, to remind me of everything when I got back, I had packed a notepad and pens. I had no inkling that once back home, my notes, despite being somewhat stilted, became of great interest, being passed from person to person. (In 2002 after being encouraged to try to turn all my notes into a novel, I had to update them as I had only written short sentences for myself. I was amazed at the amount of things I still remembered, and even more amazed at what I'd left out.) Throughout the trip I came across the names of towns, States, and rivers just as I'd read about them in my cowboy books.

I finally went to bed, not expecting to sleep, but I did.

Tuesday 14th September.

Stephen, my friend's husband and a taxi driver, came to pick me up first at 4.30am, packing my suitcases into the boot of the car. We drove round and picked up Sarah her family waving us off, then went to get Andy. His family were waiting at their gate to see him off too, their dogs barking.

He sat in the front with Stephen and we set off down the Thanet Way to the M2, on to Detling Hill, the M20 and headed for the airport. I was nervous and shaky, but Sarah was excited, and Andy was already used to going abroad. He assured me that the planes were much bigger than the short haul ones going to the Continent.

We were due at Gatwick three hours earlier than our 10am flight and had left in plenty of time, wary of heavy traffic or road works, so that when we hit the usual traffic rush hour just before the airport, we weren't inconvenienced.

Eventually we stopped at the departure drop off point. Andy found a cart for our luggage and we followed him through the concourse. I was used to the moving walkway having brought mum and dad several times when they went on holiday to Spain, but going through the x-ray machine was novel, and passport control. At least it took my mind off the thought of flying-nearly! I was petrified, still trying to think of ways I could get out of it even as we went through customs and through to the departure lounge. Even walking round the shops couldn't help the sick feeling in my stomach.

The sight of the big silver American Airlines plane through the lounge window terrified me. Andy had said they were big, but to me it wasn't. I couldn't believe it could actually fly through the air. I tried to put a brave smile on my face, but it must have looked strained. Sarah was fascinated and really looking forward to it.

We lined up when the numbers of our seats were called, walking down a long carpeted metal corridor to where the cabin crew were waiting in the doorway. As we shuffled inside, I tapped Andy on the shoulder and said, "I thought you told me it was big!"

"It is," he replied, "compared to the smaller flights to the Continent." I felt claustrophobic.

We bundled our hand luggage into the cupboards above our seats and sat down. I was shaking, trying to get interested in the bag of goodies given to us for the flight on the seat, with a blanket and a small pillow.

The stewardesses gave a demonstration of how to put on life jackets, pointing to the emergency exits and toilets. As the plane was a non-smoker, they stated that smoke detectors worked in the toilets and must not be tampered with. I was thrilled by their American accents for it was almost like being in the States already.

Finally, after telling people to turn off any portable phones or players and checking that everyone had their seat belts on, the plane began to move backwards. I kept wishing that I had the courage to scream let me out, but was afraid of looking a fool. I shut my eyes, too afraid to look up in case I could see out of the closest window. The plane taxied out onto the runway. Andy had already told me that once into the air, not to worry if the engines went quiet, they had to make as little noise as possible over the houses. The plane stopped, the engines began revving, and then it began to go faster and faster, finally lifting into the air.

*"Oh, ****. "* I prayed that I hadn't thought out loud!

The motion made me feel sickly, and when I opened my eyes, everything seemed to whirl, making me feel extremely sick. I prayed that I wouldn't be ill—how embarrassing. Eventually, as the plane stopped banking and levelled out, I felt a little less ill, but still terrified at the knowledge that there was nothing below my feet. Once permission was given, Sarah put on her headphones to listen to her CD player, while Andy was reading the magazines from the pocket in front of him. Overhead, in several places down the aisles were TV screens for the in-flight movies, and a handset in the armrest to use them also had buttons for music channels.

Not long after we set off, the stewards and stewardesses came down the gangways with a trolley, asking if anyone wanted a drink and handing out packets of pretzels. I was so petrified that I couldn't eat and refused everything, but Andy warned me that I had to drink as much as I could to stop dehydration in the recycled air. A few hours into the flight, Andy began sneezing-the beginning of a cold.

Despite people continually getting up to go to the toilets, I was far too worried to move, frightened the plane would tip if I did, which was stupid as lots of other passengers were all moving about. Finally, I had no option, making my way nervously to the back. The toilets were occupied so I had to wait, holding onto the wall for safety, where I spotted a map of the route we were taking stating the speed of the plane, and the temperature outside. We were going at 550mph, and it was minus forty-six outside. Finally, my curiosity overcame me when I saw something through the window across the gangway, and without leaving go of the wall, I leant forward, fascinated to see snow and green coloured lakes below me. Greenland! I called to Sarah to come and look.

After eleven hours, and arriving late, we landed at Dallas International airport. What a relief. I couldn't get off the plane fast enough. It was very hot in the metal and glass corridor from the plane, but I gazed fascinated across the runways at the flat land that danced with heat hazes. Texas! I was totally enthralled at being in America, at last I was in my magical land, somewhere I had always wanted to go, and I couldn't stop looking around for anyone in cowboy hat and boots.

We were due to leave for Kansas City at 15.45 from another part of the airport and had to run through the concourse, dodging people and carts. We handed our tickets in at the desk, our main baggage having been sent across automatically to our plane. I nearly had no time to get worried, until, once inside, I saw the plane was smaller. I nearly freaked. We struggled into our seats, doing up the seatbelts, listening once again to the instructions again on life jackets, etc. Then the plane taxied out onto the runway. I shut my eyes and prayed, gripping the arms of the seat tightly. Sarah was looking out the window, delighted to watch. It was only one and half hour flight there, but to me it took ages. I couldn't eat, but I did force down a coffee. Finally we reached Kansas City, once an early cattle town, at 17.15pm.

After the Civil War when the southerners returned to the Texas and New Mexico ranges, they found that although their cattle had increased alarmingly, they were actually 'cattle poor' with nowhere to take them. The animals sold for cents for just their hide and tallow until someone decided to drive a herd to the newly started railheads in Kansas where the rising population in the east were crying out for fresh meat.

In 1869, the Atchison, Topeka and Santa Fe Railroad had come through from Chicago on its way to Pueblo, and stockyards were built for cattle arriving from Texas. The Kansas Pacific Railroad ran north of Kansas City, coming in from Denver and serving the cattle towns of Hays, Ellsworth, Abilene and Sedalia, then on to St. Louis and Chicago. During the cattle boom, which lasted between the end of the Civil War and 1890, only 25 years, ten million head of cattle were moved up from the south to Colorado and New Mexico, serving the forts and the Indian reservations before heading on to Kansas, Nebraska and the railroads.

Once through customs, we discovered the carousel and retrieved our cases, Andy finding a lady at a kiosk to arrange a shuttle bus to take us to the Amtrak station. We sat in the glassed lounge overlooking the roadway until it came, a big people carrier. (All the motels/ hotels had free shuttles to and from the airports, but for places like the Amtrak station we had to pay.)

The driver was a 'Huggy Bear' type character in sunglasses, straight out of the Starsky and Hutch TV detective series, who had a tremendous sense of humour, making us laugh as he pointed out the various sights, seemingly able to drive without actually looking where he was going.

I was impressed by how clean the roads and sidewalks looked, and I couldn't see any graffiti around, although we did pass through a dingier part of town, rather like the East End of London. Several people got off at various hotels before we were left outside the train station.

We had to go down several flights of stairs to the waiting room which was quite small, with a booking counter, a little shop, rows of metal seats to wait on, and closed shutters behind which was the luggage area. Luckily, the lady behind the counter allowed us to leave our cases for we now had a seven hour stop over before our train arrived, what on earth were we going to do?

We took the elevator back up to the street, a wide four-lane road with a large hotel to our right and another big building opposite. To our left, over a bridge, was the skyline of city buildings, and I took my first photo in America. We all started to cross the road where we were, but I was worried that we were jaywalking by not using the intersection.

Further down, traffic lights were hung on cables strung across the road, the lights going from red to green without the amber we had. The street names were either hung on these cables or on metal poles over the road making them difficult to see if you were driving I thought, until I got used to them in Dodge City.

We wandered round the building to a green park and crossed it to more buildings that turned out to be a huge mall, evidently still in the process of being built. Despite the time, several shops were still open, not uncommon in America we found, unlike Britain.

We discovered an Italian restaurant and ordered a meal. It was lovely food, especially as I was starving, and the bill was paid with a traveller's cheque, getting change in return. Andy worked out the tip at the end, ten percent of the bill normally. These cheques were changed with no problem, and after a few days we finally gave up asking if shops took them. It was thrilling being handed American money. The five cent piece turned out to be bigger than the ten cent piece which made it rather confusing, while there were quarters (25c) and pennies, plus the paper bills (bill folds) of $1, $5, $10 and $20s which were very similar, despite the denomination. I had to carefully check the number at the top every time. I did ask for the Ladies room, and after a slightly confused silence, the waiter told me that the Rest Rooms were round the side.

Wandering about the complex, we emerged into a huge hall with an attractive waterfall two stories high with real trees, rocks and bushes, making the humidity rather high. We still had two hours to wait and were getting very tired having been on the go for nearly 24 hours, while my feet were aching with all the walking.

We finally returned to the station in the dark, lots of windows in the surrounding buildings brightly lit, to find several people now sitting in the waiting area. We were all fed up, and poor Sarah looked beat.

We retrieved our cases and sat chatting, occasionally getting up to read the notices on the boards for something to do. I strolled over to the glass doors overlooking the darkened station when I heard a train approaching and to my delight it was a large double decked train, silver coloured. The people alighting onto the platform used small plastic stools placed there by the conductors.

As it pulled out, I noticed numbers and wording on the sides: the baggage car, the dining car, the sleeper cars, even an observation deck on the top of one coach, its windows dark. According to the brochure, this was a non-smoker. All baggage had a weight limit like the airports, although nobody weighed ours.

Eventually our train pulled in at 23.20, the South West Chief, exactly the same as the one I'd seen earlier. The steward helped us on with our luggage, storing it away downstairs before showing us upstairs to our recliner seats. The area was in semi-darkness and the steward whispered so as not to disturb other sleepers, telling us we would be wakened before our stop, Dodge City.

Once settled, I could see that along the gangway beside each seat ran luminous strips, guides to enable you to find your way about.

We slept fitfully and uncomfortably, not only being disturbed by the stewards going back and forth, but from being next to the doors between the carriages which continually rattled and banged. When the doors were opened, the noise was loud from the tracks below. I noticed that there were pads on the doors, one halfway up and one at the foot, and while watching, I saw that to open the door you could either push the pad in the centre, or, if your hands were full, kick the lower one. They automatically closed after.

We slept through Emporia, Newton and Hutchinson, old cow towns, missing Ellsworth and Hayes that were further north. Eventually, a lady steward tapped me on the shoulder and said quietly that we would be pulling into the station very shortly.

Chapter 2

Cowboy Country.

Wednesday 15th September.

In 1872 when the railroad arrived the name was changed from Buffalo City to Dodge City after the nearby Fort Dodge for there were already many towns called Buffalo in the county. Fort Dodge had been established in 1865 on the Santa Fe Trail between two major Indian crossings on the Arkansas River and had given protection to wagon trains as well as being a supply base for troops fighting the Indians. Kiowa and Cheyenne amongst others had lived in the area, which had abounded with game then, including huge herds of buffalo. Wagons and even trains could be halted for up to two days as just one vast herd passed by.

Buffalo hides had become much sought after when new techniques back east could turn the tough skin into soft leather, and inside three months, forty thousand hides and one million pounds of buffalo meat were shipped out. Between 1872 and 1874 an estimated eight hundred and fifty thousand hides were sent back.

Winter could be hard, one year a hundred buffalo hunters had frozen to death out on the plains. It was hard to imagine the hardships that people faced in those days just to make a living. The mass slaughtering of the huge herds, not only for their hides and meat, but to bring the Indians to their knees and force them onto reservations, nearly saw the end of the buffalo. By 1875 they were almost gone, their place taken by the cattle herds coming up from Texas. From 1875 to 1886 over five million cattle were driven up the Western Trail alone.

In 1877, Ed Masterson became Marshall, while brother Bat was Sheriff of Ford County, Dodge being the county seat, then in 1878, Wyatt Earp became the assistant Marshall. On one occasion, two cowboys were leaving after a trail drive, rather inebriated, when one began firing his gun in fun, shooting up the dancehall where Doc

Holliday and Bat Masterson were playing cards. Everyone apparently 'dropped to the floor in seconds.' As the two raced out of town, one was shot and wounded, dying a few weeks later. Lawlessness became common, fights often ending in shootouts and creating the need for a Boot Hill cemetery.

In 1883, after the famous shootout at Tombstone a gambler called Luke Short was run out of Dodge City by his rival, so his friends including Bat Masterson, Doc Holliday and Shotgun Collins among others, drifted into town 'just visiting.' The rivals decided to back down, and the friends rode quietly back out of town.

By 1879, the cemetery had closed, Fort Dodge was abandoned in 1882 and by 1886 the great cattle drives had ended after only twenty-five years.

We arrived at Dodge at 6.15am where it was dark and raining. I was really excited, I was actually in an old cow town from the cowboy era and I already felt I knew America from the books I'd read. To actually cross the rivers and see the towns was just unbelievable.

We took our cases into an old wooden station to find that an elderly man was in charge, George, who turned out to be very religious. I remembered that Frank from work, who had first started me thinking of going to America after he'd been, had mentioned an elderly lady he'd met here last year and, when we talked to George, she turned out to be his wife. Andy offered to send him a postcard of Canterbury Cathedral when we got back home. George informed us that no cabs ran anymore, but offered to take us to the Best Western Silver Spur Motel for ten dollars. We crammed into his car and he dropped us off outside.

At the reception we booked in, and had to go out across the car lot (car park) to our rooms, Andy's across the way from ours. Sarah's and mine was comfortable and neat, with multicoloured bedspreads, wooden furniture, a small cupboard between the twin beds and wall lights either side of the headboards. These I had trouble with trying to find out how the switches worked. It seemed that the very small button had to be twisted, one click for on (dim), once more for bright, and again for off. The main switches on the wall worked opposite to ours back home, being pushed up for on. It was the same for the standard lamps, too. I spotted the trail of thin wiring on the floor to the standard lamps and TV's that couldn't happen in Britain today with our Health & Safety rules. There were also two wooden framed armchairs and a wooden table.

All the Best Western's turned out to be basically the same style. In all the different motels and hotels we ever visited, I had great fun trying to get the various coffee machines, where supplied, to work, as each were different. There were also air conditioners in the rooms, some quiet, some noisy, and they gave you no idea of the heat to expect outside the room. Most of the time, even with them on, I only slept with a sheet over me.

Once we'd settled in and it became lighter outside, we returned to the reception to ask about a restaurant. The man pointed across the car lot to a small, old fashioned looking wooden building, a wonderful diner. Crossing the grounds, we passed an outdoor swimming pool, empty, as it was the end of the season.

As soon as we sat down at a table, the waitress came over and gave us large glasses of water, which happened everywhere we went in America. We enjoyed a lovely cooked breakfast during which Andy suggested that we get a rental car to see the sights.

Back in reception, they kindly phoned up a local company and the car, a Buick, was actually brought round for us. Andy quickly bought a street map to help out.

Andy drove, thank goodness. It felt weird being on the 'wrong side' of the road, and very nerve racking at first. I kept my eyes out for the speed limits that ranged from 15 mph outside schools that were in session to 75 mph on a lot of the Interstates, and we had been told that we could turn right on a red light if the road was clear. Strange. But what a brilliant idea as it kept the traffic moving. All the big intersections had traffic lights, much better than roundabouts, I thought. The directions were confusing as the roads were sign posted south, north, west or east, which was alright if you knew which way you were going. Cars could also undertake as well as overtake, and you mostly stayed in the lane you were in until you needed to exit. During the times that we drove in America, I was saddened to see dead racoons, deer and gophers on the roadside, so different from the smaller English animals. Like ours, they had no chance against the swiftness of cars and trucks.

We drove around until we found the famous Boot Hill Cemetery, parking in a large car lot fenced off with wooden post and rails. It turned out that there wasn't much of the graveyard left as most of it had been dug up in the late 1890's, with the drifters, buffalo hunters and others being reburied north east of town. 'No one famous had ever been buried there.'

We passed through a door into the main building, a reconstruction of the Great Western Hotel, housing the museum, a store, admissions counter and an orientation theatre. We paid our entrance money and went through to the museum. Coming to a glass case, it housed a partly erected tepee and artefacts of the plains people with some moccasins and other decorative wear, showing how the Indians had first lived on the land. To one side hung a huge black, shaggy buffalo hide. One case showed how the early settlers and cowboys had moved in, another held a firearms collection, and one held the eastbound goods. Notices gave information about each.

We browsed in the shop before going outside to the cemetery, where the sign beside the door announced: 'Boot Hill Cemetery. Final resting place for buffalo hunters and festive cowboys.'

We came to an old white painted, wooden jail with steel bars, authentically dated from 1865 that had been at the fort until 1953 when it had been donated to the museum. Andy managed to video me through the barred window at the front, standing in one of the cells. I didn't like to imagine being shut in for real as the cells, two of them, were very small, dark, and cramped.

We strolled round the plot reading the wooden markers, real or replaced? One of the markers was for a man named Mac McDermott, which happened to be the name of the Personnel Director where I worked. Another marker bore the legend:

ONE NIGHT HE
TOOK A POT
SHOT AT WYATT
EARP.
BURIED ON BOOT HILL
AUGUST 21, 1878.
"LET HIS FAULTS,
IF HE HAD ANY
BE HIDDEN IN
THE GRAVE"

Heading back out towards the car, there was a long line of wooden buildings that looked like a real town. Apparently this main or Front Street had been faithfully rebuilt from photographs after the originals had been burnt down in 1885. We walked along the wooden sidewalk with its shingled porch overhangs and went into some of the shops, full of old tools, dry goods and furniture.

Geo. Hoover's saloon and cigar store-there were several saloons all on Front Street-had been the first commercial business in Dodge, opening in 1872. By 1877, he was receiving as many as five thousand cigars a week to sell. The tonsorial parlour, or barber's shop, was the first stop for cowboys straight in off the trail, dusty, longhaired, and bearded after their journey. Here, they got a haircut, shave and a bath before 'treeing the town' with their high spirits. The barber was usually a mine of information where they could get news about almost anything.

The gunsmith shop, Zimmermans, had had a saddle makers out back while a drug store housed the Post Office, and a grocery, furniture and undertaker's suppliers was next door. The first newspaper office had been opened here in 1874. Of restorations, there was a superior schoolhouse from Kansas, and a 1903 Santa Fe locomotive, a huge black engine with a cowcatcher on the front. Fantastic. The actual blacksmith and wheelwright store is believed to date from the 1800s. The Boot Hill stage had run from here taking passengers, mail and freight out to the Panhandle on the Texas plains.

At the end of the street was an old building, the Hardesty House. Built in 1879 it was typical of the 1880s showing a middle-class family home. Around the outside ran a white picket fence, while beside it a covered wagon stood. During the summer months, there had been demonstrations of printing and black-smithing, shoot-outs, and stagecoach rides, but unfortunately for us, these had closed for the season.

We left and drove along to the shops, also wooden buildings with post and rail fencing in front. The assistants were very nice with "hi guys, how're you doing?" the minute we entered and ending with "have a nice day" or "have a good one," even if we bought nothing-a lot more pleasant than some of the shop assistants in Britain. They were fascinated when they heard our accents and asked if we were English, wanting to know where we came from, how long we'd been here, and where we were going. All the people we met in America were interested in us, and very friendly, possibly because most of the places we visited were where the British never went.

Further down the main street, West Wyatt Earp, I spotted a clothing store, the Western Discount Store, and Andy turned into the parking lot, which, like most of the frontages, seemed to be dusty rutted concrete with lots of weeds. The whole street looked about 75 five years behind the times.

Inside, I found some lovely cowboy boots, and Andy got himself a white Stetson, which I thought suited him. The lady owner was intrigued by our accents too, and we ended up chatting for ages before we left. She very kindly gave us all a small stickpin angel for good luck that I still have.

Driving back the way we had come, we got slightly lost despite the map, but came across the huge stockyards full of cattle. We drove on for quite a way looking for the old Fort Dodge site where some of the original buildings are now part of the Kansas Soldiers Home. Following the signs, we drove slowly round the quiet roads looking at the peaceful buildings set back under the trees, many with beautiful, flower filled gardens, before heading back to Dodge.

The town of Cimarron was about fifteen miles further on, on the I-50, a straight wide, two-lane highway with very little traffic that passed over hilly grasslands. Like everywhere we went, there didn't seem to be any litter and I found out some time later that many of the Interstates and freeways had each mile being adopted by either a person, or a firm, and they each cleared their part. On top of that, litter dropping was a fining offence. Great idea, we should do that back home

We stopped in Cimarron, parking on the slant on the wide street just like they do on TV, alongside several white police cars. The drug store had a mixture of groceries, drugs, gifts, and a small cafe area, and we browsed through the souvenirs before sitting and having a coffee. Afterwards, we strolled up and down the sidewalks looking in the shop windows.

On the way in I'd seen a sign for the Santa Fe Trail, so on the way back to Dodge, Andy went into the parking area. We walked up a long winding concrete path to a sign that stated that indents from the wagon wheels from all those years ago could still be seen. Despite my imagination, there was practically nothing to be seen and I was a little disappointed.

The trail had been used by settlers heading west, starting in Independence, Missouri, what they called a jumping off point, and leading on to Oregon and California. It followed the Kansas River for a while, passing Fort Dodge. From here, one branch followed the Arkansas River, before taking a mountain route, better suited to mules, to Santa Fe. In 1824, despite a group of men suffering from Comanche attacks and a lack of water, a route was forged through the Cimarron, becoming known as the Cimarron Cutoff. In late seasons this had been prone to rainstorms that caused flash floods and rockslides, turning the dusty flatland into a muddy bog.

At Santa Fe, it branched into the Old Spanish Trail to Los Angeles, Sutter's Fort and San Francisco, through either the Donner Pass or Carson Pass. The Gila (pronounced Heela) River Trail went to San Diego. This site is owned and maintained by the Boot Hill Museum, who also maintained Point of Rocks five miles east. This had been a rounded hill with a large rocky face protruding on the south end, a major landmark for settlers, but had almost been destroyed by a highway widening improvement in 1981.

The Middle Crossings of the Arkansas River aren't visible any more due to the sandy soil shifting in frequent floods, but settlers could cross almost anywhere due to the shallow waters, and here numerous Indian raids took place. The Trail only lasted from 1821 to 1872 when the railroad arrived.

The rolling grassland stretched as far as the horizon and I could imagine it going on and on endlessly. The noise of the grasshoppers was astounding, and when I spotted one on a wall, it was twice the size of ours.

We drove on back to Dodge City, stopping at a Pizza Hut for a pizza and salad from the salad bar. There was a large choice of both, and again we were served the usual glasses of water.

Finally, Andy headed to a gas station for petrol before returning the car. He seemed to be ages rattling about at the back before getting into the car, laughing. He said he couldn't believe the cost of the gas, $13 for a whole tank, and had kept trying to put more in. I was surprised that they had unleaded petrol here as I had the impression from home that the Americans weren't environmentally friendly, but watching a TV programme a couple of years later, I spotted that unleaded was already being used in 1989, well before I'd even heard of it. Back at the motel, the rental people came and collected the car.

We managed to phone England after a lot of difficulty as America has several different phone companies, to let Sarah speak to her dad, then later that evening had a meal in the little restaurant again. Andy arranged at reception for their shuttle bus to take us to the train station the next morning.

Chapter 3

Heading West.

Thursday 16th September.

We awoke to a dark, wet, cool morning. After showering, Sarah and I met up with Andy and took the cases to the shuttle. I paid for the motel, as here, Santa Fe and Albuquerque, weren't already done by Thomas Cook, and then driven to the Amtrak station.

Our cases were taken and placed in the lower part of the carriage by the sleeping car attendant, while we wended our way up the narrow stairs to our seats, recliners with a fold-down tray attached to the rear of the seat in front. There was an overhead luggage rack, foot, and leg rests, overhead lighting, and the carriage was very clean, light and airy with panoramic windows. Below, in the next carriage along, was a small café with seating where we could get hot and cold drinks and snacks, although our tickets included the price of our meals.

We didn't stay here long, heading straight along to the observation, or Sightseer car. This, in daylight, would prove to have wraparound windows, big windows with the glass curved above, giving a brilliant view. The lounges showed either movies or cartoons for the children. The tannoy was brilliant, informing us of everything from the snack bar opening, to the times of the meals in the diner, approaching stations and, for those sleeping, when their beds would be turned down. They also gave information for when we crossed State lines, and when we had to change our watches as we passed through a Time Zone.

For now, it was very dark, but the seats were comfortable. The train travelled through Garden City where street lamps shone yellow pools of light onto the damp sidewalks and buildings. There were already a few cars on the roads.

Slowly, dawn began to lighten the sky and I could make out more details of the land before, to my astonishment, it became black again. I suddenly realised that I'd just seen the pre-dawn that I'd read about in cowboy books. Finally the true dawn came showing the land to be flat and almost monotonous. We passed small homesteads, all of which seemed to have their own private car wrecks and looked rather run-down. The train followed alongside narrow country roads and dusty tracks for miles and miles, and the accompanying telegraph poles, at half the height of ours, looked really strange, more like grave markers.

Then came the Arkansas River with its deep washes and run-offs scarring the ground, the sandy banks covered with scrub bushes and trees almost to the waterline, and muddy coloured water. I tried to imagine the herds of cattle splashing through on their way to the stockyards. In full flood, this must have been terrifying to the cowboys, most of who never learned to swim, and where they would have used their swimming horses. Like people, horses had preferences for some types of work, and cowboys would have had their own string allotted to them by the ranch. Some worked well at night, some were better at cutting cattle from the herd, while others were good on bad ground. Paints and white horses were never used around cattle as their brightness in sunlight or moonlight could spook the whole herd into a stampede.

We passed a huge reservoir that gradually grew shallower, finally giving way to marshlands. Here, blue sky began to appear in the breaks between the clouds and the sun began to come out. I spotted several hawks or kites flying, while buzzards lazily glided on the thermals, circling overhead just like in western films.

As the train began to slowly bear left, ahead and to the right of us were snow capped mountains, the Sangre de Cristos, or Blood of Christ, we were told later. Strange name. It turned out that due to its peace and tranquillity, early Christians gave it their most sacred name, Blood of Christ.

Andy went off to the little snack compartment downstairs, coming back with coffees and sweet Danish pastries.

We crossed the Kansas / Colorado border, passing through Lamar and Los Animos, nearby was the famous Bent's Old Ford, crossing the Purgatory River, and on into La Junta (pronounced Hoonta,) where we passed into Mountain Time, putting our watches back one hour. We were allowed to get out onto the platform for a walk, the train being ahead of schedule. On the far side of our train a goods train began passing—and passing—and passing, apparently about one and a half miles long!

Andy strolled about filming the long silver train, the station and the road behind the buildings. It was fascinating seeing all the different shapes of the American cars, and still odd to see them driving on the wrong side to us, of the road, although there appeared to be less traffic than back home. Perhaps it would be different in the rush hour.

At last we were told to board and we rushed back to get a good seat in the observation car before everyone else. Good job we did as the seats were filled completely as the train pulled out. Slowly it started heading towards the mountains.

The dining car was opened and we were called for our meal. The tables had white linen tablecloths, china place settings, silver cutlery and vases with flowers. Pretty! There was a choice of three main meals with a small salad for starters, three choices of sweet, and coffee or a cold drink to follow. Due to the lack of seating, people were being asked to share tables, and we were joined by an American. After telling him that we were touring, he told us that we were heading for Tony Hillerman country. Hillerman, who I'd never heard of, was a modern western style writer who wrote his mystery/crime novels based around the Navaho country near the Grand Canyon in Arizona. He also revealed the places and the country we would go through on our way to Santa Fe.

Outside, the clouds were drifting over the flat brown plains like fluffy balls of cotton and so close, you felt you could just reach up and touch them. I saw a small herd of pronghorn, slender antelope, and then a sandy coloured dog. A coyote?

We stopped at Trinidad, another old cow town, where the station looked very ramshackle with some of the windows boarded up. The train then re-crossed the Purgatory River, passing through an untidy, sprawling industrial site before crossing the Colorado/New Mexico border near Raton and then over the Cimarron River. Raton had old, Spanish style buildings with arched fronts and painted in pale pastel oranges and yellows. Main Street seemed to consist of a long block of buildings, similar to Old Dodge, but some in either concrete or brick as well as wood.

The train slowed as it began heading up a long, winding track into a rocky mountain area whose slopes and valleys slowly became covered in pines or spruce. I could imagine the flat-topped ridges adorned with Indians riding along the rim on their coloured ponies, brandishing bows and spears. The rocky outcrops slowly changed from a sandy colour to a reddish brown. The scenery was amazing and so restful, no wonder the Native Americans wanted to keep this land. I felt sad for them being pushed out into the unwanted parts of America. We slowly clattered past maintenance men at the side of the track who waved as the train slowly curved round past them, and I waved back.

I began to feel slightly headachy and my nose began to run, so I took some Paracetamol I'd brought with me. Oh dear, I'd caught Andy's cold.

We went through Springer, crossed over the Canadian River, and wended our way through Wagon Mound, Las Vegas, not THE Las Vegas, Los Montoyas and on to Lamy, outside Santa Fe, reaching there in the afternoon.

We stepped out onto the tiny station platform where birds were twittering in the trees and shrubs, and crickets, or cicadas, chirped. Off the cool train, it was very, very hot. We had to wait here for other passengers arriving from an incoming train, and with only one track, and the trains running daily, they had to have special places where they could pass. One of these was here, so our train had to wait further down the line until the incoming slowly chugged into sight.

Once the other passengers had arrived, our cases were put into a box trailer behind the shuttle bus, and we were driven into Santa Fe several miles away, heading down dusty roads and through rolling green covered sandy hills.

Santa Fe lay in the foothills of the Sangre de Cristos' mountains surrounded by lovely views. With a mixture of Spanish, Pueblo, Western, and European peoples, it is also the capitol of New Mexico. Trade here 'legally' started with the Americans in 1821 just after Mexico became independent from Spain. Before that, the officials would ambush any traders, confiscating their goods if they tried to get through. It is still a mixture of American and Mexican cultures, and part of the famous Route 66 road runs through here as well as Albuquerque.

At 15.50pm we reached the Best Western Lamplighter Inn that was very nice, similar to the Silver Spur. Here, at an elevation of 7,000 feet, it turned out to be chilly in the mornings, but for now it was very warm.

We settled into our rooms then quickly changed and swam in the indoor pool, the first time for me in years, before Andy and Sarah crossed to the hot tub. I'd never been in one before and wow, as I slowly lowered myself into the bubbling water, it was very hot. I finally felt as if I was unwinding, and Andrew looked more relaxed, as did Sarah. She and I both agreed that the soft water in America was making our skin feel very smooth.

We went for a meal at a little restaurant across the road and I arranged with Andy that I'd ring him about 7.30am before we all retired to our rooms. Friday 17 September.

We rose at 7.30 and went down for an early swim, wrapping ourselves in our towels against the chilly air, and meeting up with Andy.

After that Sarah and I showered before dressing and going for breakfast-complimentary-in a small Mexican style restaurant joined to the motel. The owner was great and kept making jokes every time he passed us, fascinated that we were English as he was enjoying listening to our accents. Once we'd eaten, Andy went to the reception area to organise a car.

The rental people came out with a shuttle bus and took us back to their car lot where we signed for a white Escort with me as co-driver. Andy took the wheel and drove round until we found the shops, although we managed to get lost again despite having a map.

The town was bright and clean with the buildings in a pinkish rendering and lots of cacti plants outside, while plazas and inglenooks housed little antique and curio shops.

We stopped outside a huge building housing the local post / sorting office to get some stamps for our postcards. A great idea, these were sticky backed for ease.

Back in the centre of town, we parked in a large square surrounded by shops that mostly sold very expensive antiques, modern art or jewellery. Along one length of the plaza, on the sidewalk and under the shade of a thatched overhang, were Indians selling delicate jewellery laid out on colourful woven blankets.

We decided to drive out of town as I wanted to find the Old Pecos Trail, part of the original Spanish Trail for traders and immigrants going west, but we got lost, seeming to drive for miles out into the countryside without getting anywhere. Turning back and following the signs for the trail straight back into town again, it just seemed to vanish!

I was still totally confused by the road signs for north, south, east or west. You could be on Main Street West, but the car compass indicated you were heading north-until I finally worked out that the roads did not always go east to west and south to north, but would meander off course. It was easy for the Americans as they grew up knowing their compass points.

Back at the motel, we changed and went for a cool swim, before going out for a meal, finding an interesting looking Chinese restaurant. The food when it came was enormous, and I was upset at the amount of food that was wasted when we couldn't finish it all.

We ended up back at our rooms in the motel, where Sarah and I sat and watched TV till it was time to go to bed.

Chapter 4

A State Fair.

Saturday 18th September.

After another swim, we headed for the restaurant for our breakfast and had just ordered when Andy suddenly realised that he had to get the car back to the rental people before we were charged for another day, and rushed off. When the meals came, the restaurant owner kindly covered his plate with another to try to keep it hot.

Andy was ages, and when he got back, told us he'd been held up in the rush hour traffic. The owner offered to warm his food for him, but Andy said that it was OK, and started to eat. He then shot up to his room to collect something making the passing café owner stop short in surprise at him having disappeared again.

From this hotel, Thomas Cook had suggested that we make our own arrangements to get to Albuquerque, so while paying the bill, Andy asked the girl at the desk which would be the best way to get there, cab or bus? She suggested a rental car would be the cheapest, so Andy rang the same people we'd used, and they came and collected us in the shuttle.

The boys in the office laughed when we reappeared, especially when they found out what we wanted, but they were very helpful. Apparently, we could rent a car here, leave it at their lot in Albuquerque, and would then be shuttled to the airport! This proved to be very convenient.

We had a different car this time, a Chevrolet Blazer, white, and very nice. It had a temperature gauge, in either Fahrenheit or Centigrade that was already showing 24C outside.

We headed SW on I-25, a big three lane freeway out into the desert where I used Andy's camcorder to film not only the big road gantries overhanging the road for the place names, but the countryside. A long mountain range lay off to our right, while to the left were long rolling hills. I just loved the huge, colourful advertising billboards we came across at the sides of the road, despite them looking grossly out of place on the beautiful landscape.

Andy decided to turn off and join another two-lane highway, part of the famous old Route 66. This road had been made in 1926 after people in Oklahoma had wanted a Chicago to Los Angeles link through their state, and they got it. Most highways in those days were little better than dirt tracks, but Route 66 was built for all weather travelling and the promotion of highway and travel together made it famous.

During a very serious drought when the flat land disappeared under clouds of dust, 'Dust Bowl' refugees all headed away via the highway.

By the 1960's, the road had such a strong hold on America that the TV series, Route 66, was made. Then, ten years later, with the increase in flying, it was decommissioned, but to the amazement of officials, there was an outpouring of support for the route.

By 1989, there were few cars using the road, but as guidebooks began including it, a new generation grew up to learn about it, and today, more than twenty thousand vehicles travel along its length.

We came across a few shops at the side of the road and stopped where, in a lovely old wooden building, I treated myself to a beautiful turquoise necklace. Further on, we pulled onto a tarmac parking area beside an old shop selling saddles, chaps and other western stuff. Inside, almost hidden behind heaps of leatherwear on tables and even hanging from the rafters, two middle-aged men were making saddles by hand. It was all very expensive and I was disappointed not to be able to buy anything.

We rejoined the I-25 again heading for Albuquerque, and after a few hours of travelling, we came to the Best Western Rio Grande. This again was lovely, but there was a problem as for some unknown reason Andy wasn't booked in, but luckily they found a room very close to Sarah and I.

Albuquerque had begun with eighteen families. It should have been thirty to qualify as a township, but the provisional governor had 'invented' sixteen more families to get it, and a petition was raised for recognition in 1706. Granted by the Spanish Duke of Alburquerque (the first 'r' had been dropped later) new buildings eventually sprang up around the Old Town.

The streets were lined with three hundred year old adobe houses, street names coming from the original Spanish land grants, Catholic saints, or historic figures. The first church is in the Old Town and still used by the Catholic population. Los Ranchos de Albuquerque-the ranches of Albuquerque-have kept their fertile fields and a sense of the past, with descendants of the original Hispanic settlers still living in homes their ancestors owned, keeping up with the traditions, arts, cuisine and music.

When the 'Iron Horse' had arrived in 1880, it had been met not only by the real cowboys of the day, but the farmers who had been raising cattle since the Spanish arrived in the Sixteenth Century. Three hundred and forty New Mexico cowboys, all qualified horsemen, were among those who, with Roosevelt's Rough Riders, had fought against Spain in 1898 and were loyal to the United States. The cowboy influence is still seen from furniture to fixtures, a lot of it hanging in most of the shops.

Tom Mix made seventeen westerns in New Mexico, and Lonely Are the Brave, with Kirk Douglas, had been filmed in the Sandia Mountains east of Albuquerque. The town also has the dubious honour of being the state capitol for UFO sightings. These must have been either shy, or having the nights off, because I never saw anything! I was very disappointed.

We visited the old part of town that looked just like Santa Fe. The buildings and streets were very clean and pretty, still in the same pinkish adobe, and with the usual cacti plants adorning the gardens and pavement edges. Beautiful trees along the streets cast shady areas especially around a delightful plaza in the centre of which stood a lovely bandstand. A couple of old cannons rested on the grass. The paths to the centre were made of red bricks, and on one of the outer railings was a sign relating the beginnings of the town.

Andy found a shop where they organised balloon trips from the map we'd bought listing all the shops in the area, booking himself in for a flight the following morning. I refused to go, being too nervous. It was bad enough going in a plane, but no way was I hanging around in a basket under a flimsy looking canvas envelope full of hot air. It was arranged that they would pick him up at the motel at 6.15 the next morning, but advised him to phone through very early to ensure that it was still OK, for if the winds were wrong, or too strong, then it would be cancelled.

I kept my eyes open for any western tack shops, but failed to see any, just clothes stores with nothing there that I fancied.

Posters around town announced that the New Mexico State Fair was being held that night and we drove round to the parking lot of a shopping mall to catch one of the specially laid on buses, rather like our 'park and ride' buses. As we got on, we had to feed our dollar bill into a machine that then issued us with return tickets. I found it fascinating the way the bill was slowly grabbed and taken into the mouth of the machine. Lots of machines in America took bills, but I couldn't imagine our five or ten-pound notes being treated like that.

The grounds inside the fencing were packed out with people, with what seemed like hundreds more streaming through the gates. A rodeo was also advertised to start in an hour, so we crossed to the booking windows first and bought tickets before walking round the rides and stalls.

I was stunned at the sickly food on offer, every other stall seemed packed with hotdogs, toffee apples covered in chocolate, pretzels with melted cheese dips, Coke, Pepsi, and our candy floss, called cotton candy here. No wonder most Americans, including the kids, are obese. Nearly all of the meals we bought had a large selection of salads so the Americans really shouldn't have been so fat. Mind you, take a look at the British these days, we're running them a close second! We did buy large paper cups of crushed ice covered with a sweet flavoured syrup which could be either drunk through the straw as it melted or eaten using the tiny scoop on the other end.

In one area we stopped to see a 'fun' ride. Two people were strapped into a chair attached to a springy rubber cable, the chair was pulled down, then released to catapult into the air, bouncing up and down to ear piercing screams from the passengers. How they weren't sick I would never know as the chair spun round and round as well. Another ride had three people face down in a sort of sleeping bag. This was pulled back high before being released, to swing them back and forth over the heads of the crowd. I made sure I wasn't in their line of fire!

I caught sight of several mounted police and went over to pat the horses, telling the lady rider that I rode western back home. She was very interested, not knowing that we did it in Britain, and she was startled when I said we also did rodeos, although not up to their standard. I also went and patted the two horses whose riders were in western gear and were riding back and forth in front of the ticket area to advertise the event.

We entered the show ring, noting statements posted on the walls that said 'no filming.' Sarah and I took seats half way up the stands while Andy went and sat near the top so that he was able to film secretly from the carrying case, placing his coat over the top. Unfortunately, halfway through, two big ladies came in and sat right in front of him, obscuring his view.

The show started with a young boy singing the National Anthem while everyone stood, the men with their hats off, and everyone cheering like mad when he finished. Boy, are they fervently patriotic over here. Not like the British who rush to get out of the cinemas before our National Anthem is played. The announcer gave a great speech about how great America was, how great its people and its ideals, to even greater cheering than before.

Then when everyone had sat down, six cowboys rode into the ring holding banners aloft, lining up three on each side. A long, long serpentine of riders, cowboys and girls wended their way through, some horses calm, some very excited. Two clowns came in last, one on a pony, one on a horse, and when they galloped back to the far entrance where the riders were leaving, the pony bucked the clown off, frightening the last few horses. One girl nearly came off but luckily another rider grabbed her reins.

The bucking horses came on first. At the end of an 8 second ride, one pick-up man rode alongside the horse to rescue the rider if he had stayed the distance while the other leaned over to undo the bucking strap. Not only do the riders score points for their riding ability, but the horses and bulls were also judged on the severity of their bucking. One horse, a lovely sorrel, was brought back into the arena at the end, her foal with her, and it appears that they now breed horses especially for their bucking capabilities, instead of finding horses that did it anyway.

Huge Brahma bulls were used for the bull riding, enormous muscular animals, with long dewlaps and a hump on their shoulders like a camel. To my disappointment, this was harder to see from where we were sitting as the bulls stayed at the far end of the arena. Considering their size, they could twist and turn with amazing speed, and one fallen rider had to run for the chutes, diving up the rails and over before the bull got him. The rodeo clowns may look funny, but their highly dangerous job was to try to distract the enraged animal away from the fallen rider, one of them having to dive headfirst into a conveniently placed barrel.

Then came bulldogging with one rider, the hazer, keeping the steer running straight, while the other rider dove onto the steer's horns, twisting its head until it fell over, when the 'time out' was called.

Calf roping I didn't like at all, the way the calf was jerked to a halt on the end of the lariat, thrown to the floor, then three of its legs tied, two forefeet and one hind, although they all got up and ran off when untied. There are now special rules as to how the animals are roped so that there is very little risk of injury to them anymore. Several cowgirls did some very fast barrel racing, and last in was a six hitch of black horses harnessed to a lovely colourful wagon.

After it had finished, we returned to the show ground again to look at the last of the horses left in the stables. This was the final night of the fair. Andy went and spoke to a blacksmith at one of the stalls who was making branding irons, only to be told that no one can have them made these days without a special licence. I was quite moved that he'd even thought to ask, as I'd always wanted one for myself. Cloud had a freeze mark number on him in case he was ever stolen, but I'd always fancied having my Boxed C brand on him.

Leaving the grounds to catch our bus, Andy was accosted by an inebriated Navaho begging for money, a sad sight. Not only had these native Americans been treated so badly that they had lost their customs and way of life but quite a lot had turned to drink or begging because there was nothing for them to do. Once back at the car lot, we drove back to the motel for the night.

Sunday 19th September.

Next morning Sarah and I went to breakfast by our selves as Andy had already left for his balloon flight. I was still full of cold although possibly due to the warmer climate I didn't feel as bad as I usually did.

When he finally arrived back, we went and sat in the restaurant with him for a coffee while he ate and told us he'd had a fabulous time. They had passed over big storm drains, the site of the annual balloon festival where hundreds of them took off once a year, and out over the Rio Grande. This long river starts in Colorado, passes through Albuquerque, drops down through El Paso and ends up in the Gulf of Mexico.

We drove back through town and on to the rental place to return the Blazer, where a member of the staff was quite happy to take us to the airport. Black clouds and lightning were approaching, worrying me considerably as we were due to fly in a couple of hours and when the rain finally hit, with thunder and lightning, the downpour was very heavy, but fortunately the storm went over before we boarded the plane, to my relief. I wondered if I'd ever get used to flying.

It didn't help when the flight became very bumpy, with apologies from the pilot for the stewardesses not being able to bring round drinks. I was absolutely petrified, sitting rigidly in my seat with my eyes shut. Then as we started to descend to Tucson airport my ears were in agony despite swallowing water holding my nose and trying to eat the salted peanuts they'd given us at the beginning, feeling like screaming the pain was so bad. Once we'd landed I discovered I was deafened, almost unable to hear anyone talking, voices sounding very muffled.

We walked through the corridors until we found the carousel, being met there by gorgeous looking Mark who'd come from the ranch, the Lazy K Bar. The carousel started operating to bring round the luggage, but broke down to jeers from people. Mark told us that it happened quite often, and when it finally it started up again, to great cheers, we claimed our baggage

We waited in the steamy heat for Mark to come round with the people carrier, while I remembered to put my watch back an hour as we had passed through another time zone. Mark loaded the bags then drove us out of the wet airport and into the dusk. The sun was heading down over the mountains shining a beautiful gold through gaps in the big black clouds. Mark pointed out Hat Mountain to us, shaped like a sombrero, in the far distance, where the ranch apparently lay at the base about twenty-five miles away. (We were told the following year that originally it had been called Stetson Mountain.)

We arrived at the ranch in the dark with the gravel drive lit by low lights and more lights stuck up in some of the cacti while, at the head of the swimming pool were two huge palms, also lit by lights shining up their trunks. The water shone bright blue and looked really inviting.

We were taken into the office in the long, low, ranch style wooden building and made very welcome, signing in and having to sign a disclaimer form so that we could ride. We were also given small torches to see our way about the ranch during the evening and night, because of snakes or scorpions, although tarantulas weren't poisonous. We were then offered dinner, buffet style with meat, salad, and slices of fresh melon with a jug of delicious lemonade. After it I had a coffee.

We were taken down a gravel path to our casitas (caseetas) small low cabins with old style wooden beds, wooden chests of drawers and a big closet, a bathroom and shower unit. The front door had a mesh screen against which the moths and bugs were bouncing. There were a lot of deep red beetles, firebugs, lying on the outside stoop, some upside down where they had fallen, desperately flailing their legs in an effort to right themselves. Despite the incessant chirping of the crickets, the tinkling of the wind chimes on the ranch porch, and the lonesome whistle of the Amtrak trains in the distance, I slept well, finding the sounds very restful and soothing. When I got home, I really missed the sounds, actually going out and buying some wind chimes for my doorway.

Chapter 5

The Lazy K Bar.

Monday 20th September.

We got up an hour early to get ready for the 7am ride, and as I stepped outside our room to be hit by the heat, it was just in time for a fantastic golden sunrise. I was surrounded by cactus, one a huge saguaro with candelabra branches, some beautiful bushes, and lovely shady trees underneath of which were three hammocks. Huge colourful butterflies and tiny, brilliantly coloured hummingbirds flitted and danced around the flowers of the bushes. There was also a horseshoe pitch and what looked like very large shove ha'penny boards. The casitas ran around stone edged gravel paths, and the gardens were flat dusty sand with different cacti, some that I recognised. Fortunately, a lot of them had name plaques. Two lovely Dalmatian dogs were lying on the porch of the ranch house.

We walked up to the corrals where the wranglers were sorting out the horses, and I was given Dunny, a mouse coloured horse. As I mounted Ed, the tall older wrangler, looked at the showy black, fringed chaps that I had brought from home and said, "great chaps, I'd like to have them."

We were offered a walk or lope ride, but for the lope you had to take a test in the corral first. Sarah decided to do the lope and passed with flying colours, while Andy and I plumped for the walk ride first.

A short way out the ride was halted while Ed came round and checked that all our cinches (girths) were tight enough. Our group was taken up and down the rocky ridges overlooking the ranch. I was nervous of the steep, narrow places, but the horses seemed very surefooted. At one point, Ed showed us the small red fruits that grew on the prickly pear cactus, skinning one with his knife and letting us taste it. It was nice, like melon, and was commonly made into either jam, what the Americans call jelly, or used in fruit cocktails.

We stopped on top of one ridge where he pointed out a jumble of wooden beams. Some time back, a film crew had come out to make a film about Geronimo and had decided to make a fake rock in amongst the real rocks for him to jump off. Once it was built, they'd then decided not to and just upped and left. I couldn't believe it, here we were surrounded by rocky terrain and they wanted fake rocks as extra!

We arrived back for the buffet style breakfast, lovely creamy scrambled eggs, crispy bacon (how do they get it like that,) biscuits (cowboy sponge style,) beef burgers, and slices of melons and other fruits. It was quite refreshing to eat the fruit and the meal together. Coffee, or their iced lemonade, which really tasted of lemons followed. We could help ourselves to both during the day, but mostly I had the lemonade, especially lazing by the pool.

There were lots of elderly people at other tables. The waitress, Rusty, who had a great sense of humour, told us they belonged to a club called the Elderly Hostel and that they came from different parts of America to visit museums and places of interest. Experts came to give them talks on anything from archaeology to the weather. The people were very nice, and very active.

We went back to our casitas, passing three friendly, black and white pygmy goats lazing in the shade under the trees, to change for the pool. The sun was very hot, and the sky a brilliant blue with few clouds, so I kept an eye on Sarah, nagging her to cover herself in lotion, and not to stay in the sun for long. Towels were supplied in a big wicker basket, and there were a lot of white loungers with plastic strips to lie on.

I hadn't swum for years and kept to the shallow end while I got used to the water. Andy and Sarah both swam well, and while we laid out on the seats, Andy would suddenly leap up from his lounger, run along the diving board and dive into the water, swimming back to sunbathe again, sometimes putting the towel over his head. I even occasionally nagged him about too much sun.

We were called to lunch by Rusty ringing the triangle outside the dining room, and after, went to lay in the shade in the hammocks. These were tricky until you got used to them, but I had to put one foot on the ground to get it to rock back and forth. The goats would come over and scratch their backs underneath which was very useful as they made the hammocks swing. Remote controlled hammocks—great.

Just before 3pm we changed for another ride. When asked by Ed which ride I wanted to do, I chose the lope, and he sent me into the small corral to try out. Dunny was fairly hard to get going, but Ed was obviously satisfied. His trot was a little uncomfortable, but his lope was quite gentle and easy.

Sarah asked Brad, another wrangler, if they had a livelier horse, and he came out with a little bay Arab horse, Leelite. Her face lit up.

While riding, I called Sarah's attention when I spotted a jackrabbit. Quickly, Brad turned in his saddle and told me that it was a jackalope, a cross between a jackrabbit and an antelope. Having read enough cowboy books to realise that he was 'joshing' a tenderfoot, I laughed at him.

Later on, he told us that a lovely ranch style bungalow, pointing to one on the slope, was his, and to go in any time and make ourselves at home. Behind me, I heard Sue, on Trigger, a rider who'd been to the ranch several times before, call out, "in your dreams, Brad," and I realised that, like the jackalope, I had been nearly taken in by one of Brad's tall tales, but he just grinned. I laughed and said, "oh yes, until the owner came home and threw us out."

Once back, we changed again for the pool to swim, before going in for dinner. This again was nice, rice, pasta, fruit, salad, pickles etc. followed by a sweet. Afterward, Andy and I lay out in the hammocks in the dark, while Sarah went out for the evening with Brad, having been asked. I was a little worried as I felt that I was responsible for her, but Brad assured me that they wouldn't be back late. Outside the small meeting room, a man was singing country and western songs to the elderly people. He was a little bit out of tune from time to time, but it was lovely to hear. While laying there, my neck became a bit itchy, and when I felt the skin, it was like tiny little raised bumps on an area about the size of a 10p piece.

Sarah returned from Tucson, and back at the casita under the lights, I noticed that despite my care, she was beginning to burn from the sun. Suddenly, she screamed and looking round, I saw a huge black spider on the wall above her bed that we thought was a tarantula (only finding out next day that tarantulas cannot climb and it was a wolf spider, so called because it hunted its prey, not spinning a web. Can't say it made us feel much better for that.)

I went round to Andy's room and knocked on the door. He suggested that we just got rid of it, but I assured him it was big. He came round and was taken aback at the size, but climbed on the bed and covered it with a glass. With a piece of paper under that, he took it outside and threw it in the bushes. Sarah and I were a bit nervous after that, but despite searching, couldn't find anything else in the room.

During the night, I awoke to hear strange screaming noises in the distance. Coyotes!

Tuesday 21st September.

We rose early again, and went on another lope ride. This time I was given a blue roan called Wrangler as Dunny had a cough. I fell instantly in love with him despite his very hard trot but he had a lovely lope and was livelier than Dunny. We rode on the plains again between creosote bushes, which smelt oily when you rubbed the leaves, prickly pear and choya. The latter was a pretty, pale green cacti covered in what looked like white fluff and jointed, like lots of sausage shaped links. According to the books I'd read, they were lethal. The spines were hooked, and once embedded in the flesh, could only be cut out. The Apache had often tied their naked victims to the clumps and left them to die in agony. There were also a lot of small barrel cacti, so named because of their shape. To my disgust, Arizona also had trouble with fly tippers leaving their rubbish out here, and Brad was furious about it, too.

I pointed to holes in the saguaros, and Brad said that that was where woodpeckers nested. Other birds then took them over when they had left, as they felt safe from snakes that couldn't climb the prickly stems. He told me that inside the temperature was twenty degrees cooler because of the water content. There were grey ribbed skeletons of dead saguaro either lying or standing like ghostly sentinels pointing at the sky. Apparently the saguaro only start sprouting their famous arms when they are eighty to a hundred years. I also spotted tiny little chipmunks, ground squirrels?

Brad suddenly pointed to one side and called out, "look, there's a jackalope!"

Quickly I replied with, "rope it then, I want to see what it looks like."

"Can't," he shot back, "the horns are too big."

"Oh yeah, you're just not good enough to rope." (That'll teach him to try to josh the English.) He just grinned back.

Returning for breakfast, I asked if there was a chance to be taken into Tucson, as I wanted to try and find a black saddle for Cloud and Brad offered to take me in, so with Andy and Sarah, we crammed into the bench seat of the ranch's truck. As he drove towards the town, he pointed out the only few tall buildings in the centre of Tucson and told us that every year the town was encroaching further and further out into the desert, getting closer to the ranch.

On the way, we had to stop for almost 15 minutes at a railroad crossing for another of the very long trains to pass.

I couldn't find a black leather saddle, only one that was synthetic which I didn't want, but I did get a lovely pair of engraved spurs with jingle bobs, tiny little weights that tinkled when you walked. On one road, we passed a man bumming for money on one of the central reservations. This caused Brad to get cross as he hated them, "our taxes pay for them," and told us that one man had been caught at the end of the day, going round the corner to his very nice car!

He was also strongly against rapists, saying they should be castrated, to which I replied, "hear, hear"!

He and Andy then began talking about a sheriff in Texas who had made his offenders sleep in tents, whatever the weather, fed them on forty cents a day, and made them wear pink underwear. Apparently, no one re-offended. I'm not surprised, and what a brilliant idea. Bet the do-gooders would whinge about their rights! What about ours? We fell about laughing at the thought of pink underwear.

Overall, we visited four tack shops without success, finally heading back to the ranch. Brad drove quite quickly over a road that was very hilly, throwing us about a bit, and making us all shriek.

"I wouldn't like to do this after breakfast," I laughed.

Further on he turned down a dusty, unmade road, "obviously you're taking us on the scenic route," before we drove up the drive to the ranch.

Arriving back, we met a new girl, April, who came from Florida. She was a real giggle, and laughed at the American accent I was trying to get, saying she'd "teach me to speak like a red neck." I knew rednecks to be like country bumpkins—and very interbred! She also laughed at all my jokes, which was very heartening as I'm usually considered useless.

After we'd eaten, I lay in one of the hammocks watching a tiny hummingbird with brilliant green/blue sheen to its feathers, no bigger than my little finger, flying from flower to flower on the bushes.

At 3pm there was a trail ride to Li'l Abner's for a drink, with a walk or a lope ride. As Brad, Sarah, Sue and I went one way, we could see the walk ride, including Andy, setting out in a long line on the other trail.

Halfway there, kids were racing their bikes up and down some concrete ramps, frightening Cheyenne and Trigger, although Leelite wasn't too bad and Wrangler didn't seem to mind. Brad shouted at the kids to stay still till we'd passed, hanging back last to check we were OK. Then we heard him shouting angrily at them. When he caught up, he told us that one boy had called to his mates that he "would get his bike and scare the horses." Brad was furious, but I told him they were probably off the new estate and had no knowledge of horses, and were just like the idiots we had back home.

Finally we arrived at Li'l Abner's, tying the horses inside a big wire enclosure and walking down to a dark wood building. It was like a real old fashioned saloon. Brilliant. I ordered a Budweiser, then Sue, Sarah and I sat and chatted to two girls who had just arrived from Slough in England, Wendy and Pippa, who were air stewardesses flying out of Heathrow. Brad came and sat with us keeping us in stitches with his stories of jackalopes, supposedly a cross between a jackrabbit and an antelope (oh yeh,) and other tall tales. The walk ride finally arrived, with Andy, and we had a pleasant half an hour before going back out to the horses. It was fantastic seeing all the horses tied up there in a line, at least twenty of them.

On the way back on the trail, Sue, in front of me, pointed out a tarantula crossing the path, very nearly being stepped on by the horses but not seeming to be in any great hurry.

We lazed by the pool and swam, then went and rocked in the hammocks. Sarah and I were pretty keen to lay out there all night, Carol having told us earlier that other guests had been known to, it was so lovely and warm, with the stars above really bright, but we chickened out at the last moment, in case of insects.

At 7pm a cookout had been organised behind the ranch house, with steaks, ribs, chicken, jacket potatoes and beans, followed by a dessert. Oil lamps on the tables cast flickering yellow lights. Brad and Andy took the rise out of Sarah with their ribs of meat, as she was a vegetarian, by constantly smacking their lips. I mentioned that I had been bitten several times on the neck, and Brad insisted that it was a "kissing bug." Despite his apparent sincerity, I wasn't too sure if he was kidding or not.

After, there was a hayride, starting out from the corrals. A large cart with straw bales to sit on and pulled by two black Percherons belonging to the ranch waited for us, two bright lanterns hanging at the front. Unfortunately, Andy missed it, thinking the pickup was from another part of the drive. Joe, another wrangler sat beside Brad who was driving.

The moon was just coming up, bathing the range in a silver light, making the choya shine like it was luminous, and there was a gentle, warm breeze.

The older people who came began singing old songs for a while, then just chatted.

Brad drove around the gravel drive, out of the gateway and down the road with Joe keeping an eye open for any cars, pointing a lantern towards them to show that we were there. Halfway round, Brad asked me if I could see the fireflies. Suspiciously, I glanced round, but could only see some lights ahead of us from houses.

"No, around the horses feet." Still suspicious that I was somehow being kidded, I looked.

"There," he pointed. It was the sparks from the horses' shoes on the road! He and Joe thought that hysterical. I silently swore that I'd get even sometime. It was a magical ride and I was sad to get back to the ranch. Brad told us that there was a possibility of doing a moonlight ride one evening, if anyone would like to go.

"Yes, please."

Andy and I went and had a look in the meeting room where there were shelves and shelves of books, and he found a row of Zane Grey's, my favourite western writer, one of which I took back to the casita to read.

Getting ready for bed, to my horror I discovered that although I had the chain round my neck, the little gold pendant watch that Les had given me years before and which I'd finally managed to have mended recently, had gone. I was heartbroken. It could have been anywhere we'd been today, and probably lost in the sand.

Wednesday 22nd September.

It was cloudy and hot when we got up and made ready for the early morning ride. I took my camera, quickly snapping a picture of Joe, who cheekily told me that that would cost me five bucks.

I said, "it's not worth it, you can have it back."

Sarah and I went on a fast ride, having lovely long lopes along the sandy trails through the brush. At one point, Brad called out, "circle the wagons," and we loped around and round in a big circle. Great fun.

Shortly after, I found my camera that I'd hung from the horn by its strap, was missing. Guiltily, I told Brad. He shot me a look that clearly said, *God help us*, told us all to wait and loped back to the clearing, coming back quickly with the camera. I just kept apologising and wishing the ground would open up to swallow me.

Back at the ranch, he told Joe in great disgust, who threw his arms into the air and said, "oh man, you've just lost three days riding privileges for that."

I pleaded quickly, "no, no, anything but that, I'll even pay you."

Quickly changing, Sarah and I joined Andy in the pool. I spotted a tiny green praying mantis on one of the floater sticks and rescued it, putting the floater next to a bush so that it could get off, before rescuing a ladybug (ladybird) as well. Heading round to the hot tub there was a huge blue butterfly by the bushes, and round by the hot tub sat a tiny lizard that flashed away under a bush when we passed by.

One of the girls mentioned that it was a hundred degrees Fahrenheit today. Strangely, despite the heat, I didn't sweat, despite drinking gallons of water or lemonade, and I didn't go to the bathroom much either. I guess the perspiration just evaporated.

Andy went off to phone the local airport, as he wanted to sky dive! Crikey, I don't like going up in a plane, but I'd never, ever jump out-he must be mad. He came back to tell us that to dive alone, he'd have at have at least half a day's training, but that he could do a tandem jump strapped to the front of an instructor, so he'd booked for Friday morning. When he'd told Paul, one of the two managers, Carol being the other, Paul had offered to drive us over and would even stay to watch.

After lunch, at 3pm I rode out with Andy, Sarah and Sue across to Suicide Pass, which Sue had specially asked for. Setting out was lovely, walking the tracks winding through the flats then heading up towards the ridges. The track was very stony and I knew that an English person would have freaked at their horses facing such terrain. I never saw a horse hurt although they got an occasional cut around the fetlocks. Then we began winding up a steeper trail cut deep in places, twisting and turning almost on a sixpence. Looking ahead, there didn't seem to be any path to follow. The horses clambered up and up, in places that seemed to go almost straight up and very smooth. It was spine chilling, but I had such confidence in Wrangler that in a strange way I was enjoying it. When I got home I told friends I thought the horses had Velcro on their hooves. How they did it I'll never know.

Finally we clambered out onto the top where there was a lovely cool breeze. The view was well worth the effort, out over a valley to the right with Tucson and the Catalina Mountains behind and across another flat valley on the left to Old Tucson and the Tucson Mountains. In Old Tucson they had made a lot of cowboy films. And everywhere stood the saguaros, clinging to the steep canyon sides, pointing out of the sand and rocks like candelabra, with silver choya, the blackish creosote bushes and the green ocotillo. Behind us loomed black clouds and I could hear thunder rolling, while a light rain began to fall over us. But Tucson was almost obscured by a very heavy downfall. Brad told us that a ten-year drought had only broken that summer which was why lots of the cacti were in flower.

We wound our way along the top of the ridges, stopping to look out over the sheer drops to the left, then began making our way slowly down. The horses were so nimble with their feet, turning and dropping down the steps of rock carefully, while we leant back in the saddles. Finally, dam, but not soaked from the rain, we arrived back at the ranch.

We changed quickly and went for a cooling swim, then sat chatting for ages with some of the elderly people. Two old ladies, who had obviously heard us chatting, and my attempt at cultivating an American accent, begged me not to lose my lovely English accent. One interesting man of ninety was called Hymie. He lived in Tucson and had come to visit his friend staying here at the ranch. He was fascinating to talk to and very friendly.

At dinner, we chatted with Carol, her son Zane, and Paul, with Andy and Zane having the same interest in fishing. When we left to go to the chalets, it was raining—but warm rain!

During the night Sarah was sick several times and was really unwell. Thursday 23rd September.

Next morning, during breakfast, I discovered that several of the elderly people had been ill, too. I walked down to the corrals to cancel our riding for the morning, telling Joe that Sarah and I couldn't go. He ribbed us about chickening out, but became concerned when I said that Sarah had been sick all night. He advised me to go to a drug store to get drinks with electrolytes in to replace the minerals and salts that she would have lost, possibly leaving her dehydrated. At the office, I asked Carol if anyone could take me to the nearest store, but she told me that there were cans in the drinks machine that had them, so I got some dollar bills and bought a couple of cans.

Sarah felt a little better later on in the morning so we decided to try and get our own back on Brad. After the rides came back, she and I went up to the corrals with plastic cups, me with a bottle of Jack Daniel's whiskey that I had bought as a present for dad, and Sarah with another bottle in her hand. We met Brad and pretended to be recovering from a hangover, asking him where he'd been as we'd had a mad party in our chalet last night. He fell for it hook, line and sinker, as Joe had obviously not told him about Sarah being ill, saying that he'd been in the bar all evening, and looking very disappointed. What a joy for us after all his tall tales. We kept on about this wild party, giggling madly, until Joe started shouting at us about, "can you hear me, is this loud enough." Then we fell about laughing. One up to the Brits!

Sarah was exhausted after this and went back to lie down for another sleep. I took a little bit of light food back to her after lunch, and she slept all afternoon while I went for an afternoon ride. When I got back, she said she felt a little better, and did manage to come to the dining room for some dinner, especially as I thought it unwise to go on the moonlight ride without any food inside her. Despite my concern, she was determined to go.

Lots of people went and it was fantastic, walking the trails up and down gentle slopes in the moonlight, the choya and saguaro glowing luminously as everything was bathed in a silver light, the saguaros casting long shadows.

That night, both Sue and April were sick.

Friday 24th September.

We were up early again for the breakfast ride, this morning heading for the cookout site. Once everyone who was going was mounted, we set off, riding up and down the ridges. I was excited thinking we'd be going for miles, but became confused as to the direction of the site as we switch-backed around the ranch, keeping it in sight from time to time. But despite taking over an hour, we ended up not far behind the ranch—only about half a mile away.

Breakfast was laid out beside a thatched, open sided shelter with wooden tables and benches under, where it and was lovely and cool in the shade. There were hitching rails to tie the horses to. Andy had walked over to meet us, using his video camera on the way. We dismounted and tied the horses, going to help ourselves to scrambled eggs, crispy bacon, beef burgers and fried potato pieces, following it up with a coffee. Brilliant. Finally, we started back to the ranch.

Once back and leaving the horses to the wranglers, Andy, Sarah and I got into one of the ranch cars with Paul and set off in the opposite direction to Tucson. On the way to the airport, Paul pointed to Twin Peaks or what had once been two conical hills. One of them had actually disappeared, taken by people excavating for minerals, a huge conveyor belt taking the rocks and debris five miles away to a factory. I was saddened to see what man could do. Further on, nearer the airfield, we passed fields of cotton, the green bushes covered with snowy white balls of fluff.

While Andy booked in at reception, I wandered round the walls of the building looking at the photos of people sky diving, before we were taken to a room to watch a video about the dangers, and the thrills, of skydiving with the instructor. It seemed very intimidating, but it didn't faze Andy in the slightest.

In the main area Sarah and I waited while Andy was suited up, then he was taken round the back of the building to get to the plane. I giggled at the sight of him in flying gear and carrying his crash helmet, despite feeling very nervous for him, but his face was alight with anticipation. With Sarah and Paul, I went outside into the heat to watch the plane take off, wanting to video it as he had left me the camera, but unfortunately, it was out of our sight around the buildings.

We watched and waited, peering up into the bright blue sky, the plane getting smaller and smaller until it disappeared from sight. It seemed to take for ages. We were told afterwards that they'd had to wait for a big plane to leave Tucson airport before they could get clearance.

Finally, someone came out and told us that he had jumped, trying to point him out to us. Eventually, I spotted a tiny black speck against the blue of the sky, but despite trying to align the camera with the nearest cloud, it seemed like forever until I got him in view. Gradually, as he got closer and closer and more overhead, I was inclining myself so far back to film him, I thought I'd fall over. Quickly, I lay down on the ground, trying to get him back into view. It was fascinating watching the two men swinging round and round on the end of the parachute, and we could even hear them talking to each other. As they reached the ground, Andy's legs seemed to buckle. Quickly he was released from the parachute harness, and eventually managed to stand up, although very shakily. Apparently, as they had swung round under the parachute, the straps round his legs had really hurt, cutting off the circulation almost, so that when he'd landed, he'd no control over them. But he was so enthusiastic, saying it had been fantastic.

As he walked back to the building with Paul and Sarah, I suddenly realised that I had left my clip-on sunglasses somewhere on the grass while I'd been filming, and went back to look, finally locating them, thank goodness. In this bright sunlight, I lived in them. Back inside, two of the men were already rolling the parachute back up on the floor to get it ready for the next jump.

We went round to the car and drove off. I was interested in the cotton bushes, never having seen it growing before and Paul stopped to let us pick some balls from the bushes. They were very soft and spongy. I told Andy the trouble I'd had trying to film him, having had to lay down to do it. He was startled, and showed me how these new cameras just needed the side lens swivelled while you watched what was happening on the screen. How embarrassing!

A few miles down the road, Andy suddenly realised that he should have been given a certificate for the jump, so Paul kindly turned around and took us back for it. We were almost late for lunch at the ranch, but everyone was fascinated by how he'd got on, and Carol said that he was the first person from the ranch to try anything like that.

We went back to the pool after lunch, and, although in the shade, I unfortunately dozed off on the lounger. Fatal. I awoke feeling sick and dizzy, like I usually do when I'd slept during the day, and had to cancel the afternoon ride because of it. When Sarah came back, she told us they'd seen a rattlesnake only a few feet from them, but the horses hadn't freaked, obviously being used to it.

At dinner we found that the elder guests had come back after a day across the border in Mexico. Apparently, drugs over there are a lot cheaper than in the USA and most old folk who could, went across and bought the equivalent. Of course you had to learn a bit of Spanish to be able to converse with the pharmacists. We stayed at the table for some time after the tables were cleared, talking to the others. April was a laugh with a terrific sense of humour, and we had quite a giggle.

After that we lay out on the hammocks for most of the evening in the dark, the breeze still warm from the day's heat, listening to the cicadas and the wailing train whistles in the distance. The stars were bright above and I could even spot The Plough formation, better known over here as The Big Dipper, a dipper being a long handled tin mug used for scooping water out of barrels on the sides of wagons, or the pails from wells. Absolute bliss.
Saturday 25th September.

Next morning we had a choice of rides or we could take part in team cattle penning. Having done the latter at home with Cloud, I was all for it. The object is for one of a team of three to ride gently into the herd of cattle and try to single out just three calves. All three riders then had to haze (guide) them gently up the side of the arena to where a three-sided pen was erected. With two people then pushing from behind, the third rider nipped up the outside of the pen to try and turn the calves into the open side of the holding area. Not easy, as cattle are very easily over faced and end up scampering back to their mates. There is a definite knack to it.

We teamed up into threes with Carol, Paul and Ed joining in, riding with us and giving instructions while Jim took out the walk ride. The calves were very nippy, like the ones at Stuart and Leslie's, who run the British Rodeo Cowboys Association I belonged to, and most of the teams only managed one or two calves into the pen. Wrangler, like my Cloud, was not impressed, refusing to lope and laying his ears back, and it took some hard work to get him to attempt to participate, but it was a great laugh as the calves nearly always won, and everyone had fun.

We put the horses away in the corral, then Andy, with Dean who was also from England, went up behind the cliff at the rear of the ranch house to abseil down the rock face, something he had always fancied doing. April, Sarah, Dean's wife, and I came around the base of the wall of rock with the wife of the abseiling instructor. She was there to shout instructions to the two boys as they descended one at a time, and also hold the end of the descending rope to slow them if necessary.

Andy wasn't too keen, edging his way down very, very slowly and carefully, but Dean was fast, going back up quickly for another go. I filmed Andy so that he could show his family back home. As Dean had come down the first time, I watched a gecko race across the face of the rocks, clinging to the stone was if it was glued. When they'd finished, we all climbed round the side of the ridge to where they had ascended, holding onto a rope hand hold battened to the wall, then sat up on top to look at the stunning view over Tucson and the Catalinas. Finally, we slowly and carefully climbed back down.

At lunchtime, a crowd of Norwegians arrived, a very noisy bunch.

Paul took out the lope ride that afternoon riding a lovely quarter horse, a lighter framed breed than in England. His lopes went on forever, and my legs began to ache even though Wrangler was very comfortable, but it was brilliant riding down the twisting paths between the cacti and creosote bushes. Ritchie, who normally went on walk rides, hadn't fancy going with the Norwegians, and despite not having loped before, actually managed to stay with us. I think Paul forgot to test him. When we got back to the ranch, I hosed Wrangler down to cool him off.

Back at the swimming pool, I managed to swim ten of the small widths straight off, back and forth. Not being a great swimmer, I had been trying to improve and build up my muscles, so I was really pleased.

Sarah and I decided to get our own back on Brad for all his pranks. We were planning to play a joke on him the following day, but at dinner, Paul told us that he'd been called away as his other horse, at another ranch, had been accidentally blinded in one eye in an accident. He would obviously be very upset, so we decided that was out.

During the early evening the Norwegians, very noisy and a bit over the top, made up a drink of 'iced tea' that sounded lethal, carrying it around in a silver ice bucket. Several of them were already more than a little merry. I get very nervous of people like that and tried to stay as far away from them as possible but they kept coming over and trying to get us to have a glass. We kept waving them away, saying, "no, no."

At 7pm we went round to the side of the ranch where they were doing another cookout with steaks, pleasing Andy as he always enjoyed a big piece of meat. The Norwegians were very merry, shouting and singing, and they sang a kind of 'Happy Birthday to you' to a lady whose husband had given her a lovely, expensive present.

The meal was great. I wasn't keen on red meat and had a piece of chicken, following that up with a lovely sweet and coffee, but Andy went straight for the big steak. Stuffed, we went and crashed out on the hammocks under the stars.

Sometime later, Carol came round, asking if we'd seen Paul, but we hadn't. Then April came, asking the same question. I was very curious, where had he gone? Eventually we were told that they had found him and taken him back to the ranch house, more than a little under the weather from the 'iced tea.'

At 10pm, reluctantly, Sarah and I went back to our casita to pack as we were leaving the following day. I had a very restless night, tossing and turning, sad that our stay was over.

Chapter 5

A Hole in the World.

Sunday 26th September.

I arose very early, going up to the ranch house for a cup of coffee, before sitting on the patio to watch the sunrise. Carol came and stood with me as we waited to watch Karen and her husband who were due to fly over in a balloon. I was very choked and close to tears. I did not want to leave. I had a long chat with Carol and she said that many people were the same, and advised me not to "take it too hard." When the balloon came sailing gracefully over the ridge, we both stood and waved like mad.

After the balloon had gone, I took a walk out to the stony path leading to Suicide Pass and back, picking up two small rocks to take home for souvenirs. After breakfast, Andy and I had to go for the rental car we had booked as Alamo are about the only rental company who don't bring the car to you. Mark kindly drove us to the airport. We paid an extra $151 to upgrade from the compact car ordered to the better looking Ford Blazer, plus extra as the drop-off point would be different, flying out of Phoenix and not coming back to Tucson.

I had expected everyone to have gone out without me, but arriving back at the ranch everyone was cattle penning again, and Carol shouted that Wrangler was in the corral waiting for me to join them. I ran to get him, putting on the bridle that they'd left dangling from the saddle horn, and I managed to get several goes in before they finished. Sarah excitedly told me that Leelite had done some cutting and had been brilliant, and I was miffed that we hadn't been there to film her. Ed had even asked her if she'd done this before, and she'd told him, "no, never."

I reluctantly walked back to the casita and took my suitcase to the car, Sarah behind me, before going to the office to check out, leaving an envelope with tips in for the staff. The girls behind the counter said goodbye, and I got a hug from one. Kim, the other waitress, also gave us a hug and told us she was sad to see us go. The secretary quickly called us just as we were about to go out the door to tell us that Brad had left a message.

"Have you found the rattlesnake he left in your cabin? He's taken the venom out!"

Sarah and I both said, "no."

I really wanted to make a cheeky reply, but we were both so close to tears that I couldn't speak, and to think that with the tragedy to his horse, he'd thought of us.

It was very depressing turning out of the drive, listening to the crunch of gravel under the tyres for the last time, and watching Hat Mountain slowly disappearing behind us. I glanced in the wing mirror to discover that Sarah looked as bad as I felt. We drove back through Tucson, and then Andy turned south on the I-10 instead of north.

"Where are you going?" I asked.

He smiled and said, "I thought you wanted to go to Tombstone." Wow!

The scenery was lovely with sand hills and the taller ranges of the Catalinas running down to our left. After an hour, we turned onto Route 80 at Benson, and finally drove into Tombstone, known for the famous shoot out at the OK corral.

In 1879, the Earp brothers and their families had arrived, drawn by the silver mining and hoping for better prospects. By 1881, with Virgil Earp now Marshall of the town, the Earps were 'at outs' with the Clantons and McLowrys who were being backed up by Sheriff Behan. Wyatt also hated cowboys after dealing with them in the end-of-trail town, Dodge City. This ended up with threats from both sides and the Earps deciding to run them out of town. So started the famous Gunfight at the OK Corral carried out on Fremont, and which had lasted for no more than a minute. I found this stunning. In films, the fight seemed to go on and on.

On the outskirts of Tombstone, we stopped at an old wooden trading post.

Outside, on the rails round the raised wooden veranda hung cowhides: reds, browns, and a black and white one. Off to one side lay the rusting rails and buckets from the old mining days. Inside the store, surrounded by racks of clothes and glass top counters, was a huge stuffed buffalo. I went over to have a closer look, never having realised just how huge and shaggy they were. With the thick, curly woolly mane of hair, fierce beady little eyes, and tiny uplifting horns it had an immense presence and awesome power.

Browsing around, there were western ornaments and clothing, everything from spurs to T-shirts, but we didn't buy anything, although I could have spent a fortune.

We drove on further down the road and pulled into the gravelled car lot in front of another wooden building bearing a huge fascia with Boothill Graveyard emblazoned on it. Inside, I bought another fridge magnet for my collection.

We paid an entry fee to go out into the graveyard and I photographed everything with names that I knew, including the graves of the Clantons and the McLowrys. It was fantastic to be here where a legend had started. Headed by wooden markers, large stones were heaped on the gravesides, the rest of the area being gravelled to walk on. It stretched for quite a distance, running away out of sight down the hillside. I loved some of the sayings cut into the grey wooden markers and coloured a dark brown.

"HERE
LIES
LESTER MOORE
FOUR SLUGS
FROM A 44
NO LES
NO MORE"
And
"JOHN HEATH
TAKEN FROM
County Jail &
LYNCHED
By Bisbee Mob
IN TOMBSTONE
Feb 22, 1884"
as well as

"DAN DOWD
RED SAMPLE
TEX HOWARD
BILL DeLANEY
DAN KELLY
LEGALLY
HANGED
MAR 8th
1884"

Another sign was for William Clayborne shot by Frank Leslie 1882, two names that I knew, and a Dick Toby shot by Sheriff Behan, the friend of the Clantons.

We drove on into the old part of town that looked just like it did in the films with dusty streets, old wooden buildings, wooden sidewalks and hitching rails, all appearing to be the originals. I found it hard to believe that even in the dry atmosphere here, wood could be so well preserved for so long.

We had missed the start of the gunfight show but as we walked down to the Main Street, we could hear shouted threats and the loud crashes of guns going off behind a walled area. Reaching Fremont, roped off to stop cars from entering, stood two red stagecoaches awaiting passengers. I wished we'd had time to have a ride.

I stopped at a saddle maker to see if they had a black saddle, but no, they only had tan or dark brown, but I did spot a lovely fancy stitched headstall with reins, and bought it. When I asked if they knew of anyone with a black saddle, they suggested I try a shop called Medicine Bow, on Main Street.

Wandering down the crowded sidewalks I browsed in the shop windows until we reached the Medicine Bow shop. Inside they had all sorts of equipment, plus two saddles, but no black one that I could see, and I looked for ages through the glass top cabinets at all the brooches and spurs, knives and guns on sale. Then, just as I was going out the front door, I suddenly looked sideways and spotted a black saddle with a white seat, metal studding, and tapaderos (stirrup covers for your feet.) It had been made in the 1930's. Would it fit Cloud? The people weren't sure, but I finally bought it for $810 (£500.) The man carried it up the road to where Andy had brought the car, loading it in the back. (Once back home, I was very disappointed to find that with Cloud being a cob and quite chunky, the saddle didn't fit him, and had to sell it on.)

Unfortunately, we didn't have much time to do anything else, having to retrace our steps to Tucson to travel on to Phoenix for the night but, being hungry, we did pull up outside a lovely little diner, just like you see on TV. It had a long wooden bar with round seats on stems, and little tables at the back with blue and white tablecloths. Very pretty. We sat at a table and ordered a meal.

Just past Tucson, Andy stopped to let me drive. My stomach curled in horror, but I had no choice. Gosh, he's brave, trusting me to drive, and on the wrong side of the road.

We changed seats and he told me which switches did what, including the cruise control. I waited for a long gap in the traffic and pulled out carefully. It felt really strange, but not as difficult as I'd thought, and I took to it better than I expected. The cruise control was fantastic. Once you reached the right speed, you pushed a button on the steering wheel, and the car took over. It was a bit frightening to have the car do its own thing, but at a touch of the foot brake, the system switched off. You could accelerate, but as you slowed back down to the speed you had been doing, the car took over again. Neat. It was magical and I was glad I learned, because I'd bought a Shogun before I left home and had no idea how to use the gadgets. In actual fact, without the stress of keeping your foot on the accelerator, driving long distances was very pleasant and even relaxing over here. With the wide roads and so much less traffic than England it was pleasant, and no one seemed to be in a hurry to get anywhere. I did like the Blazer. It handled very well.

I pulled in for gas, giving Andy a traveller's cheque to pay. He was quite a time, but finally came back to the car to say that they needed to see my driver's licence as it was a dud and that they'd called the cops! Oh, ha, ha, ha. What a fright. I drove on again.

The scenery changed often from flat plains and rolling hills to mountain ranges, although some of their mountains would be called hills in England, while slowly the bright orange sun began to dip down towards the horizon. Despite this, according to the temperature gauge, the heat outside actually began to rise, it was now between 94f and 103f (37C.)

Finally I joined a four-lane freeway on the outskirts of Phoenix and found it intimidating in all the traffic that had suddenly begun to build up. At one turn off I misjudged steering the car to the right at the corner and bounced off the kerb and was very embarrassed.

I had to stop once for Andy to ask in a shop for directions, before we managed to come across the Hilton Point hotel at 8.30pm. This turned out to be an enormous, very smart hotel on North 16th Street that made me feel rather badly under-dressed. I drove round and round looking for the reception area, Andy having to ask again before finally finding the entrance.

Getting out of the car, the heat really hit me. It was more like the steamy heat we got back home after a storm, only worse.

The reception area was very large and everything looked like it was made out of marble. We waited a long time at the counter while they sorted out our booking, then we were asked by a man to follow him. He got into a type of golf cart and drove ahead of us to our casitas.

One was a two floored, terrace style house for Sarah and I and very, very plush, while Andy was across the way in a smaller studio room. I wasn't comfortable in ours, feeling very untidy and touristy. In the fridge were sweets and biscuits, and bottles of beer, but the price list was exorbitant. So was the price to watch the films on the TV channels.

Once settled in, Andy came over rather annoyed to say that the big swimming pool had shut at 6pm but that he had found a small pool/hot tub behind his room. In such a plush hotel, he'd expected to be able to have a swim. Sarah and I got changed and followed him round the back of his apartment block. Through a gateway was a small pool, dimly lit by lights, and to one side, a hot water pool. We gladly got into the water to relax and cool off for a while.

Back at our room, Andy came in for a coffee. Once he'd left, Sarah took the bed upstairs while I had a pullout sofa bed downstairs and I slept very comfortably.

Monday 27th September.

We woke early, checked out at reception, and drove out to find the I-17, heading for the Grand Canyon. The road gradually got steeper as we travelled up through lovely passes with Ponderosa pine covered slopes and pretty flowers, wooden chalets and houses scattered about. A sign stated that we were at 3,000 feet.

Looking at the map, we decided to take the scenic route through the mountains, turning off onto a smaller road to Cottonwood for Sedona via Route 260 and 89A, travelling through Oak Creek Canyon and on into Flagstaff. What a strange, exciting feeling reading all the names from my western books.

We passed through a varied landscape of canyons clothed in pines or spruce, with grey rocks, flat mesas, scrub covered flats and sandy red rock formations, passing places with fantastic names like Horsethief Canyon,

Bloody Canyon, and towns called Black Canyon City, and the amusing Bumblebee.

We came across a sign for Montezuma's Castle which sounded interesting, and turned off up a small winding road that went up and down like a switchback, seeming to double back on itself several times. It finally ended at a long, narrow car park full of coaches, pickups and cars. Parking up, we got out to the heat and incessant noise of cicadas.

We paid the entry fee at the shop, browsing round the souvenirs before heading out the far side, taking a winding concrete path that circled under a red rock wall on the right, and beside a bubbling creek in a deep wash on the left. Lovely big green trees shaded the paths.

Coming around a corner, we discovered that Montezuma's Castle was actually a pueblo. It had been built half way up the wall of rock, under an overhang, and looked totally impregnable from where I could see. It turned out that early explorers and settlers had believed it to have been built by the Aztec emperor Montezuma, but had turned out to be a five story building built in 1100AD by Sinagua Indians.

According to the notice by the trail, people had been allowed up to see inside until it was realised that hands and feet were doing untold damage, and now you could only look at it from below.

We continued to follow the path back to the shop where I bought a small booklet about its history, then drove back down the small road and rejoined Route 89A.

As we got closer to Sedona so I saw more and more red outcrops towering huge and craggy above us, banded by different colours of black and grey, totally awe inspiring, and bearing wonderful names like Chimney Rock and the Giant's Thumb. Wow, was this part of the Grand Canyon? No, according to the map, we had miles and miles to go! If all this looked fantastic, what would the canyon be like?

Sedona was a lovely little town nestled between these red buttes. We strolled round the shops, and as usual I had to be dragged out of the bookshop where I was looking for any of Zane Grey's books that I hadn't got. Unfortunately, like Britain, westerns were obviously not in favour and I couldn't even find any new Louis L'Amour's.

Outside, Andy was trying to decide whether we had time to visit the Imax cinema. I'd never heard of one before and couldn't believe it when he told us that the screen was possibly three or five stories tall. Instead, we climbed a wood and steel tower in the centre of the plaza to see the views over the tops of the stores. The towering crags were both beautiful and breathtaking.

We carried on up the road, climbing to 5,000 feet into the Ponderosa pine covered mountains with their red rocks and white limestone cliffs. According to the temperature gauge in the car, as we got higher so the air was cooling, and now it was down to 83-86f or 26C.

Continuing along the winding road, we headed down into a wide green valley, before climbing slowly back up higher and out onto a vast plateau, the Coconino, before travelling on into more pine covered mountains at 8,084 feet. Then slowly we began descending, heading for Flagstaff. Lots of the pines here showed signs of fire in the past, but already small new trees were appearing.

We stopped at a huge, deep valley next to a Ranger Station, getting out to walk along the edge, holding onto the metal rails to peer down at the seemingly tiny creek in the dark depths. The valley was a steeply sided V shape, coming in from the left and abruptly turning off to the right.

I drove from here to give Andy a break, stopping the car several times by the side of the road to get out and photograph the lovely bubbling stream that tumbled through the rocks. Oak Creek.

At 6,000 feet we reached the town of Flagstaff that looked enormous spreading out before us, and the roads looked very busy, especially with the Interstate joining from our right.

We went on into town and parked at K-Mart, a large store. It was a lot like our Tesco's, but along with food, there were toys, clothing, household goods, fishing and camera equipment, jewellery, cosmetics, drugs, almost everything.

From there we drove on further into the town and stopped at Walgreen's, another large store and basically the same as the K-Mart. Inside was a nice cafe area and we sat down for coffee and a meal before wandering around the store.

Setting off for the Grand Canyon we managed to get slightly lost again as the signposts came up too fast for some of the junctions and we got pulled along with the rest of the traffic. But how nice and easy the roads were with traffic lights and no silly roundabouts. American roads were so easy going and well maintained, and with no sign of impatience or road rage.

Finally we reached Route 180, which eventually turned into the 64, and followed the signs for the Grand Canyon, climbing out onto the flat plateau to drive through more pine forests with many clearings.

At Flintstone Village, where we had to turn right at the T junction, we were amused to see a Fred Flintstone café and decided we'd come back sometime to look round it. It looked fun. Next to it was a big hanger with various old aircraft parked round it.

Finally we were heading down into Grand Canyon Village passing the airport and the helicopter pads. Andy was looking forward to going up in a helicopter and wanted to book as soon as he could. The long street had stores and the usual fast food places like Wendy's, Pizza Hut, and MacDonalds, then near the end on the left, next to another big Imax cinema, was the Quality Inn, another really smart hotel although not as plush as the Pointe Hilton.

We parked up and booked in at reception, taking our suitcases up in the elevator to our rooms, Andy wanting to go and find the canyon to watch the sunset. First though, he drove back to the airport to book a helicopter ride for the following day. There was no way I was going up in one of them, and Sarah hadn't got that kind of money with her. He was very lucky, they were normally booked for months ahead, but had just had a cancellation.

We turned back past the hotel and drove up the road for some way, coming up to some tollbooths where it cost $20 to go through to the canyon, but the ticket covered us for seven days. They also gave us a map of the area. A little further on we turned right heading for Desert View. We seemed to drive on for ages and ages through the thick wood of pines, and I was just looking down at the map again to see how far we had left to go when I suddenly heard, "**** ***, look at that," from Andy.

My head shot up as he slowed the car and then, through a gap in the trees, in the far distance over a vast empty space, was a huge wall of colours; red, grey, green, blue and black—sort of smoky looking. Andy swung the car over and parked beside a low wall. We got out, and I just stood there, stunned. I just couldn't take it all in, it was if I had even stopped breathing.

The canyon was immense, stretching away into the distance and off to both sides in a series of yellow and cream crags, steps and buttes, pinnacles and pointing spires. I sat down on a rock near the edge and just could not seem to accept what I was seeing. Across the yawning chasm the sun was setting, turning the tops of the walls to gold. A deep blue haze started to fill the depths and as the sun slowly sank below the rim, the temperature began to drop. As shadows slowly crept up the walls to the top, the rocks began to turn grey and brown, and then the deep gorge became black with all the rocks and crags fading away. It was breathtaking.

It also became very chilly and we were glad to get back into the car where the temperature gauge registered 48f 9C. What a change in temperature from

Phoenix to here!

Andy drove back to the hotel where we left the car and walked to Wendy's, a couple of blocks away, for a meal. Afterwards, in our room, Sarah and I sat watching TV while I scribbled my notes down at the same time. I still couldn't get used to the amount of commercials that came up during the programmes without any warning at all, even immediately before the closing titles. Those came after. Weird.

Tuesday 28th September.

I woke to a sunny but cold day.

Downstairs in the restaurant we had a cooked breakfast before driving out to the airfield where it was nice and warm inside the building, with lots of people queuing. We sat in the lounge area watching the helicopters coming and going through the windows. Outside there were eight round concrete pads with helicopters coming and going almost continuously. It wasn't until we went outside that I realised just how noisy they all were, it was deafening. Andy joined the queue for his gate while Sarah and I sat on a bench watching the people having their photos taken before they got into the helicopters, but Andy waved aside the chance for his to be done. Then, as the wind was quite cold and we didn't have warm jackets, Sarah and I went back inside.

Andy finally climbed into the helicopter, the doors were shut, the blades started turning faster, and then it lifted up and hovered slowly backwards out over the grass. Once away from the other machines, it turned to face to our left and slowly lifted into the air, heading out over the trees.

Sarah and I sat and had a coffee before going to look round the little shops there, finally waiting in the lounge to watch the helicopters coming and going until Andy got back.

When he arrived, he told us it had been fantastic and that he'd videoed all of it. He hadn't realised it at the time but he could have plugged the talk from the pilot into the video, instead of which, all he'd got was the continuous noise of the engine. No wonder they all wore headphones! He also told us that the tiny white strip that ran round the edges of the cliffs, just under the rim was actually thirty stories high! Looking across from the rim it had appeared about two inches high. He said that the helicopters were only allowed to fly over the canyon these days because over recent years several aircraft had crashed due to turbulence from the thermals rising from the depths.

From here we went down the road we had come in from yesterday heading for Williams to try and get a trip on the train out to the South Rim of the canyon, passing Flintstone Village to reach the town, again a very dusty old style town. Andy parked up in a big car lot outside the station.

Walking round to the ticket office we discovered to our dismay that the trains started out at 8am every day. According to the poster there was a show during the ride, the special highpoint being outlaws 'holding up and robbing' the passengers. Unfortunately, we would be leaving the next day and couldn't go.

Driving further on, we came across an interesting looking store on what looked like the Main Street. After browsing inside for ages, I pounced on a rifle boot, dithering about buying it, and wondering where on earth I would pack everything I'd bought for the flight home. The storekeeper and a couple of other people standing at the counter were curious that I was buying it.

One man asked, "I thought in England you weren't allowed guns?"

I told them it was just for show for that reason, but that I would have liked to have hidden a Bowie in it because I rode alone a lot of the time in wooded country and that in England we weren't actually allowed to protect ourselves with a weapon. They looked startled and told me that in America, if a weapon was on show, that was OK, but if you hid it like that you could be jailed.

I also bought a pretty little dream catcher, a round hoop with feathers attached and a kind of net affair in the middle. The Native Americans believed that if hung in a doorway, they would catch bad dreams but let the good ones through. Hope it works.

Sarah and I also found a postcard of the infamous jackalope.

We drove back towards the canyon, stopping at the café at the crossroads where I photographed Andy sitting in Fred's wooden car that was towing a bright blue Bedrock caravan.

At the shop doorway there was a cut out of Wilma and I snapped Andy laughingly holding her hand. Inside we wandered up and down the rows of trinkets and gifts before sitting at a table in the rear of the café for a meal and a coffee.

Back outside, we tried to look over the high pink painted wall to see what was on the other side, but it was too tall.

To the right of the village was an old aircraft museum and we went over to have a look at the planes. One was a Ford Trimotor as in the Indiana Jones movies, one was a Grumman Tiger, a Blue Angels display jet similar to our Red Arrows and another was a Mitchell Bomber from WW2.

Back at the canyon, we parked outside the Information building where I bought two books about the canyon's history and geography, and then we strolled about a quarter mile to see the views. The stunted cedars with their gnarled barks were twisted into distorted shapes, their branches blown by the prevailing winds in one direction away from the rim. On a point of rock jutting out sat a ground squirrel, unconcernedly gazing out over the rim and so totally unmoved by our presence, that he had his back to us all the time we stood there. We walked on another mile, stopping to watch a family of chipmunks playing among the rocks at the side of the trail. Soaring above and below us were large, black birds, their calls echoing among the rocks.

Eventually, we came to a big wooden store and just inside the entrance was an open display cabinet with a large piece of highly polished black meteorite. We walked around but the shop seemed to be selling exactly the same gifts as everywhere else and I wanted to buy something different.

We slowly walked back towards the car and I collected a couple of pieces of rock to take back home with a small piece of grey sage that smelt like lavender. We must have walked for another hour before we realised that we had missed the trail to our car park and were entering another we didn't recognise. Never able to walk far, I was getting tired, but we had to back track for a long way before we finally found the Blazer. The ever-changing views were incredible and I still couldn't get used to the immense depths of the whole canyon.

We drove further on to a place called Desert View, a watchtower of brick over-looking the Colorado (Spanish for Red River.) In the far distance the river looked like a silvery ribbon running along the bottom of the canyon. Another gift shop come café was set back from the road where I bought a Grand Canyon T-shirt, maroon with galloping white horses emblazoned on it, before we went to sit outside with a lot of other people, all waiting to see the sunset. Sarah only had a small top on and I lent her my T-shirt to wear, for as the sun began to dip down behind the rim, the air was becoming chillier.

As I gazed down into the smoky depths, I was amazed that yet again the voices of the people were very muted, almost reverent, as we sat and watched the dark shadows creep up the walls. Above the shadows the golden rays of the sun slowly got smaller and smaller as the sun sank below the rim to our left. Finally, still to the sound of whispered voices, everything went black and the first stars began to appear overhead.

We were grateful to get back to the car and put on the heating. After having the air conditioner on for days, this was almost novel.

I drove out onto the road following the line of cars before me. A couple of miles on, seeing brake lights coming on from several cars ahead, I also slowed, and as I came up behind the last car, I could just make out in the headlights, a herd of mule deer leaping across the road. That made me rather nervous about driving in case anymore ran out in front of me.

We drove back past the hotel and stopped at Wendy's for a meal. Andy wanted to go to the Imax cinema next to the hotel, so when we'd finished, we drove back and parked outside it.

Inside were rows and rows of seats set at a very steep incline with an enormous deep grey screen in front of us, too big to take in all at once. Andy said it was five storeys high. Unbelievable. The film was a documentary/re-enactment about the exploring of the Grand Canyon by John Wesley Powell.

Powell, who'd lost his right arm during the Civil War at the battle of Pittsburg Landing, had set out in May 1869 with a team of 9 men from Green River, Wyoming to explore the Colorado River, using boats. Not many had made it through to the end for one reason or another and after just one month, an Englishman left after they'd lost a boat to rapids.

The men had not risked their remaining boats to some of the rapids by either lining them down the sides or portaging boats and supplies through the rocks alongside. But some they had no option but to run.

At Separation Canyon, three more men left because of the dangers, only to be killed by Indians, while, two days later, Powell and his remaining men got to the mouth of the Virgin River, now under the manmade Lake Mead.

The screen was so big that it was difficult to know where to watch, but it was almost like being there and I expected to get splashed with the water at any moment, it certainly felt like you were being swept into the screen. As usual with cinemas, the sound was so loud that I had to sit with my fingers in my ears or I'd have had a massive headache within a few minutes. Why do they do that these days and ruin the films? With the swirling waters in close-up, and the banking of the helicopter views across the heights and crags, it also made me feel very motion sick, and I had to shut my eyes as well. Andy and Sarah loved it, but I was glad to get out.

Sarah and I, giggling, carefully painted the eye of the jackalope red using nail varnish, and posted it back to the ranch for Brad.

Wednesday 29th September.

This was our very last day. After packing everything neatly away in my suitcase, we loaded up the car, before driving back past the canyon and Desert View for the last time, heading down Route 64. It was almost as sad as saying goodbye to the ranch. As we turned away to head south, it was amazing that such a huge canyon could disappear from view so quickly, leaving just the walls of Echo Cliffs jutting up. I tried to imagine what the first people had thought when they stepped through the pines and found themselves suddenly at the edge of such an awesome sight.

We slowly descended the rolling green hills heading for the Painted Desert, so called because of the many pastel hues of the sand and rocks. We passed the end of the hills and out onto the flat plateau before climbing up into pine covered mountains with red cliffs and rocks, broken shale at the foot. Dry washes coming in from the right showed where torrents of water flowed in the wet season. Far away, out on the plateau floor, I could see a long grey crack making its way toward the Grand Canyon.

Here, we passed rows of wooden stands, stalls where the native Indians were selling jewellery.

Once onto the flat we got closer to the crack in the floor and Andy found a place to turn off so we could park up to go and have a look. We walked along a dusty trail until we reached a lot of flat rock with a metal pole fence around the edge. Gazing down into a deep twisting canyon, eight hundred to a thousand feet deep according to the sign, I could see the thin line of the muddy red water of Little Colorado, a miniature Grand Canyon. I sat for a while, lost in the views, looking down into the depths or across to the colours of the Painted Desert.

We rejoined the road, carrying on until making a right turn onto Route 89, a long straight road at a height of 7,000 feet towards Flagstaff. It was beautifully sunny, and the temperature slowly began to rise outside. We dropped down off the plateau and entered pine and spruce clad slopes with fields of grass and flowers, alternately going up long hills to the top and then dropping back down, slowly descending towards Flagstaff. Driving into the town, once again I realised how much I hate concrete roads and buildings, especially after all the quiet beauty earlier.

We managed to get lost getting to the centre of town, heading out somehow on the wrong road and having to turn to come back, but we eventually found our way back to K-Mart. We all put our films in to be developed and waited in store for them to be developed. The poor man nearly had a fit when he saw how many films we had between us, but it was so much cheaper to do it here than home—plus the fact we wanted to see them all as soon as possible. Andy also managed all his shopping here for the family back home, trying to buy up half the store!

We collected our photos and left to head for Phoenix, this time taking the I-17 and bypassing Sedona. The road wound slowly downwards through canyons and valleys, climbing steep inclines then turning to drop again through the most beautiful wooded and green countryside. Gradually, as we got lower, the green fields began to change to the dryer grasses and plains of the high deserts. The temperature had now risen to a muggy 96f 32C despite the sun dropping towards the horizon. As the sun disappeared and it turned dark, we reached flat land to head along the four lane Interstate, looking for the Pointe Hilton hotel again.

We had different rooms this time, and again the large pool wasn't open to Andy's disgust. I gave in my MasterCard, and after waiting ages, they informed me that they'd had trouble getting it accepted as it was very near the limit. I wasn't sure how, have I really spent that much. So Andy paid part of it by Travellers Cheques for the deposit. We were not happy about it, I felt a bit like a criminal, and we made it rather obvious to them.

After finding our rooms and changing we met to splash about in the small pool before dressing and going for a meal in the café, where I watched the usual TV screens around us. How the Americans can have several large TV screens going whilst trying to eat I shall never know especially as no one seemed to be watching them, and they had no sound anyway. What a waste of electricity.

We returned to our rooms and I climbed into bed for the last time in America, trying to stay awake for as long as possible to relive all my time here.

Thursday 30th September.

We got up and met for breakfast before Andy drove us to the airport through the rush hour traffic, which was just like Canterbury except for being four lanes deep. We left the car at the rental booth, while a porter took our luggage on a cart to the check-in. There, Andy had to tape up his mailbox after stuffing it with lots of presents, and I had to tape shut my holdall as the saddle was a bit big, wrapping towels over the horn to protect it. The luggage was only just underweight, so we managed to get away with not having to pay any extra charges. Andy and Sarah also helped me out by packing my bridle, spurs, and rifle boot into their cases between them.

We went through security and I managed not to set off the x-ray machine bleep by taking off my hat and belt before hand, passed through passport control, and arrived in the waiting lounge. I only had a coffee, already getting very nervous about flying again. The flight was called, we joined the line of people getting on board, and after struggling to get our hand baggage into the luggage racks above our heads, along with everyone else trying to do the same thing, I sat down in the seat and strapped up. Yet again they went through the process of telling us of the emergency exits and the no smoking rules, etc before we were backing up and taxiing out onto the runway.

It was a two-hour flight to Dallas and I was relieved when we landed, still clutching the small bag of peanuts we had been given at the start. We found the carousel and waited for our cases to come round, but they didn't. Andy went to ask, only to discover that they were already on route to our homeward flight.

As we were making our way down the corridors to find the departure lounge, Andy nudged me, pointing to one of the driven carts that people used to get from place to place. On it was sitting Dolly Parton, and she was as pretty as on the TV.

I waved, shouting, "hi," thrilled when she called back "hi," and flashing us a lovely wide smile.

We didn't have long to wait before our flight was called, and then once again we were inside and settling in our seats, listening to the stewardesses again. Not long into the flight, the sun began to go down and people closed their window blinds. Shame really as I would have liked to see what the stars or moon looked like from up here.

The films showing weren't my type of entertainment at all, but I managed to find some symphony music on the radio and I settled down to doze, trying not to feel so sad and lost at leaving America. I let my mind drift over the past weeks, and if nothing else, it helped take my mind off being nervous at being in the air.

After a long tiring flight, we landed at Gatwick to a dull, cloudy sunrise. We fought our way to the carousel, grabbed the cases and a cart to put them on, and walked straight through customs, meeting Stephen outside. After the brightness of America, England was dull, depressing and wet, and I had to get re-used to us now driving on the left side of the road, but the fields and trees were a brilliant green after all the deserts and plains.

Gosh, how busy the roads had become and, even worse, the driving seemed to have become quite manic, with cars weaving in and out dangerously and the drivers thinking nothing of slipping across the nose of our car to reach the slip-way off the motorway. I hadn't realised just how pleasant it was to drive in America. In fact, two days after returning home, I was re-organising the residents in Bullockstone Road into fighting hard for a 40 mph speed limit after being forced off the road by a white van. It had cut in off the bend on a blind corner at the top of the road, and I only just avoided a brick wall!

We talked all the way home, being excited at reliving our experiences. Andy was dropped off at his home, Stephen dropped Sarah off at her door, and then I was finally home.

I quickly phoned my dad and sister to say I was back, before going to get the dogs, anxious to see them again. I paid the money I owed to the lady while the man went to get them, saying, "watch them playing on the grass. The brown one loves to rub her face on it."

Cody bounded towards me a little unsure of who I was at first, but Callie. She was scraping her face on the grass, desperately rubbing her bad ear on it, moaning. I looked in her ear when I forced her to get up, and it looked as if the drops were still being put in. After three weeks? I got them into the car and started for home, but Callie was screaming and whimpering. Desperately, I drove straight to the vet's. They could see her in about an hour. I hung around in the car park, trying to calm her until I could take her in, crying myself.

Her ear was very, very bad. The vet gave her more drops and antibiotic tablets and told me to come back in a week's time when they would be able to anaesthetise her and wash her ears out. What an end to a beautiful holiday. I had to drive home with her constantly crying in pain.

Fortunately, the drops worked fairly quickly, and the following week she had the ear washed out under anaesthetic. The vet warned me that if she ever had it that bad again, she would need an operation to shorten the ear canal.

I never thought to cancel my cheque, being so frightened for her, but I've never recommended the kennels to anyone ever again. In fact I would sooner stay at home than allow anyone to look after my dogs again.

Everyone wanted to know if I'd enjoyed myself and it was great to relive all my memories, especially on how I'd thought the Americans and their way of life so stress free and easy going. It came as no surprise to people when I keep saying that if I could I would go and live over there, and I always refer to myself now as an 'un-adopted American.'

I was deeply moved by the strength of patriotism the Americans have, with their flags flying and their stirring speeches at the rodeos, as in Britain it seems that showing you are proud to be British is almost antisocial.

Going into shops I found myself thanking shop and bank assistants with a cheery, "have a nice day." At first I got stunned looks from them, but the smiles I received, and the surprised "thank you," I got in return, was well worth it.

I also found that I'd picked up a few different names for things. And I kept being told off by friends and relatives for confusing them with pants instead of trousers, gas instead of petrol, lightning bugs instead of fireflies, sidewalks instead of pavements, and railroad crossing for the barriers at railway lines.

I had felt a lot safer in America too, with police everywhere, giving me a wonderful feeling of being protected. Their being armed only heightened that feeling.

The sense of space, even in the towns and cities had been astonishing as there were less people on the pavements, while the width of the roads gave a wonderful sensation of freedom after the crowded, stressed roads of Britain. And everywhere looked so clean that anyone who watched the video that Andy had taken, noticed it.

Would I go over the Big Pond again? Oh yes.

BOOK 2000.

Chapter 7

How to do it Yourself!

In April 2000, I was asked by Andy if I would like to buy a computer, and jumped at the chance, especially as he was quite good with them and offered to set it all up for me at home.

I'd only ever used a computer at work and that had a package already set up for me, where I entered information from forms sent to our department. I work for the NHS in the Mental Health/Learning Disabilities sector. I'd heard of e-mail and the Internet, but they were complete mysteries to me, like listening to a foreign language being spoken. It had been the same with mobile phones until Andy had given me one for Christmas when he'd been worried that I rode alone, mainly in the local woods.

He showed me how to get into the Internet as well as how to send e-mails, and kept adding different options into the machine, half of which I still haven't played with. One I used was the National Geographic Trip Planner for America. At first I was very nervous, but as I played around, I gradually began to enjoy what I could find out. I think it was his idea to plan this next trip to America, bypassing the travel agents.

When I told Daphne that I wanted to visit America again, she jumped at the chance of having the dogs, refusing to allow them into kennels having heard what had happened the last time. So Andy and I decided to make up our own itinerary.

We sat over several evenings deciding where we wanted to go, finally choosing New York, Texas, Chicago, Monument Valley, a boat trip on Lake Powell, another week at the Lazy K Bar ranch in Tucson, then on to San Francisco. We had to juggle the dates a lot to tie in with where we wanted to be and it was no wonder the travel agent had had to keep changing things last year. The trip planner was fascinating; pick any city, bring up all the different hotels and motels to stay in, with their details, and it even gave places of interest to visit for up to 50 miles around. Then you went into their website to find out dates, and even book.

For New York, we worked our way down the list of motels for fairly cheap prices. Finding one, I entered their web site, but after trying to book, discovered that we could only book one room at a time, so when it couldn't give us a second room, we had to cancel the first booking and try another motel. We got lucky with the Econolodge in Newark, New Jersey.

We entered our details with Andy's Mastercard number and when the booking was accepted, we immediately got a confirmation number by return e-mail. Some places did take the money from our account first, but others we had to make a note of to pay when we got there. The only stipulation for Andy was that hotels had a swimming pool!

We needed to fly to Dallas from Newark, but the only flight we could get was three days later, so we ended up staying in New York longer than we'd expected. We booked the flight to Dallas, Texas with American Airlines, receiving details of the terminal, departure and arrival times, flight number, and even the seat numbers. It seemed strange using a credit card for no money seemed to change hands.

We browsed through the web sites for several car rental companies at Dallas before choosing Enterprise who had the most reasonable rates. We could even choose the type of car we fancied, another Blazer like last year. I wanted to tour Texas, in particular Abilene, Big Spring, which was the town I'd chosen for my childhood story many years before, San Antonio because of the Alamo, Waco for the Texas Ranger Hall of Fame, and back to Dallas to see the famous Southfork Ranch. However, like everywhere I went, what I wanted to see was not what I got. Time had marched on from the cowboy era, but if you looked beyond the cars and tarmac streets, a lot of the buildings were still in the same style and the streets in the same layout. For the five days in Texas, we would check into hotels as we went, depending on where we were at the time.

We booked another flight with American Airlines to go to Chicago. Here we would take the Amtrak train, with overnight sleeping cabins, to Grand Junction in Colorado. The flight looked OK, but the train hadn't any reservations for the day we wanted and we had to settle for the following day, which meant only half a day's visit in Chicago itself. But I did find rooms at the Day's Inn at O'Hare airport.

The booking gave us the train, car, and the bedroom numbers, and we could pick the tickets up at the station. At Grand Junction, we reserved a car with National and were able to leave it at Tucson, but we had to pay extra for the going one way. We booked the Econolodge at Page, Lake Powell, but the boat trip had to be booked by phone, getting the number from their web site. Andy discovered that the number was wrong, but the lady at the other end was obviously used to this and gave us the correct one. He booked a half-day boat trip to visit Rainbow Bridge that I'd read about in the Zane Grey books.

In the early days of the century, it would have taken three weeks riding over very rough country to get there, guided by the Navaho, to whom the archway was very sacred.

It would take nearly two days to drive from Grand Junction to Tucson, which was a tight squeeze, and we had to rely on finding a place to stay somewhere between Grand Junction and Page. From there we could drive to Tucson, where we booked a week at the Lazy K Bar ranch again, e-mailing them through their Web site.

A flight would take us from Tucson to San Francisco with South West Airlines, and I booked the Radisson Union City hotel. This was quite a way out as hotels closer to the centre of town were very expensive, but on a map Andy had, the Bart train, like a Metro, ran from close by right into San Francisco and was very cheap. The main external flights Andy booked through an agent, and this time we would fly with Virgin Atlantic out of Heathrow.

I made up an itinerary, listing the dates, flights, cars, train and hotel details with the times of departures and arrivals, the confirmation numbers, how much we paid, and whether it was already paid or not, and this turned out to be really invaluable. I also made another page of the itinerary for places of interest covering each city or town we were visiting or passing through.

The whole thing took us about a month as it was only done when we had the time, and although it was quite fiddly and time consuming, it was fantastic watching the holiday grow.

HOLIDAY 2000

Chapter 8

New York.

Thursday 31st August.

Again we had booked Steven to take us to Heathrow airport for our 4pm flight with Virgin Atlantic. I packed my suitcase and bag into his car and we collected Andy at 11am, needing to be at the airport three hours before hand, and allowing ourselves plenty of extra time in case of heavy traffic. This wasn't quite as bad as last year and we got through to the drop-off point at Heathrow quite quickly. Approaching along the M25, I was amazed at how low the planes were flying, right over our heads.

Andy found a trolley for our cases, and we gave Stephen the date and time of our homeward flight, getting his mobile number so that we could call him when we landed. I'd only ever been to Heathrow once before with Les and Ann-Marie, when Les had brought us in for a meal to watch the planes, and I remember being stunned at how small Concord looked against the other planes. The layout for shops, walk ways, and the check-in point were a lot different to Gatwick, much bigger and busier, but Andy seemed to know his way about, taking us straight to the check-in desk.

We found a stationer for Andy to get some newspapers and magazines, sitting and having a coffee until it was time to get to customs. I was a bit nervous as last year I had tripped the metal detector machine by wearing things with metal on them, like my leather belt with metal buckle and my hat with its silver coloured conchos. This time I remembered to take them both off before letting them go through the x-ray machine with my hand luggage.

We had a look round the duty free shops before wandering through to wait in the boarding lounge where Andy filmed the front of our plane through the big glass windows. This sported a large transfer of a girl on it. Lady Penelope. (Coming home, the plane had a transfer of Austin Powers.) The plane amazed me with its bulbous top and windows for the upstairs lounge, unfortunately only for the first class passengers.

Blocks of seat numbers were called to stagger the amount of people going in, and then we were going down the carpeted tunnel to the plane, being greeted by the stewardesses. The seating seemed a bit wider than American Airlines, and set into the back of each seat we had a TV screen. On the seats they had placed a large, pale blue plastic bag with socks, an eye-patch, notepad and pen, and a tiny toothpaste and toothbrush. After we had stowed our hand luggage overhead, which was difficult to do with everyone else trying to do the same, both along side and opposite, I settled in and did up the seatbelt.

I was still nervous on takeoff, but not as bad as last year thank goodness, though I still didn't like it when the plane banked, and I still couldn't look out of the windows for I didn't like the ground going away from me. That's when I knew there was nothing between me, and Mother Earth.

The TV had a choice of eight different movies and some Sky programmes, plus a map of the land the plane was flying over, like American Airlines last year, so I could follow the distance, time, speed, and the outside temperature. I still can't believe how cold it is on the outside. The in-flight meals were really nice and the supplies of drinks came quite often.

We arrived at Newark airport, New Jersey at 18.30pm. It was hot, but without our humidity. We followed the crowds down to get our luggage from the carousel, fighting for space to watch for the cases coming round, before queuing up to go through passport control. I had a nice man who was slightly taken aback by me wearing a cowboy hat. He asked why I was in America and where we were going. I told him some of the places we were visiting, including the ranch, and he wished me well.

We then followed the signs for the hotel shuttle service phones. Andy spoke to the Econolodge, asking if they were the Econolodge at Carlstadt.

"Yes." They would come and pick us up.

It was getting dark by the time they arrived for us, and the traffic seemed horrific. We stacked the suitcases inside and climbed in. The trip seemed very short and Andy remarked to me that it had looked longer on the map from the Trip Planner. Then we found out why. Trying to book in at reception, they hadn't heard of us. The man's accent was difficult to understand, but it turned out we wanted the Econolodge at Meadowlands, Carlstadt. I had already been worried about whether booking by Internet was going to work, now I was getting concerned—we had a whole three and a half weeks before us yet!

The man ordered us a cab, which would cost about $30, but we were tired and wanted to get there quickly. The other Econolodge was about eight miles from New York and the driver had trouble finding it, but with Andy helping by map reading, we finally got there. Even in the dark, the roadsides looked rather shabby and run down.

The main entrance was a bit of a mess as builders were working making a new counter. We signed in and were told we were on the second floor, no ground floor in America, and we had to drag our cases up two flights of concrete stairs for there wasn't a lift. The rooms seemed a bit smoky, but clean. I remembered that the wall switches either pushed up to turn on, or on the lamps, twist round.

We went down to the reception for a coffee but there was no room for the machine, which had been advertised, with all the work going on. Andy asked the man behind the desk if there was a restaurant nearby and was told we could either catch a bus, due at about 10pm, or we could order a meal to be delivered from the printed menus in our rooms. He also admitted that it was not the best of places to visit at night.

The bus went past as we stood there, so we decided to order a meal in. Back up on the balcony, Andy found a cold drinks machine and fed in a dollar bill for a can of Mountain Dew, but I still had some bottled water left over.

We ordered a Caesar salad and garlic bread, I had chicken strips with mine, by phone, and Andy ordered a drink with his. It took a while to arrive, and, not knowing what a Caesar salad was, I was a bit disappointed when it turned out to be mostly lettuce with croutons and a dressing, but it tasted nice. Once Andy left to go to his room, I showered and went to bed, sleeping well despite the air-con being a bit noisy.

Friday 1st September.

It was very humid and overcast when I woke at 6am, my usual time at home despite the time difference. I washed, and watched TV until I thought I should ring Andy at 8am, as he'd wanted a lie-in.

We walked across the long straight road outside the motel, pausing for a gap in the traffic in the middle where central lines were painted, then waited at the bus stop outside a gas station. Andy bought two large orange juices from the stand that was supplying some trucker, and I found the men intimidating for they looked rather rough. When the coach came, costing us $2.55 each, it was very clean, and as no food or drink was allowed inside, I had to throw the last half of my OJ away. We found a couple of seats and sat down. A lot of the passengers, mostly coloured, were dozing.

The bus took us into New York down a long curved road and through a tunnel, then between massive freeways with new shiny, tall buildings rising from a jungle of drab concrete houses. We got off at the last stop to go down concrete steps into a large mall with shops.

Going down an escalator I heard chimes and discovered in the centre of the shopping mall, a large glass cabinet with pool balls running along rails. As they ran down the inclines, they hit various targets, the hammers making different chimes. Reaching the bottom, the balls rolled into hoops and were taken back up to the top to repeat the process. I was fascinated at the precision.

We emerged on the streets where I found the buildings very dingy, a lot like London, crammed full of people and cars, and very noisy, and I was glad I'd persuaded Andy it wouldn't be a good idea to hire a car here. We'd have got nowhere! There were lots of yellow cabs, but of a more modern design than I expected after watching films on TV. I was also very surprised at the amount of coloured people about who seemed to well outnumber the whites.

Walking up a street, Andy was approached by a coloured ticket tout for the Greyline open top tour buses. For $59 dollars, you could get on and off where you wanted, but also included was the price of entry to the Empire State Building, the Twin Towers, and the Statue of Liberty, with an evening Twilight tour at 7pm any evening.

We reached the nearest stop, waited for the next bus to arrive and climbed to the open top deck. The ride was very bumpy. There must have been dreadful potholes in the road. Some of the road signs and traffic lights were almost too low and I felt like ducking as we went under them, craning my neck to see the huge buildings towering above us. We passed through Times Square, and reached the flat iron building, an unusual triangle shape like the bottom of an iron.

The adverts in lights were amazing and very colourful, covering just about all the buildings bar the windows, and there were two continuous newsreels running round one building.

I couldn't believe just how many people were crowded on the pavements.

There was a band in colourful caftans and hats at the side of one street (the Brotherhood of Islam), but it turned out they were shouting out their own brand of religious, and the tour guide made it very obvious that he disliked them intensely by shouting rude remarks across.

The bus stopped at a small park where we climbed down to the pavement to look for the ferry for the Statue of Liberty. The path through to the quay had several drinks/food stalls, and quite a few selling T-shirts, which Andy browsed round. He videoed the grey squirrels running along the grass looking for food to bury. They looked quite tame, but I knew from back home that they could be nasty.

It was windy when we joined the queue for the ferry, the sea grey and choppy. While we waited, I watched a skinny, black contortionist putting his legs behind his neck and swinging on his hands, before squeezing into a small glass box. Another man with him was giving a very funny running commentary in a jazzy voice, and I found them fascinating. Afterward, they came round with caps collecting tips.

We boarded a ferry to the island and as we neared the statue, people crowded over to one side to get a better view. The statue was amazing. As we got closer, it got taller and taller, and appeared a very pale green. Apparently the salt air has oxidised the copper. The flame in a holder, held straight up into the air, was painted gold.

Strolling around the island, despite the distance from the mainland, I could hear the cicadas (si-kar-das) chirping in the trees. We browsed around the gift shop where I bought a fridge magnet of New York for my collection, and then had a huge meal, similar to a MacDonalds, sitting outside on the patio with pigeons, sparrows and seagulls looking for food. It isn't allowed to feed so they didn't pester like the ones I knew back home.

We boarded another ferry that stopped at Ellis Island. Here in the lovely, old red brick buildings, many years before, incoming immigrants had been processed. We decided not to get off and look round.

Back in New York, we walked to the twin towers of the Trade Building through lots of streets and gloomy back alleys where my legs began to ache despite having put my trainers on. I never have been able to walk very far, and these days I found it very tiring, especially walking on solid pavements.

We found the entrance, and after a long wait in a queue, went to the top in an elevator that took 58 seconds and travelled at 25mph.

At the top of a set of stairs, there was New York stretching far, far away into the distance, a sea of buildings with the river winding its way through. As the windows went from floor to ceiling, I wouldn't go too close for I hate heights, which is why some of my photos have window frames in them! Over to one side, on the horizon, I could see a large black ominous cloud.

It was mind blowing to look out on each side of the Tower block, towards the far horizons, and see nothing but a sea of buildings. My thought immediately was, *'where does all the millions of tons of waste go, and the sewage?'* And the acreage of earth that was covered in concrete and steel-it was totally stunning, making me feel desperate for the fresh air and open prairies of Texas and Arizona.

We walked back to find a tour coach to take us back to the bus terminal and once there, entered a subway. Andy bought tickets to reach the Empire State Building. I found the Metro trains and station were similar to London's Underground as we went down the stairs and escalators to the trains-very dirty, dingy and as frightening to me as London, but I actually felt safer as security guards and police all had guns on their belts.

The tickets were fed into the front of the entry stalls and almost immediately popped up through a slot on top. Pulling it out, the gates opened to let us walk through. The sound of the trains coming and going into the stations started like a low roar followed by a clatter. The doors hissed open and shut, and then they roared off again. I knew when one was coming as it pushed a puff of hot wind before it, blowing loose clothing and hair about.

After finding seats on the next train, we arrived at our stop, taking the flights of steps and an escalator to the street above. It was a long walk to the Empire Building, but as it turned out to be very close to closing time, we decided to have a meal in the café below instead. It had got quite dark by the time we left there.

We got back to the subway and got on the train, but just before the doors closed, I realised I had forgotten my hat, which was very embarrassing, as we had to walk all the way back. The coloured cleaner inside smiled and said, "I thought you'd be back for your hat."

Back at the hotel, the man at the desk told us that not only was it Labour Day on Monday, the day we were leaving, and a national holiday, but also that State leaders were here for a Summit, so the middle of town would be closed off. No wonder I'd seen so many stretch limousines about.

Saturday 2nd September.

It was dull and muggy when I got up, and I sat writing my notes before phoning Andy, then sitting and watching the TV while he got ready.

Again we caught the bus to town, but which turned up twenty minutes later than we'd expected. Was it a Saturday timetable?

Once in town, we waited to board a tour bus uptown to Harlem. The tour guide was very interesting, telling us local history and sights of interest, stopping once for us to get out and look at a huge cathedral that was still in the process of being built. On the way back, he pointed out the block of flats outside where John Lennon was shot.

Getting off at a stop outside Central Park, we started a long walk past posh hotels with smartly dressed doormen and stretch limousines outside and one had huge concrete blocks around the roadway entrance. It was very hot and I had trouble keeping up with Andy who was striding out.

Coming to a diner, we had a lovely meal, and again I stuck to a chicken salad. I can't get used to the huge meals they bring and was rather put out that I couldn't manage one of the delicious looking deserts.

Across from us, horses and carriages lined up at the edge of the road, all the horses having a tarpaulin under their tails for the manure-no wonder the streets were so clean. They were drooping wisely in their harnesses, only livening up when someone climbed into their carriage.

We strolled through the park. The green grass and the trees, with grey rocks pushing up out of the ground, were very restful after the buildings and streets, but we had to hide under some trees from a heavy, warm shower. As it stopped, a man strolled past on the path with a colourful parrot on his arm, pausing to talk to a woman with a small boy. The boy was allowed to have the parrot on his arm, holding his arm out very gingerly. It was obvious that the man told the child he could stroke its head, but the parrot had other ideas, leaning so far back that I thought it would fall off.

We walked on until there was another heavy rain shower, hiding under an ornamental archway that had lovely murals painted on the ceiling. From there we could look around a fountain in an ornamental pool out at the lake and the small boats on it. Lots of people were sheltering as well, and one man came round to his captive audience collecting on behalf of the Battered Women in Central Park, NY.

The shower eased off and we set off up the concrete steps and out along the path, but after a few minutes it started again. I tried to hide under a tunnel of grapevines, but got wet from the water dripping off the leaves, so we decided to carry on walking. Some time after I'd returned home, I watched the film, Kramer v. Kramer and spotted the same place even though it was covered in snow. Eventually the rain stopped altogether and the sun came out to dry us off.

As we approached the lines of carriages I went to pat one of the horses, and was so overpowered by the heavy sell of the driver that I walked off. But further down the line, I couldn't resist patting a lovely big grey, Big Jimmy, harnessed to a pretty white carriage that sported colourful plastic flowers. The Italian driver was really nice, with no pressure on us to get in, so I persuaded Andy to have a go. I couldn't come to New York and not have a drive through Central Park. To be truthful, I also fancied a rest.

There were quite a few carriages already going round at a walk and we took our turn in the queue behind several others. Our driver was really nice and very chatty, telling us he was a naturalised American, originally from Italy, turning round quite a lot to talk while Big Jimmy plodded slowly round following the carriage in front. I was fascinated by the huge shoes Big Jimmy had, steel at the back, and rubber at the front. With all the roadwork they did the driver told us, he had to have them replaced every few weeks and I found out that it was much more expensive than having Cloud done. In places the road was very potholed, and despite the springs, we did get bounced around a bit. At the end, the driver took our picture sitting in the carriage, and then standing with Big Jimmy, giving me carrots to give him. With a last pat, we went down the road to catch a tour bus to Times Square.

The pavements were jam packed with people and we had to walk through shoulder-to-shoulder crowds that made me nervous. I'd always disliked being with lots of people, preferring more open spaces. The roads were absolutely full of cars, cabs and buses, bumper to bumper, making me wonder how anyone got anywhere. The whole scene was claustrophobic.

I bought some CD's in the Virgin shop; Phil Collins' Serious Hits, Live, along with Jan Hammer's Drive and Escape from TV. This last one I liked being soundtracks from Miami Vice, the TV series with Don Johnson.

Back outside, I heard a loud roar and turned to see a cavalcade of police cycles passing by escorting a limousine, but with its blackened windows I couldn't see who was inside.

Andy hailed a cab to take us to the Empire State building, where we joined a long queue for the elevator, shuffling slowly forward. Once crammed inside, it became very hot, but at the top and outside, it was a lot fresher. An edging wall ran round the outside at chest height with wire fencing above it making me feel more secure so I didn't mind looking outward rather than down. But the only way I could take a picture of the street below was to hold my camera over the edge, hoping that it came out OK. (It did, but it included a small ledge below full of water and cigarette butts.) Off to one side, out on the horizon, I could see lightning flashing in the gathering black clouds.

Going back to the bus station for the 7pm Twilight Tour, we were dismayed to discover that the Grey Line coach had left at 6.45pm. We were very annoyed about it, and had no option but to wait for a bus to take us back to the hotel.

Not long after we arrived back in our rooms, the storm broke outside with tremendous thunder and lightning.

I slept well, but my legs were aching, especially my bad right knee. This was already swollen and painful after having walked along all the hard concrete the day before.

Sunday 3rd September.

Next morning, we only just caught the bus by running over the road, dodging the traffic. I worried if this could this be jaywalking, and was it illegal?

Once in town, Andy hailed a cab to take us to Grand Central Station as I'd heard that it was lovely. Inside, it was very impressive with marble walls, huge wide stairs and floor, and beautiful chandeliers, while overhead the ceiling was painted like the night sky, lights depicting the zodiac star signs. The hall was very busy with people bustling around and it echoed to the sounds of voices and feet.

Back outside, we walked the streets looking for a café, stopping for a welcome cup of coffee before catching a cab to Central Park. Getting out at the wrong corner, we had to walk a very long way to get back to the main entrance, passing alongside the Park on one side with a small zoo, and tall houses and hotels on the other. I was so pleased to come across a diner and go in for a meal. We found spaces on round stools at the bar. I ordered a chicken salad which, when it came, was huge but delicious.

While I was eating, I could hear the waiters getting cross with someone and gathered that they were unhappy with a customer just down from us, an elderly lady. Chatting to one of the men behind the counter after, we found out that she apparently came in nearly every day and always complained about the coffee, just smiling back at them when they got mad at her.

We crossed the road and sat on a bench in a small circular area with a statue and fountains, inside the centre of five converging roadways. Looking up, I nudged Andy to show him that over the tops of the skyscrapers there were heavy, black clouds looming. We decided to get under cover quickly, crossing back over the road and entering a small shopping arcade, where

Andy bought a T-shirt for himself, and I found a small one for Vicky, my niece, with New York written on it in attractive coloured embroidery. I also spotted an elephant for Brenda, a friend of Andy's and mine, who collected them.

Back out on the street, Andy hailed a cab to take us to the famous Macys department store. On the way over, we were held up by a coloured cyclist screaming abuse at a cab driver ahead of us, smacking his window, spitting, and forcing the car to stop while he continued shouting. Our driver managed to get round them luckily, before dropping us off outside the store just as the heavens opened. We ran to get through the doors.

Browsing round the ladies wear department, I came across some beautiful silk blouses, fawn or pink, and decided to treat myself to a pink one as they were at a very reduced rate. I had to stand and wait for ages to pay for the queue was very slow moving.

We continued upstairs using escalators, the last two being beautiful old wooden ones, and I hoped that they weren't being replaced by boring modern ones. We slowly made our way back downstairs, finding ourselves in a cellar where there was a small café area among the goods on sale. Andy bought some cups of coffee that turned out to be the worst we had ever tasted in America up till then, and despite being thirsty, we both had to leave it.

Out on the street again, I could hear the rumbling of thunder from the departing storm, while the streets were wet. Andy tried to hail a cab, but they cruised past, all busy, so we set off walking. I was feeling exhausted, but when we came across Toys 'R Us, Andy went in to see if he could buy some Pokemon cards for the children back home. There were none there that he wanted, so we left the shop to find crowds at the edge of the road with police and an ambulance in attendance. I could only make out a pair of legs on the pavement from somebody who'd apparently collapsed.

Coming to a subway, we went down the stairs, buying a ticket and getting onto the next train, but we must have misjudged the stops as we got out somewhere strange. Andy asked directions from the ticket operator, but we found it confusing between with 'across the block.' Is a block between roads, or each building? We couldn't find the subway he'd mentioned, but after a long walk, eventually found another one. This was locked.

We had no option but to carry on walking down a long street trying to find a cab to hail but they were all occupied. I was getting more tired and my knee very sore. At last, just as I'd come to the conclusion that I really loathed N.Y, I realised that we were only a block from the bus station. I was so pleased to get into the bus to go back to the hotel.

At reception, Andy ordered a car for the morning to take us to the airport and they promised to call when it arrived. Back in my room, after a long, hot bath, I sat on the bed watching TV. Gosh, The weather forecast for Texas was very hot—100 to 110f or 41C.

Chapter 9

Heading for Texas.

Monday 4th September.

I was awake early and finished my packing before ringing through to wake Andy. We took our cases down the stone steps to reception where Andy paid the bill, just before the car turned up. This turned out to be a very smart limousine with a suited driver! I felt like royalty.

We were dropped at the airport, and went to the desk to check in. The lady there was intrigued when she heard our accents, very interested when we told her that we had booked the flight through the Internet, and surprised at the good deal we had got through it. We went down the corridors and through the security check, where I was nervous as I expected the machine to bleep at me, but luckily nothing happened.

It was a nice flight to Dallas, but coming down to the runway seemed very bouncy. Then, just as the wheels should have touched down, the plane pulled off, frightening me to death. Andy suggested that either the plane had gone too far down the runway, or it was too bumpy because of the rising thermals from the heat as the temperature was between 43-45C, making it overshoot the runway. We circled for ages before we were allowed to land, this time making it, to my relief. We retrieved our luggage from the carousel and boarded the free shuttle coach out to the rental car parks, some way away.

The people at the counter were great, very jokey, and fascinated that we were English as they had hardly ever seen anyone from Britain before. They were even more amazed that we were intending to drive around Texas, asking where we were heading, and in only five days. One of the lads took us out to see the car, a white Ford Explorer, and gave us directions on a map on how to get out of Dallas, as well as how to get back five days later.

As we set off, the doors locked automatically as the car was put into gear. Great idea, although back home, I always did it myself every time I went out. This became such a compulsive habit, that I inevitably locked my passengers in as well.

We tried to follow the directions and got lost on the freeways, but finally finding the I-20 to head west for Abilene. The road signs are strange, the I-20 West or I-20 East can head north or south, according to the compass in the car, which took me days to acclimatise to. The junctions had road names not the towns that were on big motorway signs that overhung the lanes.

The land was very flat, intersected by dry washes and arroyos. Wooden trestles crossed them carrying the railroad tracks although road bridges were made of concrete. There were green shrubs I later found to be creosote bushes and mesquite (mes-keet), with trees of scrub oak and palo verdes. The latter was Spanish for green tree, and they had lovely green trunks and branches.

We drove a hundred and eighty nine miles to Abilene in Taylor County, crossing the Brazos and Leon Rivers. Incredible! Here were names of towns and rivers that I'd read about in my western books and seen in films. (When I got home, I had to browse through the map, because when I'd been driving, I hadn't been able to write anything down.)

Looking around the countryside, I tried to imagine taking a herd of cattle through the scrub and brush. How relieved the cowboys must have been to reach any water, although drives usually started in spring after the wet winter weather. They must have been very tough, and it was no wonder they changed horses every two hours. I began to understand why a horse thief was hanged for murder, as no one could have survived for long out here without a means of transport.

We managed to get rooms in a Best Western, the Mall South at Ridgemont Drive that was very nice and had a swimming pool outside. Although it was getting dark, the temperature was still 115f 43C. The pool was lovely and cool, and I enjoyed the swim before going back to my room to shower and change. From there we went out to the restaurant next door, and I had a chicken salad.

It was still very, very hot by bedtime, thank goodness for the air con. Tuesday 5th September.

7am and it was 'smoky' hot outside. There was a free Continental breakfast of cereal or toast and coffee, and to my amusement, iced buns or doughnuts, although occasionally we could have muffins, and every Continental breakfast offered seemed to be the same. Yuk, doughnuts for breakfast. No way.

9am, and outside it was already 31C. Taking the cases out to the car, we found a note on the windscreen, 'We appreciate your using the Best Western, have cleaned your windscreen.' Wow.

I drove, heading south on Route 84 to Buffalo Gap historic village. This turned out to be a collection of original old wooden buildings, with two of brick, all donated from different parts of the county. Most had been due to be destroyed by new development until they ended up here.

We arrived a bit early having to wait outside until 10am for it to open, when we walked through the iron gates and into the wooden trading post. Built in 1910, it had originally been the baggage depot for the Texas & Pacific Railroad at Clyde, Texas, but is now the gift shop. I bought a book of reminisces collected from real, old time working cowboys, then stood chatting to the elderly lady behind the counter before starting the tour at the Old Taylor County Courthouse and Jail. Built in 1878-79, it was the second oldest building in the county, the oldest public building, and brick built.

The Knight-Sayles log cabin built in 1875 followed, being the oldest building in Taylor County and the single pen log cabin typical of the frontier, something I recognised from Westerns.

The Doctor's Office, 1920, included a collection of instruments, medicines and machines, very basic by today's standards.

From there we went into the Bradshaw Post Office, 1880, and on to the barber's shop.

Next came the Clyde railroad depot, with its wooden veranda. Built in 1910 it had originally been used by the Texas and Pacific Railroad.

The Village Gallery had glass top cabinets containing a historic map collection that I found fascinating, showing the open prairies, the few towns, some of the rivers, and county boundaries. Some also showed the original Indian reservations, and these were a lot different to where they are today for the tribes were moved from place to place when the Government took back what they had given.

The cabinet shop next door had lots of old carpentry tools that interested

Andy.

Another was the dentist's. I'm petrified of them, and this old one sent shivers up my spine. How bad could the pain have been to actually sit there and have a tooth pulled, and with none of our modern drugs and anaesthetics.

There was a blacksmith shop, 1881, with the tools that were used, followed by a wagon barn crammed full of implements and furniture used in frontier life, including two lovely old horse drawn Surreys.

The print shop had a couple of early printing presses from West Texas.

The Chapel, 1902, had been the first Nazarene Church built, but we couldn't go in as the lady had reported a big bees nest in the spire.

The Buffalo Gap Post Office, 1950, was the first free standing P.O., and had a whole wall taken up with metal boxes, some with keys, with the names of families on them.

Round the corner was the Bourn Texaco service station, 1926, built in Winters, Texas, when gas had been 9 cents a gallon.

The Cottonwood Flat School, 1908, was a two-roomed school from Scurry County, near the Clear Fork of the Brazos River. Andy and I had a quick sit down at the small wooden desks facing the blackboard.

From there, we went into the two-storey Marshall's house, 1881, one of the first homes built in Abilene, where most of the internal contents were original. All the buildings were beautifully preserved, and were a fascinating account of an old, long gone lifestyle.

I drove back down the road, stopping at a general store for Andy, where I picked up a local newspaper as a souvenir. What a wonderful fresh paper.

The front page title stated: 'It's a Wild and Woolly Weekend with the XIX Chili Superbowl Cookoff,' and was an account of the cooking and judging of chili, chicken, ribs and even beans.

Included on one of the pages was 'The Shootout,' the story of several men, who had broken into the First State Bank in 1919 using nitro-glycerine, and taken a lot of cash and Liberty Bonds. They'd been chased by the local lawmen, as well as some brought into the county to help out. Tracked down, a gunfight started in which one man was shot and the rest escaped, but they were all eventually caught and jailed. The rest of the news and adverts were wonderfully simple, with local weather and 'gatherings,' and an article on foot odour.

Driving back down the I-20, I mentioned to Andy that I didn't think the car handled as well as the Blazer last year, as, "it seems to wander," but he thought it could be that the tyres were quite big. We stopped for gas, 13 ½ gals for $20.10. While there, Andy phoned Enterprise to check that the tyres on the car were OK as we'd heard over the radio that certain types were breaking up at speed. They assured him that they had been checked and were OK.

At lunchtime, I parked up outside a truck stop diner for a meal. Again it was a long low wooden building with steps up to a veranda with wooden rails around. Inside, the walls had old cowboy photos and big sweeping horns from longhorn cattle. How on earth the cowboys had roped one I couldn't imagine, the noose had to be enormous.

I ordered sausages, eggs 'over easy,' (I love saying that,) my favourite biscuits and gravy, followed by a coffee. Great. There were a few people already seated, and from one of the nearby tables, despite their voices being muted, I heard them discussing the drought and the effect on their animals.

From there, we crossed Elm Creek, which was dry, and the Clear Fork, nearly dry, and went through Sweetwater, crossing the Colorado River (not THE Colorado.) After passing Lake Colorado City, we reached Big Spring in Howard County after a hundred and ten miles where t he temperature was now hitting 42C at 4pm. Due to our fixed time, we weren't able to stop, which was very disappointing, but at least I could see the countryside as I had tried to imagine it in my school days dream story.

We drove through hills and on past Sulphur Springs, over Mustang Draw to Midland on the I-20/80 and then the sixty two miles to Odessa in Ector County.

I was surprised at how few cattle we saw on route considering I had always heard that Texas had the biggest cattle industry in the country. Driving along, Andy suddenly put his hand out of the window and remarked that it was like putting your hand into a hot oven, so I tried it too, and he was right.

Here, the land changed from flat land to rolling hills with red sandy outcrops and rocky mounds. The lakes and reservoirs were drying out exposing large expanses of white sand or baked earth. Off to one side was a long streamer of dust, the black speck ahead of it appearing to be a truck.

I enjoyed the driving again, like last year. If I indicated, the Americans pulled back to let me in, and once in a lane, you stayed there, they either over or under took you. Better and safer than weaving in and out like at home especially as the traffic was very thin on the ground over here.

We found another great Best Western hotel, the Garden Oasis on west I-20. The rooms were lovely, and I had a good meal in the restaurant, salad and chicken.

Wednesday 6th September.

I awoke with a bad headache, taking a couple of Ibuprofen that I'd brought with me, and only managing to drink a coffee for breakfast. I suffered from these every so often, having fallen from a set of steps while wallpapering and knocking myself out a few years back.

My daughter, Ann-Marie, had taken me to Accident and Emergency at the Kent and Canterbury Hospital after looking at the wound and realising there was nothing she could do. While the doctor was putting stitches into a gaping wound at the base of my head, he'd asked me if I'd been unconscious. I'd said, "no," not realising that I had been, until I got home and saw a pool of blood on the carpet. So I wasn't x-rayed.

It wasn't for some years after, having had an awful lot of time off work due to bad headaches that I was told about Jill Weightman, an Osteo-Muscular-Remedial-Therapist at Dargate between Faversham and Whitstable, Kent. She gently manipulated vertebrae into place without the creaking and twisting of an osteopath. She discovered that I'd put out the top two vertebrae in my neck and had put them back into place. Although I don't suffer so much since they were corrected, I still have to go to her occasionally, especially if I lay wrong in bed or fall asleep in a chair and put them out again, I occasionally wake up with a headache that leaves me feeling sick and dizzy.

Andy drove from the hotel while I tried to doze, heading for the meteor crater a few miles away that I'd spotted on the National Geographic and wanted to have a look at.

It was just a shallow depression, and I was very disappointed until I read the poster in front of it—it was fifty thousand years old so it had naturally in-filled with dust and earth. Apparently, a great shower of nickel-iron meteorites had collided with the Earth, scattering over about two square miles, the biggest piece found weighing about three hundred pounds. The largest of the craters is about five hundred and fifty feet in diameter and a hundred feet deep, being the second largest crater in the United States, the biggest being at Winslow, Arizona.

A sudden movement caught my eye, two little quail running about in the brush with little feathers above their heads like bobbles on a stalk. I broke off a small branch from a bush for a souvenir. It smelt funny, like oil, and later I was told it was a creosote bush.

We crossed miles and miles of flat fields with lots of metal nodding donkeys stretching off into the hazy distance, then turned off to look at Monahans Sandhills, lonely sand dunes covered with scrub grass, before heading on down Route 18 towards Fort Stockton.

Andy suddenly pulled off down a dirt track to get close to a nodding donkey so that he could video it. I was embarrassed, it was private land and we had no business being there, but luckily no one was around, so we got out for a closer look. The metal arm was very screechy as it turned, making the place feel very eerie. The temperature had already risen to 34C 94f and it was nice to get back in the car.

We crossed the Pecos River, its headwaters coming from north of Santa Fe, New Mexico, and then the Leon River. By 11.30 the temperature had crept up to 36C 98f.

With the cool air from the air conditioning, my headache slowly receded luckily, as it had been known to keep up for a whole day, and at last I began to enjoy watching out of the windows at the countryside passing by. After the junction with the I-10, where we turned east, heading for San Antonio, we started crossing more dusty plains with flat top mesas on the horizon. Texas seemed so flat, and vast and empty, but despite it, I longed for a horse so that I could ride for miles and miles. Mind you, I'd rather ride at night—in the cool!

Andy pulled off at a pretty rest stop under some trees where he filmed a family of tiny ground squirrels (chipmunks) racing back and forth over the road, bouncing like little rubber balls, their fluffy tails carried jauntily over their backs. I felt a lot better now and took over the driving.

The countryside began changing with rocks, scrub (low bushes), creamy stone ridges, dry washes, creeks and arroyos. The road was long and open with little traffic, and once the car was in cruise control it was so easy to just sit and be able to look about. We crossed the dry Comanche River and re-crossed the dry Pecos River, but Howard River did have some water in it.

Up ahead, I spotted a billboard for western wear and pulled off the road towards a mock wooden fort. It appeared deserted when I drove into the wooden stockade, so I drove back out and round to the other side to where there were several stores. The long front looked like an old time western street with its raised sidewalk, only this was built with new cream coloured wood.

I was looking for some boots in one store, wandering up and down rows of cardboard boxes, when a lady came to help. She brought over some lovely goatskin ones, far too expensive, but further down the store were more rows and rows of boots-from floor to ceiling, all cheaper versions. I finally found a nice pair that fitted. I also asked for two nice black hats for myself. To my embarrassment, my hat size of 6 ½ was actually a children's size, but they were only $10 each, cheaper than the adult sizes. Then I spotted some cream coloured straw hats, buy one get one free. I got two in a bigger size hoping they'd fit my friends, Shelia and Helen.

I drove on, well pleased, crossing the Johnson River and stopping off at Ozona when we saw a sign for a Davy Crockett monument. This turned out to be just a small statue in the middle of a grassy park. The grass was green, but crunchy and more like straw, being very coarse and wide bladed, like most we came across.

Further on down the road, I turned off onto a dusty lot in front of a little diner come drug store. Inside to the left was a long wooden bench and stools, with several long counters of food and drugs. We sat down, ordering chicken salad sandwiches and a coffee from the printed menu card. They were nothing like sandwiches we knew. The lady toasted some bread, layered some chicken spread out of a tin onto it and added a little salad. They were quite tasty.

I bought some mint sweets in a box to suck, but they tasted peculiar, just like Germoline and Andy spat his out the car window. Actually, I grew to like them and bought some more the following year.

We went on through lovely flat country, coming across a billboard for the Sonora Caverns and turned toward it, crossing Buckhorn Draw. The road went up into rocky red sandstone hills like a roller coaster ride, up and down until we reached a quaint wooden building nestling under cottonwood trees. Getting out of the car, the heat hit me like the blast from a furnace, 44C according to the car, and it seemed to be more stifled here by the enclosing dusty, dry hills.

Inside, we discovered that we had to wait for the next tour, so I walked around the counters looking at the gems and crystals they were selling.

The tour guide came back with the other party, and then, together with several other people, we were taken across to a metal door set in the hillside, through it, and down into the caverns. Here the temperature was a pleasant steady 70f that apparently remained constant throughout the year. The formations were just beautiful, and the guide asked us not to touch anything as the sweat on our hands destroyed the calcium deposits. She turned the lights off behind us as we passed through the tunnels.

Ahead and around us the lights sparkled off the most incredible formations of stalactites and stalagmites, and long glacier like rivers of creamy white calcium that looked like ice. At one point, she asked if we would like to have the lights turned off, and when she did, there was just blackness; no flicker of light, nothing, and no sign of my hand in front of my face, even when I touched my nose in curiosity. That was creepy. Back at the main building, we bought an icecream before getting back into the car.

We carried on, crossing the North Llano and the South Llano Rivers, passing through Kerrville where the road wound through lovely green hills with rocky outcrops, and on over the wide Guadalupe (Gwardaloope) River that was full of water. Here we passed a billboard for the Cascade Caverns.

Finally we reached San Antonio in Bexar County after crossing the San Antonio River, having travelled four hundred and forty eight miles. The freeway was the usual large four lanes each side. Andy put more gas in the tank, which took just $24 to fill.

We found a Best Western, the Ingram Park on NW Loop 410 for $80 ($40ea), and which had a swimming pool on the patio overlooked by the hotel buildings. My room was neat, but the air conditioning was very noisy. I changed, met Andy outside, and went down for a swim, but the water was over chlorinated and smelt and tasted horrid.

There wasn't a restaurant with the hotel, so Andy ordered a meal in. I had a salad with a cheese garlic sauce.

Thursday 7th September.

I was up at 6am, and after showering, sat and watched TV, writing my notes until it was time to call Andy. There was a free breakfast available, but I only fancied a coffee and toast before we packed our cases back into the car and set out. Andy drove until he found a car park by the river. Here the temperature was a cooler 31C.

We wandered through the clean, fresh looking streets, coming to a paved road with a large stone paved area across the way. There, strangely tiny against the huge modern buildings was The Alamo. Painted white, the top of the building was scalloped and it had an arched frame with a wooden door and two sculpted pillars either side. Originally a mission built by Franciscan monks in the 1700's, it had been named after a grove of alamo or cottonwoods.

In 1835, when the influx of Americans had become irritating to the Mexican government, especially as they wanted to become the State of Texas, Santa Anna was sent to stop the unrest. Colonel Davy Crockett was one of many who answered the call to battle, and Sam Houston sent an already sick Jim Bowie to blow up the mission believing it to be too badly built and poorly armed to be defended against the oncoming army. Bowie decided otherwise, and set about holding it with a hundred and twenty three men until reinforcements could arrive. William Travis, with his men, took command, and on February 24, 1836, replied to Santa Anna's call for surrender with a cannon shot. On March 6, with Jim Bowie already lying in his sick bed, over two thousand, five hundred Mexicans charged the walls, and despite a brave fight, the one hundred and eighty three outnumbered Americans were overrun and killed.

In a courtyard to the left and through an archway in the stone wall grew a huge Live Oak, its low, heavy limbs supported by steel cables, and surrounded by flowerbeds full of brightly coloured blooms. Entering another courtyard, I spotted some old cannons. To the left of the first courtyard was a long, low building housing a museum and several rooms with screens showing films of the re-enactment of the battle of the Alamo. Quite a few people were sitting engrossed.

Across the way was a stone water duct, part of which actually followed the original watercourse that had fed The Alamo mission. In it swam some big carp fish. Another building housed a souvenir shop, where I bought another fridge magnet, a map of Texas.

Around at the front of The Alamo building, I could see a faint line between the original standing walls that had remained after the battle and the parts that had been rebuilt. Inside, the atmosphere seemed somehow brooding and chilling. Parts of the building were being repaired, and there were what appeared to be still bullet marks in the old painted walls. We could have joined a guided tour, but decided not to bother as we were pushed for time. Outside, as we headed away, we passed two stone placards set in the grass, one reciting a letter sent from the defenders begging for reinforcements, and a huge statue to the fallen.

We headed back down the streets to the Riverside Walk, descending a spiral of black metal stairs to the sidewalk below. On either side of the river that ran between concrete walls, the forecourts of the cafes had tables outside with pretty parasols and tablecloths. Across the river a man was feeding large black fish in the water, and two shiny blue/black birds were hopping about near him, a kind of jay? We strolled along until we found a long flight of steps up to the roadway and were able to get back to the car.

Driving off, Andy had trouble finding the I-35 heading north, going in completely the wrong direction at first and getting lost in the grimy back lots of the town for a while, making us feel a bit nervous. Once we'd doubled back and found the sign we wanted, we started out of town, crossing Mud Creek where I noticed a billboard for fireworks: 'Buy 1 Get 11 free,' which made me giggle.

We re-crossed the Guadalupe River, and went over Cypress Creek, where at Blanco, the land became hillier. The Blanco River was full, the waters held back by a small dam. Reaching the Little Black River at 11.30am, the temperature had cooled to a mere 27C 84f.

We drove through New Braunfels and past McKinney Falls on the wide Perdonales River, whose headwaters started way up in Colorado. Andy finally pulled onto a dusty car lot before a long wooden diner for a meal, where I sat and watched several buzzards through the windows, lazily circling over the trees and plains. I had eggs, bacon, French fries, and toast, a choice as usual, of wheat or rye bread, not white but brown.

From there we drove past Marble Falls and re-crossed the Colorado River where the temperature had risen to 34C 93f. A hilly road was sign posted for the Longhorn Cavern in the State Park, but despite looking out for any further signs, we never found it. Then, stunningly, over the tops of the pines rose the tips of minuets—a magnificent white chateau! *Rather exotic for Texas,* I thought

Past Inks Lakes, that sparkled blue in the sunlight, and with sailboats and speedboats dotted over the water, they consisted of several large sections of water set in a series of valleys surrounded by red rocky outcrops and cliffs.

Andy began sniffing badly and stated he'd got sinus trouble, probably from the over chlorinated water back at the pool, so I took over driving while he dozed.

Then I saw a billboard for the Inner Space Caverns, and turned back off the Interstate to find it, parking in the car lot before a low, dark wooden building. Booking in, it turned out we would be the only two in the group! We waited for the guide to come back with the tour before us and after, checking our tickets, he took us down to the beginning of the caves in a small cable car.

It was very similar to the Sonora Caverns but with several different deposits, and again very, very pretty. The caves had been found by accident when drilling had taken place to enlarge the I-35 above and the bit had gone through into the cavern. They had been dated to around eighty thousand years. The glitter from the formations was beautiful in the lights.

The guide pointed out a tiny brown bat that looked as if it had been glued to the wali on the other side of a huge hole in the ground that was extremely deep, and from somewhere, I could hear the gentle echo of water dripping. The guide also pointed out some tiny transparent frogs then, further on, clinging to a metal pole, were transparent crickets with waving antenna, making me feel itchy. Once the lights were turned out, they were all living in total blackness.

Near the end, preserved in the rock, were paintings of a giant sloth, a sabre toothed cat and something called a glyptodont, a sort of armoured armadillo with a wicked looking spiky tail. I'd never heard of it before.

From there we drove the two hundred and eighteen miles to Austin in Travis County to find a Best Western, the Executive on North I-35, which had very posh suite rooms at $160 ($80ea.) The elevator that took us up to our floor had a glass back so I could look out over the dining area.

I laid my case out on the stand in my room and sat down on the bed to watch a bit of TV. To my delight, there was a programme called Emergency on, starring Robert Fuller, my favourite actor. No chance for Andy to call for me while that was on!

We went out for a meal after getting directions from the people in reception, driving through the half empty streets to a tarmaced parking lot. Getting out of the car, I was horrified to see that the ground was crawling with crickets hopping all over the place. Yuk. I had to look carefully where I was going, afraid I would step on one.

The meal consisted of either English or Chinese food, all you could eat for $11, and was set out in a square, buffet style layout. I was constantly distracted by the crickets not only hanging from the ceiling, but flying everywhere, making me duck when any came too close, while what appeared to be hundreds of them were scurrying along the edges of the walls. One or two even landed on our table, and although the other diners seemed to take it as a matter of course, I was only too happy to leave.

We got lost on our way back to the hotel and Andy seemed very nervous in some of the darker streets in an estate, saying it was a very dangerous area, but eventually we found the hotel. He went off to bed after I said that I'd ring him in the morning.

Shortly after getting into bed, I was disturbed by the sound of a fire alarm ringing from outside. Going out onto the balcony, I meet several other nervous guests and, looking down to the ground floor, I spotted a lady walking hurriedly towards the entrance in her nightgown, pulling a wheeled suitcase behind her. I asked what was wrong, but no one seemed to know what was going on, so as there was no smell of smoke, I went back inside my room.

Suddenly, lights started flashing as well as the alarm sounding. Worried, I went down in the elevator to the desk, where I was told that there was nothing to worry about. The two men there didn't seem at all concerned. I returned to our floor, then smelt smoke, and saw above in the rafters, a blue haze. I quickly rang through to Andy's room to wake him, and while waiting for him to come to the door, a man told me that he'd been told the popcorn machine had burnt the popcorn, and there was nothing to worry about. I told Andy what had happened when he finally came to his door, by which time everyone else had drifted away.

Friday 8th September.

I phoned Andy's room at 7.30am and he sounded awful, having gone down with a cold and was all bunged up, so after breakfast, I drove while he slept on and off in the passenger seat.

At lunchtime I pulled off onto the dirt parking lot beside a roadside diner. Inside, it was very new and clean, the food cabinets made of glass and shiny stainless steel. I had an enjoyable lunch of chicken, cornbread, broccoli and corn. Including the soup, which was all Andy had wanted, it came to $13 plus tips. I wasn't sure whether to clear the table but I saw someone else get up and leave the plates, so we left ours.

I carried on driving across flat, dusty looking plains, passing between white rocky outcrops where the road had been chiselled through. We crossed the Colorado River again, and the Little River, finally arriving at Waco in McLennon County after two hundred and forty four miles. It was here that the Waco Indians had first settled on the banks of the Brazos River in the late 1700s.

I finally spotted the sign I was looking for, the Texas Ranger Hall of Fame, and excitedly drove round to the parking lot, scattering some shiny blue/black birds strutting about on the road and under the trees. They were scruffy looking and had a very comical stilted gait.

Andy wandered about with the camcorder while I headed straight for the two rangers on horseback, a lady and a man, who were resting in the shade of the trees alongside the building. They were very friendly, and interested when I told them that I did western riding in England.

"I had no idea that the English did it," said the lady. I asked if they still policed the area.

"Yes, we still do, we ride mainly round the parks and open areas, and we still uphold the traditions of the Rangers."

From there I went into the stone building for the Hall of Fame, browsing round the glass display cabinets, thrilled to note the names of rangers I had only ever read about in cowboy books. In the glass cabinets they even had the original saddles, bridles, guns and other gear that the real Rangers had used.

In 1823, Stephen F Austin had signed up a few men to protect the settlers mainly from the Indians and they ranged, or policed, vast areas. Then, in 1835 the first Texas Rangers were set up to patrol the Republic of Texas' borders from Indians, outlaws and Mexican bandits. They were eventually disbanded because of highhanded activities, 'not related to their official work' and corruption by politicians, but were reformed in 1860 under Captain Leander McNally after Mexicans from the south began raiding into Texas. From there the Texas Rangers seesawed between disbanding and being re-instated until 1874 when they were finally restored to being an official police force by honest politicians.

I drove on towards Dallas on the I-35E, unfortunately without the chance of seeing the suspension bridge that had been built in 1870 and been the only span across the river for the cowboys and their herds of cattle, with Andy reading the map. We passed Waxahachie, another cowboy town.

After a hundred and eighty four miles, I began driving down from the hills into a big valley where, in the middle of the spread out city, rose the famous glass buildings as seen on the TV series, Dallas. Fantastic! The long, straight Interstate headed straight toward them.

As I drove closer I found myself on a huge six-lane freeway! That made me nervous, but again the drivers were quite courteous, holding back when I indicated I wanted to exit to the right. There were miles and miles of road works going on, it looked like they were making a huge spaghetti junction.

I followed Andy's directions out into the countryside, turned down a road, and suddenly saw a metal archway with the magical name Southfork Ranch where, set back in flat fields stood the famous ranch house, gleaming white in the sun. It was amazing driving down the tree lined drive, but instead of the house before us as I'd expected, there was a huge white building that turned out to be a very large souvenir shop. We parked up and went in.

Andy bought tickets for the tour while I got myself a T-shirt, neckerchief, and a car registration plate with Southfork Ranch on it. For Mrs Kay, who I'd worked for as a domestic for nineteen years until she moved to London to be with her family after the death of her husband, I bought a blue, gold trimmed mug with the name of Southfork on it. We had been great Dallas and Dynasty fans, and every coffee time, mid morning, we'd happily discuss the previous evening's episodes. We had become great friends, she had supported me on Les' and Ann-Marie's deaths, and I still went to see her several times a year with her other ex-staff.

We took our places in an open carriage, one of three pulled by a big tractor

101

that took us round to the main house and I got Andy to take a photo of me sitting at the patio table where the Ewing family had always had breakfast. The swimming pool turned out to be amazingly small in real life.

We went inside where a lady told us the history of the ranch. Apparently, after the start of the series, the original family had been very upset to come home and find their once quiet home a Mecca for Dallas fans, who were walking round the grounds and even swimming in their pool. They had moved out, going to live somewhere quieter. Eventually they sold out to a rich Texan who'd remodelled the ranch in the style that he thought the Ewings would now have had it. I was deeply disappointed, as I wanted it to look just like it had on the TV, although it was still pretty exciting to walk round. She made us all laugh telling us that as the swimming pool was so small, Bobby Ewing, who swam the most, had actually been tied to a long elastic band where, filmed from different angles, he looked like he was in an Olympic size pool but never got anywhere. Also, that the body found floating in the pool after being pushed from the balcony couldn't have happened, as the pool was on a different side of the house to the balcony. The stairs also weren't on the same side as the TV series, and not even round, but square, following the walls.

After the talk, we were allowed to wander round and take photographs. I talked to her for a while after to discover that she had only held the job for three weeks and was still fascinated by meeting English visitors, wanting to know where we'd been and where we were going.

Everything in the house was so plush and absolutely amazing with the huge dining table set out with silver tableware and crystal glasses, and each bedroom named after a character from the series.

We strolled down to look at the corrals where rodeos are held during the year, and passed a huge building used for meetings and conferences. Inside a clothes shop near the back of the house stood the big Lincoln car that had actually been used in the series by Jock Ewing, played by Jim Davis.

On the way out, Andy and I took photos of each other standing under the Southfork sign.

Not long after we got caught up in very bad traffic jams making me unsure as to finding the time looking for the Fort Worth stockyards for the rodeo and entertainment before getting a hotel, so we continued on to the Best Western hotel, the Executive on the I-75. We booked in, went for something to eat in the restaurant nearby, and retired to our rooms, where I slept better as the air conditioner was quieter.

Chapter 10

Chicago.

Saturday 9th September.

Going went down for breakfast, I found it was already cloudy, hot and muggy outside, and Texas had been without rain now for over sixty-six days.

We drove out early to the stockyards, then along cobbled streets of the old town before turning under the stockyards sign hung between beautiful old western style wooden buildings, parking in the large car lot opposite the Tourist Information shop.

The stockyards had once been one of the stopping off points on the Shawnee Trail for cattle starting out from Brownsville on the Gulf of Mexico and going through to Kansas City and St. Louis. These wooden yards covered a huge area and to get to them we had to go through a big covered square housing lots of shops. Unfortunately, probably due to being open late at night, they wouldn't be open till 10 or 11am. Through here ran a set of train tracks for the Tarantula Railroad's restored 1896 steam engine that pulled six original passenger cars. Out the other side I was excited to find a corral with about fifteen real long-horned cattle, weighing about a ton and with horns that reached a spread of six to seven feet.

A mounted policeman, Jerry, came along on a pretty bay horse, and when I asked if there were any western clothing stores nearby as I wanted to buy some chaps, he suggested that I might find a shop selling them back on Main Street. He asked if we'd seen the rodeo last night, and was genuinely disappointed for us when I told him that we had gone straight to our hotel due to the bad traffic jams. I mentioned that we had to leave at 10am to make the airport in time for our flight, and he said that we should come back some day and really spend time wandering round, "there's a whole lot to see in Fort Worth."

We didn't even have time to watch the cattle being driven, old style, from their pens to the feeding grounds on the West Fork of the Trinity River, going right through town, but I did try the shops he'd mentioned. Reid's was very expensive and only had one pair of black batwing chaps, but I preferred the slim shotgun style with fringes. Another shop had nothing in stock, and the third wouldn't be open till 11am. Reluctantly we had to leave, and it was a good job that we did, as the traffic jams, not helped any by a car accident, were very bad, and we only just arrived at the airport in time.

We followed the signs to the Enterprise rental lot, parked in the line for returning cars, and got out our cases. Unfortunately, the man booking the cars back in had to charge us extra as we had forgotten to fill the gas tank up before returning it.

My baggage was getting more difficult to manoeuvre as it got heavier, mostly due to my new hats, boots, and presents as well as the little soaps and conditioners I accumulated as souvenirs from the different hotels.

We boarded the shuttle to the airport but were left at the wrong gate and had to take a driver-less train to the next terminal. It still felt a little un-nerving bumping along in a small carriage with no one in front driving.

We checked in at the desk and went through security, where I was suddenly taken, with my bag, off to one side. Despite being frightened out of my wits, I was puzzled when the two girls, wearing gloves, got what appeared to be a damp tissue in some tongs and wiped it all over the edges of the pockets and the handles of my bag. They then handed it back and waved me on with no word of explanation.

"What on earth were they doing?" I asked Andy.

"They were checking for traces of drugs anywhere your hands would have been!"

As we boarded the plane, we were given paper bags with a small snack meal inside, as it would only be a short flight to Chicago. It turned out to be a short, but very bumpy ride, scaring me.

As we prepared for landing, Andy suddenly asked, "where are your hats?"

Puzzled, I tried for ages to remember where I'd last seen them, until I remembered having put them through the security machine at Dallas airport. I had only picked up my handbag not having seen the plastic bag they were in come out the other end and, what with being dusted for drugs, I had completely forgotten them. He said we could phone the airport when we reached our hotel and get them sent on.

We landed at Midway going straight round to the carousel, but Andy's luggage never appeared. He went off to the gate to get it checked out, leaving me to keep watching, acutely embarrassed due to losing my hats and then him losing his luggage. Had it had been stolen? Surely not right from under our very noses. Unfortunately, it could happen! He came back to say that the staff would check with Dallas and that he should phone them from our hotel.

The hotel wasn't easy to find. I had had no idea there were two airports at Chicago and we'd landed at Midway while I'd booked the hotel at O'Hare, so we had to take a shuttle for $17 each.

Once there, Andy phoned O'Day's to ask for the free shuttle to come and get us. There was a lot of building work going on across the road so, because of the gusts of wind stirring up swirling clouds of dust I sat inside the doorway while Andy waited outside.

Once we reached the hotel, which was only just outside the airport, Andy phoned through to Midway airport. Luckily, they'd found his luggage was still at Dallas, but said it would be sent on to him at the hotel via the next Chicago flight, probably late that evening. He then phoned Dallas airport to ask about my hats. They'd also been found and he arranged for them to be sent Fed-Ex to the ranch, our next long stop.

We had a nice meal at the hotel restaurant where I had battered chicken strips with BBQ sauce and a salad with 1000 Island dressing, while Andy had huge beef strips and potato waffles-all for just $14.

I slept OK, the air conditioning not being too noisy.

Sunday 10th September.

Another free breakfast, cooked this time. Eggs, bacon, toast, jelly (jam) and coffee, before the shuttle took us back to the airport. We boarded a light clean railway (Metro) to Chicago for the Amtrak station-19 stops to Clinton station for $1.50 each. For several miles it ran between the middle of the freeway before eventually going underground. At Clinton we had to ask directions to the Union station.

We dragged our cases to the building that sported a 'built in 1926 sign' above the doorway from where the train we would be catching, the California

Zephyr, would be doing a round trip of two thousand, four hundred and twenty two miles, right through to San Francisco. I'd love to have gone all the way. At the departure lounge we managed to leave our luggage in the Left Luggage office so that we could go out and see something of Chicago.

The streets were cleaner and brighter here than New York with the buildings almost as tall, so again I had to crane my neck to see the tops, making me feel slightly claustrophobic and overpowered. Walking over the river on a metal road bridge felt strange as it vibrated with the traffic passing over.

Andy headed for the Sears building, once the tallest in the world but apparently now beaten by a new building in Asia, but at the entrance we were told that the cloud cover was so low that day, with visibility nil, that we decided to leave it and carry on. We came across Grey Line tours just like in New York and spent nearly half an hour waiting for a bus, chatting to the coloured ticket lady about England and our impressions of America. She said that she would love to go and visit Britain, and I told her to, "go for it one day." While waiting, we were caught in a shower of warm rain, and hid in a nearby shop doorway.

When the bus finally arrived, the young coloured tour bus driver/guide was very comical and enlightening with his remarks about the history of Chicago and I wished that I could have recorded the things he said during the trip. He also pulled in to the side of the bay so that people could take photos of the Chicago skyline across the lake.

Further on, we passed several very large marinas with their beautiful expensive yachts, before stopping at the pier. There were lots of shops including a Macdonald's where we sat and had a meal watching a juggler/comedian entertaining the kids. He was pretty good and made me laugh.

We waited ages for the next tour bus, but this time, the driver hardly spoke at all, and when he did, what with his difficult accent, he made things sound boring.

Walking back past the Sears building, the top still covered by the thick mist, we returned to the train station. Retrieving our luggage we went to the departure lounge, already crammed full of waiting passengers. As the different train announcements were made, huge queues formed in the doorways, people slowly shuffling through to the various platforms.

Luckily we found a couple of seats for we heard over the tannoy that there would be a thirty-minute delay in the train's arrival, but this stretched on to an hour, when we were finally allowed to board at 4.30pm. I struggled down the long platform towing my case, following Andy to our carriage to mount the plastic step, while the sleeping car attendant helped me pull my case inside. We then had to drag the cases up the steep spiralling stairs to the next floor where another attendant showed us to our compartments.

Mine was quite small but comfortable, with a seat either side of the little pull down table located under the big window. This would be put down to the height of the seats at night to make a bed, made up by the coloured attendant, Larry, who turned out to be very cheerful and helpful. Meals were included in the ticket price, and we could have used the personalised service for coffee or breakfast to be served in our rooms, but preferred going along to the dining car. Wow, this is living.

I found a leaflet about the train and its journey to Grand Junction and San Francisco on the table with interesting facts about some of the stations it would be stopping at, as well as places of interest.

The train pulled out, and for some time we crossed fields and woods just like Faversham or Sittingbourne in England except that the pretty houses looked like they were boarded with planks of wood. Even the built up areas and work yards looked the same. It was dark by 7.40pm, but as I kept glancing up from reading my book, I was able to see the wide Mississippi River with the silver moonlight shining on it, as the train clattered across the long, long metal bridge.

Earlier, Andy had gone along to the dining car to get a number for our meal, and at 8.30pm we were called for the final sitting. The dinner was great, and we shared a table with two men, friends, one from Lincoln, Nebraska, who would be leaving the train at 2am, and one from Denver. They were very friendly and chatty, and again, interested in where we came from. I spent most of the time comparing with them the differences between England and America, and they were genuinely pleased at how well I thought of the people and countryside.

The bed was made up when I got back to my cabin, and I discovered an interesting pastime in trying to brush my teeth in a rocking carriage, my knees jammed against the cupboard. I climbed into bed, put my watch back an hour for Mountain time as it would change during the night, and slept well, rocked to sleep by the motion of the carriage and the clicking of the wheels on the track.

Overnight, the train crossed the Missouri River at Omaha, once the westbound crossing for settlers, and the birthplace of Marlon Brando, Fred Astaire and Malcolm X.

Monday 11th September.

I had set my alarm for 6am as I didn't want to miss looking out of the window first thing, but I needn't have worried for I was awake at the first signs of daylight coming through the curtains. I opened these once I'd washed, dressed and put my makeup on, although how I thought anyone would be able to see in, I don't know.

Colorado. It was cloudy with a little sun. In places the land was either flat with stands of timber and ponds with ducks, or rolling hills with beautiful rocky outcrops. The grass was a dusty beige colour with clumps of darker spiky types. There were lots of cattle in the fields, more than I had seen in Texas, and we passed by a stockyard with cattle and cowboys. Occasionally ridges of stone cut off the sight of the distant low hills. The train crossed deep dried out washes, evidence of flooding in the wet weather, and followed alongside dirt roads.

We headed for the dining car for breakfast once Andy was up and about, where I ordered biscuits and gravy (wish we could get this back home.) I handed Andy a birthday card that wished him a happy birthday in a voice that sounded just like Prince Charles and hoped that my sister Sue liked hers— open it up and it emitted a rude 'raspberry' noise. We crossed more plains with large stands of timber, and mountains began to rear up in the distance. The flat land turned to farmland as we approached Denver where the train trundled across a bridge over a creek, the clear water splashing over rocky bedrock.

As we slowed for Denver, passing a very large area of empty wooden fenced stockyards, before the train slowly curved round almost back on itself, to ease into the station. We had a longish stop here for some baggage cars to be unhitched.

Slowly we eased out of the station, heading out into a long wide valley, leaving Denver behind to climb up into the foothills, snaking round in large S shaped loops. As we got higher, the pines and spruce began to get thicker. At one point, we had to wait a quarter of an hour for a goods train to come down, passing us. I counted two engines, approx. fifty trucks filled with coal, another engine, another fifty trucks and two more engines. I couldn't believe my eyes. It was enormous.

Above and to the left on the skyline, chalet style houses were perched on the hillsides supported at the front by log poles that looked very fragile. To the right I could see the wide valley with the tall buildings of Denver sprouting up like fingers looking similar to the Dallas skyline, while the rest of the town spread out over the green valley floor.

The train began moving more slowly as we climbed further into the mountains, passing so close to the rocky walls that I felt I could reach out and touch them. Canyons opened up, pine clad, with slides of rocky shale, and huge boulders looking as if they'd only rolled down recently making me wonder how often trains were delayed by rocks actually on the lines. Huge crags loomed overhead. The whole terrain looked wild, untamed, and so beautiful. I tried to imagine what it would have been like to try to find a way over them mounted only on a horse.

We started heading through several tunnels in the rock, some quite long. Then, as we came out into the open, across a rocky valley to our right, I spotted a dam. We began following the course of a wide creek with its white water rapids that ran back the way we had come.

Some time later I was puzzled when I noticed that the creek now seemed to be running the way we were heading! Looking at the paper map that had been supplied in my room, I realised that it was the beginning of the great Colorado River.

Wooden road bridges spanned the water, and chalet homes had been built nestling under the aspens, oaks and maples that were starting to show the pale yellow and gold of fall. Where the river went into the valleys, the waters grew wider and slower, and on one stretch, people were paddling kyaks on it. Another train passed us, two engines, one engine and then another two, with a hundred and seventeen trucks between the first and last.

The next tunnel was very long, perhaps one or two miles long. It seemed endless, and as we emerged, I spotted a ski lift, the silvery cables running up towards the heights. The train began to dip downward heading towards the town of Fraser. Set in a large, flat valley surrounded by pine slopes, the Fraser River cuts through the Arapaho National Forest and Fraser Canyon. The town was made up of wooden chalets, obviously newly built as the wood was still a creamy tan colour, and had a schoolhouse and playground. The station served the Winter Park Ski Resort, better known as 'The Icebox of America' due to its winter temperatures reaching down to minus 50f.

We continued down the valley through rich, green pastures before the cliffs closed in again, with sheer drops to the water and the river narrowing to form white water rapids over huge boulders. Dropping down one rapid I could see a rubber raft, the people frantically paddling to keep it on course. Across appeared a two-lane road built under the cliffs, the cars and trucks looking totally out of place in such beautiful surroundings. I watched out of the window as the train curved round the bends, the leading engine disappearing into the black holes of the tunnels.

We halted at Granby station, gateway to the Rocky Mountain National Park where, at nearby Windy Gap Dam, evidence had been found of stone-age people dating back to 3000BC, much earlier than even the Anasazi or the Native Americans.

Going along for our meal in the dining car, I ordered a salad followed by spaghetti bolognese, and then cheesecake and coffee. We were lucky to share a table with a couple that were great fun and very chatty, laughing with us as we told them stories about England. I never ceased to be amazed that the Americans' knowledge of Britain was about as bad as the British ideas about the USA.

The train halted again for Glenwood Springs where the famous gunslinger Doc Holliday is buried, and where the American president, Teddy Roosevelt, loved to visit.

Back in the observation car, I watched spellbound as the landscape began to change yet again as we passed between looming red rocks and cliffs, catching sight of a bird that had the same black and white markings as our magpie. We came across another small dam, and a canal with a sluice gate at the other end. The river began to spread out onto the floor of another valley breaking into several wide channels with islands between, the water turning a dirty brown colour (Colorado is Spanish for red, for which it's named.) The hills to my left were sandy coloured, with tall red bluffs on the right.

The call for Grand Junction came over the tannoy, and reluctantly I went back to our car to find that Larry had put our luggage by the door ready to leave. We thanked him, having given him a tip earlier, and as we left the train, he said he was quite sorry to see us go.

Grand Junction is at the fork of the Gunnison and Colorado Rivers, and also the gateway to not only Mesa Verde National Park and the Colorado National Monument, but Grand Mesa National Forest, places I would love to visit one day.

We walked into the station and Andy tried to use a phone to call a cab, but it didn't work, so we had to wait till the other was free. While we were waiting, he bought a map of Grand Junction for directions to Page.

We climbed into the cab, the driver putting our cases in the trunk. He was very chatty about Grand Junction, obviously very proud of living there, and telling us of all the celebrities who flew in to go skiing. He then became very rude about Texans, said no real cowboy wore boots, he must have known full well that I was wearing some, only sneakers, and told us his son was amazed anyone wore boots. Unusually for me, I kept quiet as I usually argue back, but I wasn't very impressed, especially as he'd already told us he was a teacher during the day. He was much too biased for me, and what was saying was total rubbish. The original cowboys couldn't wear sneakers as they hadn't been invented and to my mind they were extremely dangerous as a foot could easily slip through the stirrup. Boots were made for a purpose, the high heels preventing feet from slipping through the wide stirrups, and if the cowboy was on foot and had to rope a calf or a horse, he needed big heels to dig into the ground for support.

He also drove very slowly so that the fare was quite dear when we finally got to the airport, and at the rental desk, they told us he was the dearest cab about. Just our bad luck.

We filled in the forms for the car we'd ordered and Andy went out to the car lot to get it, but when he pulled round to pick me up, the oil light was on. Having a lot of distance to travel, we considered it was too dangerous to have a problem, so I went back to the desk and got it exchanged for a black saloon, a powerful Pontiac Grand Prix. Very smart, and very comfortable, although there was only just enough room in the trunk for two cases, everything else being piled onto the back seat.

It was getting dark by this time, and driving out of the airport we had trouble finding the road we wanted, but by keeping the setting sun on my right, I knew we were heading southward. Once it went down, a full moon rose ahead of us. In the dark I was having trouble seeing the road as the headlights appeared to be set too high, and Andy was too, having to slow whenever we went over bumps in the road.

Flat land slowly gave way to the black shapes of cliffs and bluffs, and when we saw the glittering water of the creek beside us, stopped to get out and look. It was very warm and still, and so peaceful with just the gentle noise of the rippling water and the incessant cicadas. The tall cliff walls across the creek were bathed in a gentle silver moonlight, criss-crossed with shadows from the rocky formations.

We drove on and came to a stretch of unmade road with roadwork signs, coming up behind another car that was sending up clouds of white dust, making it very hard to see. After quite a few miles we finally reached the end, joining a tarmac road again. Andy stopped at a gas station so he could clean the windscreen, and I saw that our once shiny black car was now almost white! We bought some biscuits and chips (crisps) at a nearby store, and drove on to Mexican Hat, a small cluster of buildings, looking out for a sign for a motel.

At nearly 11pm, Andy spotted one and parked up, going across to see if they were still open and had any rooms available. He took such a long time that as I could see him talking to some people I went over. Apparently the couple were French, on honeymoon, and had a room booked, but couldn't get through on the phone to the emergency motel number. Finally Andy managed it, and the lady owner came out from a building on the left. Yes, she had a room for Andy and one for me, indicating we should park round the back. We parked up beside several very large motorcycles in front of the raised veranda.

I pulled my case up onto the short steps and opened the door to my room, just as Andy called over asking me to call him early for he wanted to get to Monument Valley for the sunrise. When I went in, the room looked so basic that it was like being in the middle of a renovation, and when I couldn't get the shower to work, I just washed and went to bed.

Tuesday 12th September.

I woke at 6.30am and phoned through to Andy's room, meeting him outside in the dark by the car. We drove over the San Juan River heading for Monument Valley just as the sky began to lighten, passing several yellow school buses headed in the opposite direction. Finally, we rounded a corner of rock to be faced by an enormous valley stretching to the far horizon with huge red sandstone cliffs and fingers of stone rising out of a red sandy floor. Both beautiful and awesome, it took my breath away.

Pulling in off the road, Andy set up the video on the car bonnet pointing towards where the sun looked like it might come up over a ridge of thin fingers of red rock. Patiently we waited then, all of a sudden, brilliant shafts of light sparkled through one of the clefts in the rocks as if shining through a diamond. It was one of the most beautiful and radiant sights I have ever seen. The video picture was spectacular we found after, having been placed in just exactly the right spot.

We headed on along the valley road passing huge crags and buttes with pillars of red stone that thrust up from the red floor. The road crossed washes and arroyos that cut through smooth slopes of beige coloured hills covered in scrubby bushes. Navaho hogans were dotted in the distance. Fabulous.

At the side of the road we came across a billboard for Goulding's Trading Post, looking somewhat sacrilegious in such a lovely landscape. We turned off, to park under the shadow of a huge, smooth faced rock marked with streaks of dark lines as if some giant hand had dribbled different colours of brown paint down it.

The buildings were the original trading post built in the early 1905-1910 by the Goulding's, Harry and his wife 'Mike.' They'd settled there, and had become renowned for their integrity, honesty and genuine concern for the Indians, establishing a hospital along with a fresh water source. The brick built cellar out back had been used several times by film makers, one of whom being John Ford, including 'She Wore a yellow Ribbon' starring John Wayne. Inside the main building, the dark back room was given over to photos and memorabilia of both John Wayne and other films that had been made in the valley.

Back outside, we descended some steep concrete steps to a store and I browsed around finding several Louis L'Amour western books that I hadn't got in my collection. I also bought a mounted sand painting made by the local Navaho, asking the girl behind the counter for an interpretation. Unfortunately, her English was limited so I only managed to understand part of it.

Driving on, we approached road works, and had to wait in a queue of cars for a truck with a flashing arrow sign that pointed straight up, to lead us past. We had to follow it very slowly for a couple of miles, passing another truck leading more cars in the opposite direction. Once away from there, the road passed through land with small rounded red and cream rocks, and boulders dotted with grey sage bushes, some of the mounds being peculiarly strange looking, like piles of whipped icecream. Then we found ourselves out on a red, sandy flat plain with slopes covered in trees on the horizon.

As the car turned a corner, there in the distance under cream coloured cliffs, tall buttes and pillars of rock, lay a long strip of bright blue water shimmering in the heat. Lake Powell. It was spectacular. I had very mixed feelings, being impressed by the immensity of what man could build, but saddened that the beauty of the canyon could be destroyed for mans' need for more and more water. Dams were now needed to take it from here to Las Vegas and other cities. Even then a lot of it is wasted with fountains and ponds evaporating in the wind and heat, and miles and miles of grass wanted for golf ranges.

We carried on, coming to the outskirts of the town, pulling into a gas station to fill up. The signs stated $1.69 a gallon. Andy and I pretended to be horrified.

"It's disgusting, that's so expensive," and "what a rip off," ending up in giggles.

Laughing, we drove on into Page and located the Econolodge on the main street. It was too early to book in so we drove down towards the lake, stopping off at a Macdonald's for a meal. While eating and looking through the windows, I noticed that sparrows seemed to be flying up from the tarmac and onto the cars' grills, and studying them, I realised that they were picking off the dead butterflies and moths stuck there. Just before we finished, a whole coach load of tourists turned up, panicking the manager and staff.

We went on, driving across an iron bridge over the huge Glen Canyon dam that, according to a leaflet I had, held back 27 million acres/feet of water that formed Lake Powell.

Following signs for the marina, we had to stop to pay an entrance fee at one of the tollbooths where they gave us a few leaflets about the area as well as a big map. We drove down to the big car lot and circled around until finding a parking space, but there were no trees and we had to leave the car in full sunlight. Climbing out, again I was amazed at how hot it was, the air conditioning kept me so artificially coo inside.

Heading to the store and straight to the desk, we picked up our reserved tickets for the boat tour, carrying on outside to sit on the patio and look out over the clear blue water with its expensive looking boats moored in the marinas. They were startlingly white against the blue water and sky. I browsed through the leaflets.

Lake Powell had been named after Major John Wesley Powell who, in May 1869, had set out from Green River, Wyoming, with a crew of ten and two boats to follow the Colorado River, travelling over a thousand miles. On July 28, they had entered Glen Canyon, which he named. Three months later, with only one boat and five men, most of who had given up because of the rigours of the travel, they emerged from the Virgin River. Glen Canyon is now a National Recreation Area that covers the whole of the new lake and includes the San Juan and Escalante Rivers.

Other leaflets warned boats to go slowly past other boats, water skiers and swimmers to prevent bow waves, and that the taking of fossils and artefacts was prohibited. Also noted in the Clean Boating Guide was that solid human waste had to be contained in plastic canisters to be emptied at the waste disposal points indicated along the lake. Others showed the type of fish to be found in the waters, as well as native flora and fauna.

Finally we were called and went down the sandy beach to a long wooden gangway and out to the boat. Looking down into the clear water with its black fish, some very big, I got a shock when I discovered effluent floating there! How can people be so dirty in such a beautiful place? My shock slowly wore off to total disgust, aimed at some of the human race. And we were supposed to be civilised.

Two Navaho girls piloted the boat, and they seemed to spend the entire trip talking and giggling to each other. Leonora was also the guide, pointing out places of interest and telling us the history of the lake. Before we had gone very far, she advised us to drink a lot because the heat and the drying wind could cause dehydration, and I was pleased to find downstairs that they had the same lemonade I'd loved at the ranch the year before.

She told us that when the dam had been finally finished it had taken seventeen years for the water to fill the canyons, backing up for 185 miles. Pointing out the white line on the rocks just above the water level, she said that this was the height of the reservoir after the spring thaw had filled it, the white calcium line appearing as the water level fell. The depth in places fell to over six hundred feet. (How nice to have everything in feet and inches, and pints and gallons here, instead of the European measurements forced on us.)

The boat was fast and noisy, and it was very windy on top, although the speed was reduced to lessen the wake whenever we came near any of the numerous low-lying houseboats. We passed beautiful rock formations sticking out of the water and I tried to imagine how much of these lovely rocks were below the waterline. The girls pointed out special places like Sheep Canyon, with the outline of a sheep's head, and Dinosaur Rock.

After two hours, the boat slowed, turning down a narrow canyon with sheer walls on either side. Lots of the rocks sported black and brown streaks from natural irons and manganese, nicknamed Navaho tapestry. Turning another corner, there in front of us was Rainbow Bridge, a natural arch rock formation and a sacred Navaho place. It is also the largest natural bridge on earth, one of the seven natural wonders of the world. We were asked to keep to the trail marked and not attempt to go under the arch in respect of the Navaho. It was as awe inspiring as Zane Grey had described it in one of his books. I was very excited and couldn't wait to get off the boat.

We got out onto wooden pontoons and walked along to the water's edge. Through the clear water were the usual black fish, which Andy filmed, and the usual effluent. How could people demean such a sacred place, a place that I had always wanted to visit, it was like soiling a church.

The two hundred and ninety foot bridge was made of Navaho sandstone at the top and Kayenta sandstone at the base, and was called 'Nonnezoshi' by the Navaho people, which means 'rainbow turned to stone.' It was already in the shade so that I couldn't see the incredible colours I had read about. Two Navahos were chanting close to the arch holding their arms above their heads and making the whole scene very moving. A guide was giving a talk, explaining the Navaho story of the long rock that lay moulded to the left side of the arch.

Tradition told of a young Navaho child playing on the other side of the river who had been chased by a bad spirit disguised as a giant lizard. She had prayed to the Gods for help and they had sent a rainbow over the river. As she ran over the rainbow to safety, followed by the lizard, the Navaho Gods again came to her rescue, turning the rainbow into a stone arch and the bad spirit into a stone lizard forever forced to cling to the arch.

We returned to the track where I picked up a piece of red sandstone for a souvenir, which I shouldn't have done but desperately wanted to take home. Following almost alongside us by the track was a little ground squirrel that didn't seem at all bothered by the people walking past. I was sorry to have to leave such a peaceful place and could have sat there for hours.

The boat headed back towards the marinas as the sun slowly sank on the left, and the rocks turned to a smoky blue. As the sun went down and we slowly approached the marina, the full moon came up, turning the cliffs and buttes to a shiny silver and leaving a sparkling white line across the now blackened waters.

We headed back to the motel, settled into our rooms, then drove around till we found a big restaurant on the main street where I ordered chicken and salad and Andy had a steak. While we were waiting, there was a loud crash when a young waitress dropped a tray of plates and cutlery. We didn't see her for quite a while after, and Andy overheard a couple of staff saying that she'd got upset and gone home. But just before we left, she was back.
Wednesday 13th September.

We left Page at 8am, to head back across the bridge straddling the dam, and climbing a long incline.

Without any warning, we turned a corner of rock and it was like the end of the world. The road turned sharp left beside a deep drop that ended in a flat plain spreading out before us over a thousand feet below. A faint gash in the distance showed the course of the Little Colorado River and tiny tracks marked the course of the dirt roads, like spider webs in the dust. We were at the top of Echo Cliffs, and I recognised the name from a Zane Grey book. The road snaked down the cliffs, twisting and turning until it reached the base, the course of the road following the range of cliffs into the distance.

Slowly, the land changed to red rolling hills covered in purple sage. The cliffs began to peter out being replaced by black mounds of rocks, the Coconino Plateau. Here we were greeted with signs we'd seen the year before at the side of the road, 'Chief Yellow Horse sez friendly Indians ahead.'

We crossed the Little Colorado just before the junction with Cameron on Highways 89 & 64, where we'd joined it last year after leaving the Grand Canyon, passing more signs saying, 'Chief Yellow Horse sez friendly Indians behind, go back.' And I spotted a grey coyote just off the road to the left, eating something!

The scrub slowly changed to bushes of mesquite, greasewood and creosote, and in the distance, half hidden in a blue haze, showed the San Francisco Peaks. Slowly we began to climb, the hills becoming covered in pine with lots of pretty yellow flowers in the grass. We reached Flagstaff on the old Route 66, making our way through to find the K-mart store, where. I had a lovely breakfast of eggs, biscuits and gravy, and coffee, $3 plus the tips. Andy had a fry-up.

We spent some time looking round the shop before I took over driving, heading down the I-17. We passed signs with intriguing names like Oak Creek Canyon, Dry Beaver Road, Verde Valley, Big Bug Creek, Squaw Creek, Dry Wash, Dead Horse Gulch, and then on through pine clad cliffs and rocky outcrops at four thousand feet and lower. Here we finally drove out onto plains.

Finally we approached the outskirts of Phoenix where the traffic began to build up, the road widening into five lanes both sides. I drove straight through following the signs for Tucson, and joined a four-lane freeway. The cars and trucks began to get less and it was lovely to be able to put the car back into auto cruise. I just loved using it, it made driving so much more relaxing. Back home there was rarely a chance to use it as the traffic was so much greater, and with the roads here so wide and clear, it made the long distances actually quite pleasant. We headed out onto flat, sandy plains where I pointed out a thin column of rising dust to Andy, off to the right.

"Smoke?" he asked.

"No, it's too straight." It turned out to be a dust devil, a tall, thin column of spinning dust, like a mini tornado.

I told Andy we needed gas as the orange light had come on, but he said, "no, it's OK, we'll make Tucson." I wasn't sure and began to worry, especially being out here in the middle of a dry plain, miles from anywhere, and finally turned off at the next junction anyway, looking for a gas station. Luckily, we just made it as the needle on the gauge suddenly plummeted. From there we headed on for Tucson, looking for the airport to return the car.

We found the road into the terminal, getting through to the drop-off point after going around the area in a big circle looking for the actual entrance. Again we were charged extra for we hadn't topped up the tank with gas. We took our luggage into the airport, finding a telephone to call the ranch to ask for a pick-up. They were somewhat confused as no flights were due in, and Andy told them we'd driven.

It was very hot outside so I waited in the cool inside the entrance to the terminal while Andy stood outside waiting, calling me when the car turned up.

Tom, who was new to the ranch, was very nice driving us to the ranch via the back roads for the freeway was already solid with rush hour traffic. When I asked about the staff we'd known last year, it turned out that Carol and Paul, last year's managers, had left the ranch as well as Brad, Joe and Mark and I felt quite disappointed as I'd expected things to be the same. Tom told us that he had given up a good salary in construction work to come to the ranch, and he felt a whole lot better and more relaxed for it. Although his friends had been very surprised at him taking on a less well paid job, but he'd decided to put his happiness first. He also helped out in the kitchens and occasionally did some wrangling (looking after the horses.)

We booked in at the office, then took our baggage to casitas (cabins) nine and ten, unpacking before going up for dinner. Rusty, Terry and Kim were still working tables, although Kim was having a couple of days off. Already there was April, who had come from Florida. She'd been the only guest there for two days and instead of the chef cooking just for her, the new managers had taken her out to eat.

I was both surprised and pleased to find that Ed, who was very tall and walked stiffly, and I remembered had been a wrangler last year, was now the resident ranch manager along with his wife, Sharon. Eventually, as we chatted, reminding him of things from last year, he began to remember us. Also there was a coloured girl, Rosemary, who had a very loud laugh and spoke very quickly, keeping me in hysterics—when I could follow her accent. There was another nice lady, Betty, who was quiet spoken, and a man and his wife whom I recognised as having organised the abseiling last year. They were also naturalists who took people out walking to see the countryside.

The meal was great as usual. It turned out that they now had a resident chef who was working on new meals and intended to trade mark them to the ranch! Andy and I also quickly got started in on their lovely lemonade. When I mentioned the fruit of the prickly pear we'd tried last year, Ed told us that he didn't do that now as one lady had actually had a bad allergic reaction, frightening them all half to death!

Back outside after eating, we lazed in the hammocks until it got dark. It only took a short while to get the hang of getting into it again and made myself comfortable without falling out the other side. While we were swinging, two people came past, introducing themselves as Jan and Eddie, from England and who were on holiday with her parents.

Being situated in different casitas this year, I had a much longer walk to get from the ranch building back to my room. Arriving back at the cabin, I found the usual big red beetles either clinging to the wire mesh outer door or laying on their backs on the patio where they'd fallen. Moths flew around the outer light. I opened my door fast and shot in to try and avoid them.

I had a shower before climbing into bed to write my notes. No TV's here again. I slept well despite the noisy air con working in the cupboard.

Chapter 11

Back in the saddle.

Thursday 14th September.

I was up at 6am and already it was very, very warm outside. The huge saguaro outside my door was tall and stately and there was quite a few prickly pear cactus with their round red fruit. Several diamond doves were fluttering around the ground with a few blackish birds that looked much like our starlings, and sparrows were cheeping just like in England. The Oleana bush was covered in dainty pink flowers, and the Red Bird of Paradise shrub with its sprays of red flowers was beautiful, attracting large butterflies, and the tiny thumb-length humming birds.

I walked up to the dining room to get a coffee, meeting Rosemary and Betty, then went back to wake Andy just before breakfast by banging on his door.

In the dining room, I helped myself to scrambled egg, sausages, hamburger, crispy bacon, and slices of different melons. A couple of the others had ordered waffles and I loved the look of surprise on their faces when they turned up as they were huge and covered the plates.

We were introduced to Joaquin (pronounced Ho-keen) from Argentina, who didn't speak very much English. Ed came in to join us for breakfast and asked, as he did every morning and afternoon, "OK, who's riding?"

"Is Wrangler still here?" I asked, hopefully.

"Yes, he is."

"Can I have him?"

"Sure, OK."

During the meal, Ed had us laughing as he was attempting to speak our very posh Queen's English, well, at least it was better than my attempts at an American accent.

Outside by the door, clouds of butterflies, some very large, were flying round a big Tamarisk tree.

We walked over to the corrals and were allotted a horse each. It was lovely to have Wrangler again, although this year, like at home, I had trouble mounting, being very stiff. Oh dear, I must be getting old. Tom had joined us as he was wrangling today, taking drag (the rear,) while Jeff took point (the front,) on the walk ride. Jim took the lope (canter) ride out with a girl wrangler on drag. It was lovely to be treated like a lady again, and have the wranglers being so naturally polite with, "yes, ma'am."

More clouds of butterflies were settling on wet patches of mud in the runoffs from the earlier rains, and Jeff told me that they'd had a lot of it in the past two months, which was why the flowers were still out. Arizona was having an unusual heat wave this year, the temperature having gone up to a hundred and seven degrees Fahrenheit, which was twelve degrees more than average.

While out on the ride, I could hear coyotes yipping in the distance. I also spotted similar bushes from which I had taken a branch outside Odessa in Texas last year. Called a creosote bush, the leaves when rubbed between the fingers, smelt like its name. I remembered not to stare straight at anything, but to sweep my eyes across the landscape to make it easier to catch sight of anything that moved, like little geckoes, and quail, and cottontail rabbits.

Once back, with the horses unsaddled and turned into the corral, we went back to our cabins to change into swimming gear, and headed straight for the cooling water of the pool. I was a bit worried by large wasp/hornet things landing on the water to drink, back home I am scared of wasps, and kept splashing them with water to make them fly off. Then I lazed on the sun lounger in the shade, being joined by Jan and Eddie. Eddie was highly amused when, every so often, Andy would suddenly get up, run to the diving board fast for the concrete was hot, dive into the pool, then come out and sunbathe again. Despite being in the shade, my face was becoming red and felt really dry, especially my chin, probably from the wind and sun on the boat trip, although the chlorine in the pools probably didn't help.

We were called for lunch by the gong, and Ed came to ask who was riding out that afternoon, and which horse we'd had.

Andy told him that, "it was brown." Everyone fell about laughing, especially when he added, when pressed for more details, "it had four legs."

We went back outside and swam and lazed again, while Jan and her mother went for a riding lesson. It became even hotter, so I went and cancelled my ride, feeling sorry for the horses anyway, even if they were used to it.

A man came over to the cold drinks machine behind us and I thought I recognised him, pointing him out to Andy. He recognised him from last year, it was Mark, and called out. Eventually, Mark remembered me, asking where my daughter was this year. I explained that Sarah was a friend and that we rode together back home. Talking to Andy, he made a joke about having only seen a short bit of England while travelling between Gatwick and Heathrow airports en-route to South Africa one year, and that he'd have liked to have seen more.

At dinner, we met Sharon, Ed's wife, who was very nice, and reminded me of Carol, the other manager. By coincidence, their surname turned out to be Wallace, the same as a distant cousin of mine who lives near Edinburgh in Scotland.

Back at the casita, I got my small scissors and nail file out that I always carried in my make-up bag as, for the first time ever, I had to trim my finger nails down. The strengthener I'd bought back home from Avon Cosmetics was working rather too well! Very novel. Perhaps it helped not being able to give Cloud the many scratches he always asked for.

That evening, the wranglers, Jeff and Tom organised a moonlight ride. Unlike last year, which had been done in full moonlight, we went out when it was quite dark, heading up towards the hills behind the ranch. I trusted that Wrangler could see the way better than I could but Val, Jan's mum, having not ridden a great deal, was very, very nervous, finally becoming hysterical. The ride was also splitting, which I didn't like. Jeff finally shouted at us to turn back, as he'd heard rattlers on the trail ahead. Turning was very difficult on these narrow trails at the best of times, and I had to help Jan's mother as, being absolutely petrified, she couldn't reverse her horse. We finally got her back to the ranch, leaving her and Jan there, and went out onto a flatter, safer ride on the plains and heading back to the ranch was cheering with the golden light shining from the tack room door and the windows of the stables.

Friday 15th September.

I was up again at 6am. When I'd showered and dressed, I went up to the dining room for coffee, meeting up with Betty who was going to go to the corrals to try her hand at roping. I followed her out to the horse corral, where in a small set aside area they'd set up a couple of full side plastic horses to sit astride, and some horns attached to a bale of straw in front, although you could rope from the ground if you wanted. I showed her how to do it having had lessons back home from a friend's daughter's husband who happened to be a Texan. It was so much easier on foot than from the back of a moving horse, although I always tried it on Cloud at the rodeos.

I went back and woke Andy, heading up for breakfast before him. When he finally turned up, Ed asked him if he was riding. Not being that interested, he said no, which Ed found highly amusing and kept joshing him about staying behind to splash about in the pool.

We rode at 9.30, and when asked, some of us voted to do cattle penning, with Betty and Rosemary grabbing me as I'd said that I did it in England. Joining us was Wendell who hailed from Georgia and was 'drop dead' gorgeous. It turned out that he had a great sense of humour and had us laughing all the time.

We all rode into the pen and down to the bottom of the corral, going through the gate to haze (move) the calves out of their enclosure. Rose, Betty and I had first go, cutting (splitting) three calves away from the herd and driving them very gently up the side of the rails so they didn't spook and shy away from us. Near the top corner, I told Rose and Betty to go to the left of the pen to turn them in, while I continued driving the three ahead of me. To my amazement, the cattle almost penned themselves, turning in quite quickly. We'd scored a quick time, and we cheered like mad.

The others all had trouble when it came to their turn, but finally three of them got their calves in quicker than us. By now the calves were starting to get fed up, galloping off instead of staying together so that it was becoming harder each time, and also the wind was beginning to pick up, blowing dust into our eyes.

Rosemary got upset when Betty and I kept calling to her to tell her where we wanted her to be, and eventually she didn't seem to be trying, finally giving up altogether. The gusts of wind were getting very bad by now and Tucson in the far distance became hidden by clouds of swirling dust. It was very hot again, and if we weren't sweating, the horses were. Wrangler got hot because he hated cattle work and I had to keep kicking him as he refused to move very fast after the calves.

Once back at the pool, we met up with Jan and Val. Val told us she'd only gone on the ride last night as the wranglers had promised the ride would be on the flat. I said that in my opinion it hadn't been a novice ride and must have been a genuine mistake. I kept telling her not to worry about it when she kept trying to apologise for spoiling the ride. Finally, to change the subject for her sake, I pointed out a pretty lizard running across the poolside, out under the gate, and into the garden area.

Later on, I walked round to the old wooden building, the Trading Post, which was now closed as all the clothing and souvenirs were being sold in the reception area. I peered in the windows and saw lots of filled plastic bags. Just outside it stood wooden posts with white tiles stuck to all four sides depicting pictures of birds and animals that could be found around the ranch and surrounding areas. I discovered that the reptile I'd seen earlier had been a whip-tailed lizard.

I wandered back to the ranch house and into the library, searching for and finding, the Zane Grey biography book that I hadn't managed to finish the year before, taking it back to my casita to read for a while.

After lunch I cancelled my afternoon ride, as again it was too hot for me. Ed came over to Val by the pool and spoke very sympathetically to her, offering to take her on a quiet ride with just him out on the flat, but she kept refusing. After he'd gone, Jim came across and spoke to her for a long time, explaining that Jeff shouldn't have gone the way he did, shouldn't have turned on the trail, and was very, very sorry. He kept gently trying to persuade her to ride again as it would be good for her confidence. Finally he managed to get her to agree.

After he'd gone, I wondered if perhaps several people had complained about that ride and went on to tell her that we'd all go with her, it would only be at a walk. I then explained how frightened I'd been of riding for years, and that as a teenager I had been so nervous that I actually used to be sick just thinking about getting on. Even with Charlie, my first pony, he had been the most groomed horse in the world until I got the confidence to actually get on his back. And this was only eleven years ago.

After they'd left, I decided to head back to read in the cool until dinner, taking Andy's camcorder back with me luckily because on the way, I spotted and filmed a Regal Horned Lizard eating ants alongside the large shove-ha'penny boards by the hammocks. He didn't seem at all bothered by my presence, occasionally turning his head and regarding me with a beady eye before returning to shoot out a long tongue to grab the insects again.

After reading for a while lying on a hammock, I headed back to sit on the patio, on the way spotting several small desert quail running in and around the bushes, each with a tiny bobble of feathers on their head. When I asked, I was told that they were Gambel's quail, better known as the Arizona 'top-knot' or desert quail.

At dinner Wendell came and sat with Andy and I, Eddie, Jan, and her parents. Eddie had us in fits of laughter with his van driving stories, he's the typical white van man of Britain-they are well known for being dreadful. My sides were aching and I had tears in my eyes, too. Wendell was almost crying with laughter, and got worse as I started to describe how the English used roundabouts.

He mentioned that one had been built in Florida recently, and that there had been several crashes, as no one really understood it. I told him not to worry for neither did the English, judging by our driving standards. I said how they're used for overtaking, and that cars indicating left go either left, straight on, or right, or when indicating right, often went straight on, or even left. Drivers even used the entire width of the two lanes to go across instead of keeping to either left or right and allowing other cars to use it at the same time. Because of the decreasing room for cars in Britain, this made people much angrier and less patient, whereas the Americans were less stressed as they had more space.

The talk became more serious when I told Wendell and Brad how dangerous it was in Britain now. That guns, and knives were being used more and more, especially if people were drunk, because then they used anything they could get. That if you were attacked and fought back, and your assailant was injured, they could sue you for damages or that you could only defend yourself or your home 'within reason,' although no one appeared to know exactly what 'within reason' was. They were stunned, as over here the police were on the side of the victim. I told them that it was totally the opposite in Britain, and that it was getting a lot worse as the law never really dealt tough enough penalties.

They were also amazed when I said that we were now governed by Europe, who were making a lot of decisions about our future and spoiling the whole way of British life, interfering in everything we did. Someone asked, "why?" and I told them that I didn't know, it was the way Blair and other governments wanted it, although the majority of English people didn't. Jan and Eddie both agreed with me, as did her parents.

I did say in return that we had heard how America was very dangerous, that visitors could be attacked or shot at any time, that it was hazardous to drive about because of road rage, and that Americans were armed and willing to use a gun or knife. I added that after coming out here on holiday, I felt much safer here than I did in Britain today, and it was pleasant to know that the other English guests were totally in agreement with me.

We were suddenly interrupted when from further down the table, Rosemary seemed to be having an argument with a new guest, a Scottish man. When they finally broke into gales of laughter, it turned out that they were trying to pinch each other's dessert.

Off to one side sat a lot of people that I didn't recognise as being from the ranch, and when the chef came out with a big birthday cake, I realised they were having a party. We were all given a piece of cake, too.

At 7.30pm we went for the moonlight hayride, the open cart being pulled by two lovely Belgium heavy horses. A man was sitting up the front on the straw bales strumming a guitar, and as we started off, began to sing country songs. The moon slowly came up over the Catalinas and bathed the cacti in a white light, making the choya glow again. This year we only went round the ranch grounds, not out along the roads like last time.

Afterwards, we sat on the patio with Jan and Eddie and she told us that she bred and showed rabbits.

When we got up to go back to our cabins, Jan discovered she'd lost the key to theirs, and Andy and I left them frantically looking for it.

Saturday 16th September.

I was up at 6.30 again and went up to the main building to get a coffee, taking the cup outside and sitting on the patio. I got brave enough to say "hola (hello) and como esta?" (how are you) to the South American looking gardener who replied, "hello." He then smiled and said, "muy bien" (very well.) I told him, "mi comprende Espanol muy poco" (I understand Spanish very little) making a little gap between my thumb and forefinger to show him how much, making him laugh. He replied with something I didn't understand, and I just shook my head.

Walking round the path I heard a strange metallic tapping and, looking up at a casita roof, spotted a woodpecker sitting on the metal cowl to the chimney, pecking away. He must have realised he hadn't a chance of making any impression, for he suddenly flew off. Further on a black bird, a bit like our starling was poking his head out of a hole at the top of a saguaro.

I heard the dinner bell and went back to find that breakfast was being served on the new patio out the back of the dining room. This had been in the process of being built the year before, and had been crazy paved with steps and a large fancy brick fireplace. Ed came over to ask if I was riding. "Yes, please."

Jan's mum showed up at the corral and nervously climbed up on a horse. Jim took the lead, and a girl I hadn't seen before rode at the back, someone, I assumed, learning to be a wrangler. I was envious and wished I could stay and do something like that. I rode in front of Val chatting away to try and help her relax, while Jan rode behind. She seemed OK until her horse decided it didn't want to cross a damp piece of mud, and got very worried, so Jim had to come back and help her across, but after that we had a very slow, gentle ride on the flat.

Once back at the corrals, I untacked Wrangler, scratching his damp back like I did with Cloud after a ride, then hosed him down with water before turning him away into the corral with the rest of the horses.

I quickly changed and went to the pool where the water was cool and inviting. Again there were a lot of bugs in the water and I kept scooping them out onto the side, until one stung my hand. Eddie came in for a final swim as they were leaving after lunch, and we exchanged e-mail addresses. I was sad to see them leaving as they had been great company and quite a laugh.

I had a light salad for lunch as we were riding at 2.30pm and I was already feeling very hot. When I reached the corrals, Wrangler seemed to be puffing badly in the heat, and worried me. Joining us came some Australians, a tiny lady with a floppy straw hat, a tall thin man, her husband, and their kids, a girl and a boy. They said they could lope, but when Jim tested them out in the small pen, the boy had no control at all, so he couldn't go on the lope ride. The father told Jim that they all loped back home but only on the straight, they weren't used to turning corners in a menage. I wondered how they ever stayed on!

It was very hot, but the winds on top of the ridges and through the pass made it more bearable. We took another very hilly route again and Wrangler seemed to be much slower than usual, still puffing and being very careful going up and down hill. I decided that if he wasn't feeling too well, perhaps I would ask for another horse next day.

Back at the pool, April asked if I knew my neck had got very red from the sun, hadn't my friend mentioned it?

"No."

Tiny puffs of white clouds began to drift along the horizon, but after two and a half hours they had hardly moved an inch. Andy went off to phone a company to arrange a balloon ride, cheerfully telling me I was going too. No way was I going up in one of those things!

Eddie, Jan, Val and George left, as did Rosemary, Betty and Joquin. Dinner was very quiet without Rosemary, even if I found her hard to understand, but I got chatting to the Australians and the Scots, Kevin and Jerri. He kept joking: "Och aye, I'm Glenn of the Campbells" in a very broad Scottish accent.

The only meat they served up for dinner were T-bone steaks, but not being keen on red meat, I just helped myself to a salad, anyway I was concerned that I was getting too fat anyway feeling stuffed with the three full meals a day we were getting. Back home I only snacked when I felt hungry.

When Rusty came to the table, she had a brown stain on her T-shirt having spilt mousse down it, and Kevin kept ribbing her about "looking to see what was on the menu for today!" that had her giggling.

Afterwards, we sat outside chatting and watching the silver moon rising. It was so beautiful, what with the spotlights shining up into the tops of the two palm trees, the twinkling stars overhead, and a soft warm breeze playing on my face. I could pick out the Big Dipper (the Plough) star sign, just like at home.

During the night I heard cattle bawling somewhere over towards the corrals.

Sunday 17th September.

I woke at 4.30am and knocked on the wall to get Andy up for his balloon ride, as he had to phone and check in case the weather was against it. When he did call from the main building, it turned out that it was too windy to go up. He was very disappointed—I wasn't.

At 7am it was cool with hazy clouds overhead. At breakfast, I asked Ed about the noisy cattle and he told me, "they're calves, they've just left their mammas." Kevin was very jokey, especially ribbing Rusty about getting her a T-shirt made "with the menu printed on it!" and the Australians also very chatty. A young boy, Jake and his father, joined us having come from Tucson, as it was Jake's birthday and his father had booked him a night and day on the ranch with some riding.

Going down to the corrals to get mounted, I spotted a lovely little burro (donkey) in one of the small pens. It hadn't been there the day before and must have arrived yesterday afternoon.

Jake was given a lope test, and although he passed it, he seemed to have difficulty in stopping the white pony, Gunpowder. The Australian kids again asked for a lope ride, but were told "no." I decided to go on the lope ride with Jake pulling in behind me.

After the first lope, he sounded as if he was hurt and when I looked back, he was holding his back and wincing. I called out to Wendell, and Jake told him he'd had a bad back, but it had been seen to, he'd be OK in about five minutes. We walked on, and finally Jake said he was OK, but just into another lope he was in trouble again. I shouted to Wendell to stop, and he decided that Jake and his father would have to go back to the ranch in the charge of the girl wrangler. I offered to take drag to keep an eye on the people in front, which he agreed to, and I went to the back of the ride. If I couldn't be a real wrangler I could at least pretend!

We carried on with loping and I was pleased to find that my legs weren't aching like they sometimes did back home, either Wrangler was an easier horse to ride or he was thinner than Cloud. I was still not sure about his breathing, though. It was a real shame to get back to the ranch as I could have gone on longer. After the ride, crossing over to the pool, a tiny little chipmunk ran across my path.

On reaching the pool, Andy told me that he couldn't go skydiving today as he'd hoped, as there was no transport available to take him. It seemed that the only other day the skydiving people could do it was on Wednesday, when we were due to be flying off to San Francisco. He was very disappointed.

It was very, very hot again, and when lunchtime came I wasn't very hungry and just picked at a small salad.

At 3pm I went out on a walk ride, and was again very worried about Wrangler. I had asked Jim's opinion before we left and he'd thought he was OK, but I was still unhappy. We took a different route over some ridges I nicknamed Suicide Pass Mk II for it seemed almost as steep as the one that I'd called Mk I. From the top, we could look down into the valley towards Old Tucson, and on up to the Tucson mountain range. Old Tucson had been used as the site for many westerns, and during the summer months they staged shoot-outs and fights for the tourists. Andy and I had planned to go there during the week, but just never seemed to find the time.

Back at the ranch we lazed by the pool till dinner. A new lady joined us at the table, Edna, from San Francisco, as had two girls who usually went to Montana, Janice and Tanya, and who worked for a US airline. They told us that the ranch up there had changed hands and as they hadn't enjoyed themselves last year, had decided to try here instead. Edna was very nice, as were the two girls, and we all got chatting very easily.

During dinner, Wendell asked me if I was OK with Wrangler and I admitted, "I'm not really, I'm rather worried about him. He's puffing very badly."

"Don't worry, I'll check him out."

"Can I change horses?"

"OK."

Andy and I wandered out to the hammocks, passing a huge bullfrog by the outside of the pool with two smaller ones nearby, were they babies? They scuttled away into the shadows. It was bliss to climb into the hammock and gently rock under the stars, but it gradually the wind became very gusty and I had to get up around 8pm as the tree overhead was covering my hair with falling needles.

Back in the casita I felt very restless and achy, too much sun perhaps? I slept on and off, but was very fidgety, lying awake from time to time listening to the wind outside.

Monday 18th September.

At 6 am when I got up and went outside to go up to the ranch for coffee, I found a branch broken from the Red Bird of Paradise bush on the path, while in the pool were broken bits of palm leaves, bark, pieces of cacti, and dead insects. I also had to step carefully round a tiny stick insect on the gravel just outside the cabin, luckily having spotted him in time.

I poured myself a cup of coffee and went to sit on the patio to find Roberto, the gardener, sweeping up. I decided again to try a little bit of Spanish and finally plucked up the courage to say, "hola (ola)" He smiled and replied "hola."

I said, "palo" (tree) then, with hand signals, something was broken and ending with "numero nueve" (no.9, holding up nine fingers.) He looked puzzled for a moment, which turned out because I didn't pronounce nueve correctly, then smiled and said, "Si, gracious" (pronounced gratheas) which meant, yes, thank you. He picked up his tools and went to clear up and I felt really pleased for it was the first time I'd ever been able to use the little Spanish I knew.

Andy, who was normally a bit late anyway, didn't turn up for breakfast so I went to check on him. When he came to the door he was holding his hand to his ear, saying he'd got earache, possibly from the over chlorinated pool at the earlier hotel we'd stayed at, so I went to the office to explain what was wrong. I asked if someone could take me to the pharmacy at Walgreens, just down the road, and Kim kindly offered.

I spoke to a man standing in the pharmacy doorway about what to get for an ear infection and he suggested olive oil, which I bought, but Kim told me she'd got something for 'swimmers ear' back at the ranch. Once back, she went and got it for me and I passed it to Andy, along with a cup of coffee I thought he could do with. He said he was worried about whether he would be able to fly to San Francisco, but when I suggested we could drive, he shook his head.

"No, we've already paid for the plane." I suggested he saw a doctor, but he wanted to wait a while.

Going down to the corrals for the morning ride, I looked for Wrangler in the corral, but Wendell told me that he was lying down on the other side of the barn. Jeff then brought out a big sorrel (deep red chestnut) called Socks, about 15hh. I guess.

I told him, "either you lower the legs on him, or I'm using the mounting block."

He drawled back, "aw, Susan, you English are just too short!"

After mounting, I heard Mark telling a lady guest to sit her 'fanny' in the saddle. I giggled as I told him in horror, "you can't say that to an English woman!"

"Why not?"

"In England it's rude, it's the parts us ladies sit on!"

"Oh no," they told me, "it's OK in America. We have fanny bags."

"Oh, we have bum bags," I replied.

They were aghast. "You can't say that in America!"

I had a great walk ride as Socks had a really lovely gait (pace,) while the couple of inches difference from Wrangler made me feel quite a long way from the ground.

Back for lunch, I chose spaghetti with chicken strips and a white sauce, and while I was eating, Andy came in to say that he was feeling a little better. I mentioned to Rusty about this morning and what the English 'fanny' meant, and she told me an English person had said to her once, "keep your pecker up!" which had shocked her, for in America, that's very rude. Everyone at the table had quite a laugh about that and we ended up with quite a discussion about what could and couldn't be said in different countries.

Wandering into the TV room, I noticed two strange people sitting at a table. They seemed very much at ease, and for some reason as I sat and chatted to Rosemary and Betty about having been at the ranch last year, I praised the staff and the improvements that had been made, which wasn't hard to do. Then found out later that they were actually the new owners.

It was very, very hot outside with only a slight breeze and thunderheads bubbled up over the Catalina's. Too hot to do anything, so I sat on the patio in the shade of a tree to watch the tiny hummingbirds. From branches the staff had hung feeders for them filled with sugar water that they hovered at, the openings painted around with flower designs to guide them.

Ed came across to tell us that there wouldn't be any riding at 2.30pm as it was too hot, but that we would go out at 4pm instead, so I went off to change into my swimming costume to have a cooling swim. After, I lazed on a lounger in the shade. Near the edge of the pool I watched a small strange lizard. Was it a baby gila (heela) monster? Gilas are the only known poisonous lizard species, so I hoped that it wasn't.

Back at the corral for the ride, I watched a boy riding past on a grey horse that I thought I recognised, then realised it was Joe from last year. I called out, "hi," but he didn't recognise me until I ribbed him about trying to charge me for taking his photo last year, which got a laugh from the other wranglers. I also reminded him about the trick Sarah and I had played on Brad, pretending to have had a wild party in our cabin, and where was he? That got a greater laugh.

As we rode off, Ed shouted, "Susan, your horse's swallowing it's bit!" I was puzzled and asked Mark, "what's wrong." He explained that Ed meant that my reins were too short. That was novel. Back home I was always being told my reins were too long.

A short way out, Mark stopped off to check everyone's cinches (girths) and handed me his reins. When he came back, he asked casually, "OK?"

"No, I lost one of its legs!" He was checking his cinch when the penny dropped and he began laughing, giggling about it for ages. He said that he could live off that for a year, and I told him I'd have to charge him commission.

He took us on a different path that seemed even worse than Suicide Pass and switch backed all over the ridges. It was very hot while we were out and only became more enjoyable as the sun went down and it became cooler.

Andy was lying by the pool when I got back and told me that he was still having problems with his ear and didn't fancy any dinner. He went back to his cabin while I went to eat, and then took him back a coffee.

Returning to the ranch house, the abseiling man and his wife were doing Line Dancing and Barn Dancing. That was great fun, and I tried to encourage

Wendell to join in, but he just laughed, although he did do the Barn Dance later on. Roberto came to watch and was in fits of laughter at us all. I took the male role in the Barn Dance because we were short on men, and was unfortunate because the girls moved partners and I was peeved I didn't get to dance with any of the other men.

When it finished, I took Andy another coffee. He said he'd go and see a doctor in the morning if he wasn't any better, and I had to admit to myself that he didn't look too good.

At bedtime, my shoulders were very achy and I finally realised just how much swimming I was doing, but at least I was gaining more confidence in the water.

Lying in bed and just starting to drift off to sleep, it suddenly dawned on me that we only had two days left at the ranch. I was devastated. I couldn't sleep at all then so got up and sorted out all my leaflets and clothes, putting them neatly into my suitcase. Finally I got to sleep about 1am, worrying about Andy.

Tuesday 19th September.

I was up early, tired and on edge, going up to the corrals to groom Socks and a couple of the other horses where they were tied up ready for the morning's ride. The little Australian lady was given Sarah's favourite from last year, LeeLite.

We had a lovely ride out towards the breakfast area and I could hear coyotes yipping again in the distance. We suddenly came across some of the calves who had got out of their corral, so Jeff and another man with us, who had worked cattle before, started to round them up to drive them back.

I was able to chat away to Wendell, who had a great sense of humour and made me laugh. At one place, he asked me to lead the ride through a gate until he could shut it behind everyone. Halting further on to wait for him to catch up, the Australians just let their horses wander through the cacti off the trail, or among the other riders, annoying me immensely as it was dangerous and extremely thoughtless.

Riding along one of the ridges, Wendell took a phone call on his handset and shouted back to me that Andy had been taken to the hospital. I was quite shocked, and then very worried.

Riding along explaining that Andy was just a friend and had been Ann-Marie's fiancée, I told him about Les and her, and he exclaimed, "oh, you poor lady." I had to disagree, explaining that actually felt that I had been really lucky to have such a lovely family and that I'd had much more than

133

some people ever did.

At the campsite, I tied up Socks, loosening the cinch, then helped the Australian lady dismount, tying up LeeLite for her and loosening her cinch. I was really worried about Andy, and despite the lovely breakfast, I didn't eat much.

I untied LeeLite, got the Australian lady up, and mounted Socks from the block. I was riding close behind Wendell until I noticed an English man getting left behind as his horse kept hesitating at several places, so I offered to take drag and keep an eye on him.

"OK," he agreed and offered to buy me a cold beer on the pub ride later in the afternoon for helping out.

Back out on the flat most of the riders wanted to jog, but the lady riding Ginger didn't want to, so Wendell asked me if I'd mind staying behind with her.

"No, that's fine."

The others trotted off with Socks anxious to follow, but I held him back, and he was really lovely to ride as he jogged on the spot, not being used to being out of line. We caught up when the others stopped to wait for us and Wendell thanked me, offering to buy me a margarita this evening. I told him that if he kept this up, anything else would cost him champagne.

Once back, I unsaddled and washed Socks down, then went over to reception to see if they had any news about Andy. None. Apparently, Larry, one of the men who worked round the ranch, had taken him to the hospital.

Sitting down with a cup of coffee, I got chatting to Leanne who was actually leaving for San Francisco on the same plane as us and was very nervous. I said we could sit together if she wanted as I was, too. We both then booked to stay at the ranch for lunch, as our plane wasn't leaving till 4.30pm.

Andy finally arrived back from the hospital having had to pay $350 for treatment that included seeing a triage nurse before the doctor. He'd had his blood pressure taken by the nurse before seeing the doctor and that had turned out to be high, probably because of the pain, so he'd had to wait twenty minutes for it to drop. After the check up, he'd been given stronger eardrops. He'd also queried about being able to fly and the doctor had said he could as he had a middle ear infection and not the inner.

He'd been talking to Larry while waiting for his treatment and it turned out that he too had also given up a good job like Tom to come to the ranch as he'd rather be doing something that made him happy.

Again it was very, very hot and some small clouds were hanging over the

Catalina's. While Andy went back to his room to lie down, I went and bought a couple of T-shirts and a mug at the reception area to take home. While paying for them, Joan mentioned that she'd heard of me!

I was curious. "Gee, have I got me a rep?"

"Oh yes," she said.

"Ah," I replied, "but about what?" She just laughed and refused to say.

I thought I'd better ring Fed-Ex to ask where my hats were and they informed me that I needed a tracking code from Dallas. I couldn't use my Mastercard to try to get through to Dallas as the automated message kept asking for money, but I finally got through to an operator, who couldn't accept a card as I was on a payphone. I then tried the extension phone on the desk, but no! American telephones are very confusing that I ended up getting so frustrated and gave up, heading back to my cabin.

I decided about ten minutes later that as I didn't want to disturb Andy as to how he'd managed it before I would go back to try again, with no better result. Baffled, I asked the lady at reception who gave me a number to ring. Hurray, I got through to Dallas airport and Lost Property. They assured me that the hats had been sent and gave me the tracking code. I re-phoned Fed-Ex who stated that they had already been delivered that morning!

I asked at the desk for a package for Andy Bucksey. After searching for ages, they finally found it under the office desk-a reused box for reamed paper so they'd assumed it was stationary for the office. It didn't help either that the name printed on it was 'Ducksey.'

I wandered round the ranch restless and distracted, eventually leaning on the corral rails to watch the horses. At 4pm I went joined the ride to a cocktail bar for drinks, chatting to Jeff for a while as we rode. Edna then asked me about 'jackalopes' and I told her that they only came out into the shadows. You would see their big ears first. Great fun, she believed me.

We got to the bar, tying the horses up outside. Wendell offered me a drink, asking what I wanted. I had absolutely no idea! Panicky, as I didn't want to look silly in front of everyone, all I could think of was a light ale.

"OK."

He brought me a Coors. Thank goodness I didn't ask for a glass when he gave it to me as everyone just drank straight from the bottle. I enjoyed it so much I bought another before we left. Kevin had us in stitches with his jokes, making me laugh so much my sides ached.

Mark led the way back while Jeff recited cowboy poems, some that he'd written and some he'd learned. It was really lovely, especially when I saw three separate mule deer does watching us suspiciously, but not frightened, from the brush. I suddenly pointed out to Edna, "there goes a jackalope."

"Where?" She stared around.

"Oh dear, you just missed it."

Suddenly she realised that I was joking, fortunately taking it in good part and laughing. Dusk began to fall, the ridges turned a smoky grey, and one lone star began to twinkle ahead of us. The lights of Tucson on our right were very bright, as were the lines of car lights glittering on the freeway as people headed home. I told Mark how lucky the wranglers were to do this job, although I did appreciate what hard work it was.

Back at the ranch, I came across Andy who had been sitting by the pool while we were out, but as his earache was starting to come back, he went back to his cabin to lie down. I went on to eat at the cookout, before taking him a cup of coffee. Everyone was having a good laugh, and Kevin and Janice were a riot as the beer was flowing freely. He very generously gave me a couple of bottles of beer to drink.

Finally they got a bit silly, he picked up Janice and took her to the swimming pool, walking into it and both coming back soaked. Wendell mentioned that he was having a couple of days off, but when I said that I'd hoped to say goodbye tomorrow, told me he'd be around sometime. On top of that I hadn't even got a picture of him or the other wranglers.

It became very windy again by 9.30pm so I went back to the casita, but I slept badly that night, tossing and turning. By 1.30am I had to take two Ibuprofen tablets as I had a headache, but then had to have another two at 5.30am. I'd still got the headache when I got up, but it slowly began to ease off by breakfast time. I wished I could stay here forever. I didn't fancy San Francisco at all, let alone the thought of going home.

Wednesday 20th September.

I went for a cup of coffee, then sat outside the cabin watching the birds and butterflies, and listening to the coyotes yipping in the distance, before walking over to the corrals and watching the horses for an hour. Wrangler was looking better as he stood in the shade, but then started puffing heavily again when he walked into the sunlight. Had he got heat stroke?

Sparrows were chirping, there was some chattering that sounded like a flock of budgies, and the little quail with their bobble head feathers ran about under the cacti. The mountains looked a smoky blue in the distance—guess that means another hot day. Walk or lope ride? I couldn't make up my mind, I just wanted to get on a horse and ride off somewhere, anywhere. If I took the camcorder it would have to be a walk ride, but if I didn't, I could try Socks on a lope ride. I finally decided on the walk, it would make it seem to take longer.

Mark took us up Suicide Pass. Gosh, it seemed worse than I remembered. Edna was a nuisance continually wanting to stop and take snaps, annoying the English couple with us. The man muttered, "I thought we were on a ride not a film shoot," but Mark was very patient. As we rode along, he told me his girlfriend wanted him to leave the ranch, as she was a bit iffy about the lady guests, but that now he was thirty-one, he wanted to settle down anyway.

Lots of little rocks had fallen on the trail from the heavy rains before we arrived and Mark told me that the wranglers were kept busy just trying to keep the paths clear. It was very steep in places, but Socks was good. I liked him lots and just like Wrangler last year, I wished I could have taken him home with me.

At a sheer drop, we stopped to look out over the saguaro clad slopes and down into the valley towards Old Tucson. Andy and I never did get to hire a car to drive out there, but still, there's always next year! From the ridge I could see the specks of riders and cattle down in the corral where the other ride was penning, then coming down the trail, I noticed three steers on the slope, grazing on whatever they could find.

When we arrived back, I washed Socks off, then went and looked at the new black and white pygmy goats in the pen nearby. They were a still a bit nervous and scampered to the back of their pen.

Andy arrived for breakfast, feeling a bit better, and after that we paid our bill. Going to sit in the TV room, we watched a video advertising the ranch done by one of the Sky channels, and Carol, Paul and Ed were in it. Finally, I went and said goodbye to the wranglers, thanking them for everything, and said that I hoped to be back next year. I got a hug from Tom. I also met one of the chefs and thanked him for the great meals.

I told Rusty that if she ever wanted to come to England I'd put her up in the caravan and take her to see Canterbury Cathedral, Leeds Castle and other places of interest, and we arranged to write to each other once I was back home.

The carpenter then drove us out to the airport and we all booked in at the desk, passing over our cases. I chatted to Leanne while we waited, as she was very nervous, making me feel like a seasoned traveller. Andy mentioned that the plane was a short take-off one so that it would feel lumpier than the big ones. He was right, and it also went up quicker than the continental planes!

We had a layover in San Diego for half an hour, where the weather was dull like in England, and then we were off for San Francisco. The clouds below were soft and white, rippled like the sand when the tide went out. Then suddenly there was a straight line where they ended and I could see the land and the bright blue sea below. The sun, going down over the horizon, was stunningly beautiful. Slowly we came down over the bay until I thought we were going to land on the water that shimmered in the last rays of the sunlight.

We collected our luggage from the carousel after passing through passport control, and went to find a shuttle service to the hotel for it seemed easier than trying to find the Bart light railway in the dark. Outside, it was humid but not hot. The hotel turned out to be quite a lot further away so the people carrier would cost us $47.

The freeways were packed with rush hour traffic, and we joined it. Turning a corner, tall buildings rose up into the black sky, their windows brightly lit. Very pretty but, oh dear, back to concrete and steel with the roads, the bridge, the industrial areas and the city spread around us. How I ached for the desert with its giant saguaros, the clean smell of the desert, the sound of the horses, and the coyotes yapping.

At 10pm we finally reached Union City and the Radissons Hotel, being dropped off outside the entrance. It looked lovely with a fountain and pond in front. After booking in at reception, we dragged our cases up to our rooms, before heading down to find the bar for something to eat. I ordered a salad, and it was huge when it came.

Trying to enjoy our meal, it was spoiled unfortunately, by a loud girl at the nearby table. One of a group of four young people, she was spouting so much rubbish she sounded as if she was rambling and we were glad to get up and leave.

It was very warm in my room, and looking out the window, despite the darkness, I discovered that I was not overlooked being three floors up, so I was able to leave the window and curtains open a little for some fresh air. I slept without any sheets over me, despite the air conditioning being on, as unfortunately, the air was being blown straight up under the curtains.

Chapter 12

San Francisco Here I Come.

Thursday 21st September.

On rising and looking out the window, I found it was cloudy but warm and I faced out to a lovely red sunrise. The window overlooked a red roofed building, with a tiny garden between it and the hotel that was smothered in white fluff from the laundry room. But it beat looking at a freeway!

After breakfast, we were given a lift in the hotel shuttle to the Bart light railway, sharing with a lovely elderly couple from New Mexico who were friendly and chatty. I amused both them and the driver by saying how nicely the Americans drive compared to the English, and was amazed when they stated that they actually thought their drivers were bad.

"If you'd come five or ten years ago, things were much better," stated the driver, while the male passenger said, "one finger doesn't mean well done, you know."

I quickly laughed and replied, "Oh, shame. Now you tell me," that made them laugh. When the driver asked if we would want a lift back from the station in the evening, Andy told him that as we didn't know when we'd get back, could we ring the hotel from the station.

"Oh, sure."

The railway station was again light, clean and airy. We bought the usual tickets that slotted in through the entrance machines, and we didn't have long to wait on the platform, the trains seemed to be every quarter of an hour or so.

Oh dear, back to looking at houses, roads, cars and factories that covered even the distant ridges. Yuk. I shut my eyes and thought of the ranch. I could feel myself gradually smiling and was glad no one was sitting opposite me. The train travelled above ground for a while, then headed into tunnels very like our London Underground, but the stations were again nice and clean.

We emerged at Daly City, went through the exit, and climbed the long flight of steps back out into the sunshine. There, in the street in front of me was sight of my first streetcar, very pretty and colourful, being moved round on a turntable by the conductor and driver to face the other way. But there were lots of bums either on the benches or hanging around the area. We came across a delicatessen that sold coffee, and bagels with a long list of fillings, but ended up settling for a Danish pastry with our drink.

Back outside, all the streetcars were full with people hanging off the sides like on TV, so we walked on until one finally came along with room. As the driver pulled the levers that caught the chains running down a groove in the middle of the tracks to go up or down the hills, it was very noisy, and it wasn't as comfortable as I'd thought, especially with the hard wooden seats.

We changed streetcars for Fisherman's Wharf, and as we jumped onto the next one, a voice called out, "hey, England, where you bin?" and it was the American couple. I waved.

"I bet we can't do that again!" I told them, when we got off at the last stop to walk to The Wharf. He told us, rather wistfully, that having been in the city many years before and having just gone back to the park to see it again, it had all changed, and not for the better, in his opinion. I commiserated.

"Nothing ever is."

We left them and browsed round the shops where I spotted a western style shop. Inside I went looking for some chaps, but the only pair they had were miles too big, and had no fringes either. Despite their hardest efforts to get me to buy them, I didn't.

We finally came across the famous Fisherman's Wharf sign that stands at the entrance to the pier, and after photographing it, found a drug store for Andy to get some more painkillers, as his ear was still aching a lot.

At a kiosk we bought tickets to visit Alcatraz for the following day, then he booked a seaplane trip to fly over the bay at 5pm, before slowly walking along the wooden pier, which I found very delightful with all its little shops and colourful hanging baskets of flowers. Several flights of steps led up to the second level and even more shops and cafes. At the far end we came across a restaurant with windows overlooking the bay, and went in for a meal, sitting where we could see across to the Golden Gate Bridge, far out in the distance. The waters were choppy in the strong breeze, and a mist shrouded the bridge making it difficult to see.

Back outside and heading for at the other side of the pier, I could smell the sealions before I heard their noisy barking. Sleeping brown seals were heaped on the flat surfaces of wooden pontoons, while others were swimming round and round them, barking. Some of the swimmers leapt smoothly out of the water onto the backs of their companions, and the noise was tremendous as they upset the ones that were resting, causing even more noise as they squabbled and complained. According to a notice, the sealions had been allowed to take over this part of the bay-probably because they brought in so many tourists that it was worth it. I lent on the railing and watched them for a while before heading back to the shops.

From the top floor I could watch a juggler/entertainer on the lower deck who had a little white dog with him. It sat beside him while he sang, "how much is that doggie in the window?" with the dog barking "woof, woof" in all the right places and making people laugh.

He then picked out five children from the crowd, got them to kneel and bend over, and the dog leapt them all. Well almost. I think he just caught the last little girl with his feet, but she didn't appear hurt. It was great fun.

At last the sun began to shine through the clouds and it began to turn sunny and warm. Andy went off to the seaplane while I wandered over to the front of the pier to watch it take off, stopping on the way to buy a coffee. Taking it to a table at the end of the pier, although I didn't think that I'd been that long, I'd found that I'd missed seeing the plane take off from the water, for it was already in the air and heading for the bridge when I spotted it. It disappeared into low clouds, reappeared to fly over the island of Alcatraz, and away toward the horizon.

I walked round the shops, treating myself to a very tasty icecream on the way, and then on to see the sealions again. Behind them, pelicans and cormorants were flying in and landing on the long concrete jetty for the night. I went to find the opening times of the aquarium, only to find that it had shut for the day.

Back at the table, I waited until the seaplane appeared in the distance, coming in to land with white spray flying up from the floats as they touched the water. With the propellers turning very slowly, it eased its way gently into the harbour and was tied up at the pontoon.

Andy came over thrilled to bits with the ride, having had had a really great time as he'd been allowed to ride in the front with the pilot, and was able to film everything very clearly. We sat and had a coffee while he told me about his trip. I told him that the aquarium had shut for the night, and so we decided we'd come back and see it tomorrow.

Now it was dusk the pier had been lit up by hundreds of colourful lights and throngs of people were wandering about. I was tired and my legs ached, but we walked around the shops again, Andy wanting to finish his present buying. From there, we boarded a streetcar to go back to the subway for the Bart railway.

On arriving, we discovered that we would have to change for Union City as after 7pm the trains didn't go straight through, and the carriage we found ourselves in had a terrible whistling noise all the way that was very irritating. We arrived at our station at 9.30pm, and phoned the hotel to ask for the shuttle to pick us up, which they did.

At the reception desk, I booked for us to be taken to the station at 9am the next morning and we went up to our rooms. Andy had just come in for a coffee when suddenly the phone rang.

"I'm very sorry, ma'am. The shuttle has already been booked for 9am, will 8.30 be alright?"

"Yes, that's fine."

When we'd finished coffee, Andy went back to his room to browse through all the brochures for places of interest we could visit while we were here. I showered and went to bed after writing up my notes, but had a very restless night.

Friday 22nd September.

I woke at 6am and watched TV, The Little House on the Prairie. (When I got home that Sunday the same episode was on English TV!) When Les was alive, he and I used to watch it on a Thursday, nicknaming it 'sob Thursday' as the programme was nearly always heartbreaking, and quite often he would make an excuse to get up and go to make the dinner.

I phoned through to Andy at 7.30am to wake him and asked him how his ear was.

"Much better."

The phone rang. It was reception.

"I'm sorry, ma'am, the shuttle was already booked for 8.30, is 8.10 all right?"

"Yes!" (This is getting silly.) I'd just had time to tell Andy, when they phoned again.

"We're very sorry, the shuttle has been booked for that time, we would be pleased to arrange a cab for you for 8.30am." I agreed in desperation.

After breakfast, we went to wait in the reception area and I could see that outside it had just begun to rain. That was novel after Arizona! We seemed to sit for ages with no sign of a cab so I went to query it, and the girl at reception had just called them again to confirm, when the shuttle driver announced we could go with him if we wanted as he could drop us off first! The only passengers turned out to be the people from New Mexico leaving, but Andy turned it down as our cab had finally pulled up outside. Shame really as the trip to the station cost us $7.40.

We bought our tickets, entered the next train, and travelled to Powell Street putting our films into Walgreen's for developing, telling them that we wouldn't be back until evening. I think they were rather relieved as I had nine films and Andy must have had six or seven. As we got back out onto the streets, the weather cleared and it became dry and warm.

We ran for a streetcar heading for Pier 41, and it was so packed full of people that we had to stand on the running boards at the side. Great! I'd always wanted to do that, and it wasn't as dangerous or as uncomfortable as I'd thought. Gazing between the blocks of buildings as we reached the tops of the hills, I could see over to the beautiful views over the bay and city, and at one stop, I could look down the steep 'zigzag street' used in so many films.

Reaching Pier 41, the shops were basically the same as the others we'd seen the day before, but I managed to buy yet more place magnets for my fridge, including the States that we had passed through on our train trip. And then I came across a small shop with every wall absolutely covered in magnets. I was fascinated by the food stuff designs that looked good enough to eat, reminding me of the colourful erasers that Ann-Marie and I used to collect, until they were stopped as being dangerous to small children. I discovered one of a hot air balloon and bought it to give to Andy as a present.

Passing a small diner we went in for breakfast. Oh brilliant, my favourite, biscuits and gravy!

From there we walked on to Fisherman's Wharf, and then to Waterworld, the aquarium, which turned out to be fascinating.

In various places, we could stand on a slow moving walkway that travelled under plastic tunnels with shoals of fish, sharks, and rays all gliding over the top and along the sides. Some of the fish were quite ugly, like the brown rockfish and the lingcod, but the leopard shark with his spots was smooth and sleek. Tentacles of an octopus were just in sight round the tip of a rock while starfish slowly crept over the plastic. Anemones clung like limpets to it and the rocks, their feelers swaying gracefully in the currents.

On the top floor were sea pools with starfish, baby rays, and sea cucumbers that you could actually touch. In the shop afterwards, I bought some very colourful plastic lizards and dinosaurs as souvenirs for my garden at home.

Back outside, we went for a coffee. Andy still had a lot of shopping to do for presents and went off alone as I was tired, but after a quarter of an hour I got bored and went to buy an icecream, finding a bench seat to sit on until he came back.

Reaching another pier, and standing for ages in a very long queue, we finally boarded a boat for Alcatraz. Once out on the water, it became very windy and I was glad to sit inside. Andy was just wondering where all the life belts were when the announcement came that in an emergency, they could be found fitted up inside the wooden ceiling.

Slowly we approached the rocky island, with its huge white four-storey building overshadowing the dock. Having originally been built for the military between 1865-67, it was virtually bomb proof having 10 feet thick brick walls. Above it was another huge brick cell-house used to keep the hardened criminals including Al Capone and 'Creepy' Karpis. The sight of those buildings alone must have made anyone coming here tremble. To the right of the dock as we disembarked loomed a restored watchtower, one of six around the island.

It was a long walk up the concrete path, passing under the oldest building on the island, the brick guardhouse. Built in 1857, it could only be reached by a drawbridge that straddled a 15 feet deep dry moat. The Sally port was a passageway with a heavy iron-studded wooden door at each end and rifle slits lining the brick walls and anyone getting this far would have stood no chance of reaching any further. The chapel was a small building on top of the guardhouse, built in the early 1920s.

Further up the path an English guide was waiting for us, and his enthusiasm about the island made the stories interesting to listen to. He told us of the history of the island from when it had been used during the Civil War for deserters, rapists, murderers, and anyone charged with treason, even incarcerating Indians captured during the Indian wars. It then became a prison in 1934, holding among the one thousand, five hundred and forty five men, Al Capone, George 'Machine Gun' Kelly, Floyd Hamilton, and Robert Stroud, famous as The Birdman of Alcatraz.

Due to increasing costs, it had finally closed in 1963, but was then taken over by some Native Americans who believed that due to an old law, they were entitled to live there. Jane Fonda, who supported them in what they were doing, had supplied a generator for them at one time. The buildings had also been taken over by dropouts and hippies who vandalised it for the lead and other valuable metals to get money to buy food and clothing. At some point, they had even set light to a couple of the nearby buildings.

He also relayed the story of three men who had tunnelled through the walls after leaving heads made of soap in their beds, escaping to the sea but were never to be heard of again.

"How many people romantically hoped that they had actually made it to the mainland?" he asked. Naturally, lots of people, including me, put their hands up. We all laughed when he pointed out "then you are therefore happy that murderers and worse could actually still be alive somewhere in America!" He stated categorically that no one could possibly have survived a swim through the very strong currents of an icy cold sea, especially with a good possibility of sharks patrolling the waters. Crumbs no wonder only a few people had ever tried it, their chances of surviving were virtually nil. In fact, even after forty years, nobody had ever come forward to say that they had survived.

Once he'd finished, we were left to roam the place. It was drear and forbidding with tiny stone walled cells fronted by iron bars, and the footsteps sounded hollow, echoing around the long corridors. Personally I think it should still be a prison and that murderers, rapists, and anybody who committed violent crimes, should be locked up here still, it would serve them right.

Lots of people were wandering about with headsets and earphones, supplied if you wanted a spoken guided tour. We wandered into what would have been the dining room, a huge gloomy area with benches and tables, the whole thing making me feel claustrophobic, and then down some steps to the exercise yard. Here were heaps of rubble and painted signs from the occupation. I could see the couple of buildings burnt out in 1970 one of which had been the warden's house overlooking both the bay and the island, the other housing the four wardens who commanded the penitentiary.

We strolled back down the steeply paved slopes to wait for the next ferry back to the quayside. Back on the mainland, we browsed round the shops again, but I'd lost interest by now, having got bored seeing the same old things.

We boarded a tram, having to change when it didn't go the way we'd wanted, and then had a long walk up a steep hill to catch another, by which time it had got dark. We reached Walgreen's and paid for our photos, mine cost $71. Wow.

We walked back to the subway to wait for the train back to our hotel, and while sitting on the seats on the platform, Andy overheard two Chinese girls behind us talking about the stop after ours, wondering if they knew they had to change halfway. I plucked up courage to tell them. They were a bit nervous at first, after all, they didn't know us from Adam, but then they were very grateful. I told them to change trains where we did. It turned out that one of them was staying in New York, while the other was going home to Hong Kong later on during the week.

We reached Union City station at 9pm, and phoned to ask the hotel to send the shuttle. Once at the hotel, we returned to the bar for something to eat, and I ordered another salad with chicken pieces. Very nice, when it finally arrived. The service was very slow, considering that there were only three customers other than us there, but it was a different person serving this evening.

Afterward, I sat up quite late in my room, sorting out all my photos, which were great, then reluctantly creeping into bed at 12.30am. I had a very restless night, torn between wanting to see if my dogs and horse were OK and wanting to stay in America longer. How I wished I could still be still in Arizona.

Saturday 23rd September.

I woke at 6am, my last day, watching TV till it was time to ring Andy, meeting him outside to go downstairs for breakfast. After, he asked at reception for a shuttle out to the Bart station.

My suitcase was very heavy, full of extra soaps and shampoos, magnets, leaflets, books and T-shirts, and I was very grateful to use the lift.

We were taken to the station, where I had trouble hauling my case up the flight of stone steps to the platform. We should have travelled to the end of the line, Daly, but got off at the wrong stop. I thought we'd needed the one before, but Andy had decided that we didn't, so again I had to drag my case down some stairs, before waiting ages to get a train back one stop and catch yet another on to Daly.

Once there, we had to sit and wait for a bus to the airport, where I watched the planes taking off and landing someway in the distance. When the coach came, the driver only took exact change, which we hadn't got, but he very kindly took us anyway. We seemed to travel quite a long way, and I guessed that we were heading for a different airport than the one I'd been watching.

We were put off at the wrong part of the terminal and had a lengthy walk through the concourse before finding the Virgin booking-in desk. The queue was enormous and behind us, to my amusement, a group of people had a large stuffed toy brown rabbit on top of their luggage. Andy went off to try and find a trolley for the cases, but couldn't get one.

At long last we shuffled our way through to the desk and I gratefully left my luggage to be put on board. Andy still needed to shop for toys for the kids back home, so I sat and waited for him after buying dad a big bottle of Jack Daniels. This had to be left in the duty free shop and I could pick it up in the airport lounge later.

Finally we passed through security, where I took off my hat and belt yet again to pass them separately through the x-ray machine, threading the belt back through the loops on my jeans afterwards. Bit embarrassing doing that in front of strangers.

I crossed to the boarding gate to retrieve my bottle of whiskey, and we had a long wait in the lounge waiting for our flight to be called. Through the windows I could see the plane had a large cartoon transfer of Austin Powers. I had no idea who he was, even when Andy explained about the film. Once everything was ready, passengers were called in seat order, the first class passengers first.

It was a very long flight, but again the meals were great. The in-flight movies looked interesting, but I decided to try to sleep like last year, hoping that that might be why I hadn't suffered from jet lag the year before, but mainly because I couldn't bear going home.

We landed at Heathrow to heavy rain and a thunderstorm! Welcome back to jolly old England! Andy phoned through to Stephen, but due to the size of the airport and not quite knowing where we were, it took ages for us to meet up outside. He told us all about the petrol crisis—when lorry drivers had reacted against the rising price of diesel-I hadn't realised how bad it had been. Glad I'd not been here.

HOLIDAY 2001

Chapter 13

Here I Go Again!

Friday 24th August.

We booked Stephen again to drive us to Gatwick airport. Once there, we paid him the fare and reminded him of the date and flight that we would be coming back on, arranging to ring his mobile as soon as we could after coming through customs.

Andy grabbed a cart for our luggage and we walked along the corridors to the moving walkway. I like letting it do the work for me, but several people, like the other year, went walking past, obviously in a hurry. Despite feeling decidedly more than a little edgy about flying, I was very excited and couldn't wait to get going and arrive in America again.

We booked our cases through at the Virgin Atlantic desk, and walked through to customs where, to my embarrassment, as I stepped through the x-ray machine it went off, despite having taken off my belt and hat. I emptied my pockets in front of the security guard and could only find a small packet of polo mints, perhaps the silver paper did it-Cloud's sweets, which I'd been feeding him before I'd set out this morning. I was waved on through.

We wandered round the shops, Andy getting his newspapers and magazines for the flight, and then we stopped at a café for coffee. Andy passed me over a couple of aspirin.

"What's this for?" I asked.

"To help thin the blood for the flight, there's been a lot of publicity over the possibility of thrombosis on long flights," he explained. As I haven't read newspapers or watched the news for years, it was far too depressing, I hadn't heard about it.

We had to take a driverless shuttle train to get to our terminal and the big departure lounge, where we had to wait for quite a while before being called to board the Virgin Atlantic plane. On it I was amused to see a different cartoon emblazoned on the side under the pilot's window, this time it was 'Barbarella.'

I stowed my luggage away above the seat and made myself comfortable, diving into the bag of goodies they give you, fastening my seatbelt, and trying not to think of going so far up in the air. After everyone was settled, the loudspeakers announced that the 8 hour flight was being delayed from 12.30 to 13.15pm. This didn't help, as I'd been feeling very nervous about the holiday from a few weeks before. Friends had asked, "are you looking forward to your holiday, it won't be long," and were somewhat puzzled by my saying, "no, I'm not. There's something wrong." This was unusual for me for I've always loved going to America. No valid reason, I was just jittery and unsettled.

Finally they announced that we would be taxiing out to the runway to take our place in the line of departing planes. Like last year the stewardesses gave us a demonstration showing us where the exits were, where we could find the flotation cushions, and how to use the air masks, etc. At the same time, a short video was also shown on the small screens in the back of the seat in front of us. Finally, the engines screamed and we were away.

The in-flight meals were very nice again last year, each course being neatly packed in plastic containers, accompanied by metal knives and forks, and I followed it up with a coffee. Andy ordered a small bottle of wine with his meal, and I decided to do the same. It was nice. Plenty of drinks also came round during the whole flight.

I keyed in to the map on the TV that showed we were flying at between 37,000 and 39,000 feet. I nudged Andy.

"How far is that in miles?"

"Seven to eight miles up!"

"Wow." That made my heart jump!

Our speed went anywhere from five hundred and four, to five hundred and eighty four mph, and overall we covered two thousand, six hundred and seven miles.

This year I was better at looking out of the window, unless the plane banked when I had to shut my eyes, and was able to watch us passing over Nova Scotia and Canada. During the flight I mostly read my books as I find it very difficult to hear the movies through the headsets, the voices always seemed so muffled.

Just after Delaware, I was startled to see a jet fly past the front and a little below us. We turned to follow the coastline, passing over land, rivers, and deltas. At one part, we flew between beautiful huge fluffy clouds that looked like puffs of smoke billowing up from a volcano, mostly below us, but some were at our height. Gosh, I never knew clouds reached this high up.

During the flight, I ordered a dumpy, VA toy plane from the Virgin catalogue for my brother Ian's son, Jeremy, to be collected on our return flight, and used my credit card to pay for it.

We arrived at Orlando airport where it was very hot and humid, crowding onto a driverless train to get to the carousel for our cases. There I found that the wheels on my case had been almost torn off. I was very upset, as Andy had bought it for me for Christmas only two years ago, but he reminded me that luggage only usually lasted about three years anyway, due to the rough handling they received. Thankfully, I had some orange binder twine, no horsy person is ever without, in one of the pockets, and managed to tie them on again. This got to be rather a nuisance, having to untie it at the hotels to get my clothes out, and retie it again each time I left. Andy's case took ages to come round on the carousel and we'd just started to worry when it turned up.

I went through the security check, and the alarm went off again, despite having taken off my belt and hat! I was so embarrassed, how I hate this. This time it turned out to be the three little metal badges on my jean shirt. The sensitivity of these machines must fluctuate between airports because they hadn't caused this problem earlier.

Out in the sunlight, I was still having difficulty with the new glasses I'd bought a couple of weeks before, they always seemed to be slightly out of focus, so I was glad to put on the old ones that I'd had tinted. That at least stopped me squinting.

We climbed into the shuttle bus to go to the Alamo Car Rental, where I waited outside while Andy got all the paperwork done, before he headed off to pick up the car from the lot. I glanced round when I heard voices, finding it really strange hearing British accents, but then Orlando was a tourist area. I found it very hot and uncomfortable, even in the shade, but then Andy came round the corner with a white convertible Chrysler Sebring. Wow! Neat. Andy's face was brilliant. It turned out to be quite a powerful car. The man at the reception gave us a map of the area, drawing arrows to show us where the hotel was on International Drive, and how to get there.

It was very breezy in the car after Andy had had fun letting the electric top down, and I told him that, "at this rate, I'm going to end up losing my new perm."

The roads were wide and clean, with palm trees everywhere—just like in Miami Vice. Where's gorgeous Sonny Crockett?

Andy loved the electronics and fiddled with the button controls on the steering wheel, finally finding out how to use the cruise control, and I watched so that I could use it when it was my turn to drive. We had to pass through a couple of tollbooths, throwing our money into conical baskets on the side. Seventy five cents and fifty cents, the first ones we'd ever gone through in America.

We found a nice Best Western on International Drive, unfortunately not the one we wanted, and Andy was directed further down the road. We passed an 'upside down' house, and one 'tilted' as if after an earthquake, 'Ripley's Believe it or Not.' Here the three lane roads were very busy. The traffic lights were hung above the road on cables where the flashing yellow indicates to 'go with caution.' From red, they always go straight to green, and I hoped there were no queue jumpers. Actually, it was very, very rare to see anyone do that, perhaps the fact that there are more police about makes sure that drivers don't.

We found our Best Western, slightly shabbier than the last one. There was a water park opposite with a tall metal framework for a splash tunnel slide and kids climbing the outside ladder for their go. I could hear their screams as they slid down into the water. Andy had great fun shutting the car roof, clipping the front down either side of the windshield. I wouldn't mind taking this home.

The lady on the front desk insisted that Andy had only booked one room, until he showed her the confirmation printout from my computer. Good job I printed off everything we needed to know, including all the confirmation numbers. She also said that the money had not been taken from his MasterCard when we originally booked, which threw out his accounting for the holiday. Some hotels did, and some didn't.

We went up to the third floor by lift. The rooms were very nice, mine had a quiet a/c thankfully, while the wires that trailed from the standard lamps and

TV were still the same thin ones with a two pin plug. Very unsafe looking compared to England. The bathroom switch was illuminated at night, which I thought a brilliant idea. The bathroom tap was central on the sink: push up for on, right for hot/left for cold. (The TV's, and coffee machines, when there was one, and the taps all worked differently at each hotel.) There was also a note asking you to conserve water: 'please hang the towels up if you would like to use them again, OK, I'm clean after a shower anyway, or put them on the floor to be changed. Sheets will be changed every three days unless asked for it to be sooner.' I didn't rate the hotel—no coffee machine in the room!

Going down for a meal in the restaurant attached to the hotel, I found it had dark wood walls, floor and ceiling, and had the usual three or four huge TV screens. The Americans don't seem to be able to go anywhere without them, but it was no use trying to watch any of the programmes as they didn't have any sound! And anyway, they were all showing something different. I ordered a Caesar salad with chicken, lovely.

We went to bed at 9pm (2am. BST) as we were very tired, and I arranged to ring Andy about 8am as he wanted a lie-in. Unusually for me, I had a very restless night, possibly because it was very warm even with the a/c on. I slept without even a sheet over me.

Saturday 25th August.

At 7am I went down to the lobby for a coffee from the machine, finding that I needed four quarters (a dollar) for it, so I asked the coloured guy on reception for change of $5. He gave me just four quarters back. When I asked for the rest, "oh," he said, "I thought you'd only given me a one." Great start to the holiday! I hadn't come across this before, but then we were in a commercialised area for tourists.

Back in my room and watching the TV weather channel, they were predicting a warm sunny day at 92f 30C. I showered, rang Andy, and we went for breakfast when he was ready. A buffet, lovely, but I overdid the scrambled eggs, crispy bacon, sausage, fried potato and two small cinnamon waffles, making myself feel very uncomfortable.

Andy drove to Discovery Cove. He'd booked this quite early on when we were organising the holiday, as they limit the numbers of people for the day. I filmed Andy closing the roof of the car, grinning.

At the entrance to the park, a young girl held a two-toed sloth with long silvery hair. It hung from her shoulders by its thin arms, and people were allowed to pet it. It felt like a coarse brush. I felt rather sorry for it, being handled by so many strangers. We queued inside for our pictures to be taken for a security card. This could be swiped at the various counters inside for food, drinks etc, this being charged to your account, and it also entitled us to enter Sea World, where we would be going to tomorrow. We were handed some natural sunscreen cream that was not harmful to the habitat.

We were ushered into a line of people and a guide led us down the pathway to a counter under a lovely thatched roof hut where we were given a bath towel, snorkel and mask, which I'd never used before, and a yellow/blue float jacket. We could keep the snorkel but the rest had to be given back at the end of the day.

The sand was silvery white, very pretty, with rows and rows of blue/white loungers and parasols surrounding a huge clear pool with palms and rocks. A rocky tunnel and waterfall was on the right of the pool, with low rocks to the left. Lifeguards were everywhere. We were shown a locker and given a key, and went and changed into our costumes in the changing rooms.

Leaving my towels draped over a sun lounger near the water's edge, I waded in and tried the snorkel and mask, but found it very difficult to get them comfortably over my glasses. When I did try to swim with my face down, water trickled in, making me panic. As I find it very difficult to breathe through my mouth, normally breathing through my nose, using the snorkel was uncomfortable, so I finally give up all together and just swam normally. The jacket was brilliant and I found that I could float effortlessly everywhere. Great, as I'm not very good at swimming! Back out of the water, lying on the lounger, I watched lots of other people arriving.

It got very hot, the sun burning the sand and making it very uncomfortable on the soles of my feet when we went to watch and film the dolphins in the next bay. There were about five or six groups, each with a trainer and dolphin. At the end of the session, the dolphins were sent out to deeper water and did some spectacular jumps, which Andy caught on tape. He had to leave his case beside a lifeguard when it was our time to go, as he didn't have time to take it back to our locker.

We sat under a thatched, open sided hut while a trainer showed us a short video, then gave a chat about what we could expect. We were then split into groups and taken down to the water that was very salty and cold, and we had to crouch down in the water until we reached the deeper part. Here we met Marius, the dolphin, who was a blue grey colour, had very small piercing eyes, tiny little round teeth, and a big tongue (like ours only larger.)

Andy and I were the first to be taken out to deeper water by the trainer who asked me if I could swim. I told her, "not very well." She and Andy kept trying to get me to push my feet down into the water, but I just couldn't get the hang of it, bobbing around in my jacket all over the place, and I ended up holding onto her shoulder. How on earth do they make it look so easy?

She whistled for the dolphin that glided gracefully in front of us then turned over for us to stroke his tummy. He felt like a hard, wet rubber ball, but not unpleasant. I was shown how to hold onto his dorsal fin while he towed me into shallower water. I'd been really looking forward to this, it looked easy and fun, but I found that I was turning onto my side instead of staying face down. But I hung on. Letting go by the group, I was asked to crouch low down in the water again, but I had difficulty in getting my balance as the water tried to buoy me up. Then Andy was towed in.

Everyone had a turn at that before we had a chance to throw a ring for Marius to 'fetch.' Andy didn't throw it very far, making the trainer laugh as everybody else had thrown it a long way. We weren't allowed to take the ring until Marius let go, and then only very gently so as not to hurt his mouth.

Near the end of our session, one at a time we held our hands out, while Marius put his chin on them and we had to kiss his bottom lip. Then he swam slowly in front of us, waving goodbye with one flipper, finally swimming out to deeper water and doing some wonderful leaps and jumps.

I didn't realise it at the time, but still photos were being taken, plus a video of everyone. We came out of the water and were led to another thatched hut where, on computer monitors, we chose the photos we wanted. $99.95 got five big photos and two key rings. The pictures were brilliant, I hadn't realised how excited I'd looked. Andy also bought a copy of the video, edited with us in it but one that could be used in England, and gave the story of the dolphins and Discovery Cove,.

The rest of the day we spent either swimming, eating or lazing on the loungers. It was bliss. As usual I couldn't sit still for long, just about getting settled when I was up doing something else again. Andy swam through the tunnel in the rock, following the river round the back. When he returned he said that there were pools with bat rays and beautifully coloured fish you could swim with, so I swam across the big pool and went over to have a look. This again was seawater, and very cold. The little blue / black rays were awesome, gliding gently through the water in large shoals and brushing past my legs. The fish were the most brilliant golds and blues.

We went to get some drinks, but my lemonade turned out to be very strong and I had to keep watering it down with mineral water. A complimentary meal had been included in the ticket, and I chose a chicken salad. I can't understand why Americans are so fat, everywhere I went there was plenty of salads to choose from. I laughed when, several times during the afternoon, a small plane flew overhead towing a banner advertising a phone company, with a picture of B.A. from the A-Team and reading: 'Phone Home, Fool!'

During the afternoon, while we sat relaxing, big clouds started gathering on the horizon, looking very thundery, although they didn't seem to get any closer, and lots of buzzards were riding the thermals as a warm breeze sprang up.

I got two coloured polystyrene sticks from a nearby bin and floated through the tunnel and round to the back where Andy said he'd gone, finding the bird area he'd mentioned, netted above the water. The river went under a waterfall and lots of children had gathered to play underneath, laughing and splashing around.

I got out at some steps, walked across the sand to the big pool and swam back over where Andy decided to go and change realising how much closer and darker the clouds were getting and the wind picking up. I wondered if we were in for a storm. He eventually came back saying that as the men's room had been full, it had taken him ages to get a shower. I found the same in the women's.

We picked up our pictures and video from the booth, gave back the mask and towels, and walked back to the car. After we pushed the button to put the top down, I drove. Wow, what acceleration! Lots of traffic again, but they do let me change lanes fairly easily to reach the junctions I wanted. How much easier than driving back home.

We got slightly lost, doing a big circuit round the roads until we found out where we were, when Andy decided to go to all the cheap shops on The Drive, for T-shirts. I began my hunt for fridge magnets, and also found an amusing plastic notice for Kristin, at Bullockstone Farm, to put up in the stable yard. It began getting dark at 8pm with all the lights going on, but despite the time, it was still muggy, registering 92f according to the car thermometer.

I drove back to the hotel. Andy had a meal, but I wasn't hungry, although I did pick at the peppers and tomatoes that he didn't like. I was very tired, but pleased that my right foot and knee were not hurting, which they'd been doing all year since I'd had to wear Wellington boots so much in the wet weather. Perhaps using trainers was helping.

I went to bed after a shower, spotting in the mirror that my skin had turned red above where my costume had been from the hot sun, despite using the suntan cream.

I had a very restless night again, most peculiar, as I'm usually very relaxed in America.

Chapter 14

Sea World.

Sunday 26th August.

I was up at 5am again and went downstairs to buy a coffee. Taking it back to my room, I sat on the bed writing up my notes before I rang Andy at 7.30am and when he knocked on the door, we went down for breakfast, another cooked buffet. This time I made myself have less food!

Setting off for Sea World, almost immediately we ran into a traffic jam for several miles, but finally reached the signs for Sea World, turning into a huge car park (gosh, will we find the car again,) even though we parked very near the front. As we parked up and shut the roof down, I heard a loud clang as a people carrier knocked over a mobile metal sign.

We were allowed in by showing the identity cards from Discovery Cove, and headed round a small lake with a lighthouse in the middle, a lovely bright painted sailing ship on the sparkling water and model sea lions on the rocks. Pretty shops, everything again clean and bright, like the Cove. Using a map we'd got from the front booth, we passed the pink flamingos, stalking about with a disdainful air on their long spindly legs, coming to a large concrete bowl with huge sea turtles. Then on to a large pool with a beach, and dolphins, and would be giving shows over the course of the day. Walking on, we came across a dark concrete tunnel that led down to thick glass looking out into the water with the dolphins swimming past. I took photos of them cruising by, through the glass. Hope the pictures come out. (One turned out to be very comical for a small boy had run up to the glass, with his hands above his head and fingers outstretched, just as I'd taken the picture. Showing up black against the creamy blue of the water he looked like something out of E.T.)

Further on were the manatees, large pink-grey, whale shaped mammals with flippers and tails like paddles. They were just wallowing gently at the side of their pool, and were much bigger than I'd expected. Being so slow moving it was no wonder they got injured, sometimes even killed, by speeding boats. White wormy things lay at the bottom of the pool looking like dead fish, until I realised it was the roots of the trees coming through the mud. We carried on a short way until we found ourselves inside a small cinema, where a video was explaining all about them.

We walked on under the water splash ride, avoiding the drips, coming to a corkscrew like frame for the Kraken Ride, a looping roller coaster. Andy's eyes lit up and he went on it (he's nuts), while I used the camcorder to film the carriages hoping he'd show up on one of them. He came off grinning, saying it was really brilliant and the best he'd ever been on.

We wandered round to a building that housed the penguins. These were behind glass in an Arctic environment (-1C) with a few seagulls and guillimots as well. Shaved ice came from three points in the ceiling, falling like snow, making me feel shivery, and I was glad to get back out where it was getting quite hot and muggy.

We came across a large rocky pool with sea lions and beautiful white egrets, and I could hear seals barking from quite a way off, due to a little shop selling fish for people to toss to them. One poor seal had only one eye. Further round, a big sea lion was lying in the water with his flippers in the air. I realised it was hot in the sun and this was his way of cooling off! A sign stated that most of the seals here had been hurt in some way, but that a few would be released back into the wild when they were fit enough.

Further on a show was just starting, The Clyde and Seymour Pirate Show, with two trained seals, an otter and, at the end, a huge walrus. It was a play, extremely comical, and really brilliant with the sea lions 'hamming it up.' The little otter had a treasure map tied round its neck and kept running across the stage and down into tunnels. When it finished, we joined a queue of people going into a low building with a glass tunnel and along it a moving walkway. Around and above us were fish, all shapes and sizes, and sharks, including swordfish, hammerheads and nurse sharks, with tuna and a moray eel.

We stopped for a drink at one of the many cafés, sitting on wooden benches beside a huge lake, thank goodness for the cooling shade of the parasols, on which was a water-skiing show, given several times during the day. Large scraggy black birds strutted about looking for food with small British like sparrows, and some that looked like our starlings. Even some beautiful white Ibis were walking around. Kids behind us were throwing most of their chips onto the boards for the birds, and it was rather sad to see these lovely birds scrounging for unnatural fatty foods.

We carried on round the paths ending up at the gorgeous open plan stables with the Budweiser Clydesdale horses. As we came back out, an eight-hitch of them came in, their metal and brass gleaming, the black leather shining. The horses were huge and very impressive, but no one was allowed to pat them.

We reached the big stadium to watch Shamu, the killer whale, climbing halfway up the stands to get a good view. Between the big pool in front and the eight or nine black and white killer whales in the holding pens behind, was a big screen. On it, they were asking questions about the whales, followed by the answers. Then the cameras began panning round the crowd. Suddenly, I spotted Andy and nudged him, pointing to the screen, and he grinned sheepishly. Then I saw myself as it panned back, so I waved, as did most people.

One of the black diving suited trainers came out in front of the screen and started off with a chat about killer whales, before four of them came in, racing round the pool and jumping out of the water gracefully together. The large screen not only showed the whales out of the water, but also what was happening under. Two whales came in after them, their trainers riding first on their backs, then on their stomachs as they swam upside down. Finally, they all dived under the water, the whales leaping straight out with the trainers standing on their noses. Wow! The trainers were also tossed out of the water and onto the side, landing gracefully on their feet, turning to throw handfuls of fish into the big yawning mouths. One trainer was pushed out of the water and slid along the wet concrete on his stomach, closely followed by the whale, which then slid back in.

At the very end, they brought in the biggest whale, after warning that anyone who did not want to get wet, would be better getting out of the splash zone, shown by several rows of seats having blue lines painted along them. Some people did scuttle for safety. The water thrown over the edge of the tank from the enormous tail was tremendous, and she went the entire length round the edge of the pool, almost drowning the nearest people. Everyone was screaming with laughter—but I bet the water was cold. Fantastic show.

We went for a meal, eating outside at tables. I had my usual Caesar salad, and a coffee. I persuaded Andy to go and see the Pirate Show again so that he could film it, but due to the amount of people going in this time, we were forced quite high up the ranks of seats and there was a pillar in the way. I hoped that it didn't spoil the fun when I watched it back home.

There were very long queues to see the polar bears in the Arctic. You could either walk or take a helicopter. I couldn't believe the latter as no helicopters were flying, where was it? Panicky, not wanting to get in one, I said I'd walk, but Andy insisted it wasn't a real one. After about twenty minutes of shuffling along in the queue, we got through the doors and went inside, where we were directed to a flight area. Gratefully, I spotted a sign saying, 'no one should go if they have a neck or back problem.' I told the member of staff of my damaged neck and he directed me down a long corridor to reach the walking party.

Everything was under soft lighting with painted ceilings of blue sky and clouds. I came to some walrus first, gosh they're huge, but one seemed to do nothing but endlessly circle, first on his back towards the glass, then the right way up back to the rocks, then over and back again. I was afraid that he was very stressed.

The lovely, creamy white polar bears were doing an endless, repetitive pacing along one wall, past the glass where we stood to view them, turning and heading back, over and over, obviously very disturbed. I found it very sad. After them were the white Beluga whales, looking like ghosts in the dark water. Andy joined me near the end. It turned out that the helicopter had been a swaying deck, which had finally 'crash landed' in the snowy wastes. It probably wouldn't have done my neck a lot of good.

We walked round the outside lake towards a big blue tower with a circular glass observation platform and a corkscrew ring from top to bottom. As I watched it coming slowly down, I saw the reason for the rings, the platform revolved as it came down. Several people were waiting in front of us, and with some joining on behind, we went in and sat down, facing outward, looking through the glass. We were taken very smoothly in circles up to the top where it revolved twice before coming back down again. I didn't like the height at all but the view was spectacular over the whole of Sea World, the car parks, and outward to the horizon.

After looking round some of the shops, we headed back to the exit, passing a stall where two men were drawing caricatures, either in black and white, or coloured, just a head, or head and body. On a whim I stopped. I could have a choice of body! Oh dear, what? Finally I just said, wistfully, "can you bring back my youth?" The young lad suggested, with a grin, a bikini.

"OK." Andy had also decided to sit and have his done.

I noticed several people passing by either smiling, or doing a 'double take.' What's he doing? Then Andy came for a look and laughed. When I saw it, well, I was stunned, he'd got my face to a 'T' and the bikini clad young body was brilliant. I couldn't thank him enough after I stopped giggling. Andy's was also great. He'd chosen a shorts clad runner. Brilliant, how do they do it. They were rolled up for us and put them into cardboard tubes to protect them while we were travelling.

We made our way back to the car that was red-hot inside. Thank goodness the top came down. I drove once the breeze had made it cooler inside, going back down International Drive and stopping at a camera shop Andy had seen advertised in one of the Orlando brochures. He examined several models, nearly buying a £1,000 tiny, digital video camera, but, despite the shopkeeper's persistence, he said he'd have to think about it and come back as it was a lot of money, although he did want a new one.

It was now 7pm and still the temperature was 93f 31C. We decided to get a coffee at the hotel restaurant, but then Andy changed his mind and we went round the cheap market shops again, finally stopping for coffee at Dunkin' Donuts. It was too hot to drink it there, so we took it back to the hotel and sat in the dark by the pool side, watching two searchlights, one revolving round and round (possibly from Universal Studios?) I wondered how the aircraft got on with them.

We returned to the restaurant where I tried a very large Fahita with chicken, a salad, and two dips, one sour cream. It was delicious. Returning to my bedroom, I sat watching TV and writing up my notes, before showering and going to bed. After all the walking round Sea World and the shops, my right knee had begun to hurt, and I was very tired. It was also very warm in the room, 91f despite the a/c, so I slept without anything over me again.

Again I had a very restless night, tossing and turning.

Chapter 15

Space—The final Frontier.

Monday 27th August.

I sat and rewrote my notes as I remembered things I'd forgotten the night before, killing a tiny little ant on the cupboard top when it caught my eye with its movement. Andy had asked yesterday if I'd seen any. I rang his room at 8am before meeting for breakfast. Lovely, another fried meal.

We then set out in the car to go to the Kennedy Space Centre, taking the SR 528 and passing Boggy Creek Road. What wonderful names over here. At the first tollbooth, Andy missed the automatic bucket with a .25c piece that rolled under the car, and had to throw another in. At the next toll booth, it misread the total of coins we threw in, insisting we were .24c short, necessitating another .25c to complete the charge. At the third toll, I told Andy to pay the lady at the check-in the $1.25 instead of using the automatic.

The drive went through tall pines, palms, bushes, some covered in creepers, and the occasional grassy meadows. With the top down I could even hear the cicadas in the trees. The roads were very straight and looked like a scene from Miami Vice. We passed a creek, unfortunately I missed the name and couldn't find it on the map, after which the land became rather swampy. We were followed for some time by a big truck until very close to the Centre, when he turned off. Here, we found ourselves at a large expanse of water, either the sea or a large river mouth, with twin towers on the horizon, launch pads? Then we passed a space shuttle/rocket mounted at the side of the road.

We were halted for a while in a line of traffic by a bridge that was opening for a tall masted ship to sail through. After the bridge, a creek ran beside the road, and I watched out for alligators, actually seeing one floating in the centre looking just like a big dead tree trunk. There were numbers of white herons by the water and buzzards lazily circled overhead.

Finally we turned towards the Centre, heading down a long twisting road to the large car lot. Andy had bought the tickets through the Internet, so we were allowed straight through the entrance and into the main building. Out the other side, we wandered towards a wooden fenced off area that had several rockets standing on their tail fins and one lying on its side. This was the Rocket Garden. According to the information on the label on the wooden boards, they were in the process of renewing it and eventually, each rocket would stand on a launch pad of its own with paths between. We strolled through several other buildings showing the early to present day space exploration before reaching two IMAX cinemas.

At the first, we were given 3D glasses for what turned out to be a story of the future, based in a space station. The second film consisted of actual views taken by the astronauts from space and was fascinating, despite my views on spending the money down here on earth first, and what about polluting the air. Later that day, Andy explained that the fuels they used were natural gases and water, although we do manufacture one of the gases in enough quantities to use for the rockets. Several times, in both cinemas, the sound was so loud that I had to put my fingers in my ears. Why do they do that? I can't even go to a cinema at home for the same reason.

From there, we walked across to what I thought was a black tiled backdrop for a rocket launch pad, but which turned out to be a memorial with some panels relating to people who had died during the space programme. This included the names of the seven who were in the rocket that blew up during take-off, including a woman.

We then entered a white round cylinder building, apparently being prepared for the first Mars expeditions, and that would be taken to some rugged terrain later in the month for everyone to practice in. I'd seen a programme about this somewhere on either the Sky Discovery channel or National Geographic.

We walked around and inside a white and black shuttle mock-up, photographing each other outside it. It was very hot walking round in the sun, and I was glad to eventually get to a cool restaurant for a drink. This was half circular and made of ground to ceiling tinted glass windows making it very light and airy, and had metallic tables and chairs to sit at. In the middle was a large revolving stand with food and drinks. I just took a container of refreshing sliced fruit and a coffee.

We climbed into a shuttle bus that took us to LC39, an observation gallery, passing a very long, wide, sandy road with two enormous flat crawlers. Apparently, the rocket is placed on one of these crawlers, and at only one mile an hour, transported to the gantry-which can take all day! We climbed the stairs to the top where we could see at least four gantries on the horizon. The one closest was the one most recently used.

Once back down, we went along to watch a video showing the earliest astronauts and the Space Race, then took another bus to the Apollo LC39B for another video. On the way, the driver told us that a lot of the wildlife, believe it or not, lived round the base. Coyotes, alligators, and manatees, which the men fed with lettuce, but weren't supposed to, all were apparently unconcerned by the noise of the rockets going up or all the work being done around there.

We queued up outside huge metal doors for ten minutes before being allowed in, standing on tiered steps around a stage. On either side they had all the old control panels from the first space flights. While they played a launch on a small video screen, the control panels gradually lit up realistically, as it would have done, finally ceasing at the final countdown. From here we were allowed to wander round the huge buildings, seeing the original Saturn 5 space shuttle suspended from the hanger roof, This was unbelievably enormous, going the full length of the building.

From there we took another shuttle coach to the International Space Station Centre where parts are already being put together for an international space station. I was very curious because years ago, having got so stressed over killings and muggings in the papers, the cheating, manipulating and adultery going on in the Government, the EEC which was taking Britain over and all the wars, that I had refused to read newspapers or watch TV news. So that I had absolutely no idea that anything like this was being done and Andy was astounded that I'd never even heard about it. The area was sealed off, except for a couple of windows where we could look down to a couple of men standing discussing something off to one side.

Further on, we stood to watch the last video screen. They dimmed the lights. A model of the spacecraft dropped on the moon's surface beside a spaceman holding a USA flag.

Finally we boarded another shuttle back to the Visitor Complex where we bought a few presents. I fancied an icecream, and we had one each as we headed back for the car.

I drove from there, having fun putting the electric roof down first, how I'll miss that. On the way, we passed two separate police cars pulling people in to the side of the road. I got slightly lost trying to get back to International Drive as we thought we were in Universal Drive.

Back at the hotel restaurant for coffee, I discovered that the nice waitress, who usually served us, had lost her voice. The waiter who came to us explained that she'd had a sore throat for a couple of days and had refused to see the doctor until that day. She wasn't supposed to speak, but had to rest her throat, so every time she came near us, I put my finger to my lips, then whispered to her, making her giggle.

We went back outside to where the temperature was still in the high eighties, looking for T-shirts for Andy again. Considering they were just for working in, he was quite choosy. I found several presents to take home for friends. Surprisingly, most of the shops here seem to be run by Asians. By now, after all the walking, my knee was swollen and very painful, but to my surprise, my foot hardly hurt at all. Must be the trainers helping.

Back at the restaurant I had a mashed chicken salad and that was very tasty. Andy decided to try the alligator tail nuggets, asking the waiter what they tasted like.

"They're quite strong tasting."

Despite this, Andy decided to have some, but thought that they weren't that strong, just tasted slightly of fish and were chewy.

Back in my room, I sat and wrote my notes for the day, remembering how nice it was to treat, and be treated by, coloured people, as if we were all the same, laughing and chatting normally. So different from England where I felt uncomfortable in the presence of most. And everyone here calls you 'sir' or 'ma'am,' asks, 'how're you doing,' or wishes you, 'have a nice day.' They're very laid back.

I had a very restless night again. I can't understand it, very unusual for me. Tuesday 28th August.

I was up at 5am again, feeling refreshed despite being having slept badly. While packing my suitcase and bag, I collected my usual soap and the plastic shampoo and conditioner bottles, keeping them for souvenirs as they had the name of the hotel printed on them. I also packed the half empty bottles to use later as otherwise they get taken away and replaced with new, which seemed an awful waste.

It began to get light about 6.45am, with a light mist and I sat writing extra notes as things occurred to me, before showering, waking Andy at 7.30am.

I only had a coffee for breakfast as I was still feeling full from last night's late meal, and we booked out of the hotel at 8.30am. Andy drove after putting the roof down.

We got stuck in traffic, the worst we've ever encountered in America, crawling along until it became less crowded. Again we managed to get lost, ending up going completely round the edge of Orlando, despite the map. Weird! We followed the signs, turned where we should, but ended up almost anywhere but where we wanted to be. Finally, we found the I-14 from Hwy 582 heading for Jacksonville. I was glad to leave Orlando, too touristy.

It was lovely with the roof of the car down although after half an hour my head felt numb from the constant tugging by the wind. We joined the I-95, stopping off to see Daytona Beach, which lay at the end of a very rough, bumpy road. We parked in a side street rather than pay to go onto the flat, white sandy beach, especially as we weren't staying for long. The temperature was registering 92f 33C.

The sea was a long, long way away across the flat sand. Along the edge of the beach were cream and white coloured blocks of flats with the occasional skyscraper, disappearing down into the misty horizon. Cars were already parking on the sand, and there were sand buggies for hire. We went into a tiny shop crammed full of dresses, tops, shorts and bikinis, and I bought a nice sleeveless top to go with my jean shorts.

I took over driving, going on down Tomaka Road back to the I-95, and passing a dead armadillo, the first I'd ever seen, dead or alive. Mostly the land was flat with palms, pines, a few lakes, and the occasional meadow, with evidence of past fires in the burnt tree trunks. The usual billboards advertised almost everything, but we came upon quite a few in yellows and reds, for 'pistachios, fruits etc. ahead.' After a long time, we passed a village of bright shacks selling the fruits and nuts. Along the side of one building was written, 'Adult Toys, Erotica Café, great food,' which seemed a trifle odd. A café and adult toys-eat and play at the same time?

I spotted a bald eagle's nest on the top of a dead tree a thick mass of twigs in the branches, and then passed another dead armadillo at the side of the road. We turned off the Interstate for food and had a choice between Macdonald's, The Waffle House, Sonny's BBQ and Wendy's, choosing the latter. Inside, about eight army people were seated there, one a girl. She was the only one who didn't clear her table when they left. Two policemen were sitting near the back looking relaxed, as if they'd only come in for a coffee and a chat.

We got lost trying to find the airport to return the car, what a surprise, but managed to find it eventually, stopping for directions at one point. I had to really speed round cars to get out at an exit, as there were a lot of cars travelling faster than I thought. Good, no cops! But wow, what a fast car. I found the Alamo Rental and gave them the Sebring back, very reluctantly. They ordered a cab for us, a people carrier, to take us to the Amtrak train. The driver was nice, very chatty. He'd actually come to live here from Tucson and loved it. *Well, there's no accounting for taste,* I thought.

Once at the station, Andy went to get the tickets we'd ordered through the Internet. Unfortunately, we had a two and a half hour wait for the train, but there was a coffee machine and one selling snacks. Quite a lot of people were already waiting. A young girl came in and sat on a seat. She had tatty, flyaway 'Rastapharian' locks, and wore a long brown flowing skirt and top, looking extremely grubby. Going out to the restroom I discovered three women sorting out their suitcases on the floor.

Back in the waiting area, Andy suddenly asked me, "where's your jacket?"

Oh no, my nice denim jacket with the metal badges, I must have left it in the cab. No, he'd surely have come back. Suddenly, I remembered putting it on the seat outside the station while we got the suitcases out, and thankfully, it was still there.

Santa Fe 1999

The Grand Canyon

Standing in front of the Blazer rental car at the Grand Canyon

Little Big Horn Mountains

Rainbow Bridge, Arizona

Patio at Southfork Ranch, Dallas

Andy, San Francisco

Alcatraz

John Wayne Point, Monument Valley

Riding in Wyoming

Custer's Last Stand 2001

Buffalo Bill Museum in Cody, Wyoming

Dolly Parton Star

Andy and a Petrified Tree Trunk

Devil's Golf Course, Death Valley

Chapter 16

New Orleans.

The big silver train was half an hour late coming up from Miami, finally pulling into the station to my delight. I loved these huge silver trains. We had to haul our suitcases up the narrow, twisty stairs to our sleeping compartments, but luckily for me, Andy helped. Gosh, it's only the fourth day and already my case was getting heavier. The rooms we'd booked were bigger than the ones we'd had last year on the Superliner Standard, being the bigger Superliner Deluxe. It had a long seat down the right, a small chair to the left by the window, and a vanity unit with radio and shaver outlets, just inside the left door. Behind it was a toilet/shower unit. There were soaps and towels in cupboards under the sink, a box of tissues on the top, and even paper cups, and plenty of room to stand my suitcase on end. Andy had the same next door, only in reverse. The train whistled, lovely, to hear that again, and we began to move off.

Warren, the steward, came to introduce himself, and to tell me that if there were any problems to call him. He offered to, "open the connecting door to your husband's room."

"No thanks, we're just travelling companions, not that friendly."

"OK," he said, wishing me a nice trip.

The train started off through awful concrete buildings, building works, roads and streets. It seemed to me to be heading the wrong way, but gradually it began to turn a half circle until the sun was in the opposite direction and shining into my eyes. I began to change my mind about the lovely train whistle after hearing it for the thousandth time! It never seemed to stop. The driver must have had a very sore arm, and been deaf.

We began to head out into the countryside, passing through timber and swampland, and crossing a river. After an hour or so, we stopped at Lake City where, over the tannoy, it was announced that the next stop would be Tallahassee, as in the country & western song, The Tallahassee Bridge.

At dinnertime, we went along to the dining car where I chose a small salad, followed by lasagne with broad beans, carrots and cauliflower, then a strawberry sundae and coffee, all included in the ticket. Delicious. During this, the tannoy reminded us to put our clocks back by one hour to Central Time for the morning. While we were eating, Warren had made the beds up. I had had the bottom bed made up for me, but Andy decided to sleep up top in his compartment. Seemed a long way up to me, and he regretted it by the morning. We stopped for a while at Tallahassee—'ciggy time for the desperate,' or what I call 'polluting the atmosphere' to the girls back at the office. It had been raining for the station platform was quite wet.

I think Amtrak was the first to invent the roller coaster. Try cleaning your teeth and washing while on the move. I managed by jamming my knees against the cupboards! It hadn't been like this last year, but I found out later that it was because this was new rolling stock and the springs weren't so firm, so making the coaches rock badly. Mind you, I slept well.

Friday 29th August.

I woke in darkness at 4.45am, the train having passed through Pensacola and into Alabama during the night, to see lots of orange lights blazing from what appeared to be a huge oil refinery. I decided to get dressed, and went to get a coffee from the end of the corridor, then sitting and reading for a while. The train slowed for a station, stopping for twenty minutes, but I couldn't see a name board, unlike back home, so I had no idea where we were.

We passed through back streets with trash and discarded shopping trolleys, then alongside pretty bungalow chalets scattered every so often. We crossed a huge river with boathouses on the banks and slightly boring looking, posh houses with swimming pools. Trash was thrown in the woods by the tracks, and how or why they managed to drive out there, I couldn't guess. The train crossed another huge river with sandy beaches and houses built on stilts, and trees began appearing draped with vines or ivy, swampland with occasional bungalows, all alternating with stretches of river, and roads. It was amazing how they'd got the railway tracks over so much water. Another river crossing, and then came the sunrise: first a glowing orange, then a beautiful pink with black clouds rimmed menacingly with red. It had been raining.

We were called to the buffet car for breakfast and sat chatting with a lovely couple, Linda and Sam. They were interested in where we were going as they'd been to New Orleans, telling us about the sights and the streets, and also recommending a restaurant they particularly liked, and we ended up swapping e-mail addresses. I was still fascinated by how quickly and easily people could keep in touch over such vast areas. Fantastic invention.

Yet another river, then a narrow strip of water between the sea and Mobile Bay, and we were crossing into Louisiana. Here were more swamps, and then we started passing flyovers with burnt out cars under them, just like home, and concrete buildings. New Orleans. We said goodbye and thanks to Warren, then to our serving lady, giving both of them tips. She was sitting in the dining car along with other buffet staff, and another coloured waiter sitting with them told me how he loved my accent.

The train slowly edged its way past a huge cemetery with large white marble mausoleums, built above ground because New Orleans was actually below sea level on reclaimed land. The train slowly pulled into a cleaner, nicer area, and stopped. Suddenly, it began backing up quite a way, finally stopping at the station where it was hot and muggy outside.

We phoned the hotel, the Best Western Downtown, for their shuttle to pick us up. While we were waiting in the huge station building, Andy discovered that his bag, with the camcorder in, was very, very wet. At first he thought he'd put it down in a puddle, but then discovered that a drinks can had broken, and he had to tip all the liquid out. Luckily, the camera and camcorder were on top of other things and escaped a drenching.

The driver of the shuttle was very nice, telling us about the weather, that was warm and wet, and about any tours we could pick up from the hotel, if we wanted. At reception, a lovely girl booked us in and then spent a while phoning round to try and get us onto a regular tour. Unfortunately, the river tour on a paddle steamer was already full, but she finally found a coach tour we could get to in time. We took the lift to our rooms on the second floor, and I immediately spotted a coffee maker in the room (a great hotel!) From the window I could see across the road quite a few signs outside the grey, concrete buildings, for bail bonds. Is New Orleans very unlawful? Back downstairs, the shuttle driver took us down to the river front for the pick-up point.

The tour driver was very nice, and quite a laugh, telling us the history of New Orleans. The green trees and grass made the place look just like Britain, but New Orleans was not quite what I expected, whatever that was. Mostly it looked quite tatty with very rough roads, but had some quaint old buildings and houses, and the trees covered in Spanish moss, which looked like our Old Man's Beard gone mad. There were canals, levies with huge thick steel floodgates, and several cemeteries, one of which we were allowed to walk round. There were huge white marble tombs, some very ornate with doors or metal gates. A very thick wall ran round the outskirts with plaques where caskets were interred.

The coach stopped at a café for us all to get a coffee, and quite a few of us sat outside to drink it. I also bought a large pretzel, the first I'd ever had, finding it a bit dry. The driver hooted for us to get back to the coach, then drove on, passing through a beautiful park, and down avenues of lovely old wooden houses with pretty gardens, the balconies hung with flowering baskets.

During the tour I'd noticed that the driver had been in touch with base on his CB, and realised he was having some sort of trouble with the bus. He pulled in to the side of the road and told us that he had a problem and we would be picked up by another bus, although he would continue to drive. When it arrived, we got in to find the seats were very tatty and quite uncomfortable.

Back where we'd started, Andy and I walked along the street where the buildings were of old concrete, heading for an open flea market. On the way we stopped for a coffee and Andy ordered some small French doughnuts. When they came they were covered in heaps of white icing sugar. Bit sickly after just two.

We wandered through the open sided market building, Andy looking for more T-shirts, me looking at the lovely jewellery. There were many stalls all selling Mardi Gras masks and outfits, some very ornate, some with lots of feathers. I loved a plain two-piece suit in knitted white cotton, but reluctantly decided that white was not a good idea. There were strange foods, some fresh, some tinned, clothes, and stuff that was just like at a British boot fair.

While under cover, we began to hear thunder outside, and as we wandered out into the street, this turned into a heavy storm. We quickly dived into a couple of souvenir shops out of the way. It became a lot cooler with the rain, which began to slow to a fine drizzle. We walked into a camera shop where I came close to buying a video camera, but again it might not have worked back home. I was very disappointed, I was dying to have my own to use.

We crossed over the road to the riverfront to see the mighty Mississippi River, which was huge, about twice the size of the Thames, before sitting outside a restaurant watching the ferries going back and forth. I decided to order a salad, and had a Coors light beer as a change from coffee with it. Afterwards, we tried to book a river cruise for the following day, but as we would be leaving in the afternoon and the boats did not return till after that, we couldn't. We walked back to the shops where I bought a couple of Louis L-Amour cowboy books to read.

On the way back, a coloured man stopped Andy, trying to sell a cleaner for white trainers, and quickly wiping them over before he could be stopped. He then demanded money by insisting they'd 'struck a deal.' I found him very intimidating and we had trouble trying to get away from him. Obviously he'd spotted us as tourists.

We had taken a map from the hotel that showed where the shuttle would pick us up, and the times, and went to stand outside a posh casino with a lovely pond in front, with alternating waterspouts. A loudspeaker was informing people of the next prizes to be won. We sat on the wall, and it got darker and later. Despite keeping a good eye out, we never saw the bus at all and I wondered if we were at the right place. I was tired, and my knee was hurting from all the walking.

Finally, Andy hailed a cab to take us back. I asked at the front desk about it and apparently, the driver called at the entrance to a hotel right across the way, though we never saw it passing. We changed and went for a swim in the pool, then went and sat in the bubbling hot tub. It was relaxing and restful, though according to the notice on the wall, you shouldn't do it longer than about fifteen to twenty minutes at a time.

Back in my room, I made myself a coffee, the packets contained enough for two people so I had enough for the morning, and sat watching TV, writing up my notes before showering and going to bed.

It was a cooler night and I actually had the sheet and a very thin blanket over me.

Thursday 30th August.

I woke at 5.30am to rain and thunder, reading for a while, before phoning through to Andy at 7am. We had breakfast in a tiny room on the third floor, DIY toast or cereal, and coffee, although this time we could take it back to our rooms if we wanted. I returned to my room and repacked my suitcase somewhat neater, ready to leave later at 12pm. By the time we went out, the rain had stopped.

The shuttle took us to the French Quarter, about two streets away from where we were the day before. Lined up by the side of the road were some mules and lovely carriages, but at $50, too expensive (New York last year had been cheaper.) We set off down Bourbon Street, which is like our Soho, and which I hadn't fancied after watching the awful man who plays Lily Savage on TV at home who had shown the seamy side. The first few shops had clothes and things that were very suggestive, so I insisted on going across to Royal Street. There the buildings were large, wooden and very pretty, with latticed metalwork verandas covered in beautiful hanging baskets and pots, all full of colourful blooms, and were mostly pubs or bars. The verandas overhung the sidewalks, supported by ornate metal poles. There were also a lot of very expensive antique shops. Occasionally there were houses that were very run down and neglected, but so were the streets and sidewalks. It gave the impression that they weren't worth the upkeep in case the sea came rushing in again.

We stopped at what we thought was a coffee shop, but turned out to be a restaurant, so the girl there directed us round the corner to a quaint old café. There they had lots of the most amazing, fattening cakes and I couldn't resist a delicious creamy almond cake with chocolate on top.

We walked around to the back of Jackson Street, coming to a small square shaped park of shady trees surrounded by metal railings, and a very ornate church to our left. Buskers of all types, pavement artists, tarot card and 'bones' readers' had tables set up.

But the best of all was a coloured singer, playing a trombone, singing jazz songs and accompanied by another man playing a guitar. They were brilliant. We listened for a while before strolling inside the church. It had a wonderfully painted ceiling, huge chandeliers, and rows and rows of candles, some of which were lit. I guessed that this was a Catholic Church.

Coming back out, Andy filmed the musicians for a while, and I went and gave them a tip. It was very hot and humid now, the air almost unbreathable, very like Orlando.

Going down to the river front, where old trams were going up and down the rails, a lady stopped us on the pavement, giving away baseball caps and a Hari Krishna vegetarian cook book. We tried to get away from her, being wary after what had happened last evening, but it turned out she was collecting for a charity for the elderly. She asked if we were husband and wife.

"No, just travelling companions." Andy gave her some money and accepted the small cookbook and a cap.

We climbed into a tram and went to the end of the line beside a big shopping mall. Mardi Gras masks and costumes were everywhere. Andy dived into a toyshop as he had spotted some great kites finally deciding on one like a biplane while I was fascinated by the little mobile toy animals held on strings, one little toy dog turning somersaults.

Suddenly, we realised it was close to 11.30, so we hurried out, looking for a cab, but spent ages waiting for one to pass. Finally Andy managed to hail one, and we arrived at the hotel only five minutes after 12pm. We quickly grabbed our bags and went down to pay the bill. While Andy sorted it out, I spotted a rack of postcards and bought twenty to send home. Again this year I'd taken labels with me with the addresses ready printed on them.

The shuttle took us to the Amtrak station, where we booked in the cases, then went for a coffee until it was time to go. Too late, I realised that my swimming costume had been left somewhere in my room. I'd checked everywhere before we'd left, but it must have been moved by the cleaner while we were out. I was cross as I'd only just bought it before I left home.

Eventually the call came for our train by the conductor at the gate, and we joined the queue, struggling with our cases along to the tenth carriage, where they went in at the bottom of the coach, as this time we would be leaving the same day. We had already been allotted seats, and were shown up to them. The train pulled out into dull and overcast weather.

At a slow speed, we started through swampy lands with channels and islands, and the ghostly white trunks of long dead trees sticking up out of the water. Tinned roof chalets and barns lay dotted along the banks of the channels. The train tracks followed alongside a concrete flyover, some of the arches covered in creepers like the trees and telegraph poles like a spooky movie. We crept slowly through tall trees, and then out over water again, Lake Maurepas on the left, huge Lake Pontchartrain on the other, o the latter we'd been told was only about eleven to twelve foot deep despite its size. We passed more trees, grassy clearings, reeds, and swamps. A long line of huge pylons stretched out into the lake, disappearing over the horizon. Slowly the lake was hidden behind the trees as the train began to pick up speed.

We crossed a huge river, the Pearl, finding more houses and roads appearing, and quite a few trains laid up in sidings, then crossed a grey looking plain with dark grey tree trunks sticking up. Again the driver either had the hooter on auto, or would be suffering a very tired arm as it went mournfully on-and on-and on.

We stopped at Hammond City, then Amite City where it became wet and misty, becoming hillier by the time we reached McComb in Mississippi. Gradually the country became intersected by more roads, houses, junkyards and trees, while the fences and posts were all covered in green creepers making it appear very eerie.

I went down to the small buffet car to get some coffee and treated us to two apple/cinnamon pastries, carrying it all back in a small cardboard tray provided. Later on, we were given a number for our meal in the dining car.

The train stopped at Brookhaven City. Each announcement for approaching stops, or for any information, was so distorted on the tannoy on this carriage that we could hardly understand a word that was said.

We stopped again at Hazelhurst City, then went on to Jackson City, where we had over a half an hour wait. Finally, just after dark, they called us to the dining car and were joined at the table by two very pleasant and chatty ladies, one elderly, who both came from New Orleans.

Chapter 17

Gracelands-A Legend.

We passed through Winona, Grenada and Greenwood, finally pulling in to Memphis, forty minutes late and it was hot and muggy. I gave Andy the printout for the Best Western Memphis, only to discover that the address read Arkansas, not Memphis. I went cold, how on earth did I make such a mistake. There wasn't even a shuttle phone in the wooden waiting room, but we did find a rack of leaflets, one showing the hotel and it was actually just across the river in Arkansas. I felt very relieved, for it would have been very embarrassing to be so badly wrong.

The man in the reception phoned for a cab for us, which had a set rate for crossing over to the other side of the river. When the man finally arrived, he took us a long, long way out to a Best Western—the wrong one, but with Andy's help, and some directions, we finally found the right one. The ride cost us a steep $34.

There wasn't an elevator in the motel and we had to drag the cases up the stairs from reception. Not even a coffee machine in our rooms, but they were nice, the whole hotel having just been recently built. Andy decided we'd change hotels the next day to be nearer the airport, as we would be leaving very early the following day at 5am, so he phoned out and arranged to stay at Knight's.

It was very hot despite the a/c and I slept without even a sheet again. Even then I was so hot, it felt like I was sleeping on an electric blanket.
Friday 31st August.

I woke up at 6.30 and sat writing my notes. After showering, I phoned Andy at 7.30am. For some reason, I was very unsettled, worrying about my dogs, how was my friend Patrick, as he wasn't very well, was my friend Corinne coping with Cloud, how was my nephew Stephen. He had a court hearing back home (actually, it was all over by the time I woke due to the time difference.) I also wondered if my garden was alright and that hopefully, they were having lots of rain like last year to save a friend from having to water all the pots and containers.

We didn't have breakfast until 8.30am as Andy had fallen back asleep again and was late getting ready. The buffet was in a building across the parking lot where, evidently, truckers also came. $5.99 for scrambled eggs, bacon, fried potato pieces, sausages etc. Andy had waffles plus warm apple and strawberry sauce. I watched, stunned, as a fat trucker piled his plate so high he couldn't have put anything else on if he'd tried, then waddled down to a table at the end of the room. Most people didn't seem to care what they looked like, lots of Americans appeared well over weight. No wonder, when you saw the size of their meals.

Outside it had started a fine misty drizzle. We packed and phoned for a cab, waiting in the lobby while Andy got talking to the Asian man who ran the motel. It turned out that he came from Luton, Bedfordshire his parents moving here when he was six years old. He told Andy he'd like to go back and see it one day and Andy said, laughingly, "don't bother. There's not much to see."

The cab finally arrived late after Andy had phoned again to check. They told him it was just turning in, but apparently the driver had stopped for gas. We had wondered if he'd ended up at the other Best Western, like we had last night. We set out for Knights, in heavy rain. The cabbie was very chatty, said he'd love to go and see England but that he was scared of flying. I told him I'd refused to fly for years for that reason—until I'd had the chance to come to America. He also wanted to take a train and go to see New Orleans and we both told him that he should go, the scenery was lovely, and the town very pretty. We got to Knights, which was very nice, but just under the flight path for the airport! We were on the second floor, just opposite the pool, which didn't appeal much as it was raining.

We phoned for a cab to take us to Elvis' old home, Gracelands, which again took ages to arrive. At one point, the lady receptionist, who was a great laugh, waved us out thinking the cab had come. We came back in when we realised it wasn't, and I joked that we'd very nearly gone in the post van parked outside, tapping my head and saying that all we needed was a stamp. She received this with gales of laughter.

We arrived at Gracelands, heading into a very large entrance hall, Andy paying at one of a line of tills. Several large TV screens were playing Elvis' concerts and everywhere we went in the buildings, they were showing his concerts, films, or playing his music. After a while it got very boring as I had never been into Elvis, but Andy was enjoying himself. It was a bit like going into a church where you felt awed by a 'presence,' but didn't actually believe in it. There were several gift shops with everything from nice, down to really tacky.

A museum housed Elvis' cars and bikes, and we then went round into a diner. This was laid out in the fifties style with a blue and white décor. We bought coffee there later on in the day, and I was really surprised to have to squeeze between a door to the restrooms and a huge trolley full of burger buns!

Andy sent some postcards from the little post office next door including to one friend who'd wanted an official Elvis stamp on the envelope from Gracelands. I bought twenty stamps so that I could write and send mine later.

A minibus took us across the highway and up the drive to the house, passing through the famous gates. At the entrance we were given audio cassette players, so that we could listen to the commentary during our tour. We passed through the ground floor rooms, the upstairs had been private, and so were being kept that way. Everything was as Elvis had left it, including the kitchen area, with TV's everywhere. Huge rooms contained his gold, silver and platinum discs, lots of his stage outfits, and everywhere they played his music.

Outside in the grounds were two horses, a palomino and a black, and I realised from a home video that they too were copies of the horses he and Priscilla used to ride. We finally passed by his graveside, including those of his family, still surrounded by fresh flowers left over from fans commemorating his birthday. We walked round and entered his jet planes, one of them having been named Lisa Marie after his daughter. This one had gold sinks, taps, phones and even seat buckles.

Back in the entrance hall, I tried to get some money out of an ATM machine, but it refused, so I guessed it was out of order. Outside, a free shuttle was laid on to Sun Studios, where lots of musicians had started out, Elvis being one, and included one of my favourites, Roy Orbison, so we went there. The ground floor was a bar where we had a coffee. We decided to walk outside when we found that the tour upstairs had to be paid for, wanting to find Beale Street mentioned in the guidebook.

The roads were very rough and untidy, and we ended up walking round the roads in a huge square, crossing several wide streets, finally finding the shops and huge office blocks. Beale Street seemed to consist of night-clubs about to open, and I found it very intimidating and worrying with rough looking characters standing about on the pavements. There were also horses and carriages appearing, lining up alongside the sidewalk. We did a bit of browsing in a couple of the shops, then walked on and on between huge office blocks, before finally coming across a T.G.I.F. restaurant. We went in for a meal, watching the rain starting to fall outside, and having quite a long wait before our meal came.

Coming out, we walked two blocks to the trams. These went along Main Street before turning into a loop line down to, and back alongside, the Mississippi. We got off at the Amtrak station, deciding to get a cab back to the hotel, but the station appeared shut and we couldn't find a way in. I tried a door, but it was opened by a lady checking people in for a conference, so she directed us round to the side, but that door was locked, too. We walked back to the street as the daylight began to fail, walking for ages, with no sign of any cabs, or even a phone. But we did reach the trams.

We had just missed one, so we continued walking until we caught it up and climbed in. Fortunately, it had been held up by the one in front breaking down, but once that was sorted out, we got back to Beale Street. Luckily, we then saw a shuttle bus that was returning to Gracelands. It was a relief to sit down again.

The shuttle went through a very poor area before arriving back at Gracelands. It was fully dark by then, and drizzling with rain. We went back to the entrance hall where they were closing up for the night to ask where we could phone for a cab and they directed us to a phone near the jets, so we walked round and Andy called the cab company. We sat under the open metal shelter watching the traffic and waiting, but after half an hour, the cab still hadn't come, so I phoned to check. The girl at the end was very off hand, stating that they would get one to us as soon as possible, but just after I hung up, the cab arrived.

Once back at the hotel, Andy asked the receptionist if she could organise a cab for 5am the next morning and she also set up an automated wakeup call. Back in my room, I sat and wrote all my postcards, listening to the airplanes coming and going overhead. Despite being tired, I only slept till 3.50am being restless as usual, then dozing until the phone rang at 5am.

Saturday 1st September.

Going down to reception, I was hoping that the weather would be dry, but it wasn't, it was pelting with rain. I went through to a little room where the coffee machine was, getting a cup for us both. It tasted awful, and we both left it almost untouched. The cab arrived and drove us to the airport, letting us off with our luggage at the United Airlines terminal. The information from the Internet paperwork had told us to come ninety minutes before our flight, but when we got to the counter there was no one there and it wouldn't open until half an hour later.

I decided to wander off to try and find somewhere that sold coffee, and I got back, Andy was talking to a man in a wheelchair, a trucker who'd been taken very ill in Memphis after feeling bad since Florida. He was on his way back home to Denver after being discharged from hospital. I offered to go back and get him a coffee for which he thanked me.

We all got talking, and it turned out that he knew both Shell and Cody in Wyoming, having driven there. He told us that it was lovely.

We went through the x-ray machine, with me stepping through nervously as usual, and off the machine beeped, making me jump. The security lady ran a hand held gadget over me, but when that didn't go off, she thought that I may have set the first one off with a bra strap. Some of these machines must be set very lightly! We went through to the lounge, and were sent across the concourse to the plane in heavy rain. It was only four seats deep, with a gangway between, and I was very nervous. Why is it I always wonder if 'Joe Smith or Fred Brown' had tightened all the nuts he should have, and are the wheels and the wings OK?

I sat there reading a book by Bill Bryson that Andy had lent me, about his experiences on returning to America from England. Apparently Bill had written several books about his trips in various countries, the latest being about Australia, as well as coming to live in Britain and his experiences here. That cured my worries. I just hoped my shaking shoulders and giggles weren't taken for fright, the book was hilarious.

We were offered coffee and biscuits during the flight and although I had the coffee, I turned down the offer of the biscuits, saying I was too scared of flying to eat. The stewardess just laughed and patted my shoulder.

Our arrival at Denver should have been 8.20am, but according to my watch we were still flying at 8.50am, before I realised that they should have reminded us to set our clocks back one hour to Mountain Time! We made a note for future bookings not to have our seats next to the toilets as people were back and forth all the time.

Andy told me that I could have brought with me a list of e-mail addresses because there are places called Internet cafes where you can hire the use of the Internet. '*Good idea, but not as exciting as someone receiving a card through the post,*' I thought.

We finally landed at Denver, to my relief. Taxiing in, we passed two terminals with what looked like a glass covered bridge between them, large enough for planes to taxi through, Andy said. He pointed out that there were four runways, so it was a very big complex.

Up in the concourse we used one of the long moving walkways to our terminal by a long, moving walkway. This part of the airport looked huge, it must have been as busy as Heathrow or Gatwick. We just had time to buy a sandwich before we caught our connecting flight to Cody, but I had no time to get any money from the ATM machine for a man was ages taking his turn. The sandwich was very dry, but I ate it in case I couldn't eat on the plane through nerves. Eventually, we were sent along several small corridors to the 59E-S-t entrance, where we were told to wait. Outside I could hear engines turning over, and peering through the doorway, I could see tiny planes with twin propellers. My heart nearly stopped, not us, surely! How can I back out of going!

Chapter 18

Wyoming.

To me it was a long, long walk over the concrete to a set of narrow steps up into the plane, with two pilots waiting to greet us and I hoped that my smile didn't look as sickly as I felt. I was even more petrified to find that there was only one set of seats either side of the gangway, and room for about ten people. The bright sunlight through the windows only made it look smaller.

My bag was tucked under my feet for takeoff, and I could feel my feet twitching. We taxied out and took off. I buried my head in a book, too scared to look up. The flight was very rocky, and I could feel every movement and hear every little noise. I didn't dare look out of a window, or even look ahead to where I could see the pilots. It was very noisy after the bigger passenger planes, and I could feel either warm air on me one minute or chilly cold draughts the next, all the way to Cody. There were no toilets and no stewardess either, probably because it was only a short haul flight. I kept praying I didn't throw up. I tried to write my notes using the little tray that pulled out in front of me, writing slowly and carefully as if I was drunk, clutching my locket with Ann and Les' pictures. We flew at 20,000 feet, and it was like being on a roller coaster with the plane seemingly being tossed around like a feather. As we approached Cody, the bang from the wheels locking down was very loud. And then we were down and taxiing to the small airport building. What a relief, I couldn't get off fast enough.

I nearly fell down the steps my legs were so shaky, but somehow I managed a smile to the pilots. The sun was lovely and warm, the air unbelievably fresh and clean. Around me were gently rolling hills to the horizon. I began to feel a lot better as we walked over and into the airport building, where Andy went to look for Chuck, the ranch owner, while I went to the restroom. The toilet was an automated flush, and every time I moved a fraction, it flushed like it was demented. I was feeling excited, this was real cowboy country and I couldn't wait to start out into the countryside. I walked out to the car park to wait with Andy.

After ten minutes a red truck turned up with a dune buggy tied in the back. Chuck was a big, elderly man, really warm and friendly, helping Andy throw the suitcases into the back of the truck, and apologising for being late as the ranch apparently, was seventy miles away. He said that he had to hang around for the next flight in to wait for another guest to come, but would run us into Cody as he had some shopping to do first. The town had been founded in 1896 by 'Buffalo Bill' Cody himself despite being born in Iowa.

Cody was a really clean, bright place, very pretty after the ugly concrete cities, with chalet bungalows mostly built with wood, and with lovely gardens. There were a lot of trucks and horse trailers on the road making me wonder if there was a rodeo nearby as one had been advertised in the ranch brochure. Chuck stopped at a big wooden chalet style building that sold outdoor clothes, and as we went inside, I mentioned that at some time I'd like to try and buy some horse tack, if there were any places nearby.

Inside the clothes store, which heaved with people, Chuck was greeted like a long lost cousin, and I noticed that everyone seemed to know each other, shouting greetings when they met up. Two young girls were serving, laughing and joking with everyone, and seemingly having a good time. Here, more than anywhere in America, was an open, genuine friendship. It felt like being part of a big family, and comparing it against the British back home, I found us sadly wanting.

I bought a thick woollen lumberjack style shirt and a pair of warm black gloves, while Andy had gone upstairs to where he'd discovered fishing clothing, and found a set of long waders/overalls for home. He was over the moon as the price would have been over £90 in England, but in the sale was $59 (approx. £35.)

Chuck finally winkled us out, taking us to an icecream parlour. The girls serving were too slow for him, there was a bit of an argument over where he had been told to queue and I gathered that some people had left for this reason. While eating, he told us that the area was in the middle of a bad drought so he'd had to sell his cattle, for there wasn't any feed for them and I was a little disappointed for I had been hoping to do some cattle work.

Finally we left there, and he took Andy and I to a tack shop while he went and got the truck washed. I found a 'Be Nice' halter for $17 (£35-40 back home), and then nearly bought myself a slicker, a yellow western full raincoat with poppers down the front, but it was a bit expensive as it was fully lined. I did find some cheap white straw hats for my friend Corinne's children, Morag and Fred, in a sale area.

Chuck came back, but when I looked round, I couldn't find Andy. However, I'd noticed a fishing shop next door, guessed he'd be there, and went it to get him, Chuck parking just across the street. We drove back to the airport and picked up Nancy, who'd come from Philadelphia. She told us she'd been to the ranch before. She was lovely and cheerful, but chubby. Us girls sat in the back of the truck while Andy sat up front with Chuck.

We travelled along quiet winding roads across a dry plain, heading towards a range of hills in the distance with flat topped mesas in creams, greys and reds, Chuck pointing out fields of dying beans. Some farmers had long pipe work mounted on large metal wheels that could be rolled across the land to water their crops, getting this from any nearby creeks that had some water left. He also pointed out a band of wild horses in the distance, but they were quite a long way off and difficult to see.

The Big Horn Mountains appeared up ahead, looking like parts of the Grand Canyon with their striped colours of blue, grey, red, and white. Pines covered some of the slopes and the tops of the ridges. Wyoming was beautiful, with very few single story, wooden houses, fields of horses and a few cattle. The drought was very evident with most of the small creek beds dry, although we crossed over a wide river, the Greybull.

After an hour we passed a lovely, dark wood building with a veranda, and surrounded by a fence, a souvenir shop and café. Dirty Annie's. I had to laugh at the name. The road rounded a rock face where we immediately turned right to the ranch, the Kedesh, passing between two wooden chalets and across a wooden bridge over the tumbling Shell creek. This had its headwaters in the mountains. Ahead was a low ranch house with two dogs lying outside and sprinklers watering the grass. To the left were empty wooden corrals, two wooden sheds, and further to the left, a long, low dusty building with the flat roof covered in white deer antlers. Behind these rose the mountains. A truck was parked outside the barn with bales of straw, and a beautiful peacock perched on top, preening itself in the sun. To the right ran a dusty trail to a circular green surrounded by wooden chalets and an old prairie schooner with grey canvas top standing near the middle. We were driven down the track to the cabins, each one with the name of an Indian, many of which I'd read.

Chuck led me into my room. He pointed out where the lights were, and opened the curtains on the far side to let the light in from the patio doors. This led into a closed porch overlooking a stony beach to the creek, and he told us that the creek was really low. The poorest it had been for years. Across the creek was the road, and in the distance reared red bluffs of sandstone. The furniture was of a nice, tan coloured wood. Andy was next door to me, and Nancy was the end of the row. Chuck told us both to come up to the ranch house when we were settled, before dinner at about 5.30, to book in, discuss the few rules and regulations, and to find out what we would be doing during our week's stay.

I went straight out back and sat down in one of the loungers, immediately being joined by a big black labrador dog who, tail wagging happily, brought a stick to be thrown. We found out later that if you threw the stick away to lose it to try and get rid of him, he'd tear another lump of bark off the nearby tree trunks, and judging by the state of them, he'd been at it a long time.

At 5.30, we wandered up to the ranch, meeting John from Delaware, and Lynn and Bill with Marshall their son, friends of Gail and Chuck from Cody who had come out to stay for a few days rest. Andy, Nancy and I booked in, signing the disclaimer for riding at our own risk and then everyone gathered in the big back room for a chat. The rules were basically sensible and the same as the Lazy K.

Chuck told us that any food not eaten at meal times would be served up the next day. Luckily I caught a slight twinkle in his eye and laughed, and the others finally joined in. It turned out that he'd said the same thing once to a group of lady guests, who'd not been amused, and he'd been taken aback by their reserve. Thank goodness for reading about cowhands and their sense of humour. What was our wrangler going to be like? Anything like the other's we'd met in Arizona? Chuck also told us to tell the wrangler if we ever saw a rattler, as it would be killed, for they didn't dare risk a client being bitten. I found that very sad, even though I could understand why. We populate these beautiful lands and yet are not prepared to live alongside animals that had evolved over millions of years.

At the dining table, we met Gail who was lovely, with a thick head of white hair held up with clips. She advised us to help ourselves to food that tonight consisted of salad, steak (hamburger,) mash, corn and a tasty white creamy sauce. There were jugs of water, and iced tea which I didn't like, on the tables, and every day there were jugs with different flavours and colours, from green, blue, pink, orange and red, and tasted great. A young girl, Jennifer, came round with the coffee, removing the empty plates. She was fun. Bill told us that he sold live fish for a living, trout mainly to ranchers all over for stocking up lakes and creeks for ranch guests and he offered to take Andy fishing with him sometime. At one point, the talk got religious, and I nearly put my foot in it for I am not, but always willing to discuss points from my observation of the Bible. Unfortunately this never seems to go down well with people and when Andy kept glancing at me, I backed down. After all, we were guests here.

He and I walked across the grass by the cabins along the dirt road to see the horses grazing in a field. To the left of them was a large wooden chalet house, up on a rise in the trees. We found out later that it was Gail and Chuck's. Behind the horses' field was a row of low hills with a large red finger of stone pointing into the sky, named Chimney Rock. It was getting dusk round about now, 8pm although it was still very hot. We'd been advised to bring something warm for the evenings, but as it turned out to be unusually warm for the time of year, I never used one all week. We wandered back to the ranch house to look at the shelves of books, as Andy had nothing left to read, passing a covered spa bath by the creek. Chuck had offered to heat it up for us the following day if anyone wanted to go in it. John fancied it, as did Andy.

Back in my room, it was very warm and stuffy, and because I kept the doors shut in case of insects, I woke at 1am with a headache, taking a couple of Ibuprofen. I managed to doze back off to sleep, propped up on 3 pillows until 7.20 just as the sun was coming up over the hills.

Sunday 2nd September.

As the sun slowly crept up over the horizon, I went and sat outside by the creek to enjoy the lovely cool breeze, writing my up notes when Nancy came out and chatted till I went to knock on the wall of the cabin to wake Andy. We went up to the dining room for breakfast once he was ready for a fried breakfast.

Riding came straight after so I had to hurry back to my room and get my chaps and boots. Zeb, the young wrangler, gave us all a quick demonstration on western riding before leading up a bay horse for Andy. I had a flea bitten grey called Queenie, half mustang and bred by Chuck and Gail. At 15.3hh she was a bit too tall for me, but I managed to climb into the saddle by standing on a rock and getting help from Zeb. Four inches higher than Cloud made quite a difference.

Zeb turned out to be nice, but quite quiet and laid back, very different to the other wranglers last year and the year before. On our way out, he told us that Chuck had had to sell all his cattle because of the drought and the lack of grazing for the stock. A lot of horses had gone too, but the ranch would be closing at the end of September, not opening again till about the end of May, and he would be going on somewhere else for the winter.

We rode out of the fenced corral with a little old fawn coloured sheepdog Annie, who was thirteen and a half years old, and who either took the lead or followed the horses on every ride, despite panting badly in the clouds of dust kicked up by the horses' hooves. Water bottles, half frozen, were taken in saddlebags for the ride, with an extra one for Annie. I automatically took drag last that for some reason is always my favourite spot, after a mild 'discussion' with Queenie who obviously preferred to be further up front.

We rode out across the horses' fields and up a slope between some trees. To the right was the red sandstone Chimney Rock, set high on a reddish sandy soil slope covered with low, blue sage bushes, very different to the grey sage at the Grand Canyon. To the left were the rocky Big Horn Mountains with their layers of greys, creams, blacks and browns. Ahead of us were soft rolling hills.

We rode up and down a lot of sandy slopes, clouds of dust being kicked up by the horses' hooves. At one point, Queenie spooked to one side as Annie came up out of a wash. I shouted and kicked her on, and she didn't do it again. *Trying me out*, I think. Along a flat piece of ground were two mounds of stones, each with a pair of upturned western boots sticking out! Very comical, I must try that when I get home.

We passed through two barbed wire gates, held open for us by Zeb, and headed down onto a flat plain towards a rocky, white walled canyon. John, it turned out, was very nervous of heights and a couple of the slopes made him very nervous. As we got closer to the canyon, green trees on our right showed the line of a small creek, and everywhere grew the blue-grey sage bushes. These smelt a lot like lavender when the horses stood on them. Everywhere on the flats, the clumps of prickly pear were small and shrivelled.

We headed into the canyon through the trees, the horses stepping carefully over fallen trunks, rounding a corner to come across the remains of a shepherd's homestead, just the chimney made of rocks left. Round a huge boulder of rock we headed down the canyon floor, stopping for a rest under the canyon wall. Along the wall opposite ran a broken line of pipe, apparently where they had tried to bring water down into the canyon. We tied the horses' reins to some scrubby bushes and Zeb handed out plastic bottles of icy cold water that were really refreshing after that dusty ride. He then led us up a short way to see, above our heads, the ancient carved and painted pictures, petrogliphs, left by ancient tribes thousands of years ago. One of them looked like a bear's paw. It was strange to think that thousands of years ago, the canyon floor would have been much that much higher up where people could stand to do the painting.

We returned the way we came, this time following the bubbling little creek until we could turn back toward the ranch. We were allowed a short trot and like Wrangler last year, Queenie's trot was very bouncy and hard to sit to.

Back at the corral, we tied the horses to the rails with their halters, and several of us unsaddled, taking the tack into the wooden tack barn where he pointed out the burros (the A shaped wooden stands for the saddles to rest on.) John told us he had used his digital camera and he that would be able to e-mail us the pictures after he got home. Crikey, such technology—it baffles me as to what all this new stuff is.

Back at the ranch house, jugs of cold water and plastic cups were laid out, and did I need it after two hours. We sat round one of the tables and chatted until the dinner bell went. A new girl had arrived Kristin, from Hertfordshire, who seemed very quiet, but nice. She told everyone she'd liked the Denver/ Cody flight. I had to disagree, and when Nancy remarked that she liked being in small planes, I told them that Andy was learning to fly.

Back sitting by the creek with Nancy and Andy, I spotted a couple of cows wandering by on the road, followed by several more. Curiously I watched them pass by, followed by a single cowboy hazing (gently driving) them somewhere. Then more cattle, followed by two more cowboys, followed by even more cattle, all of who were wearing the Circle Triangle brand, which I could see on their flanks. They took over half an hour to wander past, with four more cowboys on drag. Working out the time scale, I reckoned it was strung out about one and a half to two miles long. Later, Chuck told us that the herds were coming down from the hills six weeks early as there was no graze up in the hills for them.

Lying out on the sun lounger, we were pestered by the black labrador, Sam again, so we kept trying to lose the sticks he brought by throwing them in the thickets, but he just tore more off the trees. He had the biggest paws I'd ever seen on a dog and wondered if he was a Newfoundland.

Dinner was a salad, followed by ham that I left, not being much of a meat eater, a cheesy/mash dish that was delicious, a bread scone, and green broad beans. Reluctantly, I had to turn down the dessert as the meal really filled me up.

Straight after was another ride. Kristin hadn't done western riding before so this was her first time on a ranch and she would be here for three weeks. I gave her advice as we rode along.

This time we went over the wooden bridge at the entrance to the ranch, across the road in one straight line for safety, and through a gate, the usual dust billowing out from the horses' feet. I kept trying to keep Queenie upwind to save her from the dust, but she was used to following nose to tail and it was difficult to keep her from easing back into line. Early on, I started covering my nose with my neckerchief as I suffer with asthma, and I guessed that I looked a bit like an outlaw, which was confirmed when I saw Andy's photos of me.

We followed the dusty trails through the small sage bushes towards a grey, rocky mesa (Spanish for table, it meant flat topped) the sides streaked with dark greys, oranges, and white nearer the top. It reminded me a lot of the Grand Canyon. Off to one side I saw two cottontail rabbits bolting off to hide. We skirted the two red cone shaped hills I could see from the ranch, went up and down the sandy, sage covered slopes, and then turned right, leaving the red hills off to our left. We headed towards the mountain range with its softer shade of pastels and lines of pine trees down the sides. We eased down a steep, dusty, stony path towards the ranch, which I knew was hidden in the line of green trees that followed Shell Creek, the pointing finger of Chimney Rock in the distance. It was slowly getting dusk, the red hills became crimson in the setting sun, the mountains began to fade to darker greys, and the sage turned from a creamy blue to black. Several stars appeared in the deep blue sky. The wind was getting up, but was lovely and warm.

All I could hear was the soft sound of voices, the pad of hooves in the dust and the creak of the saddles. It was so peaceful I wished I could continue forever. We rode alongside a deep, dry wash with branches and tree trunks caught in the steep corners where flash floods had driven them, arriving back at the stables after carefully crossing the road, where we unsaddled. My legs did ache.

Everyone was discussing getting into the hot tub, which I really fancied, feeling quite upset at missing out because I'd lost my costume, so I went and had a hot bath in the cabin instead. It was even hotter inside due to the sun having been on my side of the bunkhouse and the doors having been shut, but Andy had told me that I would find a big square fan in the cupboard space. I got it out and plugged it in for overnight.

Chapter 19

Horses 4—Cowboys 0.

Monday 3rd September.

I awoke at 5.15am but didn't get up until 6.30 when it began to get light outside. There was a cool breeze when I opened the door, and it was lovely to hear the sound of the creek tumbling over the rocks outside. I woke Andy about 7.30, and we went for breakfast when he was ready. Another fried one, but this time with slices of melon, which I love.

When we'd first arrived, I had asked if there were any rodeos as had been advertised in the brochure, but apparently the ones at Cody had finished for the season. However, Chuck mentioned one being held at Meeteetse today, so he and Gail took us all, including Jennifer and Zeb.

We drove out through Shell (pop. 50!) and Greybull (pop. 1700,) out into a scrub and tree covered plain with the usual creamy blue sage and dry, brown coloured grass. Some of the fields that had cattle in them had no grass, just barren earth. Occasionally we passed wooden shacks, some empty. I'd have loved to have bought one and done it up to live in. Dead trees rose like white skeleton fingers from among the live ones that followed the course of the creeks, most of which appeared as dry washes. Chuck told us that Wyoming was one of the least populated of the States and I could understand it seeing the open terrain and near empty roads. What bliss to live here.

The countryside varied from grey rocky ridges like miniature Grand Canyons, out into flat basins intersected by dry washes and arroyos, then between rolling hills where the grass and feed stuffs were green, watered from the creeks by long rows of pipes mounted on huge metal wheels. Along on our left ran low hills, while ahead hazy blue mountains pointed up into the blue, almost cloud free sky.

The road began to rise between crags and rocks of pale creams with sandy pinnacles of rocks to the right, some balancing precariously on each other. To the left were mounds of sand looking just like a giant hand had scooped them up into sandcastles. We continued out into a long pretty valley for about ten miles before reaching rocks and sage covered slopes with green, grey mesas to the left, where Chuck pointed out a small herd of mustangs on the flat. Clouds were beginning to fill the sky and I hoped that my worries about being too hot in the sun would be unfounded.

We finally reached Meeteetse, a quaint old time, wooden shacked town on the Greybull River. All the people were dressed in colourful western clothing, and there were trucks and trailers everywhere. As we parked at the side of Main Street, a crowd of shouting, cheering people could be seen and heard on the other side. Chuck told us they were holding a competition for tossing cow pats as far as possible. Dry, I hope.

Gail told us that we would be free to wander about for half an hour before heading out to the B-B-Q.

Andy entered a store to ask if there was an ATM machine in town as we were out of cash to go to the B-B-Q and rodeo, but the main stores and bank were shut for Labour Day, a holiday out here.

Heading down another road, we wandered round in a square of streets to finally rejoin the others back on Main Street. Chuck drove us out to a park near a huge open sided marquee, waving us all through the gateway, and giving us each a ticket to get food. I became nervous as there were lots of wasps, known as yellow jackets, around and I'm terrified of.

At a long trestle table, I was handed a paper plate with a big burger bun on which was heaped shaved beef, baked beans, a red coloured coleslaw. Further along I took a plastic beaker of lemonade. Looking round, we eventually found spaces at a long wooden table when some other people moved off, trying to fend off the wasps that quickly gathered. Chuck glanced round at all of us then laughed and said to me, "at least you look the part." (I was dressed in the usual western clothing that I wore back home) and added, "that the others looked like tourists."

Kristin and Jennifer suddenly spotted a man who looked like the film star Kurt Russell, the actor, and went over to get his picture, giggling like school kids. They stayed for ages talking and having their pictures taken with him. I began to regret not buying the camcorder and risking it not working in Britain, but at least Andy had his.

Finally we drove out to the rodeo grounds, joining a long queue of cars. Chuck parked up, and we walked over to some metal seats that were on the side of a slope overlooking the big main arena and the corrals, but we had to sit on the grass for they were already full.

People were already riding in the arena and horses were being exercised up and down the track in front of us. All the horses appeared to be American quarter horses, not to be confused with the English type which were finer, and how I wished I could be in there with them. Some of the riders were good, and some a bit heavy handed on the reins, just like in Britain. There were also several girl riders in blue and white, carrying flags, apparently a display team, some of them not looking very competent. The announcer called for everyone to leave the arena, and we all stood for the National Anthem, the men removing their hats.

The first event was bucking horses, bareback. A few riders made the time, eight seconds, being helped off by the pick up men. Quite a few riders got thrown, and one horse had a great time evading the pick up men, refusing to go back into the pen with the others. The announcer was brilliant and kept offering to sell the animal, including the saddle, if it could just be caught, and they couldn't restart the next rider until it was removed, so there was a bit of a hold up. All the way through the show he came out with very amusing comments, making us all laugh.

One bucking horse ran head first into the side of rails near us but fortunately wasn't hurt, while another bucked so hard, it nearly knocked one pick up man's horse over.

Calf roping came next, when the calf had to be roped, thrown on its side and three of the feet tied with a pigging thong, the time being called when the roper's hands flew into the air. The horses were great, backing up and keeping the rope tight so the animal couldn't get up. Chuck came over at one point to ask me if I knew what was going on, and I was pleased to say that I did. Although at the end of it, I did go to ask why the cattle had strange hoods on, and he told me it was to stop rope burns. The animals were obviously used to it as they came out of the chute flat out. I was amazed that after being roped, they just stepped nonchalantly out of the loop and walked or ran to the end of the corral to where the others were.

Once the teams had finished, the calves were driven back between two rows of fences in front of us, where children were standing to watch all the events. One little girl made the crowd laugh when she took fright at their approach and ran crying back to her mum.

Next came 'heading and heeling' where one rider roped the head of the steer and the other roped both back feet, points being lost if only one back foot was caught. The cattle also seemed used to this, getting up, skipping their back feet out of the rope and trotting off down to the other end and into the holding pen.

Then four teams of three men came into the ring and stood with a saddle for each group by the chutes in which was a horse being held by a long lariat. As the gates were opened, the horses came out fighting. The idea apparently was to get a saddle on each horse and try to ride it across the corral and around a barrel to win. The fights were both thrilling and awful as the horses threw themselves about, fighting the ropes. One of a team of men, with a pretty paint horse, was kicked over into the dust, but got up apparently unhurt. Another man eared the horse down so that the saddle could be put on. Meanwhile, two other horses had got away from their tormentors and were running freely about the corral.

The man climbed onto the paint and it took off bucking whole-heartedly, throwing him into the dust. Another man grabbed the rope round its neck, and they had to start all over again. One loose horse was caught by the lariat and was bucketing down the fence dragging a man behind him, squealing with the effort of pulling. Again they got the man into the saddle of the paint, but it took off with the other free ones, running round the corral fencing until the man fell off onto the ground again. At the end of the time no one actually won, but luckily no horse or rider was hurt. The crowd was laughing, cheering and screaming all the time, with occasional "oohs" as someone fell off a horse.

Then came the bull riding, and boy, are they huge this close. Like the horses, they each had an individual style of bucking, and one man stayed on really well as his bull just bucked in a straight line. Others bucked in circles until the rider lost his balance and fell, while several just jinked all over the place. One rider was tossed by a bull's horns, as was one of the rodeo clowns (twice), but fortunately again no one was badly hurt.

Several children had goes at barrel racing, taking turns riding fast round three barrels in a cloverleaf pattern, followed by three girl riders. One of them, on a lovely grey Arab, won the adult section. I've never seen a man riding barrels, it seems that only the girls compete. Again the commentator was shouting and encouraging us to cheer them on.

That finished the day and we had been really lucky with the weather with enough cloud passing overhead so we didn't get too hot. We headed back to the minibus and set off home, stopping only briefly to use the local toilets.

On the way we passed a dead coyote, and Chuck also stopped to let us try and take pictures of a herd of pronghorn near the road, but they spooked and ran off as we backed up. It had been a fabulous day and everyone had been laughing and joking all the way.

Once back at the ranch, I relaxed and read until dinner, a salad followed by beef ribs, corn, jacket potato and a bread roll. Halfway through, a piece of food got caught in my throat and I began choking badly. I was petrified, knowing I couldn't cough because I didn't dare breathe in, in case it went further down my windpipe. Andy was really concerned, asking me if I was OK, then trying to smack me on the back, but I couldn't speak. I became terrified. When it finally became dislodged, I had another ten minutes of coughing before I could get my voice back. Only Zeb noticed, the others had carried on talking without realising, and he'd looked very worried, too. I was really embarrassed afterward. Jennifer, who had been watching me in great concern, assured me she not only knew how to do the Heimlich Manoeuvre but CPR as well. I joked that I'd thought I'd needed it.

I couldn't face eating anymore after that, so frightened of it happening again. Over coffee, which I would only sip, we all sat and chatted, before Gail asked who wanted to go to Dirty Annie's for icecream. All but Chuck went, Gail driving.

I ended up buying yet another fridge magnet of a map of Wyoming, and a beautiful T-shirt with a picture of Shell, and after a coffee, Andy bought us both an icecream. It was dark by then, and Gail took us back to the ranch.

I had a hot bath as my legs and butt were still aching from the last ride, and after getting ready for bed, I sat up writing my notes before reading for a while, having turned on the fan as it was so hot. I slept restlessly again, waking with a bit of a headache at 6am.

Tuesday 4th September.

I showered, and sat outside by the creek before waking Andy by banging on the wall again. During breakfast, I ate very slowly and nervously, and we all went out to the corrals for the morning ride. I lent Kristin a neckerchief as she was also finding the dust overpowering. It was getting quite warm, and I rode in a shirt again.

Down the drive and out across the road again, we headed across towards the red hills with clouds of dust swirling up from the path, so I tied my neckerchief over my nose. Poor Annie was again in the dust when she wasn't running in front, occasionally stopping in a patch of shade to pant, but she never failed to catch us up.

We followed red sandy paths and on into a deep wash where only the horse in front could be seen as they went round the corners. Bushes and scrub cedars managed to grow there, making me wonder how on earth they fared in the heavy rains with water pouring down in a torrent. Gradually the red sandstone walls grew higher and higher, dwarfing us, the horses climbing over ridges of red stone. Awesome! I tried to get a piece of broken rock off the shelves to take home as a souvenir, but it crumbled in my fingers.

We wove in and out, climbing higher and higher, one wall almost straight up, the other lined with softly curved ridges. Andy's horse, Whiskey, suddenly stopped, and Andy said he'd heard a rattlesnake. I rode over to him, and looking down, saw a grey shape sliding off under a bush. Whiskey refused to pass it, and I went in front to encourage him to follow me, while the others stopped ahead and were waiting. I shouted that it was a 'rattler.' Eventually, Whiskey decided to follow me and we caught up with the others. I wondered why Zeb hadn't come over to kill it, but he just turned and led off, and we followed.

Eventually we stopped before a long, steep dusty slope where Zeb told us to hang on, lean forward as we went up, and not to let the horses stop. John was very, very nervous, but followed him. Queenie struggled a bit, but after the ridges in Tucson, this was easy for me and I found it thrilling.

Once out on top of the mesa, we turned right, following a little winding path along the edge of the canyon. It was fantastic looking down into the depths, but I couldn't see very far back down the winding trail. At the far end, we stopped and climbed off the horses to have a drink, and the cold water in the bottles was wonderful. Zeb watered Annie.

Twice while Andy was filming, Whiskey lay down, and Zeb had to get him up in case he decided to roll on the saddle, which could have broken it. Standing here and looking back, I couldn't see the canyon we had come out of, it was completely invisible from where I stood! In the far distance a line of green trees outlined where Shell Creek and the ranch lay, behind them rolling green hills and the Big Horn mountains off to the left. A gap between them showed where Shell Canyon ran.

After a twenty minute break we got back into the saddles, retracing our steps almost back to where we came up, but then Zeb turned right to go down a long, winding, stony path towards what seemed to be a flat plain. This was deceptive, because as we got closer the grassland lay in folds, the pathway rising and falling like a gentle roller coaster. Again I had to resort to my neckerchief, and I could see Kristin ahead doing the same. We crossed and followed dry washes and arroyos, finally arriving back at the road and the ranch. We'd been out two hours, and when I asked, Zeb thought we'd done about seven to eight miles. Was that all, my legs reckoned about twenty!

After unsaddling, Kristin told me Zeb was letting her turn the horses away for the afternoon, and to take their head collars off. Three of them decided not to leave and came back into the corrals, but as we were trying to chase them out and down towards the field, Zeb returned. Oh dear, he'd wanted her to leave the collars on! But he told her that it didn't matter, he'd catch them up later.

We all went back down to the ranch house and sat chatting until the gong for lunch, where again I ate very slowly and sparingly, frightened to swallow. Afterwards, we sat in the big wooden chairs in the lounge. Gail and Chuck announced that they had some friends they'd known for years who were doing a dinosaur dig about an hour's drive away, did anyone want to go and see it. I would have loved to have, but decided it was likely to be very hot there so Andy and I went and chilled out by the creek. I had a shower first and had to change as my clothes had been covered in a fine layer of red dust from the ride. Lazing outside, I sat and watched a dipper flitting from stone to stone, diving into the water for grubs, the first time I'd ever seen one outside of a TV screen. There were also two black birds, a little like our blackbirds except they had rust coloured breasts.

I decided to have a paddle in the water after they had gone. Gosh, it was freezing, so I sat on a rock instead watching tiny little baby trout swimming at the edge of the water. While glancing up at the road, I was just in time to see the truck coming back with the others, and waved before going to meet them. The gong sounded for dinner as I almost reached the ranch house.

The others had really enjoyed the dig, but said that it had been very hot there so I was pleased I hadn't gone after all. I wasn't very hungry as I had been drinking a lot of water all afternoon, but I did manage a little bit of salad, then some chicken, rice and peas. I had to eat something for I knew that Gail and Chuck would have noticed and been concerned as they were very observant and caring about their guests. Again, I was careful and very slow at swallowing.

I did have to refuse the dessert because I knew that as we would be riding afterwards, I would have felt uncomfortable. It was strange that we'd ride as it seemed to be getting very late and I knew it would be getting dark quite soon. Andy didn't come with us this time for the ride in the morning had been enough for him.

Up at the corral we had to wait while Zeb finished saddled the horses, then we mounted and headed out across the dry fields, up the slope and past the upturned boots again, heading towards White Canyon. Passing through the two gates, we rode down the slope to branch off alongside a fence, heading for Echo Canyon. Off to the right over the lower part of the Big Horns the setting sun shone golden behind the black clouds, among which I could see bright flashes of zigzagging lightening. We had no slickers (riding raincoats) and I hoped it didn't come any closer.

We crossed a small creek, with clever little Annie crouching low into the shallow water to cool off, then went up and down several dusty slopes, heading along a straight path on a sage covered plain. Ahead lay the green rolling hills I'd seen before, with a red sandstone butte, and Chimney Rock to the right, the mountains now behind us turning crimson in the rays of the sun.

Chief, the appaloosa Zeb was riding, suddenly shied, so we stopped while he got off, apparently suspecting a rattler. Eventually he found it among the sage, and killed it. I knew why, but it seemed very cruel and heartless.

John had heard that Echo Canyon was quite high and, because one could look over the edge, didn't fancy going any further. So, as I didn't like leaving him alone, I offered to stay, especially as I didn't know if Prince, Queenie's son, would like going back alone in the dusk. The two of us turned back down the track, heading for a gate in the far, left corner of a triangle shape of fencing.

Queenie was much more alert than usual, surprise, surprise, in the lead, but was quite willing to go where I asked, and this time I had to keep slowing her for John to catch up. We reached the gate just as it was getting very dark and waited, chatting quietly.

Suddenly, the horses suddenly both had their ears up, looking over towards the hills. I had no idea where the others would appear, but eventually I spotted something, pointing out to John the vague white shape coming, a dust cloud in the far distance. As it got closer, so we could just pick out voices, and I was amazed that sounds could carry so far in the clear air. It was fantastic to watch as the ghostly forms of horses and riders became clearer. Our horses were brilliant, just standing and watching intently.

We all joined up and started back for the ranch. It was quite dark now and I had to trust that Queenie could see better than I could as, in several places, all I could see was the brown butt of Tree, Kristin's horse, in the white clouds of dust. Once I tried to guide Queenie as she seemed to be negotiating a long slope that I remembered, too far up. That was a bit scary, but she knew where she was going.

Over the mountains to the left now, the black clouds and flashing lightning was getting much closer, and there were even some flashes to the right as well, although overhead the sky was brilliantly lit by millions of white twinkling stars. Kristin called back that she was very scared of storms.

Finally, ahead in the dark, I began to make out the lights of two houses, and I thought I could also make out the Kedesh among the trees by the creek. We arrived at the fields and rode along the winding trail to the corrals where we unsaddled, put the tack away, and then turned the horses back out down the trail to their fields.

At the ranch house, I was so thirsty that I drank two cups of iced water straight off, trying to wash the dust out of my throat. Then Gail announced that they had kept dessert for us. Great! We all tucked in, having worked up quite an appetite. Chuck meanwhile, had been trying to work out where everyone wanted to visit this week, as I particularly wanted to see as much as possible. It was decided that Andy and I would be taken to Cody in the morning, to visit the Buffalo Bill museum. John had already been inside, but he said that he would come along just to keep Chuck company.

I'd mentioned that I'd also wanted to be able to visit the battlefield of the Little Big Horn and Custer's Last Stand. This apparently, would be an all day trip as it was over the State line into Montana, so it was arranged for Thursday.

Chuck was interested to learn that we would be driving back to Denver when we left here, and was astonished that we hadn't realised the distance we would have to cover in two days, showing us on a map. He said that through Yellowstone Park the speed was only about 35mph which would slow us down considerably, and I hadn't been able to take into account, then pointed out a slightly different route that would be a little quicker, but still interesting. I told him that we would be doing a slight detour to see Old Faithful, the famous geyser, and we'd also hoped to drive down through Jackson Hole, being part of the Outlaw Trail. Gail chipped in that Jackson Hole was now very built up and posh, and that there was nothing much left of the old town to see anymore.

While the others were deciding to get changed and get into the hot tub, Kristin and I began discussing England, fascinating Chuck, and he kept laughing at our accents and the things we told him of life there. Andy persuaded me to go into the hot tub too, and as I only had underwear, I wore my long white shirt over the top, especially as it needed a wash due to the red dust from the trail. Gail supplied us all with towels.

I climbed in carefully. Boy was the water hot, but once I was in and sitting up to my neck in bubbling water, it was really quite relaxing. It was a real laugh with Kristin, Nancy, Andy, John and Zeb in as well, all splashing around and laughing and joking. There were several jets of strong water at varying heights and to get a chance at each one, we all kept shuffling around every few minutes. At one point, John and Zeb dared each other to jump in the creek, and did!

Lightning was still flashing overhead and occasionally the stars were blotted out by dark clouds when several times there was a few small spots of rain, but that was all. It was a great end to the evening. I finally climbed out at 11pm, wrapping myself in a towel and putting on my trainers to go back to the cabin, where I had a short shower.

I fell into bed, leaving my notes till the morning for I was quite tired. But I made a mental note to ask Zeb sometime why he'd killed the rattler tonight, but not the one in the canyon, especially as Chuck had said at the beginning that any we spotted should be pointed out to him.

I woke at 3.30am with a headache despite the fan being on and had to take two Ibuprofen tablets for it.

Chapter 20

Buffalo Bill Museum.

Wednesday 5th September.

I woke at 7am waking Andy half an hour later, banging on the internal wall as usual. We had breakfast at 8.30am before Chuck took Andy, John and I into Cody.

Over halfway there, I could see black clouds off to the left with the dark shadows of falling rain and hoped that it was heading for the ranch. I asked Chuck what the big, snow capped mountains were ahead in the distance and he said that they were part of the Rockies, with the Wind River Range to the left and in front of them.

While he was chatting with John, I heard him say that they'd had a big prairie dog town on the ranch, and as the holes were dangerous for the stock, he had poisoned them all. I was really upset about it for I knew that gophers were getting scarce in America due to all the ranchers trying to exterminate them. Did that mean that he'd had to go out and fill in all the holes to prevent injury to the stock afterwards? That could have been difficult as some towns could be up to a hundred square miles wide. I didn't like to ask.

Chuck dropped us outside the museum, a lovely new brick building with a bronze statue of Buffalo Bill outside, coming in to pay for the tickets, and saying that he'd meet us outside about 2pm. He also very kindly offered to take the films I needed developed, plus my camera, which had jammed with a film in it and I was unable to rewind. That had been very upsetting to me because Les had bought it about fifteen years before, and it was a really good one. I hoped it wasn't broken.

I mentioned to Andy that I needed some money at some time, and he spotted an ATM machine in the entrance for when we came back out.

To the left, we passed into a long, low building with loads of corridors, and the most amazing collection of guns I'd even seen in my life. From the very first ever made, they went through the Civil War and on into the modern age of WWI and WWII, and even the Korean and Vietnam Wars. It was fascinating for a while, until I found it a bit boring as they went on, and on. Everywhere I looked, the walls were covered in glass-fronted cabinets, and rows and rows of firearms inside.

There was also a mock up of an office with the original benches and paperwork for either Henry Remington or Sam Colt. Unfortunately, I didn't write down which it was.

Whilst we were walking under a glassed over walkway to the next part of the building, I was suddenly aware that it was raining very heavily, and could even hear the thunder overhead.

From there we went into the Native American section with several models. I was very interested, enjoying all the exhibits of their way of life that I'd always admired, from their clothing to their culture and their nomadic way of life. They destroyed nothing, and lived off the land, believing that they were only there to borrow the land and animals, unlike the white man who had to own and fence everything.

After a coffee in a small cafe, we headed out and down into a wide amphitheatre with a tepee erected in the centre where, against the back wall, was showing a film about the Indian way of life. In large glass cases were the beautiful war bonnets belonging to some of the chiefs, one of which being Little Shield's, plus the lovely ceremonial robes that they dressed in, including ones worn by their horses.

Further round they had the Buffalo Bill section with pictures of his life and the posters for his Wild West Shows. He had been a pony express rider, wrangler, gold seeker, buffalo hunter and Indian fighter amongst other things, before turning to stage shows of the West when, during 1882, whilst in North Platte, he heard that festivities had not been organised for the Fourth of July. He organised his very first Wild West Show for the cowboys to show off their skills at roping, shooting and riding bucking horses.

In 1883 he started the proper Wild West Shows, going on tour around America, and even to Europe, including Britain, where he performed before Queen Victoria and Prince Albert. With him came Little Miss Sure Shot, Annie Oakley.

In 1885, the famous Sioux chief, Sitting Bull, joined him, but only for four months, eventually tiring of it and going back to his people.

The exhibits included a real life stagecoach with four imitation, real sized horses, or 'four-hitch' as it is called. In front of it was a chuck wagon and bed wagon. The chuck wagon would be filled with provisions and implements for the trail and this was where the cook prepared the meals, usually assisted by his 'louse' or assistant.

The bed wagon contained the sleeping blankets and tarpaulins for the cowhands, used for their beds. If a cowboy threw his bedroll into the wagon, he was announcing that he rode 'for the brand,' with unswerving loyalty to his boss or hefe (efe) and the rest of the wranglers.

In two cases, one completely glassed, there were the most fantastic saddles, bridles and trappings. Each saddle must have weighed a ton, being covered in silver. There was also a picture of his magnificent palomino horse wearing it, and I wondered what Cloud would have looked like in such trappings. Andy took pictures of them for me as I had no camera, as well as me standing beside the stage.

We kept a watch on the time as it was getting close to meeting Chuck, and finished off the visit by headed into the gift shop. It was very expensive, but I spotted a CD of Indian Chants and Music. Handing over my card, the lady kept trying my MasterCard in the machine, but it refused to accept it! I became quite worried, knowing I'd already used it to get money out of an ATM machine before, but it became so embarrassing that eventually I had to call Andy over to lend me the money.

Back outside I tried the ATM machine three times, with no joy. As you only swiped the card, it wasn't swallow when things went wrong, unlike the push in ones, but I was getting extremely worried by this time. In America and no money!

We met up outside with Chuck and John after Andy had taken my picture standing beside the statue of Buffalo Bill, and I told Chuck what had happened. It was even worse when he told me I owed $40.41 for the films, but he said that he would add it to our bill at the end. Very embarrassing. It was suggested that I go up and down Main Street for an hour to see the shops, and to go into a bank to try and find out what was wrong. We could then meet him and John at a bar down the road.

Inside a bank I explained that I was having trouble using my card, so the lady took me outside and swiped the card in the machine there. No go. Back inside, she passed it to a girl cashier who also tried. Then she came over and tried to explain that it was out of date, we were now in September and the expiry date was 09/01. I was aghast, how on earth had I managed not to bring the new one with me. But I just couldn't remember having got a new one through the post. I was practically in tears.

Walking along the street, Andy suddenly pointed out that they had been muddled with the dates, the 09/01 was our month and year, not as they do it, the month followed by the day. She thought it had ended at the beginning of September, not the end. I felt a little better knowing the card should have been OK date wise, but why wouldn't it swipe? Andy suggested that we try later to ring the emergency number on the card to find out what was wrong.

Stopping at a café for coffee, Andy decided he would ring up and try to get our rental car today instead of coming in with Chuck on the Saturday morning, that way we could leave the ranch earlier and be on our way at least an hour or two quicker. So at a phone booth at the side of the street, he rang the Hertz Rental, based at the airport, having difficulty hearing them because of the traffic going past. He was startled when they asked, where was Cody? It turned out that the phone line went straight through to the main office, hundreds of miles away. He explained the situation to them and was annoyed to find out how expensive two extra days would be, almost double our original quote of $250, and he decided not to do it.

Down the road at the bar, we met up again with Chuck and John, and when Andy told them about the problem with the car, Chuck suggested calling in at the airport and speaking to someone at the desk there, which we did. I wandered off to try their ATM machine, with no more success than last time, except that now it told me my pin number was inadmissible.

Andy was out in the parking lot looking at a car we could have on rental, although not the make we'd originally chosen on the Internet, and at first it turned out that the rates were better than that quoted on the phone. Then the boy at the counter added on the extra insurance's. Over here you needed insurance not only for the car you were driving, but also one to cover someone hitting you as well!

I had to pay for the car as Andy had forgotten to bring his driving licence with him, and when I explained the trouble I was having with my card, the boy told me that that wouldn't be a problem, he would ring my bank from the desk.

Meanwhile, it appeared that the girl across the way had a new Lincoln Continental waiting to be returned to Denver that we could have at a much cheaper rate, $280. So Chuck came back and began arguing with the boy about how expensive he was, and how much cheaper Budget was. By the time he went back to Budget to try to arrange for us to take the posh Lincoln, the boy had cleared things with my bank, unfortunately putting the phone down before I could ask if they could clear my pin number, and I signed for the lease.

When Andy and Chuck came back over, things started getting a little heated, especially as the boy announced that I had now signed, and I went to stand outside to let the men sort it out. Andy finally shouted me back in nearly three quarters of an hour after we had arrived to sign another lease for it appeared that Hertz had a policy that they would match any other price given by another competitor.

Outside, Chuck told Andy he would be in deep trouble with the law if we were stopped with him driving and he couldn't produce his licence. Andy said that he usually didn't carry it, thinking it was safer left in his room, and hadn't realised the rules over here. This meant that I would drive back to the ranch. Great!

We found the car in the parking lot, a very nice sporty Ford Taurus four door saloon, again with doors that locked when you put the car in drive. I followed Chuck's truck back to Greybull where, when we stopped at the lights in the high street, John suddenly leapt out and got into our car, Chuck wanting to get some gas and do some shopping. We arrived at the ranch just in time for dinner, being over an hour later than we'd expected to be. Kristin, Nancy and Zeb told us they'd had a lovely long ride to Shell Canyon that morning and, despite being very disappointed, I knew that I just couldn't have made it that far.

After dinner, we mounted up to ride to Chimney Rock, which Andy had wanted to see. We took another branch in the trail, walking back through the small creek where Annie had laid in the water before. Ahead, I heard Zeb mention trotting and called back to Andy for I knew he was filming the ride. Good job I did, for after a very short trot, the horses started loping. Oh what bliss after Queenie's bone jarring trot, she was gorgeously comfortable and so easy to sit to. Once we slowed down, I kept looking back to keep an eye on Andy as he slowly trotted up behind.

Finally, we scrambled up a long red, dusty slope to the foot of Chimney

Rock, stopping where the red pinnacle towered over our heads. I was quite worried about John for I knew he didn't like heights, but he seemed to be studying his horse's ears very intently. We did tease him a little to try and ease his worry, and I well understood his fear for I was scared of looking out of high buildings, let alone flying. Everyone else seemed to take planes as a matter of course.

Zeb pointed up to two small swifts' nests, very similar to our swallow's nests, stuck to the wall under some cracks. After ten minutes rest, we turned the horses and began making a slow descent down another path, with Andy filming from behind, and it wasn't until we got home and I transferred the filming onto VHS that I realised how much he'd done. It took me ages. Silly boy, he could have been hurt if his horse had spooked. Good job he stuck to the back of the line where no one could see him.

Reaching the bottom, we were faced with several small hills, and managed short lopes up the slopes. We also came across a sad sight. A deer had tried to jump the wire fencing and had obviously got caught up. It had died there, and all that was left dangling was the skin and bones.

It began to get dusk as we neared the ranch, but not as dark as last night.

Andy had run out of film while on the way home and ran the tape back. Zeb caught him listening to the Jazz player from New Orleans and told him to stop. Good job his horse was quiet, it could have been dangerous.

Queenie's ears shot up shortly after that having apparently spotted a deer feeding near the chalets and which had run off at our approach. We unsaddled by the corrals and turned the horses out again before heading back to the ranch house where Gail and Jennifer had again kept dessert for us all.

Chuck gave me my photos, and we browsed through them. The stuck film in the camera had come out OK, but one reel of film was clear, obviously I hadn't used it at all! (When I had the next lot developed while in Los Angeles, I ran across a film that had been double exposed. What a nuisance.)

Chuck managed to get everyone's attention and told us that we would be starting out after breakfast next day to go to Custer's Last Stand. After he and Gail had retired, I queried the entrance monies and Jennifer said that the ranch usually paid for all the trips out. Wow, how kind.

Later, after I changed into my shirt, we all went back into the hot tub. It was hysterical, with everyone telling jokes, even Chuck coming down and joining in. Zeb wasn't going to get in, but we finally persuaded him, and I had them all trying to work out two different puzzles that I knew. The short one couldn't be worked out and I had to tell them the answer, but eventually they worked most of the second one out, with Kristin being good and Nancy brilliant.

After Chuck had left, I plucked up the courage to ask Zeb why he hadn't killed the snake Andy saw in Red Canyon, and he said that he hadn't realised what we'd said, just thought that Andy's horse was playing up.

I left the hot tub at 10.45pm, had a shower, and went to bed just after eleven.

Chapter 21

Custer's Last Stand.

Thursday 6th September.

I slept right through to 7.10am to find that on getting out of bed, my room seemed cooler, probably why I had slept better. Quickly I wrote up my notes, before waking Andy at 7.30. I tried putting another film into my camera, but again it refused to work. Oh dear, what a shame.

Going out of the door to head up for breakfast I realised that the weather had turned, it was dull, drizzly, and cold, so went back and grabbed a jacket. Meeting Andy, he had a look at the camera and reckoned that the battery had gone.

"When was it last changed, it's a very old type."

He was stunned when I said that as far as I could remember, it hadn't been changed for at least fourteen years, as Les had been gone for thirteen and I'd never done it! He offered to look around the shops to see if he could pick another one up.

After loading picnic hampers and boxes of drinks into the back of the open truck, we drove out of the ranch entrance, turning right this time. I was sitting in the front between Chuck and John, Andy at the back with Kristin and Nancy.

Immediately around the bend was a huge rocky canyon, completely different from the landscape behind us and was so unexpected that I was stunned. The rocks and boulders were streaked with blacks, greys, rusts, and creams, and the walls towered above the twisting road. Chuck told us that we would have to look out for rocks on the road as the rain usually loosened some into falling. Small dustcart size sweepers were parked in several places along the road to be used continuously to clear the road in wet weather, but any large rocks would have to be moved by bigger equipment brought in when necessary.

Not far along the road, Chuck stopped at a parking area so that we could get out and see Shell Falls, and a couple of us climbed down a lot of concrete steps to stand at the railings and watch the falling water. Even with little water in the creek, they were impressive. Going on he pointed off to the right, where a wide straight line of newly growing pines showed where a tornado in 1957 had flattened all the original trees. He'd been at this ranch for twenty two years having moved there from Casper having lived most of his life in California.

Thick clouds were hanging across the road as we climbed higher with some drifting along the valley beside and below us. Granite Pass. We crawled round and round, higher and higher, for nearly half an hour, finally reaching thick stands of trees with clearings, some with cattle that had been missed and left behind. These were the last of the herds, waiting to come down for winter although some would be trailered down rather than herded. It had been one of these herds that had gone past the ranch the other day. Chuck had told me then that they'd been very tired, and I could see why, we'd already travelled for miles. He told us to keep a lookout as we went along as sometimes we could come across a moose at the side of the road or even crossing it.

I noticed with interest that there were a lot of signs signifying the ages of the different rocks, from 280-325 million years (Jurassic), 325-355 million years, and anything up to 2.5 billion years.

The terrain kept changing, from rocks and hills to trees with clearings, and back again. The tips of the mountains were shrouded with white clouds like a thick mist, and from the heights, small bubbling creeks ran down, although a lot of the washes were dried up. We passed five mule deer grazing beside the road that were very shy of our car, bounding away in fright. One leapt over the fence easily as if it wasn't there. There were also a few areas of broken and dead trees, apparently torn down by what Chuck called, mini burst storms.

He pulled up at the side of the road as we neared a cloud filled valley for John to change places with Kristin as he hated looking down, and then we started down into a magnificent gorge, half filled with low lying clouds like billowing steam. At one place was a sprawl of huge rocks known as The Fallen City. Despite the drizzle, we were allowed to stop to look and take pictures, but it was quite cold and windy and we weren't out there for long. We followed the road down and down in a snaking zigzag, going under the clouds and emerging out into a huge wide valley. Chuck pointed to one sloping field that overlooked the valley to tell us that hang gliders normally took off from it. We stopped at a diner at Dayton on the Tongue River, for coffee.

Further on we stopped to read a sign for the Bozeman Trail, used by the immigrant wagon trains as well as being a cattle route up to the Wyoming and Montana ranges. Once again I was impressed by the fact that yet another historical place was well marked for tourists, and with a place in front of it for cars to stop to read the notice.

The land slowly became less wooded and flatter with soft rolling brown hills, and then we crossed the State Line into Montana. All the way there I'd been surprised at how few homesteads, ranches, and ski lodges there were about. I knew that Wyoming was the least populated State in the US, but from the looks of it, Montana would run it a very close second. The roads after the passes were now long and wide, and I mentioned how nice they were to drive on after England. When Chuck heard how crowded our roads were, he said that there was no way he could live like that and Kristin and I agreed whole heartedly, both of us wishing that we could remain here. She and I both said how we'd not come across road rage here, but that in Britain you met it constantly.

Chuck pointed out the site of the battle of the Rosebud and the Bighorn as we approached, and I tried to imagine the plains filled with tepees, smoke rising from campfires, children playing, huge grazing horse herds, and warriors bedecked in their feathers and finery. I began to realise now that I was here, how both the Indians and the soldiers could be ambushed in the folds of the land, and I could imagine the shouts, the rifle fire, the thundering of hooves. I found it immensely moving. To our right was a large ravine, the site of the Battle of the Rosebud.

We turned up the hill, Chuck paying our entrance fee at the small hut and chatting to the girl inside. As we breasted the rise, before us was a huge graveyard with hundreds of white rounded gravestones, and three tall, off white tepees standing to one side. Across the plain were scattered very small headstones.

Above us on the rising hill rose a huge monument, while in front of it was a fenced off area with more headstones. The actual area of Custer's Last Stand!

Chuck parked up and we walked across to listen to a ranger narrating the story of the battles. It was cold and windy as we were outside, and I was very glad of my coat.

In 1876, General Phil Sheridon had sent the army to drive the Indians into the agencies, with Brigadier General George Crook going north from Fort Fetterman, Colonel John Gibbon going east from Western Montana, and the 'Boy General' Custer, with the 7th Cavalry, moving west from Fort Abraham Lincoln. With Custer was his second in command, Major Reno, and Captain Benteen, both of whom did not get on with him. By June 6, three thousand Lakota Sioux and Cheyenne had gathered, camping on the banks of the Rosebud. On June 17, Crook was attacked by five hundred Indians, and after a fierce battle, the Indians retired to the Little Bighorn believing they had done well. Crook also withdrew.

June 21, Custer, Gibbon and Brigadier General Terry were informed by their Crow scouts that the Indians were to be found at the Little Bighorn. Gibbon was sent out to go up the Yellowstone and the Bighorn to block the Indians' way, Custer was to go up the Rosebud, catching them in a pincer movement. Custer pushed his troops very hard, arriving quickly at the Bighorn, unaware that the Indians' ranks had now swollen to six thousand, including the Hunkpapa, Oglala, Blackfoot, Northern Cheyenne and others.

June 25 Custer tried to see the camp through a telescope, but with most of the Indians around the bend, he couldn't see their extent, so he decided to attack, sending Benteen to the south, and Reno to pursue any fleeing Indians. Reno attacked the village whilst waiting for Custer, who didn't appear. He had no idea that Custer had decided to push on to another ridge, and had had to fall back under attack.

Despite his surprise at the number of Indians, Custer had attacked but, to a man, they had been wiped out by Crazy Horse's Oglala Sioux while a third of Reno's men had been killed by the time Benteen finally arrived to support them.

After the narrative, we trouped downstairs into a small room to watch a short film of the battles.

Back upstairs in the shop, I bought a map of the battlefield showing the places of each marker laid for a fallen soldier.

Back outside Chuck got the picnic out and we ate well, although I was amused to find English style sandwiches, with hard-boiled eggs, large filled rolls, and plenty of drinks. Delicious. But three of us sat in the truck to eat and keep warm.

After that, we walked up the steep hill to see the fenced off markers, white ones for the fallen soldiers and one near the centre with a black placard for General Custer. Standing, gazing down on the stones, I was conscious of a powerful silence and a sombre, chilling atmosphere. I borrowed the video camera from Andy to film the hills about us, amazed by the amount of scattered grave markers everywhere; in the folds of the earth, on the hills and down in the draws, singly and in groups. Almost everywhere you looked there were some.

Chuck wanted to get going, so we clambered back into the truck and he started driving slowly around part of the roadway through the battle ground, slowing for us to look at some of the information posts. It was going to be a very long trail, and as we had to get started back for the ranch, he turned round to head back for the main Interstate, stopping at the Trading Post.

I browsed among the books for ages before finally buying one about the life of Crazy Horse. Outside there were small and large tepees for sale, which I fancied, but Chuck mentioned that he sold small ones at the ranch. Much as I would have liked to take one home, there was nowhere to put it or anyone young enough to give it to any more.

The slight misty drizzle began to turn to heavier rain on the way home. Suddenly, Chuck pointed ahead and turned off the road to pull up as he'd spotted a moose trotting over the road and away towards the horizon.

It was huge, even at this distance, and had big broad antlers, while his shambling gait made his legs look like they were totally disjointed as he trotted along. I also spotted two large hawks, one sitting on a fence post, and another flying in to land on the post next to it.

At last the rain began to fizzle out, the sun came through the clouds, and the road steamed. It was a long slow haul back up the mountain, and we drove back up through low laying white clouds. Halfway up, where the cloud had dispersed, we stopped at a ski lodge to use the restrooms and get a drink from the remains of the picnic.

Finally we reached the down gradient into Granite Pass that was now a lot easier to see as the cloud from the morning had gone and I could gaze down into the deep gorge on our left where Shell Creek ran. Sitting on the opposite side of the truck to when we came up, I could see the huge boulders with slopes of broken rock (scree) looking as if they could slide at any moment onto the road. Unfortunately, we caught up to a slow moving car whose driver was obviously very nervous and kept the brakes on most of the time.

We arrived back at the ranch in time for dinner, and followed this with a ride to White Canyon again, as Kristin had not seen it, and this time Andy didn't come. It was very chilly with a slight drizzle in the air and my hands were very cold, so I kept trying to warm them under my arms, one at a time, having forgotten to bring my gloves. Kristin kept niggling about how slow the ride was and pointing out places where she thought we should lope.

On the way back, I leaned over to pick a sprig of blue sage to take home as I already had some grey sage from the Grand Canyon, and that also smelt like lavender.

We unsaddled, turned the horses out into the trail to go down to their field and walked back to the ranch house, where I had two hot coffees to try and warm up. Great, some dessert had been left for us again.

Chuck told us that there would be the chance of either a long three hour ride, which I couldn't do as my legs hurt after two hours these days, or two short ones. He also mentioned that in June the following year, the Cody Powwow would be held when thousands of real Indians turned up. I fancied coming over to see that. Someone then suggested playing games for the evening, so we all sat near the log fire in the huge wooden framed chairs.

'Sticks' consisted of two decorated sticks of wood and was a game of concentration. The sticks were passed from person to person, either held crossed or side by side, and you had to watch what the person did, and say whether the sticks were crossed or uncrossed. This was confusing as sometimes the sticks were passed on uncrossed, I tried to reverse the way they came and pass them on, only to discover that it was the opposite! I got it right three times, by accident, and after that got it wrong lots of times, eventually losing the plot completely and in the end, having to give up. Andy tried for nearly an hour, hardly ever getting it right but fighting gamely to understand.

Eventually, Kristin and Nancy started getting very frustrated, wanting to tell him and even exaggerating their movements. At last he twigged—to screams of joy from the girls. And it was so simple, but not what I expected.

Chuck did the next game, 'The Man in the Moon.' He outlined the shape of a face on the carpet with a stick and the idea was that you had to do it exactly as he did. I was well chuffed to get it on the second go, and this time Kristin took half an hour to get it, making us rib her for being so rude to Andy! I won't spoil it and say how they were done.

Jennifer wanted 'Psychiatrist' with Zeb offering to be the psychiatrist. He left the group, Jennifer told us the plot, and on his return, he had to come back and guess what was wrong with us. It was hysterical and great fun, but he discovered it in the end.

John and Andy then decided that they wanted to go to the nearby aeroplane museum for broken or/and repairable planes based outside Greybull in the morning. I wanted to either ride tomorrow, depending on the weather, as I had no slicker, or go into Greybull with Andy to see if I could get a battery for my camera, and also try to get some money from the bank. Eventually I decided to go to Greybull.

After that we went off to bed. I didn't need to use the big fan, but did pull the sheet over me as the air felt chillier. I couldn't get to sleep, sitting and reading for ages till just after twelve, but even then I was very restless, tossing and turning.

Friday 7th September.

Our last day, I rose at 6.30, writing up my notes and reading till I had to knock on the wall to wake Andy. I kept smelling faint wisps of lavender every so often, wondering where it came from, before discovering that the sprig of sage I'd picked was still in my pocket and almost under my nose.

Meeting Andy outside to go up for breakfast, there were wet marks on the cabin veranda from rain overnight although the ground had soaked it up so that it still looked dry.

We had breakfast, and as I had decided to go to Greybull with John and Andy, Zeb, Kristin and Nancy were left to go out on the long ride. That meant that there would be no riding that evening. Coming out of the ranch house, a fine drizzle had started.

We set off in the car, and not long after passing Shell, the drizzle stopped, replaced by cloud and sunshine instead. Andy drove straight to the museum, across the Big Horn River, and while they browsed round, I sat in the car reading until they returned, sitting with the door open as it was warm in the sunshine.

We parked in Greybull, and I went into the bank where I had no trouble drawing out money on my card. Strange! In a nearby western wear shop I bought a nice, bright yellow slicker, a new white straw hat, and some socks.

We headed back towards the ranch, and as we got closer, I spotted some really nasty, black looking clouds sweeping towards us from the Big Horns. Andy turned into Dirty Annie's just as the heavens opened, and we ran for the shingled porch and the inside of the store. Watching out of the windows, I saw the cars and the landscape disappear from sight under a curtain of white hail, worrying me about the riders, were they back?

We ordered coffee while we waited and when the hail stopped I took a photo of our car covered in ice. Back at the ranch I found that fortunately, everyone had returned just before the storm.

As Andy drove down to our cabins, I noticed that the once clear creek had turned a red colour from the flash flood as the water rushed down with sandstone mixed in it, and that water was pouring over the riverbanks and into the creek. Not long afterward, the waters slowly changed to a white colour. Different colours sands from the mountains.

All afternoon it rained, sometimes light, sometimes heavier. It was a dreary end to a lovely holiday, but well in keeping for my sadness at leaving in the morning. We all met for lunch, laughing and joking over the differences in what you can say or do/or not say and do in different countries. Like their 'fanny bag' that we can't call them, but our bum bag, as that was rude here.

Andy was chatting to Chuck, and from the sound of it, Brad, from the Lazy K Bar in Tucson the first year we'd been there, had been wrangling on the Kedesh this summer! Wow, small world.

We went out to the back room and played games again, which became hysterically funny, Jennifer joining in having come back after a day off. We'd said goodbye to Maureen, she was off till Sunday having alternated with Jennifer, then went to pay our bill. In the office, I bought a beautiful T-shirt with two horses on the front as well as a thick Kedesh Ranch short jacket.

Back in the main room, John had fallen asleep in one of the chairs so Jennifer splashed him with water, and he got up and chased her with a plastic cup of water, but she ran outside. Andy went off to pack while Jennifer and I sat in the ranch house, the others sitting out on the porch, chatting.

Just before dinner, the people from the dig came, mostly German, with 2 girls who were very quiet and hardly spoke English unless pushed. I thought them rather unmannerly for they made no attempt to join in.

We sat down for dinner and they started serving up the most enormous steaks! I hardly ever ate red meat, preferring chicken or fish, but Jennifer told me that there was no alternative. As I didn't like to appear impolite, when asked how I liked it cooked, I just said, "well done," and throughout the meal Jennifer kept looking at me and joking about 'how fast it was going.' I did manage almost half, and had to admit that it was very tasty and vastly different to what we had back home. It seemed such a waste, especially when Andy said that it was really good stuff and would have cost a fortune in Britain.

Kirby, from the dig, had had his birthday earlier on in the week, so at the end of the meal, Gail and Chuck gave him a lovely cake and a present.

Zeb, Jennifer, and Kristin had arranged before hand that after the meal they'd put in their 'Billy Bob' false teeth, disgustingly ugly ones and with Zeb and Jennifer's 'red neck' accents, they were hysterical. Kristin did well, although both she and Jennifer had to dive on the floor several times when their teeth kept falling out and they had to keep pushing them back in. Every time I thought I couldn't laugh anymore they started up again. Kristin, John, Nancy, Andy and I were all laughing, but I was almost crying as well, and my sides really hurt. The diggers just kept looking up and smiling at us. What a brilliant end to a wonderful holiday.

After the coffee, the diggers sat round the fire, while John, Nancy, Zeb and Jennifer played cards, twenty ones (our blackjack?) Andy and I watching. Jennifer was the banker and kept getting ratty whenever she had to give any money out, making us laugh. By 10.30pm I was having trouble staying awake, and by 11pm, everyone started to leave, the diggers going off to a motel for the night.

As we were leaving early next morning, there were hugs and kisses from Chuck and Gail and everyone, with promises that we'd try to come back next year, money willing. E-mails had been exchanged earlier before dinner. Gail and Chuck seemed genuinely sad to see us go, saying we were great, and Kristin was upset as John and Nancy would also be leaving after breakfast, leaving her the only one there.

Back in my cabin, I had a shower and packed the last of my things.

Chapter 22

Buffalo, and Geysers.

Saturday 8th September.

I slept badly, and was finally awakened at 6am when our roles were reversed and Andy knocked on the wall. It was cold outside.

We went up to the ranch house and had coffee with John, Chuck, and Nancy, who would be going back to Cody with Gail. On our way down to get the car we met up with Kristin and said our goodbyes.

Andy and I left at 7am and I was deeply saddened yet again, just like leaving the Lazy K Bar, and couldn't bear to look back. We drove out of the entrance, turned left head back towards Cody, passing through Shell, Greybull, and the tiny Emblem (pop. ten.)

As we got closer to Cody, I could see that the mountains in the distance were snow-capped and looked really lovely, shining white in the sun. Slowly the green ridges were left behind. Andy had wanted to photograph Indian Mountain, which Chuck had pointed out a few days back and looked like an Indian's face looking upward, but somehow we missed it.

We went through Cody (pop. 7,900) passing a sign for an old Western Town advertising trail rides, and headed out towards a rocky ravine. This led up into the mountains, crossing a bridge over the wide, rocky Shoshone River and surrounding us with huge grey crags. We followed the course of the river for a while, pines and spruce on the hillsides looking like fluffy Christmas trees, and passed through a long tunnel, emerging next to a huge reservoir.

I got out to film all round us, but was glad to get back into the car as, despite the sunshine, it was a chilly 44f 7C. The road carried on out into a lovely valley where we were gradually climbing higher, snowy peaks to right and left slowly coming closer. I wondered if we'd actually reach the snow line on our drive.

We crossed the North Fork of the Shoshone passing the town of Wapiti (wapeetee) where, round a bend, there were huge rock formations like hundreds of chimneys or organ pipes, rising out of sage covered slopes, grey crags and a carpet of pines.

Andy fancied breakfast and turned off onto a small trail, heading up a dirt track between dark, gloomy pines before reaching an old wooden chalet. White frost covered the wooden pole fencing and the ground. Gosh, what a change in weather from the ranch area.

We parked up and went inside, waiting to be seated, where I listened to two hunters talking, and then were shown to a wooden table with chairs made of rawhide and wood frames. When I went to order, the waitress apologised that they had no biscuits and gravy as they had run out of biscuits, so I settled for French toast with gravy instead.

There were skins and antlers on the walls, and a lovely warm wood burner at the far end of the room, crackling away. Two more men came in, and one told the other that it had been 30f—1C last night. It was so peaceful and cosy, it was a shame to get up and leave.

We carried on, getting closer and closer to the snowline, passing through more and more wooded areas, the mountains towering over us. Ravines and canyons opened out on either side of us, some with slides of broken shale. The road wasn't busy, but most of the traffic was RVs while at several parking spots were trucks and horse trailers. I guess people had gone out riding the trails.

At Pahaska, we followed the Shoshone River again for an hour or so through tall pines, and there was a sprinkling of snow beside the road. A notice informed us that we were now entering Yellowstone Park at an elevation of 8,559 feet and we pulled up at a small tollbooth to pay the $20 entry fee.

Yellowstone had first been discovered in 1867. Then, in March 1872, after Mammoth Hot Springs were seen, a bill had been passed to make it a National Park as people wanted it preserved for future generations and kept in its natural state.

In 1882, Phil Sheridon had discovered that the park had become a shambles, with wildlife being slaughtered in the thousands by poachers, and had launched a national campaign to put it under federal control. In1886, the army had taken over, put the park back into order, and restocked it with buffalo from the Texas rancher Charles Goodnight's private stock, thus helping to save them from extinction.

We passed a long open valley to the left, with snowy peaks behind it, following the somewhat bumpy, twisting road, before turning a corner to see Yellowstone Lake in front of us. There were several little beaches with people in coats walking about, and then a walled parking bay. Andy stopped, and I got out to film a plume of steam coming from beyond it, somewhere down in a crack. The smell of sulphur was horrid.

Continuing on, we passed orange/yellow sulphur ponds and dried up beds, all steaming. Nearly everywhere I looked, white steam rose in wispy plumes, and Pelican Creek wound its way across a yellow grass plain. We passed a huge buffalo sleeping by the road but nowhere to stop and film it, so I hoped that there would be more of them further on. Andy pulled in for gas, then drove on to Geyser Basin, a beach stretching from the road and around to our left, steam plumes all the way along it. An awesome sight and a strong reminder that we were actually in the middle of a still active volcanic area, in fact in a 80x40 mile huge sunken Super Volcano. One of the geysers was fenced off round the hole for safety.

There were huge areas of dead pines, some standing, a lot like a sea of fallen matchsticks, and we passed miles and miles of them. Patchy snow began to show again at 8,390 feet.

We drove on up and down hills, past clearings, dead pines, forested areas, rocks, until finally I spotted a large thick plume of steam rising over the tops of the trees where we turned off the road to follow the signs for 'Old Faithful.'

Unfortunately, we found that the plume I'd seen had been Old Faithful, and it wasn't due to go off again for about one to one and a half hours, and we had to leave before then. The regular sounding off of steam wasn't as accurate now as it used to be, for a mild earthquake had hit the region in the past couple of years.

I walked down the path to a ring of seats around the mound where the geyser was gently smouldering to photograph it, then went back and met up with Andy for a coffee. I also bought a fridge magnet of Old faithful in the gift shop, before we returned to the car.

I drove out and away, back down the road we'd come in from. Following a long line of traffic, I got stuck behind a truck towing a trailer belching black smoke and going very slowly up the hills and quickly switched off the car fans to stop the smell coming into the car like I did back home. Eventually, he pulled in to let us all go by. Not long after that, we passed a couple of buffalo grazing beside the road, again with nowhere to stop.

We turned at the junction to head for Pinedale, passing through beautiful forests and around sparkling lakes, and the steam jets slowly began to peter out. I slowed quickly as a little chipmunk ran into the middle of the road, only just missing it. The range of mountains off to the left that we'd come through gradually began to be left behind, but even bigger ones were appearing on the right. The Grand Tetons.

We stopped at a big wooden lodge beside a half empty lake for a coffee and a meal. The snow covered mountains stretched along the horizon behind the lodge, and there was a wonderful view of them through the windows. A boat slowly cruised across the blue waters leaving a long line of white ripples.

I drove on for miles following a snaking road that see-sawed up and down the hills, stopping once to film a lovely waterfall and creek running down a hillside, the banks lightly covered with powdery snow.

The landscape began to change from wooded areas with more miles of dead pines to flat plains to our front and left, a mountain range far in the distance to the left, and the huge snow capped mountains to our right.

I drove down into a canyon following the rivers of Hoback and Green where there were several miles of road works, slowing us considerably. No sign of any buffalo, antelope or mule deer. The roads were nice, but the speeds were a little slow, I guess because of the animals, anywhere between 25-55 mph.

I stopped at the town of Pinedale, parking at the side of the road and headed for a nearby café. The lady behind the counter couldn't have been more miserable (the first time I'd seen this in America) and the coffee was so awful, we got up and left it, going across the street to another restaurant, bigger and much busier. I wasn't hungry, but did enjoy their coffee.

We continued on to Rock Springs, travelling across the Wind River Basin where there were herds of pronghorn on the sage covered flats. Finally, we came across a Day's Inn, booked two rooms, and ate at the restaurant there before going back to our rooms to sleep. Great, there was a coffee machine in mine.

I had to switch the heating on overnight instead of having the cool air con.

That was novel.

Sunday 9th September.

I woke at 4.15am having slept much better than usual, made a coffee and watched the TV, flicking through the channels, before writing up my notes. Hearing a familiar voice, I looked up to see Murder She Wrote with Robert Fuller, watching until it was time to ring through to Andy's room at 7am.

We met outside the rooms and went for breakfast, another DIY, but this time with bagels, which I halved and toasted, spreading on butter and cream cheese. Oh dear, rummaging through my pockets I came across the key to my chalet at the ranch! I must post it back. We were packed and on the road by 8.15am, stopping for gas, then following Route 191.

It was lovely and sunny but still cold as we were at 7,000 feet here, with great grey crags to our left and rolling green hills to the right. The rocks gradually changed to hills and then we were driving down through a dry, sandy, sage covered valley with clumps of trees, dry washes showing where the water ran in the rainy season. Over a ten mile stretch, running alongside the I-80 Interstate, three long trains were at a standstill with one more following. The Union Pacific Rail Road. Having joined the Interstate 80, it was quite boring after the prettier, smaller roads.

More snow-capped mountains showed on the horizon, the Sierra Madre to the right and the Ferris Mountains to the left. We passed through Rawlins, staying on the I-80 before joining Route 287 to Medicine Bow and Laramie and then ahead lay the Elk Mountains, again snow covered as they climbed to 11,000 feet.

Across the North Platte River that wound across the plains intersected by deep washes and arroyos, we came to Carbon City, where the snow lay on the hills to our right, half a mile away and only five hundred feet higher. Suddenly, Andy spotted a herd of buffalo wandering alongside the road on the other side of a big wire fence, and managed to pull off the road so that I could film them.

From 10am onwards the radio was playing old sixties records that I hadn't heard in years, certainly not played on Capitol Gold or Invicta Gold back home, and it was brilliant. I tried hard not to hum along—it would have frightened the buffalo!

Around 11am, we pulled off the road at a rest area where there was a sprinkling of snow on the ground, to get something to eat, but it turned out there wasn't anything there but toilets. At Arlington, turning off the Interstate, we found a nice little wooden shack that advertised food, and had eggs, hash and toast washed down with coffee. It was a very nice meal.

From there we drove out into a wide basin surrounded by distant snow capped mountains, the beginning of the Rockies and somewhere nearby I guessed lay Denver.

At Laramie, after crossing the Laramie River, we drove down a long, long straight main street. The map we had showed where the old Laramie Fort lay, but as it turned out to be over a hundred and sixty miles out of our way, Andy decided that we were unable to visit it. Oh well, something for next year!

We walked round some of the shops, K-Mart in particular, had a coffee and a meal, and drove on, up into red rocky canyons with pines on the slopes, reminding me a lot of Sedona. Light snow was still on the ground as we reached Medicine Bow National Forest, and here huge grey rocks thrust up between stands of pine. Then out onto another plain, the ground lying in folds like a gentle swell on the sea, and headed down towards the town of Cheyenne.

In 1866, Charles Goodnight, a Texas rancher who had already experienced trail driving, decided to break a new trail north, being joined by Oliver Loving. He started west from the Texas Panhandle, went into New Mexico Territory following the Pecos River, then turned north through to Pueblo, Kansas and on up to Cheyenne that became known as the Goodnight-Loving Trail. During the drive, Loving was ambushed by Indians and killed.

At Cheyenne we spent a couple of hours looking around the shops on the long main street before we started heading along through more rolling green hills with rocky outcrops pushing up through the grass. Incongruously, a large model buffalo adorned one ridge.

Gradually the two-lane road became busier as traffic increased the closer we got to Denver, when I noticed Andy starting to look uncomfortable. He said that his stomach ached.

Slowly we began to see more and more houses and factories, and the traffic got even heavier, slowing down to a crawl several times. We had booked a Day's Inn for the night via the Internet, but had a bit of trouble trying to find it on the little map we had so, as the gas indicator light was on, we found ourselves driving down dingy back streets until we found a gas station. Andy was in the station a long time and I was getting quite worried, despite having locked the car doors, by the time he wandered out having bought a map of Denver.

Finally, after driving out onto a flat plain and down a long straight road, we came across lots of newly built hotels, and down near the end, was the Day's Inn. It was very smart, with an indoor pool. Andy booked us in and we took the elevator to our level. Leaving the bags in our rooms, we came back down to the reception area to ask directions for a restaurant. There wasn't one on site, but the man at the desk told us of one just across the road. Andy decided to take the car, which was just as well, as the restaurant was closed.

Further down, we came across the Courtyard Marriotts, parked up and went in, to be shown to a table. I had a tasty meal of chicken on a bun, French fries and a salad. Andy didn't eat much as his stomach was still hurting so, after a coffee, we returned to the hotel.

Back in my room, I sat watching TV, but then I began to feel quite sickly and wondered if I'd caught a bug that Andy had. I finally went to bed leaving the bathroom light on with the door half ajar just in case I needed to get there in a hurry. But I slept really well until 6am.

Monday 10th September.

I watched TV for quite a while, writing up my notes until 8.30 when I rang through to Andy's room to wake him. The usual way was just to dial the number, but this didn't work and after a couple of tries I rang through to reception, and they told me that I had to put an eight before the room number.

At breakfast there were toasted bagels with butter and cream cheese, but I found the bagels very dry and doughy, and just two made my stomach feel bloated.

We drove to the airport rental car lot, cleared out all our stuff, while one of the men came and noted the details on his handset, and went into the office to pay. It was much more than the boy at Cody airport had said, apparently they had added on several more things, so we would have been a lot better getting the Lincoln Continental after all. Andy was quite cross, and I decided that I would e-mail a complaint when we got home.

Waiting for the shuttle bus, Andy pointed out to me a man parked at the side of the road outside the car lot with a tow truck behind him. To his amusement, the car had three flat tyres, apparently having been driven out over the metal rods the wrong way. Oops!

The shuttle took us to the airport where I shoved my warm coat into my case, not needing it where we were going, while the cases were taken straight from the road onto a conveyor belt, and from there to the plane for us, very easy and convenient.

Inside, the terminal was light and airy with a high canvas roof, lots of shops, and a large pond with fountains in the centre. A driverless train took us to our concourse where, using the long moving walkways in the terminal, we found that we would be leaving from boarding gate 53. Slightly sad as just a week before we had left for Cody from gate 55!

Chapter 23

Tragedy.

After an hour's wait, having grabbed a coffee while waiting, we were called for our flight and went down the carpeted metal gangway to board. The plane taxied out onto the runway, and then we were up in the sky again making me feel quite dejected for I was now heading for another 'concrete city.' Looking out, I could see below us a snow clad mountain range then, not long after, Andy caught my attention, pointing out the window. We were flying over what looked like the Grand Canyon but looking at the maps when I got home, although it turned out to be part of the Colorado River, this was called the mini Grand Canyon. Wow, it was fantastic from the air, all the greys, greens, blacks, creams and rusts of the Grand Canyon, but looking as flat as if it had been rolled over by a giant steam roller. Then we were over flat plains. A desert? I checked the map, it was the Mohave Desert, and crossing it was a long thin, dark road, with shadowy places. Rocks?

Andy had been reading a newspaper and he pointed out to me an article about a mild earthquake that had shaken Los Angeles, breaking windows. Nice one. Thanks, Andy!

Coming in to land at John Wayne Airport in Orange County was soul destroying after Wyoming with all its houses and roads, miles and miles of buildings stretching to the hazy horizon. I found it hard to believe that so many people lived on the planet, let alone one city. New York had been the same—concrete from horizon to horizon.

We had trouble finding the Alamo Rental building, but eventually discovered it downstairs in the basement. While Andy was sorting out the car, I looked around and noticed that in several places, palm trees were growing up through the roof. Well, they'd built round them.

He came out of the office to say that they hadn't got the Blazer we'd wanted, but they had a white people carrier, an Oldsmobile Silhouette. Wow, big. It had a sliding door behind Andy, with another one behind me. It then transpired that I hadn't been included as the other driver on the paperwork, so it meant that Andy had to drive all the time we had it.

L.A. turned out to be a high rise city from what I could see as we drove out with lots of palms and looking remarkably like a scene from Miami Vice. It was hot and muggy outside the terminal. We headed out onto the six-lane concrete Interstate heading for San Diego. Off to our left were rolling green hills with canyons going way back, and on the right, after a few miles, I could see the Atlantic ocean when it became slightly foggy, then cold and breezy.

About halfway to San Diego, Andy pulled into a restaurant overlooking a marshy area with a creek running out to sandy dunes and the beach, for a coffee. Further along the road, another creek opened up on the left as well where there was a lot of bird life.

We found the Best Western San Del Mar, ten miles before San Diego, and while Andy was in the reception, I sat and watched a tiny, bright green humming bird flitting from flower to flower of the potted Busy Lizzies.

Our rooms were in a lovely spot on the first floor overlooking the pool where there were trees, palms and bushes in all the courtyards. The spa could be reached through the gym area. We both fancied a go at some time, but never managed to find the time.

Once in his room, Andy phoned through to confirm our balloon trip and wrote down the directions to get there. Just a forty-five minute drive north up the I-15 and we had to reach a vineyard at 6.30am to be picked up. He also phoned through to confirm his parachute jump, having to arrive at the airport by 12pm, where he would get a one and a half hour training session before jumping with two instructors at 4pm. After that he booked the Best Western Mid-Wilshire in Los Angeles for the following two nights.

Back downstairs in reception, he asked directions to the shops, or any nearby malls, getting directions. We tried to follow them, but came to a dead end! He tried the next road, but this just went in circles. We ended up joining the I-15 southbound, where there was lots of heavy traffic heading towards San Diego and the drivers were weaving in and out like England, the worst driving I'd seen since Orlando and very unusual for most of America.

We did spot some well-known shops, K-Mart and Walgreen's over on the right, but when we left the Interstate, we somehow ended up back near the hotel with no sign of them. Finally we came to a Carl's Jnr (like a Macdonald's) and stopped for a meal, where I had a nice salad and a coffee. The girl was very pleasant and gave Andy directions to a Wal-Mart, back along the I-15 northbound for a while then take the next turn off.

We did it! The road name was slightly incorrect, and it was on the wrong side of the road, but we were there.

Andy put his films in to be developed at the 1-Hour section, before wandering around the aisles. It was weird, I felt that I'd been here before until I realised that Walgreen's, or even K-Marts, were the same layout, so that when you went to another store in another city, you knew where to find things. On the other hand, that made it boring, as it was nice to wander round the shelves and have a look everywhere.

Andy browsed for ages among the boating gear for things were so much cheaper over here. After three quarters of an hour my knee was hurting badly, so I sat down while Andy did a bit more searching for presents to take home. He retrieved his photos and was very disappointed as a lot of them were out of focus. Because of the zoom? It was a new camera.

Going out through the checkout, Andy was asked for his ID, "a passport?" I said, "everything is in the car, I'll go get them," but the girl asked me what Andy's surname was. I spelled it out and she said, laughing, "OK guys, if you're cheats, you deserve to get away with it!" and let us through. It was dark outside now, Daylight Saving Time, their Summer Time.

Back at the car, while trying to open the side door behind the passenger seat that still seemed to be very stiff, I discovered that although the sliding door behind the driver was manual, the one behind the passenger seat was actually electric. No wonder I had had trouble trying to open and close it.

We managed to get back to the hotel OK this time. I watched TV while Andy went across to the hot tub for a while, and when he got back, he helped me set my hotel clock to 4.30am when we needed to leave. I showered, wrote my notes, and watched some more TV until 11.30pm, trying to make the time drag as I didn't want to sleep. Going home was getting closer.
Tuesday 11th September.

I had a very restless night, tossing and turning, and was finally woken at

3.40am by what I thought was Andy banging on the wall! I thought I'd misheard until he started tapping on my door. It turned out his room clock was set wrong, having gone off at 3.40 instead of 4.40am. Another person must have set it an hour out.

I dressed quickly, we packed the cases into the back of the carrier, Andy paid up at reception and we drove out to join the I-15 in the dark. The road was a lot clearer of traffic at this time, which was pleasant, but not far along it began to get foggier, and I hoped the balloon trip would be called off. I didn't fancy hanging below a balloon, it was bad enough flying.

We reached the vineyard which was shrouded in thick fog, three quarters of an hour too early so we dozed in our seats on and off till 6.30am.

The radio had been turned low, and I vaguely began to hear the news that a plane had crashed into the World Trade Centre in New York, about 5.45am our time here, while we were parked up. I felt sickly, we had been up there last year, and wondered how on earth the pilot hadn't seen such tall buildings, having a rough idea from last year about where the airport was. Why was the plane so far off course?

Rusty and Kevin then arrived in an open backed truck with a wicker basket standing up in the back. I thought it looked rather small and fragile looking. They introduced themselves and said that the fog shouldn't be around by the time we reached the take off site, as it was further up into the foothills. We climbed into the back seat of the truck and set off, but then we heard on the radio that another plane had hit the second tower. Alarm bells rang. Twice, was peculiar. My stomach knotted as I felt for all the people who must have been in the building. We were all shell shocked, what was going on? I just couldn't comprehend it was happening. I felt even sicker as I was worried about being up in a balloon basket, too.

All the way to the site we kept talking about it, listening out to the radio to try and understand what had happened. Gradually we heard that it had all been done by terrorists, who had hijacked the planes, and just flown straight into both buildings. How could anyone be so sick? How could anyone be so brainwashed that they could watch themselves drive into a building at five hundred miles an hour, and to know that hundreds, perhaps thousands of people would be murdered by their own hand. They had to be drugged up to the eyeballs.

Finally, we drove out of the fog and up to the take off site, where Rusty and Kevin pulled a long blue tarpaulin out of the back of the truck and began rolling it out onto the scrub grass, for the balloon to rest on, Andy told me. A huge fan was brought out and set up on the grass to begin blowing wind into the balloon while Rusty held it open, and slowly it began to inflate. When the basket was taken down from the truck, Rusty had us stand beside it for our picture to be taken with the open end of the balloon behind us. We would get our pictures and a certificate for flying at the end of the flight.

It was a beautiful morning, clear where we were with the fog lying in the hollows lower down. I couldn't believe that on such a beautiful day, thousands of people had been killed deliberately. They were saying that on a working day, up to fifty thousand people could be in there.

Rusty laid the basket over, ignited the burners, and began directing the hot flame into the balloon, which began to billow and rise very slowly. Finally it was up over the basket, swaying in the breeze, and we were allowed to climb in. I clung to one of the basket's four cables with a grip of iron. When the burners were roaring hot air into the balloon above us, it was really hot. Although I was rarely to be found without my western hat, even at home, I was so glad Andy had mentioned how bad it had been the first year he went in a balloon. I joked with him over it, especially as he had very little hair on top to protect him.

Suddenly, very gently, we began to rise. It was very unlike a plane as it went straight up, but I was still extremely nervous, especially when someone moved and the basket wobbled. We hovered for ages almost over the same spot for there was very little wind, looking down at Kevin folding up the tarpaulin. He would pack up and try to follow us to where we could land, and it could be almost anywhere, depending on the wind's direction!

Then the mobile phone rang, it was Rusty's wife, asking if he'd heard the news, and did we know that a third plane had hit the Pentagon, with a fourth plane still in the air, having also been hijacked. I was stunned. Like everyone, I thought America to be one of the safest places in the world. How could this be happening?

Rusty dropped the balloon a short way down to try and catch a breeze so that we could move or, as Andy said, laughing, "Kevin needn't try to follow us, we'll just stay overhead and come down in the same place." I was very surprised at the silence up here, especially when no one was speaking and the burners were turned off.

Slowly we drifted over dusty, scrub covered grey hills, criss-crossed with tiny tracks, coyote trails, Rusty informed us. There were also square lines laid out ready as plots for more houses to be built, and I found it very saddening that such a lonely and beautiful area would be ruined by buildings.

Rusty suddenly pointed out a coyote running below, like a tiny dog from this height, and then discovered a mule deer that was startled and kept trotting away from us, finally trying to hide in a clump of rocks. I also watched a couple of cottontails bolt into the brush.

Rusty was trying to direct Kevin by walkie-talkie as he was having difficulty in getting onto the fields for some of the entrances to tracks were stopped by chains or bad ground. Finally, we saw him double back and get onto the fields to our right, sending up a dust cloud behind him.

Eventually, we started to drift down towards a trail, where we hovered for a while, but as Kevin approached to meet us, a fickle breeze picked up, sending us away from him and down towards a gully. Rusty turned the burners on so that we rose again, and we sailed on over, heading for another hill in front of us. Kevin had quickly reversed the truck, and Rusty told him which way to go. I was genuinely pleased that the trip was continuing, and couldn't believe that I was actually enjoying myself up here.

Slowly we began to come down again, and Rusty warned us to hang on. The basket bumped over the ground, not too badly, and came to a halt, luckily staying upright. Slowly the balloon began descending, the breeze taking it out away from the basket and it began to sink to the ground. We were allowed out of the basket, standing back while the balloon deflated and flattened onto the ground. Rusty and Kevin began laying it out tidily, then Rusty went to the truck, coming back with a red chequered tablecloth, a folding table, a champagne bottle and some Danish pastries—our champagne breakfast. He gave us a toast, and recited the Balloonist's Prayer.

Once the balloon was folded up and put away, he came over and gave us our photos in a folder to say that we were now Aeronauts! He commented to me, "you're a little more talkative now! Would you do it again?"

"Probably!" I wanted to say, yes, but thinking about what was happening in New York, I just couldn't feel pleased about anything.

They drove us back to our car at the vineyard, where we heard over the radio that all flights in and out of America were now grounded, with external flights being diverted or turned back. Andy mentioned his parachute jump for which Rusty thought unlikely to be on.

We drove out to the airfield anyway and Andy went to see what was happening. When he came back, he said that that nothing was in the air but that they might be able to refund his money so he'd told them to put it towards a disaster fund.

Back at the ghastly concrete Interstate, we headed for LA. Everywhere I looked there were houses, buildings, and offices, and we passed several of the huge storm drains. We just couldn't stop talking about the crashes, and I suddenly realised that my sister Sue would be frantic even knowing that I was nowhere near New York. I would try to ring her when we got to the hotel.

The hotel was found fairly easily and we rushed to our rooms on the 3rd floor to turn the TV on. It was worse than I'd thought. They showed one tower burning in the middle with a plane appearing behind the other, and there was the terrible flash of an explosion with a ball of smoke as the second was struck. I couldn't believe that someone had caught it on video, but then tourists were always around. People there were screaming and running about in evident shock. We were both appalled, and I kept wandering from my room to his and back, just glued to the TV channels.

I phoned Sue when it was 8.30am there, 12.30pm here. She was frantic, and so relieved, as distance didn't matter to her. I was, "in America somewhere." I had to smile when I saw the funny side of her saying that it had happened yesterday when it was today here. I explained that we were about three thousand miles away from New York, but she just kept repeating, "it doesn't matter, you're still in America." She promised to ring Daphne, who'd already phoned her anyway, and I also asked her to let Kristin know at the stable yard, giving her the farm number. I was hoping that we would be home on Friday as Andy had already confirmed with Virgin Atlantic for our flight, but later on the TV news stated that LA airport would not reopen until at least Wednesday.

We went out to Denny's, just round the corner, for lunch. It was similar to Wendy's and better than Macdonald's, while the food and service were good.

After that we drove around the roads for nearly three hours trying to find the famous 'HOLLYWOOD' sign on the hill, but somehow, in all the traffic, we missed it. But we did drive up and down Hollywood Boulevard, Sunset Boulevard, and Wilshire Boulevard, and spotted the signs for Universal Studios.

I'd always wanted to visit Hollywood Boulevard as this was where all the actors and actresses had their names in stars embedded on the sidewalks, so Andy parked up and we set out walking. I was very surprised at how dingy the place looked with the smaller shops looking like our lockups back home with each shop having metal grills over doors and windows. I'd expected something a lot smarter. Looking quite out of character was the inevitable Macdonald's on Sunset Boulevard.

I treated myself to a very fancy Hollywood emblazoned T-shirt with lots of glitter in one of the shops, another car number-plate for Daniel, and a pretty thimble for Daphne. There were lots of grubby bag people and bums sitting or lying on the pavements, several with supermarket trolleys full of rubbish, and one man in a dirty old torn coat was pawing through a garbage basket. How lucky I felt to have grown up in better circumstances. I had had a lot to be grateful for.

It was getting dark by then with all the street and shop lights coming on, so we drove along the Boulevards before starting up a narrow, steep hill in low gear, turning very sharp corners between houses and blocks of apartments. By the time we finally reached the top and seemed to be heading nowhere, it was pitch black, so Andy turned round and we started back down. Not far into the descent, I got him to stop the car and got out to take a photograph. The whole of Los Angeles to the far horizon seemed to twinkle with millions of lights, hundreds of feet below. It was absolutely stunning.

We continued the descent carefully, meeting very few cars coming up fortunately. How any car could do this ascent and descent more than twice without wearing out both gearbox and brakes, I couldn't imagine, as I don't think our people carrier enjoyed it much.

We drove back to Denny's for a coffee, then continued on to a Wal-Mart, two blocks away, where I bought two cartons of powdered lemonade for $2.99each (fifty pints each when made up with water,) hoping it was as nice as the stuff at the ranch.

Back in my room I switched on the TV and I sat trying to write my notes. It became very difficult to concentrate for almost every channel was showing films of the planes hitting the towers, and people running, and the towers falling, over and over and over again. My mind just switched off, I was beginning to watch it without it seeming to register. Flicking through the channels, I discovered every one either covering the disaster, or closed down, but then found the BBC. It was strange to watch the British version, stated in our dignified English way, comparing it to the emotional Americans who were threatening dire consequences to whoever had been involved.

Amtrak trains, Greyhound buses and all the airports were now closed-America had ground almost to a halt. The whole thing was incredible and almost inconceivable. Eventually I went to sleep around 11.30pm.

Chapter 24

Jaws.

Wednesday 12th September.

I was up at 6am and made coffee, then sat watching TV.

No. Yesterday hadn't been a dreadful nightmare. It was real! More amateur film from different angles, more news of people lost, police, ambulance and fire crews that had all rushed to help. People jumping from the towers, unwilling to wait to be burnt, falling to their deaths.

I called Andy at 7.30am and went down to the 2nd floor for breakfast when he was ready. In a tiny little room set with a few tables and chairs, was a choice of cereals, toast, or the inevitable donuts and pastries.

Then we were off to Universal Studios, Andy opting for the dearer $12 but shorter walk to the entrance, instead of the $7 fifteen minute walk, parking in an underground lot. The entrance fee was $39 each extra to get in.

We walked around for a short time, going down about five escalators to a building lower down but I found, like many of the rides there, that I wouldn't be able to go on because of my bad neck. In some cases I was really grateful. Once back up again, the loudspeakers announced that it would be advisable to take the guided tour round the sets early because of inevitable long delays later, so we queued up to wait for seats on a three trailer road train.

Conveniently placed TV screens hung from the ceiling with Ron Howard from 'Happy Days' giving commentary about the various sights we would see on the tour. We also had a live tour guide with us at the front with a microphone.

They drove us around the sound sets first, big buildings with large numbers on each. Several were in use at the time, but despite all the people moving about, there was no one I recognised.

The carriages slowed down and turned towards a dark entrance to one of the buildings, passing through big sliding doors. Ahead in the darkness I could hear a roaring sound, and then sparks flashed ahead. A helicopter suspended from the roof was firing at an enormous figure of King Kong as it climbed up some bridge supports. It was very close and absolutely brilliant, but the eyes suddenly started flashing red and that rather spoiled it for me.

Back out in the sunshine, we went round a cul-de-sac of famous houses from programmes like 'Murder She Wrote,' and 'Uncle Ben's Cabin.' From there we headed through different streets including the Roman Empire, the gangster style Chicago, Olde England, and others before heading into another black set, an underground station.

Suddenly the train began to shake and tilt—an earthquake! Passengers squealed as cables broke and sparks showered around when a generator cupboard broke open on our right. Opposite, a huge petrol tanker slid down towards us, just stopping short of the train. Then a metro carriage fell down, bursting into flames. On the right again, a huge cascade of water poured down the passageway, through the turnstiles, and under our train. All the time it kept shaking and rattling, and tilting. Absolutely brilliant! Then we were out and into the sun.

We threaded our way round roads and buildings to arrive at a Mexican village. As we halted, there were lightning flashes and crashes of thunder, before sprinklers came on like heavy rain. Suddenly, down the cobble stone street from behind the corner house, a torrent of water flooded down and under the train, making us all jump. The commentator was at pains to tell us that all the water is, apparently, recycled.

We circled the Bates Motel, the Psycho house just beyond it on a hill, just a shell like all the others, the inside scenes all being done in the huge sound sets. Wending our way past a lake, the Black Lagoon, we came to another with a replica submarine anchored in the middle. Just after that the train stopped. The commentator announced, "and this is where we do the parting of the seas," and where the road dipped and climbed again, the water began to drain away, leaving the lake water held back by metal gates. Driving through, the water was actually at eye level. Fantastic.

Finally we reached a town and another lake, this one with fishing boats on it. The spooky Jaws music came on, a model diver surfaced in the centre of the water, then a shark attacked with the diver going down screaming and the water bubbling up red. Slowly we continued on past a jetty with gas tanks, arranged in an 'L' shape, and here a huge model Jaws came swimming alongside the carriages, rearing up and splashing everyone in reach. Andy jumped back, but not quickly enough and his camcorder got a bit damp. He wasn't best pleased.

Once off the train and back near the entrance, we had a quick meal beside a huge lake watching water skiers doing a show. Beautiful little white egrets were stalking about on their long pink legs, greedily eating chips the kids were throwing who I reckon threw more than they ate. What a waste of food, and it was really sad to watch such delicate, pretty birds gorging on rubbishy, unnatural food. The scene was a replica of Sea World in Orlando.

Just round the corner we came across the Wild West Show I'd wanted to watch, and which turned out to be a glorified slapstick comedy stunt show, with the hero being pushed around by a bad family consisting of a bossy mother and two sons. Mother was pushed down a well, sides of buildings fell down, and the hero was beaten up before he scrambled over the rooftops to slide down a rope. It was very well done, and quite fun, but by now the sun was getting rather hot for sitting and watching shows comfortably in the open.

We shopped in the little arcades where I bought some popcorn, then turned when I heard and saw approaching old black and white police car with its sirens blaring. Inside, I could see two men in dark suits and black hats who drove up to the stage and leapt out to run up onto it. 'The Blues Brothers,' a singing and dancing show. They were really good and we were lucky to find two empty seats at the back to stay and watch. Eventually, police sirens could be heard in the distance, they raced back to their car waving to the crowd, and drove off.

We went further on to watch the Animal Channel show, where a conure parrot flew into the audience and took a $1 bill a man was holding, taking it back to the trainer on the stage, before returning it. There were performing dogs and other animals, but at the end, a chimp refused to do almost anything, finally escaping and climbing up into the rigging above the stage. Everyone was asked to leave quietly, but lots of us hung on to see what happened, again being asked again to leave. I guess they finally coaxed it down after we'd gone.

Finally, we queued up to watch Waterworld, and I was glad to sit down again as my knee had become swollen and painful after the long wait. Wow, the show was incredible, being based on the film. The set was made up of metal bits and pieces, looking exactly like a junkyard, with towers and ropes, and speedboats and water skis on the water in front. The stunts were fantastic, the explosions noisy, and near the end of the show, the water was set on fire from underwater gas pipes. Even a seaplane was catapulted across the water, ending up on the other side of the pond near the audience.

During the day, various characters appeared on the streets, stopping to have their pictures taken with visitors. Dracula was fantastic, very real and spooky, enveloping the women with his long black bat cape. There was a very realistic Doc from 'Back to the Future, three of the Marx Brothers, one of them being my favourite Harpo, and several other characters.

Eventually, we left through the entrance, only to discover to our left a long mall of shops, so we spent another hour browsing up and down the street. One shop had lovely little mechanical walking animals, dogs, cats, horses, a zebra etc. wandering about tethered on strings. In one shop I came across a very large remote control with extra big buttons for dad to use with his TV and video as his eyesight was failing. I just hope he can use it. (Alas it wasn't compatible with our television back home.)

We bought an icecream cone each and went back to the car where, on the radio, they started playing a new Enya record with voice-overs of the disaster. It was very moving, and was played every time we turned the radio on.

Back at the hotel, switching on the TV in my room, they were still showing the disaster and holding lots of phone-ins and interviews. One man, whose firm had occupied several floors, had lost all his employees, only being saved himself because he'd had to drop his son off at school. He felt so guilty at not being with them, it was heartbreaking to listen to him.

We drove back to Hollywood Boulevard and bought a map showing where all the stars were positioned on the pavements, walking up and down some of the sidewalks to try and find Robert Fuller's. Unfortunately, in some places, the pavement was up due to building works going on and I never came across it. Andy did find a shop selling suitcases and bought another travelling case for all his presents and T-shirts.

Back at the hotel, Andy phoned through to Virgin Atlantic, who told him that no planes would be going out before at least Friday, although the TV had stated earlier that even then there would only be a few internal flights. Andy said that he wanted to be put on the first flight out and was told, "so does everyone, we can only take every person in turn."

He then went down to the reception to ask for another night's stay, which was OK with them, but wondered if we would be covered by our insurance for the extra rooms, car rental, food etc. He also phoned Alamo about the rental car and got it for another day, but would have to ring every day after to ask again.

We decided to go back to Denny's for a meal, but when we went out to get into the car in the underground lobby, Andy felt the car vibrating slightly and pointed to a glass mirror on a cabinet on the wall, which was shimmering, too. That made me nervous, and I was glad to get out. As the security guard wasn't around I couldn't ask if it was a mild earthquake.

At Denny's, we were served by a very friendly Asian girl, but when Andy's meal came it was huge as it also included three pancakes and two slices of toast! I'd settled for another salad. After a coffee, we went back to the hotel.

I felt very, very tired and drained, glad to shower and just fall into bed, dozing while I tried to watch the TV a little longer, flicking through the channels to see if anything good was on. I managed to stay awake long enough to phone Sue at 11pm to say that there were no flights till at least Friday, I'd just have to keep in touch and let them know what was happening when I could find out.

Thursday 13th September.

I didn't wake up till 8am when I turned on the TV for the news and they stated that L.A. airport was due to be opened at 12 noon, but that long delays of anything up to 4 hours were to be expected. We went for breakfast, but I wasn't very hungry and just settled for a coffee.

It was hot outside again. This time we headed out for the L.A. Zoo, missing the signs for it as they weren't very clear, and we overshot the entrance. Alongside the road, just past the zoo was a fenced off sand track, and inside a girl was riding in western gear. I wished I could be back in Wyoming.

Andy bought a map of the zoo area and we began wandering round the exhibits. The animals seemed to be in very small, sparsely grassed enclosures, which I thought was unusual for zoos these days, although some enlarging appeared to be going on. I stopped for a coffee at a kiosk, grateful to sit down for a while as my knee was aching quite badly, especially after yesterday's walking, but it tasted very bitter and we both ended up throwing most of it into the trashcan.

The orang-utans were much bigger than I expected, but very disdainful, mostly sitting with their backs to us behind their protective glass panels. The elephants were also in a very small dusty area and I felt sorry for them, they were swinging their trunks aimlessly and looking bored. We came to a round building with glass cases, surrounded by a wooden fence. Inside the cases were different species of snakes, with an enormous boa constrictor in one.

Confined animals of all sorts make me feel claustrophobic and I felt so sorry for all we saw all over America and Britain, although we now have lots of safari parks. Humans can walk where they want on the earth, while animals are trapped.

Slowly we wended our way back down to the entrance, browsing in the shop where I bought two rubber snakes with rattles in their tails to put in my garden. It was hot, the car registering 80f 24-25C when we got back to it, so we headed for the beach at Santa Monica, stopping on the way at a Carl Jnr's for a meal.

As we left, just round the corner, we passed a fire engine, with police and paramedics treating someone sitting on the ground. It looked as if a car had turned in towards a parking lot and the pedestrian had been knocked over. On the ground, around the car, red glowing flares were laid on the road instead of the cones that we use.

Andy stopped once to phone Virgin for any information, only to be told that there was no further news and to try later, either that night about 11pm or on Friday morning, but that we were definitely on the waiting list to be first out.

Over the radio, we heard that men with false pilots' papers had just been arrested in New York. This was scary, were there maniacs out there still trying to hijack planes?

We drove through Beverley Hills on a three lane freeway, passing lots of beautiful homes, some with ornate metal railings and gates, all with tall palm trees as well as beautiful flowering shrubs and green grass, finally ending up parking in a lot near the beach.

Along the sand was a cycling, skating all weather pathway. This was Muscle Beach with volleyball nets and gymnastic rings, but not a sign of a muscle anywhere, to my disappointment! Out toward the sea were the lifeguard huts—just like Baywatch, and ahead of us was a long wooden pier stretching out into the beautiful blue sea.

We walked up the steps and along the wooden flooring of the pier, from the sides of which we could look down at the big breakers running in under the metal pillars. It felt just like being on an English holiday, and looked like it too with the stalls, the cafes, and the fishermen along the sides. The air smelt fresh of the sea. Bliss!

A roar from over the sea made us look up, startled, for way up, a seaplane flew overhead, the first we'd seen in days. Great, perhaps things would start moving now. At the end of the pier we stood looking down for a while, before walking back.

Andy drove along a bit further where we found to my amazement, a roundabout and it was weird trying to go round it on the wrong side. He found a marine shop, parking up and going in for forty minutes while I sat in the car and wrote up my notes. Around, were lots of cars and trucks, and even police cars all flying the American flag that I'd wanted as well, but we never did find any, most of the sellers seemed to be standing in the central reservation where we couldn't reach them.

Further on we came across a grocery store and bought some drinks before getting salad from the bar which we could make up ourselves for $4.99 a lb filling a plastic container with anything from the many various selections offered. A brilliant idea—until Andy mentioned some time after that anyone could have been standing over the food, coughing or sneezing, and handling things, despite plastic spoons being provided.

Returning to the hotel we sat watching the TV in Andy's room while eating the salad, and I made cups of coffee from the machine provided. Andy tried ringing Virgin Atlantic, but only got through to a recording saying that the office was closed (of course, it was three hours back where they were,) but that all flights were still suspended. I went back to my room, showered, watched TV till 10.30, and went to bed.

Friday 14th September.

After breakfast, we went back to our rooms and Andy tried Virgin Atlantic. They again informed him that nothing was known as yet, and advised him to try later that evening, so I phoned through to tell Sue. She said that she was going to meet Daphne, Tony and Daniel at their caravan that evening, as they had never actually met each other before, and that Daphne had stated she might stay on the site for the week, if I wasn't home by the weekend.

We booked out of the hotel, planning to move to one closer to the airport to save time, driving down to the ocean first. Andy parked in a small street backing onto the beach, and we trudged out to the sea on lovely clean warm sand, passing between two of the towers used by the lifeguards, now closed and shuttered. What a disappointment, where's David Hasselhoff?

Sitting on the sand, I watched the incoming waves, while the avocets and gulls ran up and down the sand as the water lapped in and out, with not a soul in sight. It was lovely and warm in the sun with a cooling breeze, so I slapped on some suntan lotion and laid back. It was so peaceful it was hard to imagine anyone hurting another human being, rather like being in another world, and it was smashing to just relax and chill out. I had been getting ratty for saying silly things, mishearing what Andy said, getting the map reading wrong, and becoming nervous of the driving, because I kept forgetting to take my Lecithin capsules every morning.

Originally used in America to bring down cholesterol levels, the only known side effect had been the improvement of the memory. I'd read about it in the Daily Mail's female page a couple of years back, and without it I would have lost my job as my concentration and memory began letting me down badly. I'd been amazed at how the stuff actually worked.

Suddenly, I looked up in amazement as I heard a plane's engines roaring, as it climbed from behind the houses and flew out to sea, followed at intervals by others. Andy thought that they must have opened up the airport, whether for just cargo or passengers, he had no idea. I went for a quick paddle, but the water was colder than it looked, and I didn't stay there for more than a few minutes.

After an hour, we walked back to the car, where I had trouble cleaning off the sand that had stuck to the suntan lotion, but I managed by brushing my legs and arms off using my socks.

At a parade of shops, after parking in the car park in front, we went to a café for a coffee and a meal, sitting at one of the tables outside. I ordered a Caesar salad, and when it came, it had some of the nicest tasting chicken strips I'd had so far. Going inside to pay, two girls were sitting inside making up red, white and blue ribbons with tiny gold pins, and having been handed one each, we put some money in a tin for the disaster fund.

Further down the road, I spotted a bank and went to see if I could get some money out, after I managed to find the doors to go in, which were hidden around back. But it turned out not to be a main bank and my card wouldn't swipe, so we continued on, coming across a Bank of America just down the road. No trouble there, thankfully, and I got my cash.

Andy headed down a long, dreary road full of shops and supermarkets, gas stations and car lots, all with big billboards or signs, but nothing that we wanted like a K-mart or Walgreen's. About 75% of them seemed to be for fast food, Wendy's, Carl Jnr. and Macdonald's amongst others. Pulling into a gas station, he filled up, paid, and just as we were about to drive off, a coloured man went into the restroom, struggling as he had his bike with him. Once in, he began singing then began throwing toilet rolls out the window, so Andy went and told the attendant. We left quickly.

Back at the hotel, I found kids next door banging on the internal walls and making a dreadful racket.

Andy tried for over an hour to get through to Virgin Atlantic with no success, so we gave up and went out for a meal, finding an Arby's. I could only manage a milkshake, not being very hungry.

Returning to the hotel, Andy tried phoning again, but this time only got the recording as the office had closed for the night, but which informed him that we should ring tomorrow, as there were possibly limited flights.

I watched TV for a while, still mainly about New York, and the scenes were even more horrendous. They also stated that the airport was now open but warned passengers to take their own food and drinks for there would be up to five hours delay.

I had a disturbed night with Amtrak trains hooting as they passed the hotel window.

Chapter 25

Home at Last.

Saturday 15th September.

I couldn't sleep after 3am and lay watching TV before finally dozing off, waking up at 7am. I phoned through to Andy at 7.30am. He started phoning Virgin, but by 8.30am as he couldn't get through due to the lines being continuously engaged, we went for a continental breakfast of coffee and donuts!

Back at the rooms, I tried as well as him to get through to the airline, but nothing, so I rang Sue. She had made arrangements with Daphne for us to ring her as soon as we landed at Heathrow and she'd send a cab for us, that way Stephen could pick us up from her place instead of the crowded airport. She gave me Daphne's telephone number in case my mobile phone's battery had gone while we'd been away.

Still no answer at Virgin so I phoned Sue back and asked her to ring Heathrow to see if she could find out anything that end. Half an hour later she rang back excitedly, it having taken her all that time to get through.

"Can you get to the airport three to five hours before 17.30pm our time?"

"Yes!"

I rushed round to tell Andy, we dragged our cases downstairs, and Andy paid the bill. On the way to the airport we decided it would be a good idea to have a breakfast in case of a long delay, stopping at a Denny's. While sitting at the counter, we chatted to a nice waitress for a while before she went to speak to a man in a uniform, obviously knowing him well, and he turned out to be a pilot with American Airlines. After telling him that we were from England, he informed us that he had relatives in Cornwall.

After that, we stopped at Ralph's to get some drinks and snacks. While we were in there, I got chatting to a coloured lady who asked where we'd got our ribbons as she hadn't been able to find anything, and had to tell her it was at the beach. When she realised we were British, she said how impressed she had been with the speech from Tony Blair, our Prime Minister, supporting the USA. It had meant a lot to Americans to know they weren't alone.

We drove round and round the perimeter of the airport before we finally found the car rental place, having a very near miss with an oncoming car at one junction when Andy swung across to the right without seeing him and making me shout out a warning. We parked up and Andy went to check to see if he could get through to Virgin to find out any news, not wanting to leave the car in case we could keep it, but again no joy, so he gave it up as a bad job. While I was waiting for him, planes were taking off quite regularly and we must have been near the end of a runway as they were very low.

The shuttle bus took us round to Terminal 2, passing through a couple of checkpoints. The men were obviously used to the driver as he was waved through. No cars were being allowed into the airport at all, but there were police cars and motorcycles everywhere.

The queue at the terminal was huge, stretching along the pavement almost back to Terminal 1. An English girl, Sam, was organising the line, and when Andy asked what was happening, she explained that she didn't know any more than we did at the moment. A TV van from Fox Sky was parked just up from us, and after walking along the queue the reporter eventually interviewed a British girl behind us.

At 13.20 the line finally started moving, although very slowly. Andy wandered off, coming back ten minutes later to say that despite having spoken to a Virgin Atlantic man who couldn't tell him anything about what was happening, this was only the stand-by queue, all those with today's tickets were in another queue further down where the line was split. Andy had explained to him that we had confirmed our flight on the Monday night, and had been told to ring and book again on Thursday, but after that we just couldn't get through to anyone. The man had reiterated that we had no option, that we had to stay in line and would have to re-register.

The staff began splitting the line, the people with confirmed tickets being allowed in the rest of us staying where we were. Andy went to look for Sam who told him that there would only be a 747 and an airbus due out today, and that even if we booked in our luggage, there was no guarantee we would leave before Monday! We couldn't leave the airport either, as we had to book in at the desk for the chance of any stand-by seats. She also told him that it wasn't true about us being definitely booked on a waiting list to be first out, as he'd been told on the Thursday when he'd phoned. That was irritating.

We got chatting to two English girls who'd managed to get through to Virgin at 9.30am and were booked to get out today. Perhaps we'd be lucky. At 14.45, we were all suddenly pushed back by police who didn't want anyone in the building, back into a crowd of incoming people for Terminal 1 and Air New Zealand. Apparently, someone had left an unattended bag.

Fox TV were filming, panning along the line, the girl reporter talking to the camera about the length of the queues and the amount of people waiting, so I guessed we must have been seen by American viewers. With no TV to watch, it was rather frustrating not knowing if I'd been seen in the background, and anyway, no one back home that I knew of would have been watching a US television news channels.

When ushered even further back by Sam and another man, who kept apologising for the inconvenience, I smiled back.

"At least it broke the boredom."

He laughed and said, "I like your attitude."

We were allowed back into line at 15.10. I sat on the floor as often as I could to try and relieve my knee, which had started getting painful again, before finally we shuffled through to the ticketing desk at 16.30. We handed over our tickets only for the girl to look confused, saying she couldn't find us on the system, and going across to another member of staff to ask him. He studied the tickets then told her to re-enter them on the computer. She also questioned a lady sitting beside her, who told her how to do it. We were then informed that we would have to wait by the far windows until names were called for both evening flights, a bit like a lottery.

Eventually they announced that the 17.30pm plane had been delayed, but our names hadn't been called at 16.30 anyway. Several young backpackers who were waiting suddenly started dancing around. They'd not only got stand-by tickets, but been upgraded to first class!

I wandered downstairs and found a Starbucks, buying a couple of coffees but it was so bitter and awful, that we both threw it away after a few mouthfuls. We waited for the next flight, the 20.30pm, but our names weren't called at 19.15pm either. Andy spoke to a man passing who told him that although we'd been booked in, it was a case of first come, first served, we would have to come back tomorrow. Andy was furious, eight and a half hours standing at the airport for nothing.

Taking our cases downstairs, Andy phoned some motels before the fifth, a Super 8, had rooms available and sent a shuttle bus. It was out quite a way, seemed to be in a dismal part of downtown and was a bit grotty. No wonder people drank, everywhere were concrete buildings and roads.

Arriving at our rooms upstairs, my swipe card for the door lock wouldn't work to open the door, so Andy phoned the man on reception, who came to mend it. So we went out to a restaurant a couple of blocks away while he sorted it out. I was nervous of walking, it was very dark and forbidding, but we found the diner fairly nearby.

The meal was nice, but very filling. I had a small salad followed by chicken spaghetti in a lovely sauce.

Back at the motel, I was given another card from the receptionist, but again it wouldn't swipe, so the manager had to come up and let me in. Not a good start, and got even worse as there was no coffee machine in the room! I tried to phone Sue but couldn't get an outside line, so I gave up until the next day.

Sunday 16th September.

I was awake at 7am and rang the front desk to arrange to have an outside line. Sue was stunned and horrified to find that we were still in LA as she'd been assured we'd be on that flight, and had even sent Stephen all the way to Heathrow to pick us up. I told her it had been a case of, "first come, first served-and we weren't it!" She said she'd try to get Stephen on his mobile to get him back.

I phoned her five minutes later to say, "it would be best not to do anything, I will call you when things are more definite, probably from the plane."

She had got very uptight, not having been able to get hold of Stephen. As he was driving, he had his mobile switched off, she couldn't call him back. She was so embarrassed. She'd already been in touch with Daphne and Tony who were going to go back home with the dogs to wait for us there, and she would also get in touch with the people at work on Monday to tell them why I wasn't there.

I rang Andy at 7.15am to tell him what had happened, then showered, and watched TV till 9.30. I was so frustrated at all the misinformation that I just wanted to get out of the room and go for a walk around, but I didn't dare go outside on my own. I hated walking round Canterbury, too. I'd not seen anything outside to look at, anyway. If we'd been in Wyoming, Arizona or New Mexico, I'd have been out, despite the threat of rattlers or gila monsters.

Not hearing from Andy, I finally rang him again at 9.40, waking him up. He'd fallen asleep after I'd first called, but had also been contacted at 7am by reception to clear the use of his card for me to phone Sue, as he was the one who had booked in. Oops!

To the right of the motel was the Back Packers hotel, where I had a generous breakfast of eggs and bacon with biscuits and gravy for a very reasonable price. From there we went across the road to a small store to get some more drinks for the wait at the airport. I had mixed feelings about getting a plane for although I disliked Los Angeles, I really didn't want to leave America.

The shuttle took us from the motel to the terminal at 12.15pm. Gosh, the queue was even longer than yesterday. We took our cases onto the pavement, where we got chatting to a couple from Hampshire who had originally gone to Las Vegas to get married and were anxious to get home to see their little girl of six months. They'd got tickets to fly and their flight had been confirmed. Andy went off again to try and speak to someone at the Virgin Atlantic desk.

A TV van drew up, Eyewitness ABC news, and a reporter with a cameraman got out. She did a commentary to the camera and then turned to ask about what was going on. I found I was being interviewed! I told her the difficulties we were having getting seats home, and what a hard time we were having not being able to contact Virgin. No one seemed to know exactly what was going, on even when we did get through.

Suddenly, everyone was being shunted back again, another bomb scare. This time, we were ushered right back into Terminal 1, squashed in with all the people flying Air NZ. All the shuttle traffic came to a halt as police cars shut off the road. I began to worry about where Andy was.

At 13.10pm we were allowed back out, but I was now further back down the line than before due to more people having arrived at the terminal, and me having been pushed into the back with the cart. Oh well. Can't do anything about it.

I found myself chatting to an Asian couple from Bradford who'd been on a Virgin Atlantic tour with their two boys, and knew what had happened. Apparently a man had got out of their shuttle bus, the driver had placed his bag on the road, but realising he was at the wrong drop off point the man had got back on the bus leaving the bag behind.

Andy arrived having been sent to the other side of the building, with no more news about any flights, but that the police had sent in the bomb squad. They had used a machine that had sliced open the bag and pulled out the contents, nothing more sinister than clothing, but it had all been taken away in a police car. Boy, was that man going to be in trouble, stupid idiot.

Someone else in the queue mentioned that there was a list being made up, with people being given a number. Andy went to check, and yes, we were tenth. He was also told that an extra plane was being laid on. Great. We finally reached the ticketing area again at 15.30pm. While waiting our turn, a man (Dutch?) came and asked if anyone had seen his bag.

"Yes," said Andy, "it has been cut open and taken away by police." He seemed stunned, but how come it took him an hour and a half to come and ask for it?

This time, the desk lady took the top copy of our tickets. Must be going this time then. We went and waited by the windows, and I sat on my jacket on the floor, before spotting some backpackers with a Macdonald's. I asked where they'd got it from and they told us it was in Terminal 4.

We pushed the cart along the corridors of Terminal 2, then Terminal 3, and out along the sidewalk to Terminal 4, I guess about half a mile away, which must have been the main one as it was crowded but more luxurious than ours. Andy wheeled the cart into the lift, then along the crowded floor to Macdonald's. We got lucky when two people stood up to go and we got to sit and eat in comfort.

We hurried back to wait for the names to be called for the first flight. Not us. We went back to wait and I got chatting to a lady from Blackpool, mentioning the extra plane. She laughed, they'd heard the same thing, but did I know it was for other people being bussed in for Virgin couldn't get planes in and out of Las Vegas.

An announcement was made that the next plane was delayed till 21.30pm. Fat lot of good that did us, if no one would be allowed to get on it.

Andy came back to say that the list was irrelevant, some people who were going had been at 98, then some at 54 and even 32, no rhyme or reason, and that others were beginning to get cross. I told him about the people coming in on the bus for the plane, he was furious and went back to find the manager.

He returned angrily after quite a while to say that the manager had confirmed that it was true and no seats would be available. He'd also checked to see if we had a confirmation number, which we didn't have. Apparently we should have been given one by Virgin when we'd spoken to them on Saturday morning!

We went back over to the desk to see what was going on. One girl was in tears, people were ready to grab the manager, things were getting very heated, and the couple from Bradford were also very annoyed as they had 2 young children with them, the smallest only six.

Andy told the manager that he was, "basically reversing everything we've heard, that it's now the complete opposite of what we've been told on the phone. What's going on?" I felt so sorry for the man, he was trying to calm everyone, and getting very ratty, but when Andy and I finally turned and walked off disgustedly, he rushed after us angrily.

"Do you know just how many people are stranded in America?" he demanded.

"Yes, we do, but there are too many conflicting stories. The list isn't being adhered to, we still have no idea what's going on."

He argued for a while before going back to the desk. As we walked away, Andy said he'd thought the manager was actually going to hit him, he was that rattled.

Back with the Bradford couple, they told us that a man they knew who'd been number 96 on the list had been called and gone for the earlier flight. We were stunned. What was the point of a list if it didn't go in rotation!

They were suddenly called away by their Virgin representative and a whole bunch of people left the queue and went over. From the voices raised, a lot of them were also very annoyed.

We went back downstairs to phone for a hotel. After several attempts, we got rooms at the Ramada, $69 each plus tax. It was usually about $120 but I guess they wanted customers. Walking outside for the shuttle area, we were approached by two girls who asked where to meet the buses. We told them to follow us, and we all went down to the red neon sign above the bus shelters.

Suddenly, I heard very loud music coming towards us slowly, from the far end of the road that sounded like the US anthem, and then someone shouting. To my surprise, it was a police car covered with small American flags. The driver was waving to everyone and giving a very patriotic speech. I waved and cheered back, along with most of the other people standing about. I couldn't see any of our police doing that.

The shuttle arrived and took us to the hotel. Wow, it was lovely. Andy found the spa inside, the swimming pool being outside. I went back down to the reception to ask if I could pay for a call to Britain using my card, although Andy had booked in using his. This was OK, and I made a quick call to Sue. Afterward, I made a coffee and stayed watching TV till midnight for I wasn't at all sleepy.

Monday 17th September.

I was up at 7.30, showered and had a coffee, ringing through to wake Andy at 8.10am. Waiting for him, I suddenly began feeling sick and panicky, the world had gone mad. I just couldn't bear the thought of joining the long, long queue and going all through the wait again, sitting on the floor, with no coffee and no information, trapped in the building with all those crowds. I think shock was starting to set in.

We went for breakfast when Andy knocked on the door.

"I rang you," he laughed, "and got someone else, I'd rung the wrong room and woken them up." I only had a coffee not wanting anything to eat.

Back at our rooms at 10.10am he decided to try and ring Virgin again and on a whim I said I'd do the same. To my surprise, I got straight through to a recording and frantically ran to bang on the wall to Andy, rushing back to continue listening to the recording, then having to gallop back for the door as I hadn't opened it for him. He grabbed the phone and actually got through to someone. He explained our situation after telling them that we'd phoned on the Tuesday to confirm our flight. I saw his face change.

"We're not showing on the computer system!" he whispered.

Suddenly, he said furiously, "you'd better be joking or I'll string someone up," then looked up at me and said, "we've come up on the computer as a no show! We weren't at the airport and didn't book in!"

He stated angrily down the phone that, "we'd been there all day, eight and a half hours we'd waited."

Then I quickly reminded him out loud, hoping that the person on the end of the phone line could hear me that the girl at the desk had had to re-enter us on the computer on Saturday. He glanced at me.

"We're now back on the list at number forty five."

"But the manager had said the evening before, we were at number ten!" Suddenly I said quickly, "ask about me being there!"

"It's OK, we're booked together." I don't know why, but I began to panic, insisting that he ask.

"I don't care, you've only ever mentioned your name."

He asked, and worriedly told me that I wasn't showing up at all, but then that they'd re-enter me. This time, he was given confirmation numbers. He put the phone down and looked at me in despair.

"We've got to go back to the airport again, and just wait."

We checked out and took the shuttle back to the airport, re-joining the long queue out on the sidewalk. All my energy seeped away and I just became laid back and fatalist, giving up worrying. There was nothing we could do about it. It didn't take long for my knee to get painful and swollen again, and I kept sitting down anywhere I could.

At one point while sitting on my case, I had to laugh when the TV van was towed away for being parked in the wrong place.

I started talking to a couple behind us who were from Oregon, heading out on a tour round England, Wales, Scotland and Ireland, really nice people.

A man with a walkie-talkie came over, asking for anyone confirmed for the 17.30pm flight. I just shrugged.

"I've no idea, we've only just found out that they lost us on the computer, we had been put down as a no-show despite being re-entered and put on stand-by, we should have left on Saturday."

He was startled and rang someone about where we were on the priority list. Apparently we were now nineteenth, but he said apologetically, that there wasn't anything else he could do. Sam also came over, I again explained the situation, and she went off to see if she could find out anything else.

We met up with the couple from Bradford again who'd now got a confirmation number for their flight. Andy and I were quite annoyed for they had been behind us on the list, (according to the number we'd been told. The American couple also had their confirmation, and they went. We wished them a good holiday in Britain.

I then got chatting to a young couple from Chatham, about twenty miles from where we lived, but I had to keep going and sitting on the floor by the windows for my knee was painful. Then John Bell, the manager, called us over to the flight desks and again confirmed we were nineteenth in line.

I went and sat outside for some fresh air, leaving Andy with the cart, watching the continually patrolling police cars and bikes, and the shuttle buses dropping off more passengers, while Andy went to hear the names called for the 17.30pm flight.

Suddenly, I heard banging from behind me. Andy was frantically waving.

"I've got our tickets, we've got to get through the x-ray machine, fast!"

We shoved through the crowds and almost threw the cases into the machine, grabbing them at the other side and taking them to the ticket line. It seemed almost dreamlike, everything was happening so fast. We showed our passports and the cases were put on the conveyor belt. Passports and tickets were scrutinised at the foot of the escalator, and then we were going up. I glanced back a little sadly to the crowds below and my last sight of Terminal 2, recalling the days we'd spent waiting in line.

Crossing the floor to the security check, we had to change from one checkout to another when the first was suddenly closed. Nervously I stepped through the x-ray machine, expecting it to bleep. It did. I was checked over with the hand held machine, but allowed through. Andy thought it was probably set higher than usual and anything tiny could have set it off. At the duty free shops I came across the man from Bradford who said that he and his family were leaving on the later flight at 20.30pm. We then met the Oregon couple in the waiting lounge had been booked on the same plane as us.

Finally, our flight was called, and we went to board. The girl forgot to tear off the green slip I had, but luckily Andy spotted it and I gave it to one of the desk people. Another of the other staff shouted out a man's name and told him he had three seconds to get his duty free before it was taken off the plane, making people laugh.

Once on board, putting my hand luggage into the cupboard above the seats, I spotted the couple from Chatham, several rows in front of us in the plane.

The pilot announced that we would have about a ten hours flight, and that the weather was dull and showery at Gatwick. What a surprise! The stewardesses checked everyone's seatbelt was fastened, and then we were taxiing out onto the runway. Oh dear, leaving America again.

As usual I dozed most the way home, only just remembering to use the internal phone (wow, £5 or $9 a minute) to call Sue and say that we were on our way, having to ask the stewardess for help for it was too dark to read the instructions. Sue reminded me to call Daphne when we were at the airport to get the cab sent for us. During the flight, I asked about the toy plane I'd ordered on the in-ward flight, but unfortunately, due to all the delays, it wasn't stocked on this plane.

Nearing the end of our flight, a couple of rows down from us in the centre block, people started milling about and over the intercom we were asked if there was a doctor on board. For a while, the stewardesses were helping out, but I never did find out what was wrong.

Then, six days after the tragedy when the two planes were flown into the Twin Towers in New York, and four days after Andy and I were originally due to leave Los Angeles, the Virgin Atlantic flight to England landed at

Heathrow airport to clapping and cheering from the passengers.

Will I go again? Oh yes, I'm already organising a sightseeing trip by car from Phoenix to the Petrified Forest, Canyon de Chelly, Valley of the Gods, Bryce Canyon, Zion Park, and Death Valley, amongst others.

HOLIDAY 2003

Chapter 26

Yet Another Trip.

Tuesday 29 April.

I got up early, excited again, made a cup of coffee, and had time to go and see to Cloud before I was ready to leave. I put Callie and Cody into the back of the car after loading my suitcase. I'd tried hard not to put too much in it this year, but with some of the average temperatures for places we'd be visiting down to 3-5C, I'd packed some warm cardigans and a coat.

As Daphne, Tony and Daniel were looking after the two dogs and my car while we were away, this time I was driving up to their house at Addlestone, Surrey and from there, Tony would take us on to Heathrow as he had a meeting after.

This year I had booked in January with British Airways as they'd had the best deals on the Internet and Daphne had wanted to know when I was going so that she could organise having my dogs.

I set off to pick up Andy and once he was in the car I gave him the written directions to their place. As we chatted away, he was upset to discover that today was my birthday, which he'd forgotten. The trip wasn't too bad on the motorways, the traffic only slowing a couple of times.

Just before Junction 10, I got Andy to phone Daphne to say that we would be with them shortly, and they were at the door waiting for us as we came round the corner. The dogs as usual couldn't get out of the car and into their house fast enough, Cody immediately racing around the kitchen/dining room area for the box of toys they kept.

Once our cases were in Tony's car, Andy and I waved goodbye to Daphne and Daniel, and Tony set off, but we were forced to return after half a mile when Daphne phoned to say that I'd left my hat behind. I was so embarrassed.

Once inside Terminal 4 and with our cases on a cart, we looked at the screens to find out when we could book our luggage at the check-in desk, but with no sign of our flight number, we walked over to the desk to ask. Apparently they wouldn't be taking the luggage until 11.30, so we went off for a coffee. As I was feeling a little sickly, still being nervous of flying, I didn't fancy anything to eat, but being back at the airport was so exciting and I felt like a seasoned traveller, much more comfortable with all the procedures.

At 11.30 we joined the long queue for the desk, and after twenty minutes shuffling through the twisting roped off aisles, we reached it. Once our cases were taken, we were free to browse round the shops.

I became a bit concerned when my bad knee began to suddenly 'click' as I was walking along, and I hoped that it wasn't going to let me down on the holiday. Andy went to find the electrical outlet to try to buy an adapter for his mobile phone, but somehow he got side tracked, later realising that it had been forgotten.

We headed towards customs. Nervously I approached the x-ray machine, and despite carefully putting everything metallic that I could think of, like my belt and necklaces, and my handbag, into the tray to go through the hand luggage machine, I knew it would go off. Andy went, then it was my turn to walk through the sensor.

"Beeeeep." Oh, God, now what.

The security lady took me to one side while I tried to say that I'd taken everything metal off, what was it? Another security guard, a man, asked me to take my western hat off, took it and waved it through the arch—which beeped. It was the metal strip that ran round the rim. Funny, it's never done that before, this machine must have been much more finely set. I was also asked to remove my cowboy boots as they often had metal inside, and both hat and boots went through the hand luggage machine.

Once on the other side, we went for another coffee and this time I managed to eat a baguette.

I decided to use the restroom before boarding the plane, but as we strolled through the corridor to the flight desk, a tannoy announced that a cream jacket had been left in the ladies. Oh crumbs, mine! We rushed back to retrieve it, then hurried down to the plane, finding our seats in the middle aisle.

Just as we got settled, a stewardess came to ask if we would mind changing our seats to save a family from being split up, so we shifted a couple of rows back. I didn't mind, as long as I got to America. Andy then realised that he hadn't got his adapter from the duty free section and hoped he could get one while we were in America. After a short wait, an announcement was made that the plane would be delayed as baggage had to be found for some passengers who wouldn't be making the flight.

Eventually, the stewardesses gave the usual in-flight safety demonstration with an accompanying movie on procedures for any emergency. Mind you, these planes can't glide as someone had rather stupidly informed me some time ago, so from that height I didn't fancy our chances.

The pilot introduced his flight crew, then informed us that the weather in Phoenix was 30C. Ooh, lovely. Slowly the plane began to back up before taxiing out to the runway. The engines began to roar, the plane started moving, and we were off, lifting back into the sky again. I was okay until the plane began to bank, which always makes me feel ill, but once we were levelled out, I began to relax. With the blinds drawn on the left windows to cut out the bright sunlight, I could only see the right hand wing. No worries about seeing the ground then.

When lunch was brought round, I chose tuna salad, a Korma chicken dish with roll and butter, and a chocolate dessert with chocolate flake pieces in it. A chocolate bar, and coffee followed. All served on a tray in small containers. I don't know why people don't like in-flight food, I'd never had a bad one yet.

I found that again I couldn't watch the films, for the screen on the back of the seat in front of me was either too close or too far for my bifocal glasses, a real nuisance, but I could keep glancing at the map shown for our flight. We flew at 36,000 feet with 30mph head winds for some time, before rising to 39,000 feet.

Later on, the stewardesses brought round a snack, two quarters of a sandwich with the crust cut off, a roll, a chocolate brownie and coffee. Good grief, too much chocolate for me after the last lot, too sickly.

Near the end of the flight, we got chatting to a very nice girl who'd been visiting her sister in Southampton. She had visited London, and had loved the old buildings especially.

Then we were landing, a bit bumpy, while I stared across at the windows trying desperately to catch a glimpse of Phoenix. Leaving the plane I was really excited and happy, it was just like coming home!

Waiting in one of the queues to go through immigration, a sniffer dog, a chocolate coloured Labrador, was being walked up and down the lines of people with its lady handler.

After getting our luggage from the carousel, Andy headed for the row of rental car desks where he asked the price for a 4x4 type at the Enterprise desk. It worked out very expensive with them, so he headed for the next desk. Waiting with the luggage, I saw the guy nodding, he and Andy had sorted out a deal. Once the price was agreed, the man took us out to the roadway, and we were picked up by a coloured man driving a minibus to be shuttled out to their garage. He was very jokey and chatty, explaining that he was a minister, and that his wife was due to have a baby in August.

We had a long wait in their waiting room while the rest of the paperwork was sorted, and then he explained that they had decided to change the oil in the car, a Toyota 4Runner, before filling the tank with gas. When he heard that we were heading out to Globe, he got on the phone to start organising a room for us at a friend's new hotel. Overhearing him say that we needed a suite, I hurriedly explained that Andy and I were just travelling companions, so we really needed two rooms.

"Oh! Ok."

I began getting edgy as it was getting dark and I knew that Globe was 70 miles away, but eventually we were in the car and Andy was heading for the I-10.

From there we turned onto Hwy 60, a small, twisting road with lots of maintenance works. By now it was pitch dark, and all I could glimpse were the dark shapes of canyon walls from time to time in the headlights, warnings signs for falling rocks, and the tall pointing arms of saguaros. There were also warning signs for 'Ice on Road.' I guess they hadn't been removed after the winter, or perhaps they were left there permanently. Another sign showed me we were crossing Pinto Creek.

Finally we reached Globe whose sign stated that it had been founded in 1826, and drove slowly through. Despite crossing several junctions, we were unable to see the road we wanted so Andy parked up in front of a gas station/store and went in to ask.

"It's at least another hour away!" he exclaimed on getting back in the car.

We didn't fancy travelling for another hour, and pulled in at a Comfort Inn, the Round Mountain Park. In daylight it would prove to be a pretty, two story cream and blue coloured building with tan tiled roof. I always felt slightly underdressed at these places, but while Andy was in reception booking the rooms, two young men walked past me and in through the door. Overweight, dressed in tight, untidy T-shirts, their arms held away from their sides, and with the 'modern' baggy shorts with the crutch at their knees showing off their hairy lower legs, they looked more like Neanderthals!

Taking my case into my room on the second floor, it proved a similar layout to a Best Western with two twin beds covered in lovely throw over covers, and a shower/toilet at the end of the room with a vanity sink and mirror. Great, it had a coffee machine.

I met up with Andy outside and we went across to the restaurant, a single storey white clapboard building with a green tiled roof, pink canopies over the windows, and pretty rose motifs painted on the gable ends. We waited to be seated, and were led to a bench seat alcove by a young and very giggly waitress.

As usual, we were greeted with a big smile and "hi, I'm Pam, I'll be serving you tonight." It was as if she was genuinely pleased to be meeting us and be able to help with our meal. We met very few staff who didn't. I ordered a ranch style salad with chicken strips, and a roll and butter. Butter? In America it's very sloppy being made from vegetable oils, and the taste is only just passable.

I was very tired and glad to retire to bed, although I managed to sit and write up my notes first. I also discovered when reading the map that we'd actually passed through Devil's Canyon in the dark, one of the places I'd wanted to see.

I woke up near midnight feeling very ill and shaky, and tried to calm myself with very long deep breaths for ages. Finally I dropped off into a very restless sleep.

Wednesday 30th April.

At 6am I still felt a little sickly, but managed to drink a coffee before going for a shower. Fortunately, a note on the wall explained that the inner spout had to be pulled down to get the water through the showerhead, quite different to ones I'd used before. When the water came through, the high pressure nearly sent me reeling against the far wall and making me gasp, but it felt really lovely and tingly on my skin. I dressed, then Andy phoned at 7.10 to say he was already up and outside. Crumbs that must be a first. I went out to meet him for some fresh air where it was beautifully warm and sunny. The Inn was very pretty in an old rancho style, the outer walls a creamy coloured adobe rendering.

Inside, the little breakfast area had tables and chairs, and on offer were cereals and toast. I helped myself to a coffee and some toast and sat listening to four people chatting about the area, one couple obviously Australian. Once they were alone, we got talking and Shirley mentioned that we ought to try to see the Apache Trail Loop Trip. Via US 60, The Old West Highway and Hwy 88, the Trail went through the original old Apache stronghold, and she told me that the scenery was stunning.

This Trail had once served as a stage coach and freight wagon route from Mesa to Globe where Indians, cowboys and minors all rode through the mysterious Superstition Mountains, and where The Lost Dutchman's Mine is still supposed to be waiting to be rediscovered in a hidden canyon somewhere. A pamphlet showed lots of interesting things to do in the area from horse riding to museums, and one of the saloons at Tortilla Flat had the bar seats made of saddles. Neat.

Unfortunately, Andy and I decided that we wouldn't have the time to go round (which was a shame as it turned out that our three week journey didn't take as long as we'd thought, given the amount of mileage.) Shirley and I swapped e-mail addresses before Andy and I left, me driving, for the Salt River Canyon on Hwy 77/60.

Just down the road, we spotted a Wal-Mart, and parked up to see if Andy could find an adapter. Entering the store, an elderly lady offered us a basket.

"Hi folks, how're you doing," she asked with a smile. I couldn't help but reply, "OK, thanks."

Despite a search, Andy couldn't find British to American, just American to European. Hopefully we'd find one later on.

The cracked and bumpy road wended its way through Gila County and its red sandstone and scrub desert dotted with grey sage and green creosote bushes where I spotted a road sign: 'State Prison—do not stop for hitchhikers.'

As the land got hillier we crossed Seven Mile Wash where the weather began to get warm and sunny, and the sky became a cloudless bright blue.

I suddenly became aware of a faint tapping before discovering that the windscreen was being hit by hundreds of bugs. Goodness knows what they ate, but trying the windscreen wipers the mess just smeared, not helped by the fact that the washers were empty. At the first gas station we came to, Andy bought a container of screen wash. Whenever we stopped for gas, he also cleaned the front windscreen with the water and sponge/scraper garages provided.

Slowly we drove up through two passes and out onto grasslands spotted with green trees, coming across a sign: 6%, with a picture of a lorry at a dangerous angle heading down a steep incline. The strange thing was that almost every single steep hill we came to had this sign—did they only make roads at 6% inclines? (Eventually, during our holiday, we did come across a couple bearing the legend 5% and one of 4%.)

We parked up overlooking the canyon to take pictures and walking to the edge to look at the view, I spotted little lizards darting away to scurry under the rocks. Below us the road twisted and turned heading down to the Salt River.

For three miles the road continued in a series of serpentines down into the green Salt River Canyon with palo verdes bearing bright yellow flowers and spiky yucca plants. Here, we left the San Carlos Indian reservation and entered the White Mountain Apache reservation.

Just before a steel span bridge, we pulled off the road to take photos of the rapids, to find that the Native Americans had their beautiful jewellery laid out on low stone walls. I was tempted to buy a necklace, taking my time to choose as they were all so pretty, before spotting some scorpion models made out of twisted gold and black coloured wire.

"My nine year old son makes them," one lady told us proudly, as I bought one for a souvenir. Andy also picked one.

Back in the car, we began the long, winding climb out of the canyon to a huge tree covered valley where I spotted a sign for Cibecue, a name I recognised from several Zane Grey books. All the way to the horizon were scrub covered hills and sandstone outcrops in mixtures of red, grey and black colours. We crossed Carrizo Creek, passed through Carrizo City and drove on to Navajo City. I loved that. Cities? They were no more than small towns. Cedar Canyon turned out to be a gash in the landscape, dotted with huge black rocks and boulders. Once over Corduroy Creek, we came to a forest of blackened pine tree trunks covered in new leaves, recovering after a fire.

Just before Show Low, we headed north on the 260W to Payson where I wanted to see the Mogollon Rim I'd read about, also by Zane Grey. As a backwoodsman, he had hunted cougars with Buffalo Jones, not to kill them for sport, but to try to capture them with lariats to send to zoos.

We crossed Cottonwood Wash into more open, flatter land, then over Decker Wash. From here, the clouds began to gather and the wind got up.

Thirsty, we stopped at Overguaard, at a brand new western style town built alongside the road. Turning left towards the buildings, I could see buffalo in corrals to our right. Driving round to the front, looking out for a café or restaurant sign, I noticed a stables advertising trail rides. Wish I had time to go. Passing the green painted Wild Woman Saloon with its wooden railed verandas, we came to a stop outside the Bakery, Twinnie's Coffee Break & Ice Cream Parlour, also painted in green.

Mounting the steps and going inside, it looked a very posh sort of tourist place, and I was amazed at the rows and rows of jars holding differently blended coffees. We ordered coffee and sat at one of the dark wood tables. Just before we left, a man came round to light an imitation gas flame fire under the alcove, where three or four bear statues sat holding sticks with marshmallows in front of it. After, we went out the far side of the room to find the restrooms, stepping into a neat square of buildings and stores.

I drove down the dusty track to the buffalo. There were about a dozen dusty brown shaggy creatures with black button eyes and tiny curving horns lazily chewing hay from a container. They were not at all interested in my tapping on the bars to try to get them to look round so that I could get a picture of their faces. They were smaller than I'd imagined, and I later read that bison were now just two-thirds the size that they had been before hunters decimated the herds almost to extinction in the late 1800s, due to inbreeding as they were rescued.

Down the road a couple of miles, I pulled in for gas where, as Andy was filling the tank, I saw him approached by a man. Andy shook his head. When he got back in the car, he said it had been an Indian, asking for money as his car had broken down, but inside the gas station they'd told him not to take any notice.

Back out on the road as we entered an area of pines and white rocky outcrops, the road improved, looking as if it had been recently laid. The clouds began to disperse, and then we were back with clear blue skies. We went through Wildcat Canyon and into more trees that looked like they'd been swept by fire, while every clearing seemed to house RV parks-they were dotted everywhere.

Down we drove into an open pine clad valley surrounded by hills. To the left was Black Canyon Rim and to the right, the tall cliffs of the flat top Mogollon Rim, its sides dotted with pines. I was hoping that we could find the unmade road shown on the map that went up to and along the Rim, but somehow we missed it, ending up turning onto an unmade road just after Kohls Ranch. This became a sandy pink dusty trail running parallel to the bottom of the cliff. Ahead of us drove a lorry, some sort of water carrier, that turned left at a fork in the road while we went the other way as it looked more promising, but we ended up at a cul-de-sac of log cabins and houses.

Turning round we narrowly missed squashing a gecko as it flashed across the track. We continued after the lorry, driving though yet another R.V. park at the base of the canyon wall, crossing the dry, dusty and desolate Tonto Creek, while Lewis Creek and Moore Creek were also dry boulder strewn beds. Through the trees, I caught the occasional tantalising glimpses of the Rim and we finally managed to stop to take some pictures where there was a break. The rocky cliff had now become thickly covered in pines. Bray Creek had a trickle of water running down it, as did East Verde River, and I wondered where most of the animals drank in such hostile surroundings with nothing but dry sandy ground, boulders and deadfalls.

After miles and miles, and just as I began to feel we'd never see civilisation again, we caught up with the lorry that had halted as another was heading in from the opposite direction. This stopped in front of the first, and one of the drivers waved us past, a narrow squeeze on the thin track. From the dampness of the trail, this last lorry must have been watering the dust. Up and down we went, twisting and turning at the sharp bends, hoping we didn't meet anything big coming the other way, the car's wheels slipping on the gravel. As Andy had given me the video camera, I recorded quite a lot. Finally, we came out onto Hwy 87 and headed for Strawberry.

This turned out to be a small town of wooden houses and chalets among the pines and we pulled into the front lot of the Strawberry Market store. Its signs stated that it sold 'gifts, videos, fishing equipment, groceries, liquor and snacks.' An American flag flew from a tall post attached to the wooden rails round the veranda, but the modern metal and glass doors looked oddly out of place. We went in, but the only snacks they did were chips (our crisps.)

Back outside and to our left was another dark wood building that looked like an old pub. Heading through the door, it was quite dark after the bright sunshine, but I could see men sitting round the bar drinking. We went over to sit at one of the several tables and looked through the menu until a blonde lady came from behind the bar to ask what we wanted. Andy ordered coffees, and when she returned with them, we'd decided to order tuna melts.

"I'm on my own, serving and cooking," she explained with a smile, "so it'll be as soon as I can do it."

"Yeh, that's fine," I smiled.

We sat drinking the coffee till the food came, after which she topped up our coffee cups. The meal was good, tuna covered in a choice of cheese, I had Swiss, tomato, and lettuce inside two slices of toasted brown bread, and fries. Cut in halves, both sandwiches were secured with long cocktail sticks decorated with twirly coloured ribbons of cellophane.

Sitting in the car, reading my itinerary and looking at the map, I discovered that having taken the back road under the Rim, we had missed the Tonto Natural Bridges Park. I was a bit disappointed, but there was nothing we could do about it.

I drove north on the 87, crossing the dry West Clear Creek. Slowly the pines began to thin until I was driving across flat plains of brown soil, silver grey grass and scrub bushes. Ridges of rock poked their way out of the ground, gradually changing to red sandstone, some weathered and splintered, the soil the same red colour. Movement showed a small herd of pronghorn antelope in the distance, and far away rose the peaks of a mountain range.

Finally we reached Winslow and headed west on the I-40. Turning south at the junction for the Meteorite Crater, I headed five miles along a twisting road out onto plains with red rocky outcrops mingling with round creamy stones that looked like the tops of giant mushrooms. Signs showing the picture of a cow warned that this was, 'Open Range.'

Buildings came into view on the side of a huge mound, and as we got closer, I could see that a high wire fence surrounded them. To our disappointment, the opening times were 9-5pm and it was past that, so Andy and I decided to carry on up the I-40 to find a motel.

Two Guns showed up on our Four Corners road map, so I turned off the Interstate at a big motorway sign, but came to a dead end with the wrecked remains of a gas station in front of us. Novel. Big motorway signs for something that no longer existed. OK.

Back on the I-40, I continued on to Two Arrows, also shown on the map, leaving the Interstate and crossing Canyon Diablo Creek. To our amazement, we arrived at the old wreck of a café with two huge painted arrows stuck in the middle of what had once been a car park. Again there had been big signs for it on the roadway. Baffled, we carried on up the road, but came across nothing else before Flagstaff.

We arrived on Main Street, a long line of motels, gas stations, parking lots and stores, seeing a Super 8 motel sign, but as we had been very disappointed with one of these before, and this did look a little the worse for wear on the outside, we continued on.

Eventually we came across a Day's Inn, The Hampton, a lovely hotel with a pool. We were both feeling tired after all the driving but Andy wanted to go out to find the K-Mart we had been to before. Unfortunately, our memories weren't all that good, and despite turning up a couple of roads that we thought we recognised, we couldn't find it, so I suggested Wal-Green's at the far end of town that we'd visited on our very first holiday and went there instead.

After spending some time in the store, I drove back to Day's in the dark, feeling more confident at driving now, even in all the traffic, but then began to worry that I was being a little over confident. That's when things could go wrong.

Once in my room, unfortunately there wasn't a coffee machine, the news on TV stated that Flagstaff now had water restrictions in force, and also that the White Mountain area was on fire alert.

Chapter 27

Canyon de Chelly.

Thursday 1st May.

I slept well, waking at 4.30 to the lovely sound of a train whistle. I showered, wrote my notes, and watched TV till Andy phoned through at 7.15. I dressed quickly and found that my new jeans, bought at Matalan in Canterbury before the holiday, had suddenly become rather loose round the waist. Had I lost weight already? I found my nice belt and put that through the loops to hold them.

When we went down for breakfast, I was put off. Donuts, no thanks! I settled for a glass of orange juice and a cup of coffee, taking them back to my room. Just as we were about to leave, Andy discovered that his wallet was missing.

"I must have left it in the dining area."

Rushing down, he found it had been handed in to reception. Wow, lucky.

It was smashing outside, warm and sunny, and I drove out towards Sunset Crater, following the signs just outside Flagstaff. To my amusement, we passed a log cabin 'cruising' down Route 89 on the back of a low loader. I'd always found it hilarious whenever we passed two halves of a chalet type bungalow being transported-but a log cabin!

We travelled through a forest of pines, arriving at the Visitor Centre where we bought tickets for the crater. With them came a coloured pamphlet warning people that 'moving or collecting pottery shards or any archaeological artefact carried a fine of $250 minimum,' as did 'defacing or destroying natural features or archaeological sites such as collecting rocks, fossils, plants or animals. Climbing or walking on ruin walls was a minimum $50.'

We continued on through pine covered slopes following the highway up and down steep inclines coming to black cracked lava flows on either side of the road. I parked in the car park and we got out before a huge black mountain, its slopes dotted with pines. At a height of 8,029 feet the 900 year old cinder cone volcano was just one of many that formed a four mile long weak spot here in the earth's crust, called a fissure. Around 1250AD it had finally stopped throwing up cinders, and these had become coloured red by the oxidation of the iron in the magma during the eruption. A notice stated that 'due to damage to the environment, walking up the crater was no longer allowed.' Thank goodness, it looked very steep.

A cinder track walkway took us over a bridge spanning a deep crack in the black lava and led on down below a huge wall of lava into a deep gully. The whole area was both bizarre and fascinating with the shapes and creases, and it was odd to know that somewhere under us could be a cave with ice inside, sealed off by the hardened surface. I struggled up the other side of the gully, concerned that my breathing wasn't good, especially in the heat. Sad signs of getting old, I guess! At the top of the track, looking across the road, I could see a tall red pillar of rock. All the hills and mountains around, including the San Francisco Peaks of which Humphrey's Peak is the highest at 12,633 feet, were extinct volcanoes, part of a 2,200 square mile area known as the San Francisco Volcanic Field.

We drove on round to the other side of the crater where the sides were a beautiful deep red. Around us were hills and valleys covered in pines stretching to the far distance, and it was awesome to know that each hill in view was an extinct volcano. Crumbs, I hope they are extinct!

We finally left heading back for the I-40, driving east back to Meteor Crater, where I parked the car.

We walked up the long flight of steps to the entrance stiles, paid, and passed through into a lovely cool museum. While I was looking at all the exhibits and pictures I happened to glance through the window to my right and to my amazement saw an enormous multihued depression. It had been formed around 50,000 years ago when a meteorite hit the earth at a speed estimated to have been between 30,000-40,000 miles per hour. Today it's 550 feet deep (equivalent to a sixty-story building), 2.4 miles around the rim, 4,000 feet across, and was once thought to have been an extinct volcano. Discovered by a man called Franklin, who'd once served as a scout with General Custer, it had originally been named Franklin's Hole after him.

Standing outside on one of the platforms, it was breathtaking looking down into the saucer like depths. A long stretch of steps went up the left side to the top of the rim, and I was almost gasping by the time I'd climbed them, but the view was spectacular, right out over the crater to the plains beyond. It reminded me of the film, Starman, when the helicopters flew towards the crater to try to capture the alien. I'd thoroughly enjoyed the film.

I descended to the lower platform where some thin steel pipes were welded onto posts pointing out over the hole to look down into the depths. Staring through them, I could make out various details like the equipment at the bottom and an entrance hole halfway up the far slope. These were very hard to find with the naked eye so the pipes came in handy.

Back inside the museum, we wandered through to the gift shop where I bought postcards, and then went into the café at the back, ordering a large baguette each. Mine ended up with beef, Swiss cheese, tomato and lettuce, etc. Each time I was asked my choice of filling and I thought he'd finished, he began listing something else. Which choice of meat, which dressing, which of the salads, etc., confusing me completely, but it was well worth the wait. It was delicious and a complete meal in itself.

Back at the I-40, I headed east for Winslow. Without thinking, I flashed a large lorry to pull in once he'd overtaken just as I did at home and was delighted to have a 'thank you' flash of his hazards.

Just before Winslow I stopped for gas before heading for the Petrified Forest National Park, crossing Clear Creek on the way. The deep cleft of the Little Colorado River ran along near the road on the right. Once through Holbrook, I noticed some odd looking stone shapes at the sides of the road inside the fencing.

"Look, stone tree trunks!"

I pulled off the Interstate and headed for the Visitor Centre, a low stone building where I wandered round the books and gifts and bought two more Tony Hillerman books. Not only did I enjoy the stories, but I loved reading about the places I'd seen, or had visited in and around the Navaho reservation. I couldn't find anything else. The trouble with gift shops was that they nearly all seemed to sell the same type of thing and it was getting a little boring.

We drove round to the ticket booth to pay the entry fee and were given a map of the route round the park.

From the height of Tiponi Point, a placard stated that we should be able to see for a distance of around 120 miles. Between Tawa Point and Kachian Point was a hiking route, and at the latter, we parked up to walk round the Painted Desert Inn, a lovely low stone pueblo structure in grey stucco with shadowed windows. It had a long petrified tree trunk outside the front wall, and I took a picture of Andy sitting on it. It was incredible to see the details of the bark and even the tree rings perfectly preserved, but turned to solid stone.

The original Stone Tree House it had begun as a small roadside stop along what was to become Route 66. Some of the walls inside still hide blocks of petrified wood hence its nickname. Due to its deterioration in 1936, the walls had had to be excavated, underpinned and lined with wood, with the original floors levelled and rebuilt. It had taken a year to harvest and prepare the pine and aspen poles used in the open beamed ceilings. The walls, built of native stone and mortar, were covered with a stucco finish to resemble adobe. Flagstone floors were laid, and the chairs, tables and soda fountain had been carved and decorated with Indian designs. Tin light fixtures imitated native Mexican designs, and glass panels for the ceiling were painted with Hopi pottery motifs like stained glass windows. The building had been closed during WWII between 1942 and 1947. The walls were white, and the wooden ceiling beams held up by poles. With the ornate iron railings and stained glass windows in the ceiling, it was enchanting, while the view over the Painted Desert to the far cliffs with their pastel hues, was beautiful.

We went on to look out over the barren lands from Chinde Point and Pintado Point, and then on to Nizhoni Point, Whipple Point and Lacey Point. At Nizhoni, we came across an area of hills that looked as if some giant had been building sandcastles before abandoning them. We stopped at some stone ruins, Puerco Pueblo by dry Nine Mile Wash to use the restrooms, then drove on to see Newspaper Rock, looking down the cliff to house sized fallen boulders on which we could just make out more petroglyphs. Looking out across the horizon, the land was flat, the foreground sprinkled with blue flowers intermingled with large white blooms like our Dog Rose but that grew close to the ground.

The Tepees were conical white, red and grey striped hill formations, the white bands were sandstone, the darker red being iron stained sandstone, and the tops clay. The darker bands had been caused by high carbon content, while the reddish bases were stained by iron oxide (hematite.) Nearby, the Puerco River was just a wide band of sand where the water ran during the wet season.

We drove on round to Blue Mesa, a three mile loop with views over clay hills and miles of 'badlands' covered by thousands of scattered broken tree trunks. These petrified tree trunks were gradually being eroded from the softer silt of an ancient riverbed that had once been a plateau of rivers and swamps. Thousands of tons of them had been carted away by visitors until 1906 when the whole area was made into a National Park.

Some of the hills were horizontally layered pastels, greys, creams and browns, while others were layered on the slant. At the foot of the cliffs were heaps of broken rocks and boulders. Despite the desolation, the whole place was both awesome and breathtakingly beautiful. We came across a stone tree trunk spanning a gully that had been supported by a length of concrete in 1917 to preserve it intact. Today apparently, the modern idea is to leave it alone until it broke naturally, which to me seemed very weird. What was wrong with supporting it for people to see for another hundred years or more?

We drove past Agate House Trail, the Jasper Forest Overlook and the Crystal Forest, another walking trail, to reach the south entrance where some of the logs were even larger. We decided to turn round and retrace our drive back to the I-40. We could have gone out of the park and turned right to go round the back of the park to the Interstate, but it looked a lot longer on the map than returning the way we'd come.

From the Interstate, we headed north on the 191 for Hubbell's Trading Post at Ganado, an old time store, but when we finally got there, it had just closed. It seems that the Navajo Reservation observed Daylight Savings Time from April through October, and had shut only an hour before we arrived.

There weren't any hotels about that I could see, so we continued heading east on the 264 towards Window Rock and the state line to New Mexico, but after a short way when we found nothing, we turned back and took a small road north towards Chinle.

After about fifteen miles, we passed through a small Navaho town where I spotted a notice, 'End of Pavement.' Odd! A few yards on, I discovered that the 'pavement' was actually the road because the tarmac ended suddenly and we were now on a dirt road. As our pavement is a sidewalk here then it seems that the pavement is the road. Unwilling to turn back, despite there being no sign of even a dirt road on the map, we drove on having to slow down as it was quite bumpy, a couple of times being passed by old pickups going the other way driven by Navajos, both men and women.

For miles and miles we went on passing the occasional homestead before the sun sank below the horizon and it began to get dark and I was getting quite worried when at last lights appeared in the far distance. With clouds of dust billowing behind us, we bumped our way back onto a tarmac road and followed it to a junction. Thank goodness, Chinle.

Andy stopped for gas and to ask for directions to a motel, being informed that the Best Western Canyon de Chelly (pronounced shay) was just down the main road. Opposite was a restaurant and store. No problem again about rooms, although we had to drag our cases up the stairs to the second floor, and very nice rooms.

Once we had settled in, Andy drove to the shops to try to find an adapter in Radio Shack, but like the other places, they had run out. While he was asking, I wandered round the clothes section, but despite seeing some very pretty things, I ended up not buying anything. Without help I was never entirely sure whether I was buying stuff too young to suit me.

Back at the motel, we crossed over to the restaurant, waiting to be shown to a seat, the usual bench seats and table, and I ordered a chicken salad. The Navaho girl came back with our coffees to say that they hadn't any chicken left, so I decided on a cheese bacon burger and fries.

Around the room were pictures of Navaho families, many showing them at a very big ceremony. Running round the room near the ceiling were tacked some pretty handmade banners with the names of Navaho clans embroidered on and typed notices underneath with the English translation.

Back in reception, Andy asked to use their Internet connection to look up his AOL e-mails. I would be able to get into mine too. He got into Yahoo, only to discover that the motel people needed to put in their code and password so he could use it. Unfortunately, they had only just had it installed and when he called them over, they kept insisting that he had to put his password in. He tried to explain that it wasn't his e-mail address, it was theirs, but they couldn't understand. While this was going on, a man had come in with his girlfriend to use it and I got the impression that he was getting rather agitated at the delay. Andy eventually gave up, telling him that if he wasn't with Yahoo, he wouldn't be able to get in, but he didn't seem interested.
Friday 2nd May.

I was up early, showered, and was ready to go over to the restaurant for breakfast where, to my delight, they had biscuits and gravy on the menu.

When we'd finished eating, we packed our cases into the car and Andy drove out to the Canyon de Chelly.

This had been a Navajo stronghold until in 1863, Kit Carson had led a brutal campaign against the Native Americans. He destroyed their cornfields, hogans and orchards, forcing them to surrender or starve, then enforced thousands to march 300 miles east across New Mexico to a barren reservation at Fort Sumner, known as Bosque Redondo, becoming known as the Long Walk by the Navajo. Although officials called this a reservation, they were basically held there as prisoners.

For five years they had begged to be allowed to return to their lands, and finally in 1868, with roughly half of the original Navaho surviving, they were allowed to go back home. There's about 80 families living in the canyon now.

I picked up a leaflet about the Navaho code talkers who I hadn't heard of before. Apparently, following the attack on Pearl Harbour and the Americans joining the war, the US Military had been having trouble keeping the Japanese from breaking all their codes and learning where troops were being sent. The Navajo Marines made up their own secret code after learning the military and field terms in English, and they created the Navajo equivalent, which was never broken throughout the course of the war. The number of American lives they saved through this work had been 'inestimable.'

At a parking bay on the South Rim at Tunnel Overlook, looking out to the beginning of the canyon, a Navajo boy had set up paintings of petroglyphs done on slate, on his car bonnet. As I stood and looked at them, he got out and came over to tell me what they all meant and how he had started painting and selling his art after he had learnt from his grandparents all the meanings. They were beautifully done and I bought one.

At the next outlook, Tseyi Overlook, we walked across swirls of rock that looked like whipped icecream to the edge of the canyon. It was a long way down to the bottom of the cliffs where the shallow water wound along the bottom of the canyon framed by lovely green cottonwood trees. Fencing mapped out the different little farms and I could see a few cattle grazing while a truck splashed through the water where the track crossed the riverbed. The whole place radiated peace and tranquillity, and I could have just sat and looked for hours. A real paradise, hidden from view until you stood on the dusty barren plateau above it.

We went on to Junction Overlook, and then to White House Overlook and Trail where the White House ruins of Anasazi buildings were tucked under an overhang of rock opposite. These houses, like all Navajo hogans, always faced east to get the rays of the rising sun. At most of the bays where we parked, we could see ruins nestling at the foot of steep cliffs or almost hidden tucked under overhangs and in caves entrances.

Tiny canyon swifts flew below us like tiny darts with their piping squeaks echoing. Two blue-black birds (ravens?) flew in tight formation, wingtip to wingtip. The beauty was overwhelming and I wished I could live here, working in the open air with no hurry and bustle, and no TV. Andy was more down to earth: no doctors, no electricity, no gas, no plumbing.

The road turned left and at the end was Spider Rock Overlook. Not having realised what this was, I was astounded to walk round a corner of the path to see the two 800 foot tall pillars of rock immortalised in the film, 'McKenna's Gold' starring Gregory Peck, rising up like two huge fingers from the floor of the canyon. The sun threw shadows at the base.

We drove back to the Holiday Inn where we had seen advertised jeep trips into the canyon, and having just over half an hour to wait for the next trip, Andy decided to drive back to the main shops to try and get some sinus tablets. On the way, I was saddened to see the bloated body of a dead dog, covered in a swarm of flies, just laying, ignored, on the sidewalk. We found a Wal-Mart, but unfortunately there were very long queues, and we ended up being 15 minutes late back. The driver didn't seem too put out when we apologised, and luckily we were the only ones going.

We climbed into a battered old jeep. Andy let me sit in the front seat, and I clung onto the roll bar above my head as we bounced and jolted along the road to the entrance of the canyon, where down by the river, the breeze was lovely and cooling. As we drove slowly out onto the sandy riverbed, our guide told us that if we'd been here a week before, we couldn't have come down, the river had been too high from the spring melt. It seems that quicksand, deep dry sand, and flash floods make the canyon hazardous to travel, and even the Navajos living in the canyon were cut off until the waters receded.

We jolted and splashed across the uneven riverbed, criss-crossing over to the other side and up onto the dry bank, stopping to see some petroglyphs, where another jeep was already parked with two people. By the end of the holiday, I was amazed at just how far flung instances of petroglyphs were, the Anasazi people must have been spread over most of North America.

We continued on, our guide pointing out more petroglyphs and Anasazi ruins, plus the Navaho tapestry, the black and brown lines of iron and manganese as they oozed out of the rocks over millions of years. It always looked to me as if the walls were crying. The driver told us that his parents and grandparents all had land in the canyon.

We bounced along the sandy trails, almost getting bogged at one point, our guide having to rev like mad backwards to get us free, passing under tall cottonwoods, driving up and down and over the river crossings, the wind throwing the spray back into my face. It felt like a very badly made roller coaster ride, but the scenery was worth every jolt.

We splashed our way along under towering cliffs, finally pulling up by some stalls under another overhang of rock. Getting out of the jeep, I found myself beside the biggest ruins we had come across so far and again these were fenced off to stop vandalism. Personally, I thought that anyone caught defacing history should have their hands cut off. One strange petroglyph looked like a half made Nazi sign, except that it had been scratched into the rock face hundreds of years before World War II.

A wagon train of wagons and riders on horses and mules was just heading out further down into the valley. With Navajo permission, camping sites could be booked, and this was just one of the types of parties that came down into the canyon. There was also a lot of hiking.

We bought some drinks and I got a couple of cookies while we browsed round the gifts for sale. The wind whipped up around under the wall and blew everything about, and I was glad of the storm strap securing my hat. Andy began to feel drowsy and rather headachy, attributing this to the tablets he'd taken.

Before we left, I decided to use the toilet facilities. Inside a concrete shed were two toilet pans fixed over a hole in the ground. With no doors and only just round the edge of the wall, I prayed that no one suddenly appeared round the corner, I'd have been mortified.

We set off back and this time the wind was coming towards us so we got sprayed every time the wheels hit a bump in the riverbed. Our guide pointed out a tall mesa, a flat topped rock up which the Navajo had scrambled trying to hide from the soldiers forcing them away from their land.

Back at the car, Andy wasn't feeling at all well, so I drove, heading north on the 191 to Many Farms, then picking up Route 59 for Kayenta. He was asleep most of the way and missed seeing the thick dust storms swirling across the horizon and on down over the road, almost obscuring the cars in front of me. For all of the fifty-four miles to Kayenta these dust storms continued, and even when the dust clouds were far off, the continuous wind swept eerie streamers of sand across the tarmac like fog in a ghost film. Alongside the road at a particularly windswept area a windsock was blowing straight out by the force of the gale. In the distance, through the haze, the flat plain was becoming split by huge ridges and fingers of broken red sandstone, white rocks covered in scrub, and golden coloured sand dunes.

Suddenly, three police cars overtook us with their lights flashing, everyone pulling over to the side of the road, then about twenty minutes later, two came back past normally. Wonder what had happened.

From the 59, I turned west, passing another wind sock blowing straight out from its post, and finally reached Kayenta, a dusty looking huddle of buildings where the sand had blown into every corner and crevice of buildings and kerbs. Andy woke up and wanted to go to the shops to try and find his adapter, but again, he was unlucky. Everything but the one he wanted.

I drove along a bit further until I saw a pretty Holiday Inn and we decided to stop for something to drink. Inside was very neat, with deep couches in a half square around a fireplace, and a restaurant area behind woven screens. Andy didn't fancy eating and I wasn't really hungry, so when the waiter came, Andy asked if we could just have coffee. The man pointed across the lobby back to the doorway and told us that complimentary coffee was available and free to everyone. I hoped my eyebrows didn't shoot up in amazement, but we thanked him, went and got a paper cup of coffee, and sat by the fireplace. Andy still didn't look at all well.

I continued on west to the 98 and headed north for Page, missing out the Navajo National Park for Andy was asleep again. As the Econolodge had been fairly nice when we'd been there a couple of years previously, I decided to see if it was still there. It was, but was now called the Economy Inn. $72.94 for two rooms.

The rooms we were given were across the road from the rest of the layout. They were comfortable, but my a/c was rather noisy. The sink tap had to be inclined upward before being turned either right or left for hot and cold water.

Andy went to bed, but as I was hungry, I walked down to the KFC and back for a chicken burger and fries. Although it was dark and I was wary, I didn't feel worried at being alone.

I sat and watched TV where I found an episode of MASH I'd never seen before. Unfortunately, all Sky showed back home were the same couple of dozen shows over and over again, and I was sick of seeing them. Even better, when flicking through the channels afterward, I discovered two episodes of 'Stargate SG1' which I adore.
Saturday 3rd May.

I was awake at 6am and went for a shower. The shower pull on the bath spout either wasn't working properly or the showerhead was blocked, because only half the normal amount of water came out.

Writing up my notes, I couldn't believe that this was only day four. We'd already done quite a lot from the itinerary, so my worry of running out of time to do everything was looking very unlikely.

There wasn't a coffee machine in the room, so I walked over to the office to get a drink, but they only did tea and I didn't fancy that. I asked about somewhere for breakfast and she told me I could go to a restaurant next door. I phoned Andy when I heard him coughing through the wall, and he said that he was feeling much better and came with me for a meal.

No biscuits and gravy, they'd run out, so I settled for 2 eggs over easy, hash browns, bacon and toast. Our waitress, Maggie was very nice and had a pleasant laugh, and told us she'd originally came from Mississippi. The elderly man on reception was tall with a big moustache and was dressed like an old time cowboy. Neat!

Through the windows I could see across to Lake Powell where dust storms swirled round the buttes and spires. Andy asked if there was a Wal-Mart anywhere and was given directions to go left on Main Street and to carry on round behind the town.

First though, he drove across the road to see if we could get on a jeep trip to the Antelope Slot Canyon that we'd missed out on a couple of years back. The first shop hadn't opened so we went down to the office on the other corner of the block and booked in there, being given a ticket with Andy's name on it for 11.30am. The trip was organised by the Navajo as it was on their land.

We drove round the outskirts of the town, Andy turned right at the lights although I thought we should have stayed on the main road, and we found ourselves driving round a very large pretty estate of bungalows, many with big cars outside. Eventually we came across the main road and turned right, and there, down the hill was the Wal-Mart in a large shopping mall. At Radio Shack, Andy tried for an adapter, but again he was unsuccessful.

At Wal-Mart I bought some new jeans and a black leather belt with several silver studs, as the jeans I'd brought from home had either stretched or I'd lost weight, and kept slipping down to my hips which felt uncomfortable.

We returned for the jeep trip, but in the office I couldn't find the ticket in my bag, and the lady was different to the one earlier so didn't recognise us. I insisted that it was in the name of Haven, but they couldn't find it in their copies of the receipts until at the last moment, Andy remembered signing it in his name, while I'd paid. They looked up Bucksey, and there we were, just as I finally found the ticket. How embarrassing.

A young Navajo lad came in and was having a laugh with the lady behind the counter, giving her a cuddle and being cheeky, and we found out that she was his mother. He had come back from university for a few days, and suddenly being a driver short, she had 'press ganged' him into taking one of the minibuses. He kept insisting that he should be on holiday not working.

Andy and I climbed into the front seat beside him, and some of the people behind us began kidding him about "had he got a driving licence?" and "did he know how to drive?" and he responding by asking where the gear stick was. In the end we were all laughing, everyone was very pleasant and funny. He followed the other three jeeps out onto the road and onto Hwy 98 south for a few miles, passing the big power station, before turning through a gate and stopping at a wooden shed. We were waved through, he put the minibus into four wheel drive, and we went out into a wide sandy wash. The wind had been picking up and the sand was billowing out from under the wheels of the jeeps in front, while the minibus slipped and slid as it hit pockets of deeper sand while gradually the jeeps began to pull ahead.

After a couple of miles we approached a sand covered ridge where other jeeps and trucks had stopped and got out, the wind whipping up the sand in swirls stinging when it hit my face. The wash had come to an end, but ahead of us there was a dark, shadowy line cutting vertically down the rocks.

Trying to hide our cameras under our coats, we trudged after the others into the entrance to the narrow slot that had been discovered by a four year old Navajo girl just eighty years before. Sunbeams shone from overhead in places lighting up the wonderful pastel colours of the sandstone that had been worn into fantastic bowls and loops where the water poured through from the melting snows. It was absolutely stunning.

Quite a few advertisements had been filmed here, and to make the sunbeams stand out even more, our guide tossed handfuls of dust into the light making it sparkle. It was so beautiful. In places where the sun hadn't quite reached overhead it was fairly dark, and some of the slot was quite confined, making our voices echo. In the occasional rays of sunlight, a fine film of dust swirled about, invisible in the darker parts, and I began to worry about my asthma.

We strolled slowly through and out the other side into another wide, steep sided wash. It was awesome to think that so much water could be channelled into such a fine slit in the rocks. The noise must have been tremendous.

John Travolta had been filmed at this very spot standing by a stolen bomb in the film, Broken Arrow.

We walked through the slot again trying to avoid the photographers with their tripods, and back to the jeeps where the wind was really gusting now, and black clouds were heading our way. Andy disappeared back into the slot for a few more shots while everyone else crammed back into the bus. Arriving back, he began trying to blow dust out of his camera, especially where the lenses screwed into it, and I could hear the fine grating as he turned them. He was quite worried about possible damage.

On the way back to town, our driver told us that his girlfriend had been in South America for two years and was due to return shortly, and he was uncertain as to whether to ask her to marry him. I said that if that was what he wanted, to go for it, and I hoped that if he did, he would be as happy as I'd been. We slithered our way back down the wash to the road and were driven back to the office.

The other shop had now opened, not only selling camping gear and clothing, but also doing short trips on balloon rafts down the Colorado, so Andy went in and booked us on one for the following morning. I was assured that there weren't any rapids. They would be leaving from the foot of the San Juan Dam and travelling down to Lee's Ferry, returning us by minibus.

Back at the motel, while Andy waited outside in the car, I went into the office to book another night's stay, but when we'd parked outside our rooms, we discovered that we couldn't get in the doors. I realised that as it was after the leaving time, perhaps the cards should have been re-swiped for another night's stay, and when I walked across to the office, they apologised and rectified the cards.

Earlier, I'd spotted a notice in a hairdresser's window for perms and decided to go across and see if they had time to do me, as the price was cheaper than Britain. Inside, a lady was cutting an elderly man's hair while on the other side a man was dealing with another customer. The lady just smiled at me and carried on working, so rather than interrupt her, I sat down to wait. A man came in with two boys and sat down only waiting a short time before the youngest boy was taken to a chair to have his hair trimmed. Finally, the lady finished, and once her customer had paid, asked me what I wanted doing.

"Could you fit me in for a perm?"

She was very apologetic. "I'm sorry, Saturday's are too busy for perms, I won't be able to do it until next week. You should have said, rather than sit there."

"That's OK, I didn't want to interrupt you. I'll be leaving tomorrow so I'll have to leave it, thanks."

"Ok, you have a nice day."

By now Andy and I were hungry and I said, "let's go back to that restaurant where the girl dropped a tray, a couple of years back," so Andy drove down there.

We found it, a long dark wood building looking like an old saloon both inside and out, and went in to sit by the big windows at a booth. I ordered a tuna melt with fries like I'd had in Strawberry. A couple of people, who had been inside when we arrived, got up and helped themselves to the salad bar at the far end of the room.

While we waited for our meal to arrive, I watched the dust storms flying across Lake Powell while the rising wind was flapping the flags on the hotel opposite. A couple of black ravens were being blown around as they soared over the road and gardens, landing on lawns and in the trees with difficulty. The meal was huge, but as nice as the last one. During the meal Andy still seemed to be having sinus trouble, constantly sneezing and sniffling.

I'd written on my itinerary about Vermillon Cliffs and Lee's Ferry, mainly because I'd read about them in Zane Grey books and other westerns, so we decided to take the 89 south to Bitter Spring and pick up the 89A west. But before we reached the junction, we had a twisting drop down the 2,000 feet Echo cliffs. Halfway down, we stopped at a recess with other cars to take a picture of the plain below where, over near the horizon, swept the dark streaks of a heavy rainstorm. Beyond that lay the dark line of Vermillon Cliffs.

We crossed a metal span bridge over the deep green waters in a narrow gorge and Andy pulled onto a parking area on the right. Walking out onto the bridge, I watched a girl swinging an antenna. I knew from wild life programmes that she would be tracking something, but what? I plucked up the courage to ask her what she was doing.

She was really nice and told me that they had released about eight pairs of California Condors into the wild and most of them were roosting under the bridge, so she and another man were out here to try and find out which ones were down there. Unfortunately, at the time they weren't flying. Andy and I joined them in peering down to where the struts of the bridge were cemented into the rocks, and then he managed to spot a bird. Hanging onto my hat in case the wind snatched it away, even with the storm strap under my chin, I leaned out quite far and saw a black spot on the ledge beneath me. Just then, the man called out that one had flown and I managed to rush across to the other side of the bridge to take a picture of the bird as it flew underneath us.

The girl offered to give me some pamphlets on the scheme from her car, so as she sorted them out, I went and got some money to give her a donation, as much for the project as to pay for the pamphlets. She was highly delighted and said that I would be able to look them up on the Internet when I got home to discover how they were getting on. She asked where we were from and when I said Canterbury, near the French coast, she said that she'd stayed with a friend in Tunbridge Wells once and had loved England.

We carried on down a small road close to the cliffs of Marble Canyon passing huge fallen boulders and rocks, a couple of them looking like giant mushrooms, before coming across a small hut with a ticket machine and a notice on how to pay for a ticket. I couldn't fathom out how it worked, so we decided to drive on.

The road got narrower and began winding down towards the river where we passed a small rapid. Just beyond that was a wide expanse of water with several pale blue balloon rafts tied up at the foot of a gangway, alongside some smaller boats. Lees Ferry.

From the dirt car park we walked down to the wooden trestle gangway beside the clear water to look across the river where rocky hills rose above the green cottonwood trees. To the left and upstream, the river disappeared around a bend between craggy rocks. Wow.

We drove back to the rapids, parked and walked down to the water's edge where I picked up two small stones for souvenirs. Back on the road, we stopped at the mushroom shaped rocks' where we took photos, each standing underneath one. I took one of him on his digital. By-passing the iron bridge we followed the road beside Vermillon Cliffs, a sheer precipice of dark red and brown stone with black shadows and enormous rocks strewn at the base, some rolled close to the road. Hope none roll while we're passing.

I'd seen a pamphlet describing petrified swirling sand dunes, but on looking at the map, I discovered that the dunes, confusingly with the same name as the cliffs, were on the other side of Page, miles away, so we turned back.

As we sped between Vermillon and Echo Cliffs with the Colorado River flowing unseen down a gorge in the centre of the plain, I knew that I had to be one of the luckiest people alive. To actually visit all the spectacular places I'd read about since a child was overwhelming, and I had to choke back tears.

Black clouds began to build behind us as we drove back over the bridge and started towards Echo Cliffs. Once up the steep climb to the top, the clouds caught us up and several times we drove through short showers.

At Wal-Mart we parked up and headed for the little café for coffee. Afterwards, I bought some biscuits so that I could take my herbal tablets, as I wasn't hungry enough for a meal. I also purchased two more Louis L'Amour westerns that I hadn't already got, a cowboy magazine, and a couple of small, cheap American flags, buying one for my car at home. I'd put a small British flag on the aerial when the football had been on, adding an even smaller USA flag underneath, but they were both getting frayed by the wind and needed replacing. Just as I got to the checkout I suddenly remembered that I needed a new lipstick and shot back to quickly chose one.

Back outside, the ground was wet and there were puddles from the rain with black clouds slowly passing overhead, but more were heading our way. It had started raining by the time we arrived at the motel and continued on into the night.

I had a shower, that was bliss as I felt itchy from the dust that had blown over me during the day, before sitting on the bed to write up my notes, then reading the pamphlets that I'd acquired regarding the Colorado River and the dams along its length.

I'd never been impressed by dams, they seemed against nature despite mans' pride at taming the river and producing electricity. I'd always heard that the ecology had been bettered by having them, but it seems that despite the brags, things were not good. The bottoms of the dams were silting up, so that Lake Powell was actually getting less water in it year by year, and by 50 years plus, it would be so silted up that it would be useless. The 275,000 tons of sediment that used to go down the river replenishing the beaches and enriching the environment were now backing up behind the dam at a massive 30,000 dump truck loads a day, making it less efficient. And with the water temperature a steady, ice cold 48 degrees instead of the varying 35-85 degrees, it was now destroying the native fish. I wasn't surprised. This magnificent river had forged its own way down for millions of years so there was no way that the interference of man was going to do any good to anyone but himself.

The Glen Canyon dam was just as bad, and after 40 years, it is one of the most destructive projects ever built. So I guess this would apply to all dams around the world.

I watched a little TV, coming across editions of MASH, and also 'Are You Being Served?' that I enjoy. Apparently, the Americans also love it.

Chapter 28

A Raft Trip.

Sunday 4th May.

I woke to blue skies and sunshine, and although there was a little chill in the breeze the air smelt wonderfully fresh and clean. I rang Andy to see if he was up, and then we went to the restaurant next door for breakfast. Great, biscuits and gravy. But I was in for a disappointment. It wasn't as nice as I'd had elsewhere in America and the white gravy was highly spiced.

We parked outside the camping shop to meet up with other people who were also coming on the trip and were informed that we would be taken by minibus to the top of the dam. There our bags would be put onto another truck to go down to the raft through a long, long narrow tunnel to the foot of the dam, our minibus following separately for security reasons. The minibus arrived outside and we all climbed in.

At the fenced off compound with its sentry box at the top of the dam, our bags were transferred and we set off into a narrow tunnel, making me cringe at the thought of all that rock above us. On the way down the driver informed us that the water in the lake was now over 100 foot down due to a three year drought, and that even the snow melts this Spring had not been up to much. The tunnel continued for two miles and during its construction a lot of small tunnels had had to be drilled out over the river for all the rubble to be emptied out. Nearer the bottom the road began to get wet from water seeping through the soft sandstone.

Once out, we were given hard hats to wear for protection from any falling stones while we collected our bags and walked down metal gangways to the raft. Once at the raft, we gave the hats back and climbed in, Andy and I selecting to be near the front. Down here the breeze was lovely and cool, and there seemed to be thousands of the little blue black canyon swifts flying along the cliffs or skimming the water.

Our guide, Mick, took the raft out into the current and while we floated gently towards the first little white water, told us about the building of the San Juan dam. How doing it had made the water cleaner, and that the temperature remained a constant 70 degrees, although the green tinge was due to no silt getting down. This encouraged wildlife and also allowed trees, especially the cottonwoods, normally swept away in the floods, to take root on the riverbanks. As we got to the shallow rapid, Mick lifted the engine's propeller up out of the water so that it didn't get damaged on the rocky bottom.

The white dam slowly receded as we drifted lazily round the first bend, the rocky cliffs towering above us looking as if they'd been made out of putty that someone had tried unsuccessfully to smooth off with a blunt knife, leaving nooks and crannies. He pointed out that the water was so clear the fish could be easily seen gently drifting with their heads pointing upstream.

He went to the front of the raft and laid down over the edge, his head out of sight, his arms reaching down into the water as he told us that you could actually catch them this way. Suddenly, he raised himself up with a thrashing fish clenched between his teeth making some of the women shriek. With great glee I spotted it was really a plastic one. What a laugh!

On one of the bends, we came across another raft beached where they'd obviously been having a picnic. He stopped our boat on the clean sand alongside to guide us up some sandy steps and along the trail to see petroglyphs on the walls of the canyon, the clearest being a line of six fat little antelope with stick legs and half moon bodies. Here, it was really hot, despite the cool breeze.

Back at the boats, he helped the girl in charge of the other boat to pack the tables and the rest of their things away while a couple from our boat wandered over to them without noticing where they were, and began to get into theirs. They took a lot of stick over their mistake, coming back rather embarrassed.

Both boats set off together, and now Mick began to go faster, the spray beginning to splash up over the front and onto me, very cooling. The river narrowed in places where the water picked up speed, and at others widened and slowed, often rippling over a stony bed. Several ducks flew off the water at our approach, similar to our mallards.

Then Mick pointed to some tiny dots on the edge of a cliff that we were approaching. People, and then I spotted the bright light of a camera flash going off. Some of us waved as we got closer, before we were gliding past and away. The other boat began manoeuvring close in under a sheer wall of rock out of the hot sun, and ours followed, Mick tying them both to rings in the wall. He reached for a guitar from his bag.

"We only do this when we have time and the weather's right," he said, tuning in a couple of the strings. He sang three songs, and he was great to listen to. With the sounds of the river gurgling past, the shrill piping of the canyon swifts and the gently bumping of the boats, it was like being in paradise. What a sad thing when he finished, packed away the guitar, and we had to start off on our way again.

As we got closer to Lees Ferry, the cliffs began to change to hills of broken shale, and then to my great disappointment, there ahead was the place we'd visited yesterday. Mick slowed the boat and came in closer to the right hand bank, where a boiler and a pipe were half submerged, the remains of an old boat that had once plied up and down the river.

We left the raft, thanking him for the trip, and climbed into the minibus. Andy had gone right to the back, and without thinking, I followed, ducking down under the roof. As I sat down in the cramped space and other people filled the seats in front, I began to panic.

"What's wrong," asked Andy.

"I'm claustrophobic in confined spaces," I said, "and I know I can't get out." I began to shake, getting a bit hysterical. He looked at me in slight amazement.

"Ask to go down the front."

But it was too late, the door had been shut. I clenched my fists and shut my eyes tight, desperately trying to pretend I was back on the water. And there I remained, silent, shivering, for the hour trip back to the shop, where I almost fell out of the door in an effort to escape.

We drove out of Page and back down the 98 to reach the 160 to Kayenta. After the rain last night several of the creek beds either had trickles of water or the sand looked wet as if they had already started to dry out, but after the junction with the 160 there was no sign of rain having fallen at all.

Just after Kayenta, close to the junction with the 163 for Goulding's and

Monument Valley, we had to stop while a Navaho and his dog drove a herd of sheep across the road to another field.

It was lovely to drive back through the Valley again and get the chance to stay at the motel by the old trading post. After all the driving, I was tired and glad to stop for the rest. Andy booked us in at $60 a night each and also booked us onto a jeep trip for the morning. A good motel, not only did we have ground floor rooms that were easier to access with the cases but they had coffee machines in the rooms.

I looked out my window to discover a small balcony with a couple of chairs facing a great view over the buttes of red sandstone standing out on the valley floor. I imagined wagon trains rolling across the vast sandy terrain, the scouts riding long distances searching for water, possibly caught up in swirling dust storms. It brought closer the perils and dangers that the pioneers went through just to try to get to a new, and hopefully better, life.

Across at the gift shop, I bought another sand painting protected by a covering of cellophane, and a small metal Texas tie pin badge, before we climbed several flights of wooden stairs to reach the restaurant.

We were shown to a window seat. Dusk was falling and the whole valley began to fade into a deep blue haze until finally there was nothing to see except a few twinkling stars. I ordered a Caesar salad. Very nice.

We went back to our rooms, but I slept badly, my back aching. Too much sitting and driving?
Monday 5th May.

I had a shower and discovered that I had a sore rash of spots about the size of a ten pence piece on the back of my neck. Not another 'kissing bug' like I'd got at the Lazy K Bar ranch the first year?

I made myself a coffee and sat out on the balcony listening to the sound of the sparrows chirping in the low bushes. I could see for miles, and it was so quiet and peaceful, it was a shame to move.

We met up to go to the restaurant where I ordered eggs, bacon, sausage and toast. Then we packed the cases in the car before joining the queue to get on the open sided tour jeep. Our guide was a pretty Navaho girl.

Crossing the 163 we were in the desert, stopping to get out to visit a Navajo hogan, where the doorway always faces east toward the rising sun. The hogans are still made by hand using local materials and regarded as a sanctuary for the family where it is still traditional for 'the Blessing Way rite' to be performed before the family takes up residence. The traditional Navajos still prepare and spin the wool the old fashioned way using dyes made from native plants. Wild plants are used for many things including medicines, with the yucca providing the basis for shoes, baskets, clothing and soap. Almost 300 Navajo still live in the valley all year round.

We all managed to get inside, standing in a semi circle around a pile of rugs on which sat a Navajo lady, weaving a rug on a board in front of her. While she was working, she was singing a Navajo chant. I was fascinated. Although I had no idea what she was singing about, I found it deeply relaxing.

A Navaho man began explaining about their way of life on the reservation and how they lived. She then turned to show us a bunch of stiff grass stems tied together that would be used as a hairbrush.

"The women sing while they are working," stated the guide, with a broad grin.

"That way we know they're not gossiping," That brought laughter.

"Who would like to sit and have their hair done in a traditional way?" he asked. Nearly everyone was elderly, and no one spoke. Embarrassed by the silence, yet eager to have a go, I offered, and was asked to sit with my back to the lady on the rugs. Getting down wasn't too bad, getting up was going to be a big problem as my muscles were so stiff these days. Oh, the joys of getting old.

Starting another sing, she began to brush my hair and pull it back, while the guide offered me several strands of coloured wool.

"Which would you like?"

I chose a deep rose pink and it was used to tie my hair back in a neat bun. I wished I could have seen it being done. When she'd finished, I began to struggle up and a man stepped forward to give me a hand. I thanked him, and turned to thank the Navajo lady. Andy looked embarrassed by the whole thing, but I was chuffed.

"I can't believe you did that," he said.

Back in the jeep we drove past empty stalls and wooden sheds that would later hold Navaho jewellery and gifts for sale, eventually stopping at a gift shop for twenty minutes to have a look round. I walked over to the low wall to take a few photos of some buttes, two of which looked like mittens complete with the thumbs, facing each other. The right one had apparently been used for an advertisement for a Jeep company, the vehicle being airlifted to the top by helicopter.

Further on I could see in the distance the huge Cly Butte, better known for the Marlborough cigarette commercial. Here a Navajo chieftain is buried with his cattle, sheep, goats, horse, saddle and bridle, all to go with him to the spirit world. Inside the shop, I bought a couple of fridge magnets and some postcards.

The jeep headed through a fence gate and down a red, dusty trail out into the huge valley of sandy soil, sage bush and sand dunes. Rising up were more huge buttes and pointed fingers of rock looking as if they'd been shoved out of the ground by a giant hand, surrounded by falls of shale and huge boulders. One was so tall and thin it seemed a miracle that it was standing. Some of the names were stunning: The Setting Hen, Brigham's Tomb, The King on his Throne, Bear and Rabbit, the Three Sisters, and Rain God Mesa, this last being used as a platform for the medicine men to pray for rain and which contained a sacred burial ground. Agathlan is the core of an ancient volcano, renamed El Capitan by Kit Carson, the Indian fighter and explorer of the 1880s.

We stopped at John Wayne Point, an outcrop of cliff overhanging the valley, used in the first film, Stagecoach, and including She Wore a Yellow Ribbon, The Searchers, How the West Was Won, the Eiger Sanction and Back to the Future III. Here, an elderly Navaho was riding a black pony out to the tip, standing still for a while, then trotting back. For a few dollars, you could have your picture taken on the back of the pony. Stalls were laid out with beautiful jewellery where I bought another necklace for myself, and a bracelet each for my nieces, Tracy and Vicki. Wandering about, I discovered under a lean-to a picketed white stallion. I knew better than to try and pat him.

From there we went to see some natural stone arches, a tall cave like overhang with a hole in the roof, and some petroglyphs. To get to one arch, we could climb up the sand dune, so naturally, off I set. Half way up I began to feel tired, and by the top my heart was pounding so hard, I could hardly breathe. Gosh, I knew my breathing was a bit bad, having industrial asthma from going into a skip for months to bag up shavings for the horses' beds, but I began to realise that it was a lot worse than I thought and got quite frightened. It was much easier to half slide, half walk back down.

Driving up and down some of the sand dunes following the tracks of other jeeps, our guide had a bit of difficulty and at one point, as the vehicle slid and slithered to the top, we cheered her efforts.

On the way back to Goulding's, the wind got colder, with a fine rain in the air and I got quite chilly as I was only wearing jeans, shirt and a jean jacket. I was really glad to get back into our car as it was nice and warm from the sun shining on it.

We drove on north through Mexican Hat passing the motel we'd once stayed at, turning left onto the 261, and heading for the Gooseneck curves of the San Juan River. The road became an unmade track along which we bumped until it came to an end. The view was stunning, miles of twisting canyon, the walls made of horizontally layered and stepped rock in pastel greens and greys, black shadows and red sandstone, the greenish grey waters of the river far below edged by green trees. We retraced our steps to the tarmac road again, and headed for Muley Point, joining another dusty track that ran for miles.

We approached a huge cliff where the road began to snake up a steep incline. The car didn't seem at all happy with the gravel and felt as if it was slipping all the time, even with the traction control, making me somewhat nervous. We stopped halfway as I wanted to take a photograph of the view stretched out below. Scrambling out of the car, with quite a crack this time, the car gave me yet another static shock, making me say a few naughty words as I rubbed my arm.

After taking my picture I glanced down, and with a shock I saw an upturned car in the rocks just above a sheer drop, before Andy pointed out two others. That scared me even more.

Eventually, we reached the top of the cliff, luckily not meeting anyone coming down, and a few miles further on reached a walled area for parking. Off to our left down another rougher track was parked an RV, so Andy drove past it and followed the trail, which became rougher and rougher. Finally, we decided that this wasn't such a good idea, turned round, and headed back to the wall. The view from here was similar to the Goosenecks, but seen from a different angle.

We retraced our route back to the cliff, made even more frightening as we were now heading downhill. Absolutely petrified, I was so relieved to reach the bottom in one piece. Andy drove back to a sign for the Valley of the Gods and turned off the road onto another unmade track that was like a switchback or roller-coaster ride, through a sandy, sage covered valley. Huge pinnacles of rocks thrust their way to the heavens and towered above us making me feel as small as an ant. Wow, where's Airwolf.

We did pass a couple of cars coming from the other direction but otherwise we could have been on Mars, bouncing along for miles and miles between the huge buttes before reaching the 163 again to head for Bluff.

Looking back from the road, the whole valley had disappeared from sight- the most amazing scenery had literally gone. If we hadn't just driven through it, I would never have known it was there.

We crossed Chinle Creek and drove into the sleepy town of Bluff, a collection of dusty shacks, trailer parks, gas station, an old motel, and according to the sign on the edge of town, around 200 people. Pulling up outside the Cottonwood Café, we gazed at it in awe. It looked like it belonged in the 1920's. We went through the door and into the shack, skirting some wooden tables and chairs to reach the counter. An elderly, sharp looking lady came from the equipment at the back of the kitchen area and glared at us.

"Yes?"

I was a little intimidated, but asked for coffee, and began reading the menu up on the board. She shuffled about getting the cups and saucers, then fixed us with her gimlet eyes. A bit taken aback, we asked for hamburger and chips. Without a word she went and got a rack of crisps, putting it in front of us.

"Oh, sorry, we meant fries. We call those crisps in Britain."

"They're not, they're chips," she stated firmly, and took them back. As she started to cook, Andy asked where the restrooms were.

"Round the side, next building," she snapped, "but don't flush it. The last person who went there blocked the cess pit and it went everywhere. DON'T FLUSH IT."

Rather than sit alone in the place, I followed Andy out and waited outside the toilet till he came out.

"Bit basic," he said. I went in determined not to pull the handle, petrified I would by mistake.

Back in the café, we sat at the table with our coffees, which were just about warm, then I got up and wandered round the glass topped cases. They were crammed full of jewellery and oddments, and the prices seemed rather steep. Andy was trying the double glass doors into another area.

"It's locked," she called out, stalking round the counter with her keys and opening them for us, following closely behind, while I wondered if the food would be alright left alone.

Even more glass top cases were full of the same stuff, there must have been a fortune in here. Was she in the pawn shop business? Andy was looking at the pile of rugs in the centre of the room, at which, having never taken her eyes off us for a second, she began turning back every one for us to have a look. We admired them, then she slowly and methodically began turning them back.

As we left the room, she reset the alarm, locked the doors, and went back to the cooking. As she passed our table, she firmly pushed Andy's cup and saucer into the middle of the table then banged a couple of the chairs back under the table beside us.

"Don't want it falling off," she stated. "They're very expensive and antique, $65 each." Andy's eyebrows went up and, having had more than enough, I had to try hard not to giggle.

"They're rubbish," he whispered, "anyway, who in their right mind has expensive cups in a place like this. I was looking at the ancient jute box over there that's got a licence on it. Guess where we are?" Puzzled, I looked at him grinning at me. A suspicion sprang to mind.

"We're in Utah!"

"Oh," I whispered back, "that explains a lot!" Utah is mostly populated with Mormons and there is a lot of inbreeding, and in some places very severe inbreeding. We both started chuckling until she finally appeared with our meals—in paper bags! Actually, mine wasn't bad, but both meals were huge.

"Had some French people in here," she told us sounding disgusted, her elbows on the counter as she fixed her grim, bright eyes on us. "Tried to tell me I can't sell French fries as they're not French." I wondered how they had the nerve to tell her.

"Why not," I asked. "They are always called that."

"Told me I can't do it," she snapped. "They were most insistent. I told them that's what we call them."

Andy explained to me, "because the French got mad and vetoed the war in Iraq, so they don't like them being called French fries any more, just fries."

As we were finishing, a girl came in and went up to the counter and I caught enough of the conversation to hear that she wanted to hock some jewellery for gas for her car. After some discussion, a price was arranged, and she had to fill in loads of details on a form. The owner definitely was in the pawn brokering business.

We paid up and went out to the car, anxious to get away, heading back on the 163 until the turning to the left for the 191 south. From there we turned onto the 160 east for the Four Corners Monument.

Pulling up alongside the fencing, we discovered that the gates had shut at five. Disappointed, we were just about to leave when a Navajo packing his car by the gate waved his hand towards the entrance.

"It's OK," he said. "Go and have a look. It's only about a quarter mile."

"Oh, thanks."

We grabbed our cameras, slid through the gap and began walking swiftly towards some flags flying in the distance, passing empty gift stalls. We finally came across a raised concrete dais with four flags for the four States, and mounting a couple of steps, found right in the centre a round brass plaque sectioned for Colorado, Utah, New Mexico and Arizona, the only place where four States actually meet. I felt a little disappointed.

"Oh, is that it?" I asked, taking a picture. As we walked back to the car, we passed several other couples and families heading for the monument. Gosh, they could have stayed open a bit longer and made some more money.

I drove on up the 160, crossed the San Juan River again and took the 160 /666 to Cortez, Colorado, a large town of around 4000-5000 people. Along Main Street we stopped at the Best Western Turquoise Inn where, in the middle of the buildings and car parking space was a waterfall and pond.

The rooms were very nice again, my room being across the other side of the square from Andy's, and I was greatly impressed by my shower area as it sported a dispenser on the wall for shower gel and shampoo. Very smart. Not only that, but there was a coffee machine on the vanity unit.

Neither of us were particularly hungry, so we decided not to bother going out for a meal and instead, I sat on my bed writing postcards, sticking on the hand written labels I'd taken with me. Unfortunately, I had an unsettled night as overhead 'elephants' kept tramping about all evening and several times in the night, plus the noise outside from the continuous waterfall.

Tuesday 6th May.

I awoke to the faint sound of a creaking bed mixed with gasps and groans above my head, and dived in the shower for a bit of peace, before having a coffee and watching TV. Andy phoned through and said he was going for something to eat, so I went across to meet him in the little room behind the reception area. There was a choice of biscuits and gravy that I didn't fancy after the taste of the last lot, cereal, or some lovely fruit bread. I chose a couple of slices of that on which I spread butter and cottage cheese. Actually it tasted quite nice.

Across the main street was a big low building with a J C Penny's advertised amongst other signs on the wall, but when we went in, it appeared to be just a huge food supermarket, so we left Cortez on Route 666 making for Monticello.

Here we entered farmland with red soil and green grasses that slowly became enveloped by a forest of pines, the San Juan National Forest. Just past Yellow Jacket and Pleasant View, I spotted what appeared to be white smoke drifting up from the trees, and as we drove further on, this elongated into a strip of fire that looked at least several miles wide.

After Dove Creek the scenery became flatter and slowly turned to desert, and I knew we were back in Utah when the road suddenly became old and patched. It was as if roads weren't the main concern here and were neglected.

Distant peaks of the Abajo Mountains in the Manti-La Sal National Forest showed ahead of us, while the La Sal Mountains to the right were snow capped. Both were the same National Forest but with about 30 odd miles between them. We crossed Montezuma Creek, about the only one we'd seen so far with water in it, and drove through Monticello, a large pretty town of almost new built buildings, to join up with the 191.

We turned left onto the smaller 211 to look for Newspaper Rock, driving up through yellow and red cliffs then down a very twisty road to stop at the car park at the bottom. It was very hot, but there were quite a few trees to walk under.

At iron railings around a rocky cliff, a group of kids were playing, noisily running about, their language a bit ripe, and spoiling the chance for me to stand and admire the handiwork of the Anasazi. There appeared what at first glance to be hundreds of petroglyphs: feet, hands, wagon wheels, buffalo, a rider on horseback with a bow and arrow, and among them squiggly lines indicating rivers or floods. It seems that every time the Anasazi passed by, they left more and more information to those following of conditions of the year's weather, hunting prospects, and anything else they thought would be of great interest.

Back on the 191 and a few miles further on, we stopped to see Wilson Arch from the side of the road. Just as I was about to take a picture, a black raven landed on the big white sign in the foreground, and when the photo was processed it looked very eerie. I couldn't have done it better if I had tried.

The land slowly changed to canyons of round rocks, and then shale, the road twisting and turning through and around them. Huge ridges of crags and spires rose on the left with rolling hills on the right that turned to tall cliffs with banks of shale at the base.

Finally we drove into Moab, a sprawling town in the centre of a long, wide fertile valley and built close to the Colorado River. The place was full of cycling, hiking, jeep and rafting businesses among the gift shops, motels, hotels, and gas stations. Andy parked on the main street and we got out to wander up and down, looking in all the interesting windows. Suddenly, he came across a sign for an Internet Café and dived inside. I had never used one before and was curious.

He bought us a coffee each and we were directed down a narrow corridor to a dark room with several tables bearing computer screens where he set me up to get into my Internet address, and bingo, there were my incoming e-mails. I was fascinated! I wrote just one e-mail about our holiday so far, adding extra bits for different friends and the girls at work, and sent it off.

Driving towards the other end of town, Andy spotted a small café and turned onto a dirt track to park in the dusty back lot behind it, under a tree. It was so quaint, a wooden veranda with tables and chairs, wind chimes, and a pretty garden to the front and side. The centrepiece was a huge cup and saucer made from concrete and completely decorated with mosaic. Beside it a girl was working, planting and weeding looking like a 1900s English lady in her straw hat and light cotton dress.

Inside the building it was so old, quaint and tiny, with shelves and window ledges filled with old and antique curios. The girl serving was friendly and cheerful. I ordered a hamburger, and when it came the meal was huge, the hamburger surrounded by lettuce, slices of tomato, sliced gherkin, onion and potato salad. Delicious.

Before we left, I asked for the restroom and was directed out back to a tiny room with chintzy curtains at the window and nets hiding the shelves of cleaning stuff. It was a real shame to have to get up and leave the café at all.

We carried on through town, crossing a big bridge over the Colorado River to turn right into the Arches National Park where we stopped at the tollbooth for a $10 entrance ticket.

The narrow road rose up the cliff in short zigzags and we followed the signs for Delicate Arch, parking in a small valley before a fenced trail. It was very steep in places and I was quite breathless clambering up the rocks and along the gravel track, but then we were quite high up. Finally, we reached a flat bed of rock.

Far in the distance across a deep canyon was the arch, looking extremely odd as it rose from a flat surface all by itself. I took a picture hoping that it would show up, not having a zoom lens like Andy. It was a little disappointing to see it so far off, but in the heat there was no way we wanted to take the three mile hike to see it closer from the other side. Luckily the downward trip back was a lot easier, and near the bottom Andy stopped to take a close up picture of the big desert ants as they scurried about the hole to their nest.

Fiery Furnace was next on the list. This was an overlook facing a steep panorama of deep red rocks and cliffs that fell away into a valley below. Quite spectacular.

We carried on to the next set of arches, Broken Arch and Skyline Arch. According to a sign these were on a one point three mile trail from a camping ground where, parked in small areas off the road, were the big RVs. Nearly all of them had a small car in tow and quite a few people had cycles. Several barbecues were going.

We parked at the side of road on a small stretch of sand for we weren't allowed to go into a parking space without a permit. Carrying my water bottle, we set off across the rocks and along the sandy trail that was marked out with piles of small rocks, scrambling up inclines and climbing down into narrow gaps. In the heat, it was quite tiring. Finally we came to what we thought was Broken Arch, both being startled as this turned out to be just two upright pillars of rock with no middle, but the arch was actually further on.

Andy was beginning to doubt that the track was only as long as they'd stated. It seemed more like two at least and, as I was beginning to flag, I was quite prepared to think the same. We passed a couple with two children going in the opposite direction and everyone said, "hi." It didn't matter where we went, everyone was prepared to acknowledge each other.

Eventually we came to Skyline Arch which looked rather fragile as it had a crack running through the middle, especially so when I saw that the trail led up a rock face and then underneath it, but we got through OK and began the downward walk back to the car. As we reached it, two rangers were standing nearby, watching us approach.

"Is this yours?" asked the lady indicating our car.

"Yes, we've been on the walk to the arches and this was the only place we could see to park," I said, wondering if we were about to be fined for illegal parking.

"That's OK," she smiled, "it's just that we've had to move a car on for parking in one of the spaces."

"Oh, we're just going on to the next sight," I explained. They both smiled and walked off, leaving us to drive off out of the campsite.

We couldn't face another mile and a half walk to the Devil's Garden, and turned back, stopping off near the end of a loop of road to see the North and South Window arches with the 'Parade of Elephants.' This was a ridge of sculptured sandstone that did look remarkably like several elephants, the outline of the eyes being holes in the rock, showing the blue sky behind.

We drove back to Moab to find a motel and got two rooms at the Best Western Canyonlands. Unfortunately, they were again up on the second floor, but my room was pretty with a lovely mural of canyons on the wall above the headboard.

Out onto the street, looking for somewhere to have a snack, we ended up in a bookshop where the girl behind the counter made fresh coffee to order. I bought two more Tony Hillerman books to read and sat down at a table with a coffee for my knee was beginning to hurt. Andy continued looking around a little longer then came and sat with me. We drank our coffee and headed for the motel, but I realised that I needed something to eat so that I could take my herbal tablets, buying some biscuits at a gas station two doors down, several teenagers moving away from the doorway as we approached.

I wrote up my notes after taking the tablets, then watched TV for a while before going to bed, turning the air con on as it was quite warm.

Chapter 29

Death Valley.

Wednesday 7th May.

I woke late after a restless night at 7.10 and had a shower. By 9am my nose was running and I realised that I'd caught Andy's cold, taking two paracetamol for it. Shut in the close confines of a car, there really wasn't any way I was going to miss it.

We packed the car, drove round to the little café for breakfast, and sat outside to eat despite the cooler, cloudier start to the day.

We headed north on the 191 again, passing the road to the Arches NP, and after thirty five miles turned south on the 313 heading for Dead Horse Point. The small road came out onto a wide plateau where we stopped at the Ranger Station and Visitors Centre. We received an information leaflet and walked round the various exhibits to find out about the geology of the land, the weather, conditions and the animals that can be found before driving further on to park in the spaces available.

Walking up the rocky path to a low wall overlooking the 2,000 feet drop to the Colorado River, once again I was stunned by the immense views similar to the Goosenecks. It was breathtaking, the canyon snaking in loops before disappearing into the horizon in both directions. Reading the leaflet, I was appalled to read why it was called Dead Horse Point. It seems that wild horse hunters would drive the animals onto the point and shut them off with fencing at a bottleneck that was only thirty yards across. Unfortunately, one set of men left a herd there and never returned, resulting in the deaths of all the horses.

From there we took the 191 again north where the land slowly changed to flat plains. At Crescent Junction on the I70 we turned west for Green River, the landscape becoming cream coloured ground with creamy cliffs.

Turning off at Green River we drove down to the town, threading our way through a lot of road works, turning off for the Tamarisk Restaurant, where we were seated at a window overlooking the Green River. I only ordered a soup and roll, not being very hungry.

The river was obviously in flood, swirling down under the bridge and racing between the wide banks, swifts darting and wheeling above it. The banks were almost all pretty pink flowered bushes seemingly favoured by the tiny hummingbirds, and when I asked the waitress what they were, she said they were tamarisks. Although they weren't poisonous, having been introduced into the USA years ago, they were now deemed a pest as they grew everywhere.

Waiting for our meal, we watched two men working at a snails pace down by the water's edge apparently trying to pull a black pipe along the riverbank. One man spent most of his time hidden by the water's edge by the bushes while the other just seemed to stand about on a small jetty, looking on. When we left after about three quarters of an hour we'd still not discovered what they were up to.

I drove back to the I-70. Andy didn't fancy any more rocks and canyons, so I decided it might be easier to change the itinerary, stay on the Interstate to Salina, then head for Kanab, leaving out Bryce Canyon and Zion Park. Andy dozed on and off while I drove.

We went up and up into the mountains with its dark red rocks to the right, creamy white cliffs on the left, and out onto a wide flat plateau. With huge canyon lands to the right, the San Rafael River valley lay to the right, to disappear into the smoky distance. As I headed down into the long, wide valley, the wind became quite gusty and I had to slow down to fifty-five mph.

The road crossed the bridge at Muddy Creek and passed through Fremont Junction before heading back up into more mountains with snowy topped peaks. The Manti-La Sal National Forest with 11,133 feet Mt. Baldy on the right and the Fishlake National Forest with Mt. Marvine at 11,605 feet, on the left.

I never tired of the views, they changed so much: from the kaliderscope of dark and soft colours, the sharpness and the smoothness of the rocky crags, the deep dusky blue of the valleys, and the deep greens of the pine forests. Coming down, the peaks and the trees were hidden by swirling mist and it began to drizzle with rain.

At Salina, I pulled off the Interstate to get gas, Andy waking up as I slowed to get off at the exit. Thick black clouds now hid the peaks.

I had to get back onto the I-70 (89) for a short distance before getting off to head for Junction, Panquitch and Kanab, but discovered that the 89 appeared to be running parallel to me. I turned off to follow a smaller road hoping it was the 89 as it wasn't sign posted that I could see, and luckily, a couple of miles on, I came across the sign at the side of the road showing that I was OK.

We cruised down a green valley to wend our way through a mountain pass, only to come to another pretty green valley with another pass at the far end. Here was a lovely creek that passed over several shallow white water rapids, Sevier River, and the road followed the course of the dreamy quiet river all the way down past Panquitch. After all the sharp dryness of the past few days, the scenery was one of peace and tranquillity. I spotted a blue jay and a magpie, and then a large bird overhead, an osprey or an eagle?

I went through Panquitch, a neat little town. After that I came to another wide valley where a bright rainbow began to form, the bottom seeming to end in a field not half a mile away. I remembered the legend that 'gold was hidden at the foot of the rainbow' and had an strange urge to stop and look for it. In one area, I passed a couple of acres of grassland covered in ghostly, grey coloured dead trees, looking very spooky. Andy took over the driving, and I could get back to writing up my notes.

Gradually we got further into forests of pines where the ground began to break up with rocks and crags. As we got closer to Kanab heading down through a pass, a large creamy pink rock canyon opened up on the left, and then, with the weather turning overcast and chilly, we were driving into the city past a Wild West town.

Kanab was another quiet, pretty place with both old and modern buildings and a long winding main street. After about a mile we found ourselves back on the outskirts having driven right through town, so we turned back, spotting the K Motel Budget Host (the old Economy Lodge.) It boasted a sign advertising rooms, a swimming pool and jacuzzi all for $39 each per night. The chalets looked a little old but quaint, and I booked us in for two nights.

The lady showed me to my chalet, a nice neat room, with pictures of Indians on the white walls, and an electric radiator. Leading me outside to the games room that also had a small kitchen area, she apologised that both the pool and jacuzzi weren't available yet as it was still too early in the season. Up close the pool was very small and still covered by a tarpaulin. Wandering about the parking lot was a strange looking man who seemed to be aimlessly checking the white lines in the parking areas. I hoped that he was the handyman.

As we returned to the office, I asked if she'd met any film stars.

"Clint Eastwood stayed in chalet fifteen during the filming of The Outlaw Josie Wales in 1976, and Robert Fuller was here last year, signing a photograph for me," showing it to me on the office wall.

"Oh no," I gasped. "I adore him. Was he nice?"

"Oh yes," she said, "he's my favourite too."

I pretended to reach out to strangle her, laughing, "oh I'd kill just to meet him. Was he easy to talk to?"

"Oh very."

After unpacking, Andy and I walked up the road to look in the shops, stopping off at a small bookshop come camping clothing store for a coffee. Then, in the small supermarket across the road I bought a yoghurt and a small box of Lunchables, tiny slices of creamy cheese, some small salty crackers and tiny round slices of luncheon meat, so that I could take my herbal tablets.

I ate them in front of the TV, sitting on the bed and writing out my postcards, attaching the address labels and the stamps.

Thursday 8th May.

I awoke sneezing and with a slightly sore throat. Outside, the day was overcast and felt very chilly as we went round to a restaurant the other side of the motel. I'd been told that if we showed them our room keys, we would get a 10% discount on our meals. I had a fried breakfast and coffee. When we asked for the bill, Andy thought it a bit expensive until he realised that they'd only taken 13 cents off instead of $1.30, having got the 10% discount incorrect. Calling the girl over, he explained, and we got an amended bill.

We drove out to Moqui Cave, after finding a novel drive-in mailbox to post my cards down the chute. The entrance to the cave had been partially bricked up with slates of rocks, leaving just a doorway. The actual cave wasn't all that deep, but was crammed full of gifts, souvenirs, and pieces of rock with dinosaur track imprints. The chap there was very enthusiastic about the history of the cave, telling us that his parents had found it originally. At the back of the deepest part, kept in darkness, there were cases and cases of colourful fluorescent rocks, all glowing with the different colours of the minerals; bright blues, greens and reds. Incredible.

From there we drove out to Paria to see a film set, taking route 89 and heading back towards Page, passing a range of red sandstone mountains with lots of box canyons.

"Gosh, we've done a complete circle," I told Andy in amazement when I realised where we were.

After about 40 miles, I felt sure that somehow we must have passed the entrance by accident as we'd reached the Paria River, and so we turned back, finally discovering an unmade track on our right that we'd overlooked on the way out. The track got bumpier and narrower, twisting and turning up and down, getting rather close to the edge where I could look down onto cream and grey rocks, and making me nervous. When we reached the end, there were just three new, empty, wooden buildings.

"Is that it?"

Getting out, we found a notice stating that the original buildings had been washed away after severe flooding many years ago, and that a local committee had recently got together to make some more, putting them above the flood line this time.

Just before we got back to town, we turned right into a canyon to look for Johnson, another old film set. We'd already been warned that we wouldn't actually be able to get close to the old town as some of the buildings were now in a state of collapse. The canyon was very restful with trees, grass, and fields of cattle, and eventually we stopped beside a fence to look across at the old shacks some distance away.

Back at Kanab, we parked up outside the Old Wild West Town. As the season hadn't started, there weren't any shoot-outs going on yet and I was quite disappointed.

To get out the back, we had to walk through the gift shop to the wooden sidewalks, passing the various imitation shops and business fronts. They could have only been about three feet in depth, but each window had authentic looking goods behind them, from ladies wear to hardware. One of the rooms was set up as the sheriff's office.

To the right were bigger buildings made of adobe that we could go inside, used in the film, The Outlaw Josie Wales. Outside a building of an outhouse an audio recording boomed out when I went near, telling passing people, 'not to disturb the occupant,' making me jump. We wandered about the gift shop for a while before heading up the main street.

There were lots of old restored buildings within walking distance of Centre Street. The Heritage House had originally been built in 1894 before being sold on to a Thomas Chamberlain. He'd had six wives, fifty-five children, and had been jailed for a term for polygamy.

The Lewis Jepson Home had had one of the only two bathtubs in town, this one often in use as a font. Lewis had also built the first motion picture theatre in Kanab, as well as installing the first individual electric light system.

The Kanab Hotel had had many movie stars to stay including Clark Gable, and they'd eventually had two bathtubs installed. One for the men and one for women.

The James W Swapp House had been ordered from the 1912 Sears Roebuck Catalogue, was shipped by train from Chicago to Marysvale, Utah, and from there taken by team and wagon to Kanab. The sections had been ready cut with the boards being numbered, and everything had been included: paint, flooring, the lathe shingles, and even a china closet. All for $640. Some of the money towards it had come from a $500 bounty James got for shooting a mountain lion.

A couple of blocks up was a gun and camping gear shop where, just inside the door, I spotted a cardboard box with old Utah car plates, of which I wanted a couple to take back to Daniel. I browsed through them, finding two fairly less battered ones, going to stand near the counter while the man served a lady. It turned out that she was buying a gun for she would be going across the state to visit relatives some way away, and was showing him her ID. I was fascinated, what a brilliant idea, at least over here you could defend yourself, but when I saw him loading it, much as I was a firm believer in protecting myself, I found I was mentally backing away from the idea. I was very surprised at my reaction, I'd always said that I would have a gun if I could, but was now having doubts. Strange!

Outside, as she was putting her boxed gun in the trunk of her car, she called to me as I went past.

"I've got an old number plate I was going to throw away, would you like it?" she asked.

"Yes please, that's really kind of you," I replied. "I get them for a friend's son."

"You're welcome. Have a great holiday."

Andy drove along main street to park outside Denny's Wigwam, a fantastic western goods store, where my eyes lit up at all the clothing.

Saddlery was hung high up on a balcony, I assumed just for display, as there was no way up there. We decided to have a coffee first in the small area just inside the entrance. Being a bit peckish, I chose a cheese and ham roll from the cooler cabinet, then left Andy afterwards to browse along the racks of clothes, finally deciding on a new jean jacket. The lady from the counter allowed me to try two on, and I ended up buying the less decorated one. She was very interested in us being from Britain and asked if I was enjoying being in America.

"This is our fourth year here, and I wouldn't go anywhere else. I just love it here," I said. Like every American I've ever told on our travels, she almost puffed up with pride and it never ceased to amaze me just how fervently patriotic the Americans are. Not back in Britain where it seems to be a crime to love your country.

Further along the road and down a side street, we came across a big bookstore, and went in. After a quick glance round the first shelves, we realised that we were in a Mormon store and all the books were religious, so we got out quickly.

Heading out of town, Andy drove to a small airport to see if there were any planes available to hire, but there weren't, being all privately owned.

Back in our rooms at 16.30, I found that my room hadn't been touched, and went into Andy. His hadn't been done either! I went to the office to ask why, but there was no one about, and nobody answered the machine on the desk when I pressed the button, so I gave up and we drove back out to Houston's Trail End restaurant. Inside, the waiters and waitresses were wearing gun belts, although one waitress had a pen and notepad in her holster.

We were offered something to drink and I had an iced raspberry that was delicious, before ordering a breaded chicken salad with noodles, lettuce, roasted sliced almonds, and a honey mustard dressing. It was so huge I had to reluctantly leave about a third! It was slightly uncomfortable to eat for the bench seats were so low my chin was almost at the same level as the food. But the meal was great.

Standing at the back of the room to pay, I could look through a large window straight into the kitchen area with the big griddles and ovens. A chef came up to the glass with a big grin, pointed to me, mouthing, "you look the part in your outfit." I smiled and called back, "thanks."

Andy drove down a road to the right and out into the countryside heading down and up a dry gully to see where it went, but with nothing of any interest at the top, he turned back to the motel. I stopped at the office and finally got the man out.

"We don't have a maid service this time of night," he stated, when I said that our rooms hadn't been done, and looking slightly surprised. "You should have hung the notice on the door handle outside to get it done in the morning."

Andy told him, "we've never had to do this anywhere before."

"And I didn't have a notice," I pointed out, sure I hadn't seen anything like it in the room. He seemed rather put out about it, so we left and went back to our rooms. When I looked around my door, I definitely hadn't got a notice, but Andy's had. I decided I'd mention it in the morning.
Friday 9th May.

I woke feeling heady and sneezing. My cold was starting to come out, so I took two paracetamol before ringing Andy to see if he was up. We met to go round to the café for breakfast before leaving Kanab. The weather was cloudy, cold and it was trying to snow, the mountains almost hidden with mist.

I took my suitcase out to the car and met up with Andy.

"Utah man just walked in on me while I was using the toilet," he stated. "He said he'd been told we'd gone and had come to clean the room."

"Oh, how embarrassing."

Just as we climbed into the car, the man wandered by and wished us a safe journey.

We headed south on the 89 to Fredonia, then turned west on the 389(59) towards St. George, a large city judging by its name being in big black letters on the map. Andy cheered as we crossed the Utah border and got back into Arizona, where the roads immediately improved. Odd. As we travelled the sun began to try and break through the mist to the east although the clouds to the west looked black and menacing.

We passed Pipe Spring National Monument on the Kanab Plateau, the road to it heading into the red and white cliffs on our right, and then passed the dirt road to Sand Dunes Coral Pink State Park. I was still fascinated as we came to the towns dotted about the landscape out on the range. Mostly they were sprawling and untidy. Colorado City, Hildale, Grafton, Big Plain Junction. In almost the blink of an eye we were through and they were gone. The larger towns had well defined main streets with rows of buildings and traffic lights at the junctions, but here these were almost non existent.

Green hills and plains swept past on the left with red and white cliffs to the right, the boulders looking very precarious as they balanced on the tops of the broken ridges. Then we were driving down a long steep, winding road into a huge valley with the town of Hurricane spreading out between the cliffs and the hills. It was quite large and very pretty, with well laid out roads and houses, and pleasant to drive through. Nearer to St. George, Hurricane Wash actually had shallow water in it.

Then, as we were driving into the outskirts of the town, five miles from the centre, a stone hit the windscreen with quite a crack, leaving a splintered mark the size of a quarter just below one that had been there when we first got the car.

St. George was lovely, bright and clean with a tall white church rising up in the centre and palm trees along the roadsides. The roads were busy, but again traffic was easy to drive through. Ahead, overlooking the town were cliffs where, on the top, planes and hangers announced the airport and Andy headed straight up there still wanting to try and hire a plane. Parking outside some hangers at the end of the road, he went over to enquire leaving me to look out over the city. Even up here with the slight breeze, it was very hot.

He came back disappointed, there were none available, although they had suggested that he try the other side of the airport. We eventually found our way round to some other buildings, but again he was frustrated.

Back down the main street, we came across a sign for the Information Centre, finding it hidden back behind the municipal buildings. The lady inside was very kind, ushering us through to another room with racks of maps and pamphlets, and telling us about all the things we could do for the day.

We plumped for the Rosenbruch Wildlife Museum, about a mile away, a long, low building of glass and metal set in a park of green grass which had only been opened in March 2001. The reception area was set between gift shops, and while Andy went round the shelves, I popped to the restroom.

I bought the tickets, the girl stamping the backs of our hands with an ink pencil in case we needed to come out and wanted to go back in again.

Inside, it was well lit and I could hear the sounds of various animals long before they came into sight, first looking round the cases in the world bug collection of long dead beetles and butterflies. The moths and butterflies were so pretty, some amazingly huge, as were a few of the beetles. The spiders made me feel creepy, even if they were dead and mounted in cases.

The walkway curled round open areas at different levels with stuffed and mounted animals, from tiny antelope to huge elk, some grazing, some leaping, some fleeing for their lives from predators, all in the most realistic surroundings, accompanied with the different sounds they made. It was beautifully done, well worth looking round.

Back outside and feeling hungry, we parked up in front of a Denny's restaurant and went in, being shown to a table and bench seats. Again I was struck by the cleanliness of the place. The meal when it came was huge, a club sandwich consisting of slices of ham, bacon and salad, with fries. Very tasty. But I was forced to turn down a second top up of coffee.

We found a Wal-Mart, doubling back after seeing the sign, finally finding a car lot for the small mall. Goodness, some checkouts were self-service! Back on the I-15, Andy was heading for a place called The Valley of Fire.

On the way he related the story about friends who'd got married in Las Vegas in the style of Elvis. The priest was dressed as 'The King' and they played his music as well. He'd found the whole thing hysterically funny.

The terrain changed from rolling hills to tall cliffs that towered over either side of the road. It followed the course of the nine mile long Virgin River Gorge that curled round and down, heading out into an arid desert of scrub bushes, tall cacti in flower, and the strange looking Joshua Trees. Lots of the bushes were covered in spiders' webs of fine orange coloured strands.

We passed through Littlefield, and then Mesquite, inside the Nevada border, still following the course of the river until it finally emptied into the top end of Lake Mead. Coming in from the east, the waters of the Colorado River also emptied into the lake. We turned off the Interstate on Hwy 169 looking for the Valley, winding our way through pastel red petrified sand dunes and arid dusty plains.

"That must be it," I said to Andy. "Bit disappointing."

He turned off down another small road, rounded a corner, and the scene just took my breath away. The ridges and rocky outcrops suddenly became an amazing deep red sandstone everywhere I looked. Made from great shifting sand dunes about 150 million years ago, it was easy to see how the valley got its name. The pamphlet explained that the winters were mild, ranging from freezing to 75 degrees but that daily summer highs usually exceed 100-120 degrees. The average rainfall was only four inches, coming from light winter showers or summer thunderstorms.

Andy pulled into a lay-by for me to use the restroom. The place was buzzing with flies and had a bad smell being only a toilet seat laid over a hole in the rocks. I couldn't get out fast enough.

We passed a few petrified logs laying scattered about on the ground, and a rock formation known as the Seven Sisters with its outline of figures, to stop at the Visitor Centre down a side road to pay the entrance fee. The little booklet we were given gave the rules and regulations for helping to preserve the desert, an extremely fragile environment that would take centuries putting right any damage caused.

We drove on to Mouse's Tank. Parking up, we walked down a narrow sandy trail between rocks, some decorated with petroglyphs, to a tank, a natural hole in the rocks where water collected.

"Wouldn't fancy drinking that," stated Andy.

"Bet you would if that was all you could find," I replied, peering down into the water only to discover some brain dead morons had thrown two plastic bottles and a tin can into it, where they floated as a stark symbol of mans' filthy habits.

I tried to imagine the lone Apache slinking across the rocks, pursued by white men, looking to see where he could lay up. It was very hot. If this was what it was like in May, what on earth was it like in full summer?

A bit further along the road, we turned a corner to see an amazing view. The top half of the rock was fire red, and in an almost a straight line the rock below was a creamy white.

Just as we were almost out of the park, we stopped to see The Beehives, conical ringed sandstone looking just like beehives.

I drove back to the I-15 and turned west towards Las Vegas, the traffic slowly building up as we got nearer. Andy pointed out the huge sprawling town in the centre of a huge dusty valley, and told me of the different buildings he'd seen when he'd flown here with friends after taking and passing his pilot's licence test in San Diego in February. It looked horrible to me, perhaps it looked better in the dark when it was lit up by millions and millions of coloured lights and flashing signs, but I was glad we weren't going there.

I turned north on the 95 heading out into the flat valley for miles and miles, before finally finding Indian Springs that consisted of a motel, gas station, and a casino with a café inside. We booked our rooms, having to drive round the back to get in. It was basic but comfortable.

Down in the mart, mingling with an assortment of gifts, motoring accessories, drinks and food, were blow up alien dolls and T-shirts, and Andy told me that we were close to Area 51. Hysterical. It was like visiting planet Mars. Andy almost bought one to take home.

The small casino had several machines in the foyer with people playing them, and the café was round to the right. We slipped into a booth along the far side, and found an 'old newspaper' with an astonishing story on the front page. A list of the food was printed inside. After ordering a cup of soup and a half sandwich, I had a chance to look round where I noticed a lot of framed newspapers on the walls, all in the same vein but with different stories.

The soup was lovely, but it wasn't until after that I discovered it was clam chowder. Not being very adventurous, I'd never tasted it before because it had sounded odd, but it had been very nice. On the way out, I got $200 from the ADM cash dispenser using my card.

Back in my room I tried switching on the TV but couldn't find any controls so I read for a while instead. What with the lumpy pillows and hard mattress, plus the warmth, I had a restless night.
Saturday 10th May.

We had breakfast in the café before heading back north on the 95. Just after passing the Nellis Airforce Base/Nevada Test Site, better known as Area 51, the road narrowed. To our left were the Funeral Mountains and to the right, the granite Bare Mountain. Between them the road ran through the flat Amargosa Desert where a red coloured mountain looked to be being mined, I'd no idea what for. Then I pointed ahead to an oncoming helicopter following the road.

"It's checking speeds," said Andy. I was glad I wasn't over the limit.

We filled the car with gas at Beattie, a cluster of buildings on a crossroads, Andy making sure that we had lots of drinks with us as we were now heading for Death Valley. Just the name sent a chilly thrill down my spine.

As we headed onto Hwy 374 through the 4,317 feet Daylight Pass between the Grapevine and Funeral Mountains on the California/Nevada state line, the clouds became smaller and sparser in the bright blue sky. Slowly descending towards the valley, the pressure made my ears ache despite trying to swallow while holding my nose.

Outside a stone building, some very smelly restrooms that had just a toilet pan over a long drop into a rocky hole, I had a joke with some other people about the wonderful facilities.

Turning left onto Hwy 178, we rounded a bend, and there was Death Valley below us, stretching to the far, far horizon. The Panamint Mountain Range towered over the shimmering white bottom of the valley-the dreaded salt flats—while the Amargosa Range ran along the left. The whole place was chilling and eerie.

Getting closer to the flat, the grass and bushes became sparser, although pretty little flowers still raised their heads to the sun. The newly laid road ran alongside salt pans that were not white close up but a dirty grey, the heat waves making everything ripple. Opening a window to put our hands out, it was like a furnace.

I spotted moving black dots out on the salt pan to our right, and as we got closer realised that a road had been scraped out into the middle of what the sign referred to as, The Devil's Golf Course. We bumped slowly across to a parking area and got out into the heat. Gosh, if this was what it was like in May, what was it like in the middle of summer! I did know that my brother-in-law Peter and his wife, Maureen, had been out here on a coach tour a few years back and they'd got straight back into the coach. Another reason I'd booked this holiday earlier than usual. But even now the heat was draining.

According to the sign, trying to go off the track was extremely treacherous, and trying to walk between the bobbles of salt, I discovered that they were in fact as solid as rock. This pan, 200' below sea level, was subject to flash floods in winter and spring that covered it in water and formed a lake. As the water evaporated, the salt was left behind, hardening under the sun.

Back on the road we continued south passing just a couple of cars, making it the most desolate, loneliest place I'd ever been to, and anyone trying to cross this at any time of year without transport had to be out of their tiny mind.

Coming across an unmade track to the left, we bounced and jolted along to park with other cars under the lip of the mountains. A sign stated that there was a long walk to see the view, and looking at each other, we shook our heads and got back in the car. Not in this heat, thanks. I headed back to the main road in a cloud of dust.

The road wound round and along the valley edge like a switchback, pools of water still left in places at the sides of the road with tall spiky grass clumps growing through it, nearly 70 miles of valley. The last half of the road was cracked and split, waiting to be laid with new tarmac.

Finally, we were heading up and over the 1,300 feet Jubilee Pass, giving me a final look back at the long valley, before driving through the 3,288 feet Salsberry Pass, where the road continued down into a green valley dotted with white rocky mounds.

Hwy 127 took us towards Shoshone, another small cluster of old buildings, shacks, a wooden water tower and trailers, palm trees lining the roadside. A notice on the gas station forecourt showed $2.50 9/10s for gas. Very dear!

We stopped outside a store for a coffee, taking our paper cups to sit outside under some trellis, watching the sparrows bouncing almost to our feet to eat the bits of crisps we threw them. One of them was being continuously harassed by its baby into thrusting food into its wide mouth, as fast as it was able.

Across the road were some old wooden buildings with a porch, under which were the rusting remains of a very old car and an even older hand driven gas pump. Inside, a wonderful museum was packed with old 1900's newspaper cuttings that made the era come alive, including the story of an elderly man who had just rescued his fiftieth person out of Death Valley. This memorabilia had once been part of peoples' lives out here-from hand written notes to an old sewing machine.

A big glass case in the centre of the back building had the remains of a dinosaur. We spent ages wandering about, and as I left, I put some money into the collecting jar.

"That was absolutely fascinating. Thank you very much," I told the girl behind the counter.

"You're welcome."

We crossed Ibex Pass, the Amargosa River, and the Dumont Sand Dunes. On the way to Baker, near the Soda Mountains, the road ran alongside the flat sandy bed of the dried up Silver Lake for miles, while in the distance I could see the shine of blue water with the reflection of mountains. But the closer we got to Baker, the more the water receded until I realised that I was looking at a real mirage! I couldn't believe that it could be so life like.

At Baker we picked up the I-15 again that ran alongside Soda Lake, another dry riverbed and a glistening white salt pan like Death Valley. This was part of the Mojave Desert with Cave Mountain and the Mojave River Wash on the left. A sign beside the road for Zzyzx Road had me in a gale of giggles. How on earth do you pronounce that?

Between records on the radio, I heard a news report that 300 tornadoes had crossed the Mid West since the 1st May and that more were expected due to a weather front passing over. Glad I wasn't anywhere near there.

While heading south-west towards Barstow where we intended to join the I-40 to Lake Havasu, Andy spotted a sign for Calico, a ghost town at Yermo. We reached it at 16.15pm, laying out $16 at the entrance hut, but just after paying we realised that the shops would be closing at 5pm. After parking, we had a very long, steep climb up a wooden stairway to reach the old western town at the top, making me puff a lot, despite walking slowly. The whole town seemed to be built on the side of a hill.

We watched a rather hammy gunfight in which the sheriff was called to the street by the lady saloonkeeper because of a brawl by some cowboys that she wanted stopping. He shot one of the cowboys.

"No," she screeched, "not that one, him," pointing to another man. The sheriff shot him.

"No, No," she screeched again, "that one." And this went on till all four cowboys were laid out on their backs on the road.

We wandered round the town crossing a small bridge to see inside the schoolhouse, where I was totally amazed at some of the questions asked for one of the tests. I didn't know some of the answers.

Back outside, I could see and hear an old style train chugging round the outside of the town. Nearby the old Margaret mine tours had just shut. A lady there informed us that although there was still about 2 million dollars worth of gold left behind, apparently it would have taken four million to get it out. Gosh, modern technology was too expensive to find it? I offered to go in and dig!

Further on down the street, drawn by the clanging of metal, we came across a working blacksmith shop.

Wandering through the various shops, I was asked by one lady about the badge I had on my jean jacket, the BRCA (British Rodeo Cowboys Association) and told her all about what we did in England.

Asking about any motels nearby, Andy was told of one in Yermo and given directions, but driving down the road, we couldn't find one anywhere. Heading back towards the ghost town, we discovered that we should have gone further along the I-15.

The motel was very nice, $114.50 or $57 each, with a coffee machine in the rooms. Just down the road was the famous Peggy Sue's diner we wanted to try, although in front of the motel was a new looking silver road car diner. In competition? What a shame.

Andy wasn't feeling too good and went to lie down for a while. Too hot in the car? Long journey? No lunch?

At 19.45 he felt better and drove down to Peggy Sue's, a fantastic old style 1950's diner with the waitresses dressed in short dresses and wearing mobcaps. Everywhere I looked the walls were covered with memorabilia of pop stars and there was a large cut out of Elvis while old records were playing in the background.

Across in the dining area, where the lighting was low from strings of light bulbs, I ordered a burger and chips. The meal again was huge and I just had to leave some or I'd never have felt comfortable.

We returned to the motel where I wrote up my notes before climbing into bed.

Chapter 30

London Bridge.

Sunday 11th May.

Mother's Day. I had slept well until the alarm suddenly went off at 6am. Jerked awake, I thought I'd pushed the right button to stop it, until it went off again at 6.10, so I pulled the plug on it. The person before me must have set it. I still had a blocked nose and the sneezes from my cold, but I had a shower and a coffee before phoning Andy. He'd only just woken so I made myself another cup.

We went for breakfast at Peggy Sue's then went round to the busy gift shop, browsing for ages looking for presents to take home.

From the I-15 west we joined the I-40 east for Havasu City, 139 miles away. Alongside us for quite a way ran the old Route 66, starting off on our left before crossing under us to run on the right. Also to the right were sandy plains and hills covered with scrub bushes and what appeared to be the remains of black lava flows that reached from the Pisgah Crater almost to the side of the road.

Almost 25 miles from the 95 and Lake Havasu, Andy decided we needed to fill up with gas and pulled off the road at a gas station. The area was very scenic, surrounded by palms and flowering bushes. The fenced off garden area had lovely plastic statues and the air was filled with bird song, a delightful place to be after the dry, sandy plains and hills.

In front of the fence on a strip of grass were several tables and chairs that looked like they were made of blue slate. The only thing that grated was a sign: 'Keep Out—No Trespassing.' Unusual for America.

Andy climbed back into the car in high dudgeon. "$2.89 a gallon," he said. "If I'd have known I never would have stopped. What a rip off."

"What!" I was astounded.

"When I complained, she said that we were in the middle of nowhere and they only had a generator for the electricity to work the pumps."

"Oh. A captive audience," I stated. "I guess they catch people because we're miles from anywhere."

Back on the Interstate we drove over the South Pass, where the lorries overtaking each other on the downgrade made me feel nervous, and on down into a valley where the winding Colorado River shone like a ribbon in the distance. We drove through Needles and crossed the bridge over the glorious blue river. Here they were re-surfacing the road, each lane being about an inch higher than the other, making the car wobble as it touched the inclines.

Reaching the 95, we turned south travelling through more lava flows toward the Mohave Mountains. Here the ocatillo was in flower and the shrubs were again covered in orange cobweb strands. The terrain began to get rockier and craggier, and soon we were back into canyon country. In the distance to our right shone the blue waters of Lake Havasu with motorboats leaving creamy white streaks in their wake, and the streets had rows of new, cream coloured bungalows.

Andy drove up to the airport on the left to ask again about flying but there weren't any planes available. He was asked to go back tomorrow to see the instructor, and then he could possibly fly in 3-4 days.

"That's no good," he told me when he got back, disappointed again. "We'll be gone by then."

He headed down a street towards the lake, then had to turn abruptly left parallel to it, finally coming across a sign for the Windsor Inn. I leapt out first to ask if there were any rooms available, getting yet another crackling shock off the car as I accidentally brushed it. Yes, $40 each.

Andy drove round to park in front of our ground floor rooms opposite a nice cool looking swimming pool where we could just catch a glimpse of the lake through the trees.

After taking my case into the room, oh dear no coffee machine but there was a huge fridge freezer and a microwave, I went outside to sit in the shade of some trees by the pool. I couldn't be bothered to change and stayed dressed in my black shirt and trousers, with my white scarf tied like a neckerchief. Two ladies were already lying on the loungers and I got chatting to them. They were fascinated by my accent, then to my amazement one asked, "are you an actress?"

"Oh no, just here on holiday. We're touring around," and I told them where we'd visited.

"Oh, you are dressed so well, I assumed you were." Gosh, I felt quite thrilled.

Andy came across to ask if I wanted to go out for a drive, so we headed out to see if we could find London Bridge.

Out to the right we finally saw the bridge's parapets in the distance flying several British and USA flags. Andy parked up and we walked through metal gates down to a large fountain with four lions spouting water like Trafalgar Square in London. I took a picture only to discover that the camera rewound the film after only the ninth picture! Oh heck, what's gone wrong? Despite the camera being fifteen or sixteen years old it took absolutely brilliant snaps, was it going wrong at last? I put in another film that I had in my bag and took another picture, which went OK to my relief.

Off to the left sat a red London bus from where they sold icecream and soft drinks, although it was shut for the moment while on the right was a big building, the London Pub and Playhouse. Wow, just like being at home.

The bridge looked spectacular. Down the pavement we went to the water's edge where the arches spanned what I thought was the river, but it had actually been rebuilt in the desert with one side on an island near the river. The land had then been excavated beneath the arches before the water had been allowed to fill the canal while the actual lake was further away behind it. Other Tudor style houses ran along the far side of the river embankment in the style of an old English village.

The water was so clear that I could see big black fish swimming about, and when some little children bought fish food and began throwing it down to them, they came straight over. Cicadas were chirping in the trees along the embankment beside the shops, their sounds mingling with the shrill piping of the little canyon swifts that were flying too and from the tiny mud nests adhering under the old arches. It was very relaxing.

We wandered along through the various shops in which one, a huge toy shop, had a train set that went through the shop above our heads, around the outside of the front door, and back into the shop.

Looking at the menu board by one café I had to smile for along with beef jerky was good old English fish and chips!

Arriving back at the hotel for a rest, I discovered that I had another noisy 'herd of elephants' in the room above me, so I went back out to the pool with a book to read until it got darker. Andy came over to join me before deciding to set out to try and find somewhere to eat.

We eventually came across a sign for Krystle's. This was a rather posh restaurant, and despite us not having booked, they found us a table by the windows where I took my hat off for the first time during the day.

Andy ordered a sirloin steak while I had onion soup, a small salad with breast of chicken on a bed of rice, and a glass of white wine, a Chablis. It was really nice and beautifully presented, although Andy found his meat a bit stringy.

Back in my room, despite the air con, which turned itself on and off all night on the thermostat, it was hot and a bit stuffy. I tried to get the TV to work, but couldn't get it going, so I knocked on Andy's door and he came round and set it up for me.

When I went for a wash before bedtime, I discovered that there wasn't a plug in the sink so I took the cellophane off one of the plastic beakers they supplied and stuffed it in the hole.

Monday 12th May.

I had a shower, and as it was already warm and sunny, sat on the bed reading with the door open. Just before 9am I went up to reception and booked for another night, then rang Andy, waking him up. While sitting and waiting for him, a big old golden retriever called Windsor wandered in the door and I gave him a pat. The lady who owned him kept trying to call him back, but he was enjoying the cuddle too much, and only wandered back to her when he wanted to, making us laugh.

Andy was ready by 10.15 and we drove over London Bridge looking for somewhere for breakfast. To the right was another large car lot from where we descended a couple of flights of stairs and walked down a long glass corridor, out onto a lovely patio overlooking the bridge.

Sitting down at one of the sets of tables, a waitress came over and took our order. As I ate, I threw little bits of bread to the sparrows that flew off with them into the bushes to eat.

We drove back across the bridge to the other side to the shops where I bought some presents to take home, and we enjoyed an icecream each. In one shop were posters about the history of London and the bridge on which it stated that 'it had been opened originally by King William IV and Queen Adelaide.' I was ashamed to say that although I knew much about the American West, I hadn't even heard of Queen Adelaide. (I felt vindicated a few months later when I realised that my American friend didn't know about either the Long Walk endured by the Navajo, or of Canyon de Chelly, or even what a saguaro was. She just knew that as cacti.

Andy suggested that we had the hour and a quarter trip advertised on a waiting paddleboat, the brightly red/white painted Dixie Bell. Climbing up the steep wooden steps to the top deck, we sat in the shade beside the barroom. It was gorgeous, although as we set off I discovered that the paddle didn't actually drive the boat, just went round with the movement of the water. We cruised under the bridge heading for the lake itself to be met with a lovely breeze.

It was perfect, cruising along the narrow channel and out into Lake Havasu where a couple of speedboats were shooting across the water ahead of us. The island that supported one side of London Bridge was fairly scrubby with small chalets and trailers and after heading out into deeper water, the boat followed alongside the beaches before rounding the point and heading back to the landing stage.

We got back to the car, set off down the road and found a small shopping mall. The car parks had lots of boats on trailers everywhere, along with jacked up pickups, their bodies two feet above the wheels, and with roaring exhausts. Everywhere were teenagers in long legged shorts, the crutch down by their knees, hands in their pockets and with the usual baseball caps turned round backwards, making them look comically like Charlie Chaplin. I often wondered if boys, even those back home, knew just how idiotic they looked—fashionable or not.

The shops were manic with lots of people about, by far the busiest place we'd been to. In Wal-Mart I bought yet another book, and in one of the clothes shops, a white top and white jeans. A bit risky I thought, buying white, but they did look nice. We stopped at Macdonald's just inside the door for an OJ each, then headed back to the motel.

While I chilled out by the pool, Andy decided he'd drive off round the boat shops looking for some parts that were expensive back home. When he got back a couple of hours later, I had a quick swim, showered and watched TV until we were hungry enough to head out for a Denny's for dinner. I had chicken strips on a large salad with honey and mustard dressing. (Hope I can buy the dressing back home.) Again there was no chance of finding room for a dessert.

"Next time, I'm not having the main course," I told Andy, "I'm going straight for the sweet."

We had a browse in Safeway's before returning to the motel. Despite it being 9pm it was still 27C 86f, and the TV weather guide was for very hot all week.

I had a restless night, waking up at 4.30am with 'elephant feet' people stamping across the floor above me and sat trying to read for a while, but found I was starting to get agitated about how few days I had left here. Finally I managed to drop off to sleep.

Tuesday 13th May.

I was up at 6.25am and went for a shower after being disturbed by the people above thumping across their floor again, then sat with the door open again to sort out all the papers and pamphlets I'd collected from all over. It was cooler today, and cloudy.

Twenty minutes before Andy knocked on the door at 10.30, a man outside started up a noisy generator so that he could hose down first a pickup and then the tarmaced car lot in front of the motel doors.

We packed the cases into the car and I got out at reception to hand in the keys. The car shocked me with such a loud crack this time that even Andy heard, and he just laughed as I rubbed my arm. We set out south back on the 95 until we reached Parker.

Just after the dam, Andy swung in off the road in front of a pretty little diner for breakfast. The doors weren't open, but just as we were about to walk away, they were opened by a lady who invited us inside. She brought us coffee then offered us roast turkey sandwiches and fries with a little bowl of pasta salad, "left over from Mother's Day celebrations." Actually, although I was a bit astounded, it tasted quite nice.

I drove from there on through Poston to the I-10. From the Interstate, we decided to head for Wickenburg on the 60 where I knew there were some guest ranches, heading through sand dunes, a craggy gorge in the Harqahala Mountains, and out onto a plain surrounded by mountain ranges. After Aguila we drove into Wickenburg an 'old style western town,' passing a sign for a ranch. We decided to look around the town before heading back to see if they had any vacancies.

Coming across an Advice Bureau, a lady told us that the ranches had all closed down for the summer, the horses being shipped north to cooler climes. Her elderly mother sitting beside her was a bit confused and kept suggesting places that were shut.

Just down the road we came to an old fashioned café like something out of the forties, very basic with a jukebox and radio playing very old records. Some I swear were as old as I was! Well, I only just recognised them! But brilliant.

I stopped for gas at $1.68, and while Andy was washing down the windscreen, I caught the whiff of an awful smell. I kept glancing round wondering where it was coming from, then spotted Andy's face. It was the water from the bucket and must have been about six months old. Yuck.

We headed south for Phoenix on the 60 and I accidentally overtook a police car tucked in front of a line of traffic. I was just touching eighty in a seventy-five mile an hour limit, but they didn't come after me thank goodness. Rather than look as if I was guilty by putting on the brakes, I continued cruising on and let the car slow to about seventy-eight. Oops!

We reached Phoenix and headed down the I-10 towards Tucson, reaching it at 18.30 after 300 miles. It was still overcast, but hot. We followed the billboard signs to the Best Western, which was lovely both outside and in, although Andy had a toilet pipe leaking in his room. It was fixed almost immediately when he phoned reception to tell them.

Night had closed in when we decided to drive around and find a restaurant, the man at reception mentioning a couple just down the road. We picked on Gus and Andy's at the corner of Oracle and Ventura. This was a smart restaurant with waitress service, and the meal was smashing, a salad with roast chicken, jacket potato, sour cream and tomato sauce. $35 for the both of us.

We managed to find our way back to the hotel again and I arranged to phone Andy in the morning. After a shower, I sat and wrote up my notes before trying to go to sleep, but again I had a restless night. I wish I didn't have to go home.

Wednesday 14th May.

I woke to a warm and sunny day with a bird singing that sounded like our blackbird and the mournful hooting of an Amtrak train. I made myself a coffee and opened the glass door to sit out on one of the chairs on the patio watching the little doves and birds like starlings flying from the trees and shrubs onto the green grass, while sparrows flitted through the rose bushes. How lovely to see the pretty flowers and the greenery after all the rocks and crags of the National Parks. Somewhere in the distance I could hear a chiming clock, a church perhaps?

I rang Andy at 9.30 and arranged to meet up for breakfast downstairs, getting there first and helping myself to coffee and toast. Three other people came in and sat down, they appeared to be having a meeting.

Watching through the glass door, I spotted Andy trying the handle, then he walked off further down the corridor, obviously not having seen me. I went out the door to look for him, then went back to finish my breakfast, only to discover the door had shut itself behind me. On rattling the handle, one of the men came over to let me back in, when I discovered that the dining room had actually closed. I finished my toast and went back outside finding Andy near the reception area. He'd been to reception ask where to come and been told that the restaurant was closed.

We packed the car, then drove down a couple of the long streets looking for a Tourist Information office, but managed to find Speedway Boulevard leading out to the world famous film studio sets at Old Tucson.

The road became two single narrow lanes, twisting and turning through the hills and valleys whose sides were covered in yellow flowered palo verdes, red ocotillo blooms, and the tall candelabra like saguaro. Lots of the roads around Tucson had notices stating, 'do not enter when flooded,' hinting at local flash floods.

I thought that the ridges to our right looked like the ones we'd ridden while on the Lazy K Bar ranch a couple of years before as while out there we'd been told that we were overlooking the Studios area.

In the almost empty lot, we discovered a lone coyote wandering about on the tarmac. Andy swung over to try and get closer to take a picture and the animal didn't seem to be at all worried until we got within a few feet, when it began to move warily away. Gosh, up close it looked just like a slim, beige coloured fox. It was very hot when we got out of the car.

To the left of the entrance to the studios was a store where the lady behind the counter told us that there were only guided tours today, the shows and exhibition gunfights being on Thursday through to Saturday. Returning to the car, we drove back out to the road and went on to the Desert Museum.

Receiving a map with our tickets at the entrance, we passed through to the gift shop/coffee shop, buying drinks and crisps, then sitting outside on the patio. A little ground squirrel was darting about looking for titbits, and we began throwing it pieces of crisps. It would run in, grab it, spin round and leap into the shade of the trees to eat. Suddenly, when it had had enough, it suddenly sprawled out on the ground, all four legs splayed out, tail laid out straight behind. A pretty little bird flew onto the windowsill behind my head, hopping along from one end to the other, but it flew off before I could take its picture.

The museum was made up of lots of different types of gardens, terrain and native animals. The prairie dogs were cute with one working very hard burrowing into the soil, throwing up clouds of debris which sometimes landed on the ones who came over to see what he was doing. They shook themselves off and went off in a huff.

An elegant cougar was laying on a ridge of rock in an enclosure the size of about half an acre. Although he had trees, water and rocks, it was very disconcerting to read on the notice that they were known to travel over tens of square miles hunting for food. I felt quite sorry for it even though it might have been shot if it had been found living wild out on the range.

Some otters were swimming in their pool, although one seemed to prefer to be on his back all the time, and there were enclosures with deer and turkey, and even a huge desert ants' nest.

We came across the entrance to a cave and wandered through, although Andy diverted off up into a very narrow cleft, meeting me at the other end. Too narrow for me to enjoy.

Back at the shop we had an icecream each and sat outside listening to a couple from England talking to an American girl about their camping expeditions, and how they'd found bears around the tent, finding that extremely frightening. They also said that once they'd come very, very close to a cougar on the trail that had fortunately, run off when it had seen them.

We walked on to the aviaries to see the humming birds. They were all different colours, flitting around the flowers, with two 'fighting?' They kept hovering, then flying at each other, and I could hear the smacks as their wings met. It went on for ages and they were still at it when I moved off. A man in front of me caught my attention as he pointed to a tiny bird sitting on a nest not a couple of feet from our heads, looking steadily at us with black beady eyes.

The car was red hot after being in the sun and we had to have the air con running for a few minutes before we could drive off. Back at a junction, we came to a gas station and I went to the pay phone to look in Yellow Pages for nearby ranches while Andy went to buy a map of the town. One name I recognised, the Tanque Verde ranch, and we decided to head for it.

It took twenty-five minutes to cross Tucson before we found ourselves heading down a long straight road and back out into the desert. Approaching the end of the tarmac to where it became an unmade track, Andy stopped so that I could ask a couple of people with horses if we were close to the ranch. They pointed ahead.

"It's just down there. Keep going."

Turning down a dusty trail to the ranch, the corrals on the right appeared full of hundreds of horses: blacks, greys, pintos, buckskins, and browns. Lean and fat ones, short and tall. All sorts. I couldn't stop watching them.

We drew up outside a big wooden ranch house. Entering the door to the office, Andy enquired about vacancies. Yes, they had some left, where had we heard about the ranch from? I told them I'd seen their website on the Internet and had remembered their name from the phone book. The price worked out at $230 a day (wow.)

Unfortunately we'd missed lunch although there was to be a barbecue tonight, while riding would be at 7am next morning for the lope ride or 7.15am for a walk. If we wanted to lope, we'd have to get there a little earlier to be given a lope test. Both rides would end up at a cookout area for breakfast. Andy asked if they had Internet access, and they pointed out the computer on the far side of the room.

He had a room by the main building while mine was back down the hill just past the corrals, so he drove me down to deliver my suitcase before going back to his. The room was lovely, very pretty, while the bed was so enormous, I almost had to have a ladder for it, but it was nice and cool inside after the heat outside.

I changed into my costume and walked back up to the swimming pool, collecting a towel from the big wicker basket box in the office, before passing the spa, and then a bar room, the Doghouse Saloon. The notice in the window offered games of pool, satellite TV, and there was also complimentary fresh popcorn with the drinks.

The swimming pool was big with a rocky waterfall on one side and it was great to slip in and gently float in the water, but after a while big black clouds began to close in and the wind became a bit chilly.

I went back to my room to shower and change for the meal, and waited to see if Andy came down. When he hadn't appeared by 7pm I strolled up and knocked on his door several times, but there was no answer. I even glanced in the laundry room, but nothing, so I headed back and followed the signs for Cottonwood Grove.

In the dusk, the lantern lights and the huge bonfire were welcoming, but I wasn't quite prepared for the amount of people gathered there. No wonder they had so many horses, if all these people were riding. A man with a guitar was singing not far from the trestles laden with food. I still couldn't spot Andy so I joined the line, helping myself to salad, bypassing the steaks and chops to ask for a breast of chicken.

Just as I sat down, I spotted him coming and waved. After telling me that he'd been in the office on the Internet, he joined the line of people for his meal. The food was tasty and I went back for some more salad. Not wanting to stay on, we walked up to the office where I looked at my e-mails—nothing from Sue, or Kristin. Strange.

I went warily back to my room to read for a while, keeping a look out for insects or snakes, finally going to sleep at 9pm as I was really tired.

Chapter 31

Old Tucson.

Thursday 15th May.

I woke at 4.45am with a headache and took some tablets, but they didn't kick in until 6am when I phoned through to Andy, waking him up. On my way up I called into the office to get him a storm strap as the rules in my room stated that all hats should have one, but he said he didn't fancy wearing his baseball cap anyway. We wended our way down to the 'Wranglers' Roost,' a wooden shack, going through to the corral where other people were already waiting for their horses to be brought.

I was given a big blood bay, Titon, and gosh he was tall, while Andy got a stocky Dutch warm blood type. Using the steps to climb into the saddle, I couldn't have felt happier, it was so good to be back on a horse. Once we were lined up, the wranglers split the ride into two, and Andy went with the other ride. Just ahead of me was a boy from London who was having his first holiday on a ranch, this week being the first time he'd ever ridden, while behind me was a very nice chatty girl.

We wended our way up and down narrow paths between flowering palo verdes, scrub oaks and saguaros where I spotted the occasional cottontail rabbit, before the wrangler stopped the ride to flush five or six big jackrabbits. At the last hill, a lady was waiting to take our pictures as we rode up.

Behind an old brick ruin, the food was ready and waiting for us. I climbed down to let the wrangler take Titon and tie him up with the other horses, joining Andy to queue for our cooked breakfast. He said that he was feeling uncomfortable-the horse was too wide for him!

We got chatting to some other people at the table next to ours, and a couple of the girls said that on the way here they'd spotted a snake swallowing a squirrel with only the rear end and tail sticking out. Urh! The wrangler had moved it out of the way under a bush. Another lady asked me if I knew what the difference was between a tobiano and an ovaro horse, and I explained that it was the amount of colour on a paint horse, more colour than white was the former and more white than colour, was the latter. She was quite fascinated.

She also told me how everyone said how Tony Blair had been very supportive of the Americans over Iraq, although I said that I just didn't like the man or his policies. Especially as he was allowing us to be forced into changing our way of life drastically by the Europeans, who interfered in everything. She laughed and said that the Americans hated the Bush family.

"No-one likes either him or his son," she said.

I told her how nice it was to drive over here, drivers were so courteous on the road.

"Oh," she said, "over here in the cities they shoot each other."

"We have that in England too, although it was more likely to be a beating, or a stabbing. And you'd understand why if you saw how bad the standard of driving has got over there."

After we'd eaten, our mounts were brought round for us, I had to use the mounting block again, and we slowly rode back to the ranch. I'd arranged earlier to go on the lope ride a bit later on but one lady told me that after she'd ridden it, she'd been sore for two days after, so I cancelled as I hadn't ridden for a year at least.

I went back to change, then went for a swim before lazing in the sun. As I knew what time the pictures would be ready, I went across to the veranda near Andy's room to see them. Mine was brilliant. Andy wasn't too keen on his but I bought it for him anyway. I had to return to my room to get the ten dollars, and while crossing the trail near the corrals, I caught a movement out of the corner of my eye.

I stopped dead when I realised that about ten yards away, slowly climbing the spines of a large saguaro, was a long, black snake with a bronze coloured head. Fascinated to see what it would do, I waited while it watched me, weaving its head about nervously. Suddenly, it decided it didn't like any of this, and half slid, half fell off the plant, disappearing at an incredible speed into the undergrowth. I hadn't even had time to be scared, I was so interested in watching it. A man and lady who'd been a little way behind me came over.

"What was it?" he asked. I took his question the wrong way.

"A snake."

"What sort?"

"I've no idea, I've never seen one like it before. It was black with a dark golden brown head."

"Ah, a copperhead," he informed me.

"Is that a type of rattlesnake?"

"Yeh."

"Wow, it was climbing the saguaro, I didn't think they could do that with all the spines. It must have been frightened because it shot off fast."

I went back and paid for the photos, had a quick shower in my room, then tried to phone Andy, which took a while as his phone was continuously engaged. It turned out that he'd found a phone book and was ringing round to see if we could get onto another ranch, this one being too big for him, too many people for him to be comfortable.

"The White Stallion is full but a place called La Tierra Linda guest ranch has rooms, they're out by the Marana airport," where Andy had sky dived from on our first holiday in 1999.

We booked out of the ranch and drove across town to the I-10 and from there to Silverbell Road. I thought I'd recognised the name, but it wasn't until we passed a Wal-Mart that I realised we were heading out towards the Lazy K Bar, and then I spotted the familiar shape of Stetson Mountain.

We took a left and drove up the road for half a mile, finding the sign for the ranch and heading up the drive through some lovely gardens. At the office, we booked in at $125 a day, riding and meals extra, and were taken on a tour of the cabins by a lovely lady.

My room was gorgeous with two tiered flooring, a little sitting area first, the big bed area down a step, and the bathroom just further on. It included a coffee machine, fridge, and even the air con was controlled with a hand held remote. I was given a phone number to call for the stables, who would provide the riding. If we needed any fruit, orange juice or extra milk containers, they could be got from the fridge in the dining room-just help ourselves.

I tried getting my suitcase inside the little closet in the bathroom but it just wouldn't quite fit, so I had to shut it up and turn it sideways on the suitcase stand. Wanting to go out, I shut the door and turned my key in the lock, but every time I tested it, it unlocked. Frustrated, I went along and asked Andy what I was doing wrong. He showed me that all I had to do was turn the little lock in the middle of the handle on the inside and shut the door behind me. The key would unlock the door when I went back.

The swimming pool was opposite Andy's room, round the corner from me, and it had a green concrete frog fountain spitting water into the pool. To the right was a huge open sided barn.

I made myself a cup of coffee, rang the stable number and arranged for a two hours ride from 8am the next morning. Putting the phone down I suddenly wondered what time breakfast was.

I couldn't ring through to Andy as each phone had its own number rather than ringing an extension, but one day I had a flashing light to say that there was a message, and sat listening to three long winded hard sell pitches. Crumbs, just the occasional double glazing sales pitch drove me mad back in England. But three!

Going outside, I found Andy was already by the pool reading. I had a swim, then sat in the shade on a lounger reading a book, laying a towel over me as the wind got quite gusty. He had lent me another Bill Bryson book, In a Sunburnt Country, which I had been avidly reading, but when I got to his description of a cricket commentary he'd heard on the radio, I began to giggle. The more I read the funnier it got until I couldn't see the words for laughing, tears trickled down my face. It was hysterical. Every time I got myself under control and tried to read on, I couldn't, and finally had to give up completely.

Eventually, I headed back to the room for a coffee, noticing that despite using suntan oil, I was going red round the shoulders, arms and neck. (It wasn't until some weeks later that I heard a report on the TV stating that suntan lotion is not spread on as thickly as it should be, as this made it very expensive to use.)

We'd decided to eat dinner in the little restaurant here, so after I'd had a coffee sitting under the parasol outside my room in a little walled off patio, I went across to the dining room and booked us a table for 6pm.

We just sat around all afternoon for it was too hot to do anything else, before heading up to the dining room. I ordered bar-b-cue chicken breast (two pieces,) pilar rice, a mixed vegetables of tiny carrots and broad beans, and a salad to start. It was really delicious.

Afterwards, we sat by the pool until it was dark, enjoying the cooler air and watching an eclipse of the moon. Walking back to our rooms I noticed around the edges of the paths ran strips of tiny lights. Very pretty.

Returning to my room, I discovered that the bathroom had an plug-in automatic nightlight. Very useful if I needed to get up in the night. After a wash, I went to bed at 10pm.

Friday 16th May.

I was up at 6am. As I'd run out of creamer for a coffee yesterday, I went up to the kitchen to get some more little containers from the fridge to take back to my room then sat outside with my drink on the patio, listening to the birds singing and cooing. One black bird had found a piece of apple and was tucking into it with gusto. Wish I knew what it was, I really must find a book on native birds. Woodpeckers were busy flitting in and out of a hole in a saguaro, obviously feeding chicks, while several cottontails were running about on the gravel between all the paths. Around the edges of the patios and paths were piled fallen pink petals from the shrubs making it look as if a magnificent wedding had taken place.

I walked to the stables, going up to the bars of the corrals to look at the burros, miniature ponies and horses, one of which was a lovely, but very nervous, paint horse who refused to come anywhere near me. Just before the small, dark wooden buildings of tack and feed rooms was a pen of different sized goats. Beyond that was a half circle of 'fronts,' very slender buildings, of a wild west town with a large wooden stage in front of them. I went into the tack room/office to find a young, chubby wrangler waiting.

"Do you mind waiting, two other people want to come on a ride, but they can't make it before nine?" he asked.

"No, that's OK. I'll come back."

I wandered back to the dining room and made some toast, not wanting anything cooked although the bacon, sausages and scrambled egg smelt heavenly. I started chatting to very nice girl who was in charge, Kirsty who told me that originally she'd come from Colorado. It turned out that Andy and I were the only ones here at the moment, but that there would be a wedding here on Saturday with the reception being held under the big open barn behind the pool and a lot of people would be staying over.

I went back to the stables where I met the other people riding, a lady and her daughter from California. It seems that she hardly rode at all, but that her daughter rode English style in California. We both saw the funny side that while her daughter rode English style in America, I did western in Britain. My horse was brought up, a big bay called Diego, and I mounted from the block.

We headed out round the back of the western town fronts and out towards the plain in the general direction of the Lazy K Bar, onto winding sandy tracks through the scrub and creosote bushes. Diego had a nice walk but continuously tossed his head, possibly because of the flies. At one point the young girl's horse spooked at some black rubber material at the side of the trail, making Diego jump too, although not badly. I told him off while the wrangler got down and dragged it off to one side.

I was shocked to see the amount of housing being built since we'd last been here, pushing the riding tracks further into the desert and it seemed odd that the gardens were walled off, surely people were coming out to see the country? And what of the native animals? Their land was slowly being taken over and they were being forced further away into the wilderness. Coyotes, snakes, lizards, birds, scorpions. And the lovely names they gave these estates: Coyote Canyon, Wild Horse Ranch. Attractive names, but where were the animals they named them for? I wondered just how long the stables or even the Lazy K could survive out here as civilisation continued to intrude into the desert.

It was the same in England, the beautiful countryside that I loved was also being covered in tarmac and buildings. I used to love sitting up on the hillside in Cloud's field in the warm sunshine, looking out over the bay, listening to the bird song and relaxing. Now all was ruined by the incessant roar of the traffic on the new bypass making me want to scream at them to go away and leave me in peace.

Diego had settled nicely by now, but his jog, like most of the stable and ranch horses out here, was very uncomfortable. Too many different riders, I guess.

During the ride I managed to spot a couple of cottontails, several scuttling lizards, and a lot of birds. Suddenly, Diego spotted some workmen off to one side working in a couple of the houses. His head came up and I tightened my legs round him, pressing him forward, but he really jumped sideways when some machinery the other side of the fencing started. I kicked him on and managed to get him settled. People were just as thoughtless of horses here as back home I see.

We finally joined a rocky, stony trail I recognised that headed for Suicide Pass, but we continued on after the turn to it, slowly circling left back towards the new bungalows and the ranch. Occasionally we passed bits of bob (barbed) wire, some new, some very old and rusty, odd air tights (tins) and bottles, some broken. Oh why does man have to be so filthy!

I enjoyed the ride, it was so lovely to be back in the saddle and I only began to feel discomfort in my legs over the last twenty minutes. Back at the ranch, once we'd dismounted and I used the mounting block, I asked about the possibility of a moonlight ride.

"Yes, we can do one most nights, just call the number for the stables and they'll organise it."

I walked back to my room, changed and went round to Andy's room to find the housekeeper with her trolley outside. She'd knocked but hadn't had an answer.

"Is your friend in?"

I glanced over to the pool and Andy waved to say it was OK for her to go in. I went and sat on the lounger next to his. He told me that he'd phoned the local airport and was going over at 1pm to take a written test, have a flight with an instructor, after which he should be able to go solo. As he didn't know what time he'd be back, he suggested that I only ordered a meal for myself in the evening.

When I went over to book, I asked if they did lunch. They didn't, but they gave me a list of restaurants I could go to. With no car that was out, but also some that would deliver. After Andy had left, I tried phoning the first number on the list and got an automated reply saying that the meal was twenty dollars. It then followed up with such long details of what I could have, that I finally gave up listening (good job local calls were free.) The man at the second place apologised and said that they didn't deliver any more.

As I wasn't all that hungry anyway, I found a dollar bill in my purse and got a cold Powerade drink from the machine. This was full of electrolytes that replace the minerals sweated out, a bit like our Lucozade, tasting a bit odd, but refreshing.

I phoned the stables to ask about the evening ride and the girl promised to phone me back, so I decided to go up to the fridge in the kitchen and see what was available. I took a couple of yoghurts, some 'half and half' milk containers for my coffee, and a glass of O.J, returning to my table and chairs to read in the shade of the parasol. The parasol wound up with a small handle. It was difficult to know what to do in heat of 90f, apart from keep jumping in and out of the pool, and I wondered how on earth the poor horses stood it in their corrals.

It was lovely to rest up, but a little boring as I liked to be on the go back home, but at least it made the time go slower. Only four days before we leave for home, but I was really looking forward to going back to the Old Studios tomorrow.

As the afternoon drew on and I waited for the promised phone call, I kept glancing up into the sky to see if Andy had managed to get a plane. At 4.30, he arrived back. He'd had to sit a one and half hour written exam and then fly with the instructor, but it had been so hot that trying to take off, climb and then land against the heat waves, had been very difficult. He was so warm and tired that it was a relief to him to come back and dive straight in the pool.

I had a short swim, then showered and changed. Just before I went up for my meal, the phone rang and the girl from the stables told me that we could ride the following evening at 8pm. Andy didn't fancy anything but a cold drink so I went to the restaurant by myself. Waiting to order, I watched a tiny hummingbird darting about the flowered creepers outside the windows.

I ordered a Cobb salad that turned out to be huge, chicken and bacon pieces, lettuce, chopped hard-boiled egg, tomato and avocado. I'd never eaten avocado before and found it lovely and creamy. Reluctantly I had to leave some of the meal as I was really stuffed, I must have a really small appetite compared to Americans.

I joined Andy beside the pool, reading until it got too dark to see, then went back to my room to watch some TV while he went off to get a snack from the fridge.

Saturday 17th May.

I was sitting outside with my coffee by 6am, watching the cottontails bounding towards the bushy gardens to stop for a drink at the ground sprinklers feeding small trees. Birds were singing and a flock of sparrows were having a mock fight around one of the flowering shrubs. As I listened to their noise I began to realise that this was one of the sounds I most missed back home. Sparrows were getting rarer, although they could still be found in the big barn on the farm. Doves were flying to the tips of the cacti and drinking from the flower heads, while the woodpeckers were busy darting backwards and forwards feeding their chicks in the saguaro. On the top of a very tall, slim conifer perched a black bird. His song consisted of whistles, caws, and tweets, while his body swayed with the tree. It was captivating.

I had time to sit and ponder as to why I hadn't had any problems with being sore after both rides, so why was I in discomfort back home? Jill had thought that my back problems were due to riding, but was there something more than that! I was puzzled. Yes, my knee ached and my thighs were a bit stiff, but it hadn't affected my riding, and I hadn't felt discomfort at the time. Was there something wrong with Cloud rather than with me? (Once back home, my suspicions were realised. Cloud was in discomfort being ridden and kept going lame, so he had to be retired at the young age of twelve years.)

I wandered up to the restaurant for some breakfast, scrambled eggs, bacon, two sausages and some toast, chatting with Kirsty again. She mentioned that there would be bull riding in the evening at one of the rodeo grounds and I decided to ask Andy if we could go and have a look.

He finally arrived, had some breakfast, and then we were on our way back to the Old Tucson Studios, stopping at Wal-Greens on the way for me to put seven films in for developing. The lady behind the counter was very interested in where we'd been travelling and hoped to be around when I called back for them. I didn't bother with the cheaper hourly rate for we'd be out most of the day.

At the Studios it cost $14.85 each to enter, plus tax. Going through the turnstile, the girl sitting there gave us a map of the town, smiled and said, "you're really dressed for it." I told her that this was the way I rode back home.

Wow, the place looked so real that I couldn't stop looking around at all the shacks and buildings with their wooden sidewalks and shingled roofs, even a cowboy riding up and down the long dusty street on a bay horse.

To the right of the entrance was the Southern Pacific Dept which ex-president Ronald Regan had used in his 1950s film, The Last Outpost. Two doors up at the Cowtown Boots and Western Wear building, I bought a white hat as my black one was making me feel too hot in the sun. Next was Olson's Gift Shop, once used as the set for Maureen O'Hara and Brian Keith in Deadly Companions (1961.)

Two buildings further up was a taxidermist/fix-it shop that over the years had been changed several times by various script writers for each film, from a store, a saloon, and even as a doctor's office in the John Wayne film, El Dorado (1965.) Behind that was a river created for the 1970 Rio Lobo movie with John Wayne and Jack Elam. Hollywood magic (and high-volume pumps) can still transform this stream into a raging river, but today it was placid.

An 1868 reproduction of the first adobe schoolhouse had been built for the 1939 film, Arizona, while beside it stood the corrals and surrounding buildings used in the 1957 film, Gunfight at the OK Corral, starring Burt Lancaster and Kirk Douglas.

Looking at the map and the legend on the reverse, the first show would be The Great Tucson Bank Robbery a fifteen minute shootout between a sheriff and two outlaws, to take place in the plaza between the bank and the central bandstand. Once a trading post this had been converted to a bank for the 1986 film, The Three Amigos. Before the show started, we had time to wander in and out of the other various buildings. One was a sheriff's office with a bunk bed behind iron bars where I got Andy to take a picture of me staring out from the inside, then stopped at a small café where I bought a nice cold strawberry milk shake.

Back outside, people were starting to gather across the street from the bank and I managed to find a little shade under a tree. Putting my drink down carefully, I got my camera ready, then found to my dismay that it had fallen over, spilling half the contents on the ground.

The men in charge of the show began encouraging people to come in a lot closer and sit on the ground to watch, so I went nearer to take pictures.

The two outlaws arrived, wearing headsets with a microphone. Very comical. One was dressed in black and had long hair. They started discussing how to rob the bank and get rid of the sheriff. Eventually, one hid while the other called the sheriff, telling him his horse had been stolen. Then they both attacked the sheriff, knocking him out and dragging him into the empty doctor's apothecary next to the bank. The two then went into the bank, but as they came out the door, the sheriff staggered from the store and began shooting it out. One outlaw was shot as the one with the long hair got onto one of the roofs, but he was also shot and fell to the ground, rolling over and over. As the sheriff stood over them, they all got up and bowed to applause from the audience.

We wandered back round some of the other buildings. In one were costumes used in the series, Little House on the Prairie, while around the walls of another were the different flags made from the very early days of American history. Some were very ornate and some quite plain.

In the playhouse, the Grand Palace Saloon at the top of the plaza where the street split into a Y shape, was a Western Movie Magic show with singing, dancing, special effects, and starring a 'ghost' called Roscoe. (just a voice.) Hammy, but great fun.

At another saloon further up the street we sat down at the bar and ordered a slush ice drink. Talking to the man next to me, a widower, who had driven across from Dallas, Texas, he said that he was driving to out to San Diego, California and from there would be going on up to Los Angeles. Seeing the cloth Texas badge sewn to my jacket pocket and my collar pin as well, he asked me if I liked Texas.

"Oh yes," I beamed. "Andy and I drove round a couple of years back for five days," and told him we'd seen the Alamo and the Texas Rangers' HQ at Waco, as well as visiting Southfork and Fort Worth.

Andy took a long swig of his drink, and I saw him wince badly. It turned out that the icy cold had hit a nerve and given him a blinding headache, which took quite a while to wear off. Carefully, I only took a sip of mine, but must have overdone it too, as I ended up in pain as well.

Eventually, we left the man to have his lunch, and carried on round the lots, where I came across a familiar sign. High Chaparral from the western series of the same name, and it was just as I remembered it. Further on round was the wonderful old Reno locomotive complete with cowcatcher, built in 1872. Apparently it had been very badly damaged in a fire here some years before and was now awaiting restoration. Originally used in Nevada's Comstock Lode, it had become a movie star in the 1939 film, Union Pacific before being used in over a hundred film and TV credits including the series, The Wild, Wild West.

Behind that were the trail rides where visitors could ride the same routes as John Wayne and Lee Marvin, passing the Phillips Ranch from the movie, Rio Lobo. It was just too hot to ride at the moment, perhaps I could have a go before we left if it got cooler. Whilst continuing our tour, we were passed by a stagecoach pulled by a four hitch (four horses) taking people for a ride round the town.

A smaller version of an old style railway engine, a CP Hunington, complete with carriages, was chugging round the back of the town and some of the film sets, so we bought tickets for it. The train cleared of its earlier passengers, we climbed into the open carriages, grateful to feel even the slight breeze that wafted over us as the train began to clatter its way round, and the driver began telling us about the area.

After that, we made our way back to an old white Mexican church adored with long sashes in the French colours and several flags, and with a round fountain in front of it, the set for the film, The Three Amigos. Facing it were tiers of wooden bench seats, and we clambered up to the back seats, only just managing to get into some shade.

The Three Amigos, dressed in their bright stage costumes of white and black, had to go up against three Mexican bandits, and was very comical, like the original film. After, the three stars sat in their cart and signed autographs.

There was quite a long time before any more shows, so we decided to leave and head back towards the ranch, stopping off for my films where it seemed that my pictures had gone down well with the staff.

"They're lovely, they've turned out really well," they enthused. "Haven't you seen a lot of sights." One lady hoped that she'd see us here again.

"Maybe next year." I must admit that I still fancy going back to the Lazy K Bar again.

Back at the ranch, I quickly changed and joined Andy in the pool to cool down, before heading back to my room, noticing that the wedding party had already gathered and the bridesmaids were having their pictures taken against a backdrop of shrubs.

I took my shower but stepping out of the bath I discovered that the tiled floor was flooding, so I quickly put the plug in to try and stem the water. It worked and I began bailing the water out into the sink with a plastic cup, moping up after with a towel. I tried gently pulling the plug out to confirm my suspicions of where the water was coming from, and quickly shoved it back in as water trickled out from under the bath again. I got dressed and phoned through to reception to tell them what had happened.

"Do you want someone to come along now, or could it wait a while?" I was asked.

"Anytime. I've already showered," I replied, thinking that perhaps the staff were all helping out in the restaurant. I made myself a coffee and sat outside on the patio, spotting the bride and groom arriving in a beautiful horse drawn carriage.

Andy and I had decided earlier to go out for a meal for a change, but before setting off, I told Andy about my bathroom and he went for a look, deciding that there had to be some sort of blockage in the actual drain. Just before we left the room, the phone rang. It was someone from the office to say that they would change my room over for me tomorrow.

Andy drove towards the Marana airport down a small twisting road hoping to find somewhere to stop and eat, but although we went for miles, nothing appeared. Finally we ended up heading back to Tucson, joining a road that ran parallel to the I-10. I was getting a bit edgy for we needed to be back at the ranch by 8pm for the moonlight ride.

Eventually we came across a Burger King, but I wasn't at all impressed with the inside or the service, it was more like a Macdonald's back home. The chicken sandwich bun was very dry, but the fries were alright.

We rushed back to the ranch and walked down to the tack room where the two wranglers were already chatting, so Andy and I roamed about outside waiting for the moon to rise. We waited for over an hour, but the sky was only filled with sparkling stars. Eventually I went back to the wranglers and said that we were giving up, could I have an hour ride in the morning instead.

"If that's what you want, ma'am," said the chubby wrangler. Somehow I got the impression again that he really wasn't much interested. During the rest of the evening, I kept popping outside to look for the moon, surely the wranglers wouldn't book a ride not knowing when it would be rising, but by the time I went to bed at 10.30pm there was still no sign of it.

Sunday 18th May.

I was up again at 6am and sat outside with my coffee sorting the photos, numbering them and writing on the backs of some of them where they had been taken. My knee wasn't feeling too good, so I had already bandaged it with some crepe I'd brought with me just in case.

Going down to the stables, I was joined by a big man, his wife with a little boy, who she sat on the saddle in front of her, and a small girl who wanted to ride by herself. But when the pony somehow upset her, she had to be led by the younger wrangler. I had a different horse this time, a big bay, C.J. He turned out to be rather trippy in front and I began to suspect he had problems with his flexor tendons just like my old palomino, Goldie. He was also shaking his head because of the flies.

It was a slow walking ride but I enjoyed it, although I couldn't get over the sight of the woman and little toddler riding with no hats of any sort. She didn't look like she'd ridden much anyway, letting her horse just follow the one in front. It gave me a chilly feeling.

Once back, I went for breakfast where I sat chatting to Kirsty, and she asked me if I'd gone to see the bull riding.

"Oh no, I forgot. We were supposed to have had a moonlight ride but the moon never came up. I could have gone after all." I was quite disappointed.

"The moon wouldn't have been up anyway," she pointed out, "it's being blocked at the moment by the last of the eclipse, and will be for the next couple of days." Oh well, that's that then.

I asked if there were any nice malls nearby to go shopping and she mentioned two. I also promised to bring up my photos from home to show her, especially of Ann-Marie and Les.

Andy found one of the shopping centres after looking at the road map and drove into the car park of the Foothills Mall. Just outside the entrance was parked a fire engine, police car, and an ambulance making me wonder what was going on, but I never found out.

I loved these malls, they were so light and airy consisting of two floors with seating areas for the various coffee shops and cafes. There were even play areas for children with bench seats for parents who were keeping an eye on them.

In a huge bookstore that also sold CDs, I bought one each of Enya and Roy Orbison to play in the car. At each section was a handy set of headphones and a computer keyboard where you could look up any disc that they had and could even listen to each track before you bought. Brilliant idea.

Going upstairs I sat reading a book on horse colouring, my goodness there were thousands of variations, while Andy browsed, but once back down on the ground floor, I suddenly realised that I'd lost the dark glasses that I'd had tucked by an arm in my shirt front. We began retracing our steps, even asking at the desk to see if they had been handed in before I discovered them upstairs on the floor beside the chair I'd been sitting in. What a relief. I couldn't do without them.

Andy wanted to buy some Nike boot type trainers while he was over here, but in all the places we looked he could never find the ones he particularly wanted. Eventually, we stopped at a stand to buy a lemonade, sitting down at one of the nearby tables. How quiet it seemed to be despite all the people, and so clean.

After wandering about for over an hour, we set off to find the Tucson Mall that turned out to be very similar to the other. Halfway round and feeling hungry, we stopped at a sandwich bar and I ordered a ham, Swiss cheese, lettuce, dried tomato and mustard bun. Huge but delicious. I sat listening to the sounds and watching the people, feeling very wistful that I would soon have to go home and very reluctant to move.

At a pet shop I was dismayed to find for sale some gorgeous Siamese kittens, two blue points, one brown, and one a mottled colour while on the other side of the door were some puppies. They were in very clean surroundings in the window, but I wondered just how stressful it would be for them. And who would buy them, would they go to kind homes? Inside the shop were glass-fronted containers with puppies, including two German Shepherds, and some Dachshunds (what we used to call sausage dogs when I was little because of their long bodies and very short legs,) some mice, ferrets and even budgies.

Further on round, Andy treated himself to some cinnamon sticks and cream while I settled for an O.J. as I was really thirsty. In one arcade, I finally found a present for Mrs Kay. While the lady was wrapping it up, she remarked that she liked my hat, where did I get it?

"The Tucson film studios."

"Where are you from?" she asked.

"Canterbury in Kent, better known as the Garden of England because of the flowers and orchards. We go home in a couple of days and I don't want to, I'd rather stay here."

"Oh, do you love America?"

"Yes. Given half a chance I'd live here although I'm not too keen on the heat."

"You'd be better off coming in April," she stated. "It's a lot better."

On the return to the ranch, I discovered my bathroom in a muddle with mops and towels on the floor and a note on the table apologising for the inconvenience, would I go to the office and they would give me a key to another room. I went straight over only to discover a sign on the door, Office Closed, but just as I was about to walk away, a man came over.

"I've come to change rooms."

"Mrs Haven? Yes, I've got the key for you."

"I've got to change as I've got a leak. Well, not me personally, the room," I quipped, getting a smile and a laugh.

I was shown to a room opposite the other one, very nice, and once I'd taken my suitcase over, I changed to go for a swim. Afterwards I showered, then rang through to book a table at the restaurant for 8pm.

"I'm sorry, ma'am. We close at 7.45." I arranged to go straight away, and quickly went to get Andy.

I ordered the smallest looking meal there as I felt so bloated despite not having eaten much all day, a veggie burger, potato wedges and sliced tomatoes. He only ate half his meal again, and I struggled. He reminded me that he was due to go flying early next morning and that he'd be leaving at 6.30am.

"I'll try and fly over," he said. "There doesn't seem to be much traffic about so I should be the only one."

"You might see me," I laughed, "I'll be the one jumping up and down by the pool!"

Monday 19th May.

I had a restless night not sleeping till well after twelve, as all I kept thinking about was that we only had today and tomorrow before we went home. I could understand people not wanting to go back home after a holiday, but surely not everyone was as bad as this?

At 3.45 I was awake and sat watching a bit of TV, drifting off to sleep until 5.45 when I got up. I made a cup of coffee, and went out onto the patio just as the sun was coming up, to find that the breeze was actually chilly. I went and knocked on Andy's door at 6.50 to make sure he would be in time to fly.

"Are you awake?"

"Yes."

I was just sorting out my photos using our maps to get them into the right order as I found that I couldn't remember which order we visited everything, when he came out to go to the car. After he'd driven off, I was startled by a big lizard shooting across under my table and over the little wall. It was gone before I could get a good look at what it was.

I went up for breakfast, chatting to Kirsty who told me that the Germans in the room just down from me had found a baby snake curled up on their patio table the morning before. These things have no hands and no feet, how on earth do they climb saguaros and trees, and even up onto a table! Crumbs, where might I find one. I got quite nervous.

I sat outside by the pool with my camera to watch for Andy, finally hearing a plane, but it was so far off I knew I wouldn't get it on film as I didn't have a zoom lens. I was very disappointed, until about half an hour later when a small white plane began circling the ranch. I guessed that that was him, but couldn't understand why he was so far up, at home he was allowed down to about 500 feet. Eventually, it flew away, but I did take some shots.

Going back to my room to make a coffee and go through my photos again, I watched two quail running across the space between two lines of bushes with nine or ten tiny babies scuttling behind in a long line, one after another.

Suddenly two jets roared across the sky. Hope Andy's out the way!

He arrived back at 10.30am. He hadn't been able to fly lower than 2,000 feet because of the Pima Air and Space Museum so he'd had no chance of seeing me leaping up and down like an idiot, but he had got a few still shots of the ranch.

He fancied going to see the Museum so we drove out to the other side of Tucson to find it, parking in a huge car lot. It was getting hotter by the minute and I was very glad to get inside the cool of the gift shop area, in the first hanger.

Andy was anxious to get outside to see the big, black, stealth aircraft that was shielded from the sun by a large canopy. The rest of the open field was enormous with planes everywhere, their windows and engines boarded up, everything from light aircraft, one of which was noted as 'the ugliest home made plane, to the biggest bombers. Standing in the shade of some of the wings, I felt overawed and intimidated, for just the wheels by themselves were as tall as I was.

We reached the presidential plane where under a canopy, a man was giving its history to half a dozen people. His voice seemed to drone on and on and I got bored, but he did know his stuff. I was grateful to be in the shade and even happier when I discovered that around the edges of the roof ran a pipe spraying a fine mist of water in several places. Oh, bliss. Eventually the other people were taken up the steps and inside.

We stopped at another canopy, no mist here, but there was a cold drinks machine and a candy bar machine. Andy put in a coin and with his chocolate bar came a dollar bill as well. I tried it—and the machine said I was 5 cents short. It was obviously a chauvinistic male.

We wandered into several hangers, one housing pictures of people as well as information of the people who had been in the various wars, while in another was a model of model aircraft flying over land with commentary from the flight team plus the roar of the engines. In each hanger was a collecting box.

I came across a floor standing mirror with a black line quite a few feet from it that made me curious. When I stood back from the line I was shown upside down, but as I stepped forward holding out my hand, I could almost shake hands as the image came so close. I was fascinated, trying it out several times. What a brilliant optical illusion.

Back outside and heading for the car, we watched at least a dozen planes taking off from the field across the road, either singly or in formation, and Andy told me they were the planes that were being used in the war against Iraq.

From there we decided to drive out to Colossal Cave, heading out towards the far hills. From the I-10, we set off north on a small road across the desert going through the town of Vail and heading for the Rincon Mountains. Pantano Wash was empty of water. We joined the Old Spanish Trail to the right where the road began to steadily climb and get narrower, ending at a long steep curving slope to a car lot.

Crossing over the road to some flag stone steps, they led down to a covered area with a gated entrance to the cave on the left. Ahead was a long, dark, narrow gift shop. I went straight to the counter outside for a cold drink, getting a lady who was obviously having a bad day. I was quite put out, as this was very unusual for America. We bought our tickets and waited on seats under the roofing until the tour before us began to emerge from the cave's entrance.

Once he'd joined us, the guide explained that the cave was a crystal filled hollow mountain between 12-20 million years old with a perfect 70 degrees inside. We had to take care descending the stairs, and as reminded that we should try not to touch the walls as the sweat and oils from our skin would damage the fragile ecology. It seems that due to a lack of water filtering down, the formations weren't growing at the moment.

We stopped while he told us that train robbers had once used the cave and the nearby La Posta Quemada Ranch, while in the 1930s the Civilian Conservation Corps had constructed the Colossal Cave headquarters as well as all the present walkways and handrails. The surrounding 2,400 acre mountain park had nearly a thousand plant species and over a hundred bird species, as well as almost half the bat population in Arizona, including both rare and threatened.

It was awesome as we twisted and turned down the narrow paths, around six and a half stories down overall, with lights carefully hidden in pockets and gaps in the rock giving the area an eerie glow. It seems that lots of the cracks and clefts were almost bottomless as far as anyone could tell.

Back outside, we made out way back up to the car and headed for the ranch, where I phoned the stables to have my last ride in the morning.
Tuesday 20th May.

I was awake at 5am and got up to find a firebug laying on its back on the bathroom floor, legs waving animatedly and unable to right itself. I found some tissue, picked it up gingerly and shook it out the door, then made a cup of coffee and sat out in the early dawn watching the sun start to rise over the horizon. The birds were singing, while a group of sparrows were noisily fighting in the bushes making a racket. Cottontails were scampering along the paths and in the bushes, occasionally crouching by the puddles of water to drink. Every now and then a horse whinnied.

I sat trying to think of a daring scheme to find a way that I could stay behind, irrational or not: run away and miss the flight, rent an RV and just drive round the countryside, get a job in a diner—anything to remain. Then the thought of upsetting dad, leaving my dogs and Cloud behind, ended that. I reminded myself of something I had heard once: 'look out, you may get what you want!' I leave that to be thought about.

I walked down to the stables for the last time at 7am to meet the big wrangler who was waiting. He'd always given me the impression that he really wasn't interested in what he was doing, and today was no different. He brought up C.J. again and we set off round the back of the mock town, heading out towards the new bungalows. After half an hour I started checking the time more frequently as we appeared to be heading back to the ranch. Perhaps the wrangler was going to go another way. No! We ambled back to the ranch twenty minutes early. I climbed down and sorted out my money, giving him just $20. He looked at me.

"We're back twenty minutes early, I'm not paying more than that."

"Oh, did we," he mumbled, glancing at the clock on the wall.

"Yes, and not only that, the horse you gave me again has problems with the flexor tendons, that's why he keeps stumbling in front. That could be quite dangerous later on if you put beginners on him. I know what's wrong because I had a pony with the same trouble and it had to be retired. I'll inform the stable yard when I get back to my room." And with that, I walked off, very disappointed.

Back at my room, I immediately phoned the yard and explained why I wasn't paying the full amount and that I wasn't happy being given a horse with flexor tendon problems. The lady seemed quite upset and stated that she would speak to the wrangler when she saw him.

I packed my case before heading up to the dining room to show Kirsty my photos of Ann-Marie, Les and Cloud, and to give her my e-mail address in case she ever went on line again. She hadn't got one at the time because her server had been trying to make her pay a bill she didn't owe, but she promised that once she was with another, she'd get in touch. She also told me that the ranch had been sold, no wonder that there was hardly anyone here, but that she already had another job to go to. After that I went to the office and paid the final bill—whoops! $1268.

I returned to my room for a shower and sat outside under the parasol until Andy came round at 10.30am. We put everything in the car, checking under the seats to make sure nothing had been missed, then set off to join the I-10 back to Phoenix. As we passed the sign that a couple of days before had made me giggle, I stopped so Andy could use his camera to photograph it for me:

INA ROAD WATER POLLUTION CONTROL

New Biological Nutrient Removal Activated Sludge Treatment Process (BNRAS.)

What a brilliant way to describe nothing less than a sewage plant!

I found it a very depressing drive to Phoenix made worse when I managed to miss the slip road to the I-10 and we had to continue on to find the next junction. All the way I tried hard not to think about arriving at the airport.

On the way, in a field, I could see lots of different sized dust devils swirling in the dust most of them looking as if they weren't moving from the spot. No breeze to move them?

First we would have to try and find the car rental place, and although Andy had some directions given to him, we had to stop at a gas station for a map of Phoenix. Coming into the city, the Interstate was the busiest I'd ever seen American roads with cars cutting in an out—very unusual. Eventually he thought we were in the general area of the garage as we followed the signs for the airport.

"Turn right here," Andy said suddenly when we reached another road junction.

As I started to turn, something caught my eye and I realised that it was one-way—and not our way! I braked just on the corner before the oncoming car could get close, and was luckily able to back up, no cars behind me. Whew.

We carried straight on over once the traffic was clear and managed to double back to find Washington Road, turning right and crossing the junction I'd nearly come out of earlier. We pulled up in front of the office.

Leaving our cases in the car as someone would take us to the airport we went into the office for Andy to pay the bill. They asked us how we'd got on with the car.

"Ok, it's a lovely drive," I said, "but every time I got out, the darn thing bit me. I kept getting electric shocks!"

"We teach them to do that," the lad replied, with a grin.

Back in the car, the driver went through the streets to the airport rather fast to my mind, but then he must have known the way very well. Andy found a cart to take our luggage and we went straight to the British Airways check-in to leave our luggage. I thought that my case would be over weight, but luckily it wasn't. The lady at the desk saw my badges for Texas and told me that she came from there, did I like it?

"Oh, yes," and I told her about the places I'd visited with Andy.

Again I was feeling very choked and desperately unhappy, and I knew that I was being quite ridiculous.

We had another three hours to wait for the flight and wandered round the shopping areas. I still had a $20 bill in my purse to spend, but couldn't find anything I really wanted, so I ended up taking it back home with me. Ever since my first trip, I've had a strange superstition that I have to keep any American money once I was home or I would never return to the USA and I've collected about $35 in change now because I always forget to take it back out with me. We ended up sitting at a takeaway for a coffee and a snack and

I had a huge tuna sandwich.

Then it was the usual trip through security and we joined the queue. I was very nervous approaching the metal detector gateway, making the security guard smile and I edged through slowly, this time making him laugh. Nothing happened.

"It always goes off," I explained.

"Never did this time," he laughed.

We walked through into the waiting lounge sitting until the flight was called at 18.50pm.

Once in the plane, I was given a choice of sitting by the window and actually sat beside it for a change, although when we took off I did have my eyes averted. It was getting dark by then, and the land under us became pitch black with only the glowing lights of the towns to be see from time to time. One big area I thought might have been Flagstaff, and a huge place possibly Denver.

After that I was asked by the stewardess to pull the blind down for people who wanted to sleep. *It was dark out there, how on earth would it keep people awake?* I thought. I had wanted to watch the stars and see if there was a moon. Still, it gave me the incentive to try to sleep. I hadn't met with jet lag yet and had no intention of suffering, having seen how long it took Andy and others to get over it.

We landed at 13.35pm and after clearing customs, I restarted my mobile phone to phone Daphne, glad that the battery had remained fully charged.

"Tony's not here," she stated, confusing me.

"Why?"

"We thought you were landing yesterday. I've got to ring the taxi cab company as they've got a man already going to the airport and he'll bring you back here."

I told Andy there'd been some sort of mix up and that we had to wait outside for the driver to contact us, so made our way to the terminal entrance. After waiting what seemed ages, we finally discovered that the man was waiting in a roadway just over from us as he wasn't allowed to pick us up by the entrance. He took us back to Daphne's.

Although I was pleased to see the dogs, after a quick sniff and cuddle they just wanted to get back indoors and play with their toys. Oh well, they've obviously been very happy.

Chatting over a cup of coffee, we weren't allowed to leave until Daniel came home from school so that he could see us, with Tony arriving not long after. It appeared that although I'd sent a couple of e-mails with our itinerary and the flight date and numbers, on the last one I must have accidentally put down that we were arriving on Tuesday 21st by accident and not Wednesday 21st. When Tony hadn't found us at the airport on Tuesday, Daphne had phoned BA in a fright to discover that all their flights from Phoenix were BA 288—every day!

Then we had the car packed with the cases and the dogs, and I drove back home. With all the places we'd already seen, I couldn't help but think about the rest I would like visit.

Go next year? You bet.

Printed in the United Kingdom
by Lightning Source UK Ltd.
108987UKS00002BB/3